Encountering Development

Editors

Sherry B. Ortner,
Nicholas B. Dirks,
Geoff Eley

A list of titles in this series appears
at the back of the book

PRINCETON STUDIES IN
CULTURE/POWER/HISTORY

Encountering Development

THE MAKING AND UNMAKING OF THE THIRD WORLD

Arturo Escobar

PRINCETON UNIVERSITY PRESS

PRINCETON, NEW JERSEY

Library of Congress Cataloging-in-Publication Data

Escobar, Arturo, 1952–
Encountering development : the making and unmaking
of the third world / Arturo Escobar.
p.   cm. — (Princeton studies in culture/power/history)
Includes bibliographical references and index.
1.Economic development. 2. Economic history—1945–
3. Developing countries—Economic conditions.
4. Developing countries—Social conditions. I. Title. II. Series.
HD75.E73   1994   338.9—dc20   94-21025

ISBN 0-691-03409-5 (cl)
ISBN 0-691-00102-2 (pbk)

This book has been composed in Caledonia

Princeton University Press books are printed
on acid-free paper and meet the guidelines
for permanence and durability of the Committee
on Production Guidelines for Book Longevity
of the Council on Library Resources

Printed in the United States of America by Princeton Academic Press

7   9   10   8   6

CONTENTS

PREFACE

THIS BOOK grew out of a sense of puzzlement: the fact that for many years the industrialized nations of North America and Europe were supposed to be the indubitable models for the societies of Asia, Africa, and Latin America, the so-called Third World, and that these societies must catch up with the industrialized countries, perhaps even become like them. This belief is still held today in many quarters. Development was and continues to be—although less convincingly so as the years go by and its promises go unfulfilled—the magic formula. The presumed ineluctability of this notion—and, for the most part, its unquestioned desirability—was most puzzling to me. This work arose out of the need to explain this situation, namely, the creation of a Third World and the dream of development, both of which have been an integral part of the socioeconomic, cultural, and political life of the post–World War II period.

The overall approach taken in the book can be described as poststructuralist. More precisely, the approach is discursive, in the sense that it stems from the recognition of the importance of the dynamics of discourse and power to any study of culture. But there is much more than an analysis of discourse and practice; I also attempt to contribute to the development of a framework for the cultural critique of economics as a foundational structure of modernity, including the formulation of a culture-based political economy. In addition, I include a detailed examination of the emergence of peasants, women, and the environment as clients of the development apparatus in the 1970s and 1980s. Finally, I incorporate throughout the text accounts of Third World scholars, many of whom tell stories that are less mediated by the needs of the U.S. and European academy.

The approach is also anthropological. As Stuart Hall said, "If culture happens to be what seizes your soul, you will have to recognize that you will always be working in an area of displacement." The analysis in this book is cultural in the anthropological sense but also in the sense of cultural studies. It may be situated among current attempts to advance anthropology and cultural studies as critical, intellectual, and political projects.

As the title of the book suggests, development and even the Third World may be in the process of being unmade. This is happening not so much because the Second World (the socialist economies of Europe) is gone and the Holy Trinity of the post–World War II era is finally collapsing on its own but because of development's failure and the increasing opposition to it by popular groups in the Third World. The voices that are calling for an end to development are becoming more numerous and audible. This book can be seen as part of this effort; I also hope that it will be part of the task of imagining and fostering alternatives.

I would like to thank the following people: Sheldon Margen, Paul Rabinow, and C. West Churchman of the University of California, Berkeley; Jacqueline Urla and Sonia E. Alvarez, special friends and co-workers in anthropology and social movements research, respectively; Tracey Tsugawa, Jennifer Terry, Orin Starn, Miguel Díaz-Barriga, Deborah Gordon, and Ron Balderrama, also good friends and interlocutors; Michael Taussig, James O'Connor, Lourdes Benería, Adele Mueller, Stephen Gudeman, and James Clifford, important sources of insights and support.

Scholars working on related approaches to development whose writings, discussions, and active support I appreciate include Majid Rahnema, Ashis Nandy, Vandana Shiva, Shiv Visvanathan, Stephen and Frédérique Marglin, and the group gathered around Wolfgang Sachs, Ivan Illich, and Barbara Duden; James Ferguson and Stacy Leigh Pigg, fellow anthropologists; and María Cristina Rojas de Ferro, also studying Colombian regimes of representation. Donald Lowe and John Borrego read and offered suggestions on my doctoral dissertation in Berkeley.

Several people in Colombia have been extremely important to this book. I want to thank especially Alvaro Pedrosa, Orlando Fals Borda, María Cristina Salazar, and Magdalena León de Leal for providing intellectual exchange and friendship. My research on food, nutrition, and rural development was made easier and more interesting by Darío Fajardo, Patricia Prieto, Sofía Valencia, and Beatriz Hernandez. In the United States, I thank Leonard Joy, Michael Latham, Alain de Janvry, and Nola Reinhardt, also for their work on food and nutrition, on which I draw. The Latin American dimension of the book received vital impetus from the following friends and colleagues: Fernando Calderón and Alejandro Piscitelli (Buenos Aires); Margarita López Maya, Luis Gómez, María Pilar García, and Edgardo and Luis Lander (Caracas); Edmundo Fuenzalida (Santiago); Heloisa Boarque de Hollanda (Rio de Janeiro); Aníbal Quijano (Lima); and Fernando Flores in Berkeley, who was instrumental in helping me obtain financial support for a year of writing at Berkeley. Funding for fifteen months of fieldwork in Colombia (1981–1982; 1983) was provided by the United Nations University.

More often than not, my undergraduate students at the University of California, Santa Cruz, and Smith College responded enthusiastically and critically to many of the ideas presented in this book. I want to thank particularly Ned Bade, and Granis Stewart and Beth Bessinger, my research assistants at Santa Cruz and Smith College, respectively.

On a more personal note (although in the case of many of those already mentioned the line between the personal and the professional is blurred at best), I would like to thank friends in the San Francisco Bay Area, particulary Celso Alvarez, Cathryn Teasley, Zé Araújo, Ignacio Valero, Guillermo Padilla, Marcio Cámara, Judit Moschkovich, Isabel de Sena, Ron Levaco, Rosselyn Lash, Rafael Coto, Tina Rotenberg, Clementina Acedo, Lorena Martos, Inés Gómez, Jorge Myers, and Richard Harris; Marta Morello-Frosch, Julianne Burton, and David Sweet at the Latin American Studies program at the University of California at Santa Cruz, where I taught for three years; Nancy Gutman and Richard Lim in Northampton, Massachusetts; and my colleagues in the anthropology department at Smith College—Elizabeth Hopkins, Frédérique Apffel-Marglin, and Donald Joralemon. In Colombia, a similar group of friends includes Consuelo Moreno, Jaime Fernando Valencia, Mercedes Franco, and their children, and Yolanda Arango and Alvaro Bedoya. Finally, I want to thank especially my family—Yadira, María Victoria, Chepe, Tracey, and María Elena. I also want to remember my father, Gustavo, who died in 1990 still dreaming of his small hometown while trying (without great success in terms of conventional economic and development indicators) to make it in the big city so that his children could "get ahead" and become modern.

The suggestions of Mary Murrell, my editor at Princeton University Press, were an important catalyst in bringing the book to completion in its present form. I am grateful to her for her trust in the project. Finally, I would like to acknowledge two other sources of inspiration: Michel Foucault, whose work provided insights in many forms and at many levels, and the vibrant sounds of many Third World musicians—Caribbean, West African, and Latin American—particularly when I lived in the San Francisco Bay Area. It is not a coincidence that Third World music is becoming increasingly important in the cultural productions of the West. This brief mention is meant as a reminder that perhaps many books—this one included—would be quite different without it.

Encountering Development

Chapter 1

INTRODUCTION: DEVELOPMENT AND THE ANTHROPOLOGY OF MODERNITY

There is a sense in which rapid economic progress is
impossible without painful adjustments. Ancient
philosophies have to be scrapped; old social institutions
have to disintegrate; bonds of caste, creed and race have to
burst; and large numbers of persons who cannot keep up
with progress have to have their expectations of a
comfortable life frustrated. Very few communities are
willing to pay the full price of economic progress.
—United Nations,
Department of Social and Economic Affairs,
*Measures for the Economic Development of
Underdeveloped Countries*, 1951

IN HIS inaugural address as president of the United States on January 20,
1949, Harry Truman announced his concept of a "fair deal" for the entire
world. An essential component of this concept was his appeal to the United
States and the world to solve the problems of the "underdeveloped areas" of
the globe.

More than half the people of the world are living in conditions approaching
misery. Their food is inadequate, they are victims of disease. Their economic
life is primitive and stagnant. Their poverty is a handicap and a threat both to
them and to more prosperous areas. For the first time in history humanity
possesses the knowledge and the skill to relieve the suffering of these people. . . . I believe that we should make available to peace-loving peoples the
benefits of our store of technical knowledge in order to help them realize their
aspirations for a better life. . . . What we envisage is a program of development
based on the concepts of democractic fair dealing. . . . Greater production is the
key to prosperity and peace. And the key to greater production is a wider and
more vigorous application of modern scientific and technical knowledge. (Truman [1949] 1964)

The Truman doctrine initiated a new era in the understanding and management of world affairs, particularly those concerning the less economically
accomplished countries of the world. The intent was quite ambitious: to

bring about the conditions necessary to replicating the world over the features that characterized the "advanced" societies of the time—high levels of
industrialization and urbanization, technicalization of agriculture, rapid
growth of material production and living standards, and the widespread
adoption of modern education and cultural values. In Truman's vision, capital, science, and technology were the main ingredients that would make this
massive revolution possible. Only in this way could the American dream of
peace and abundance be extended to all the peoples of the planet.

This dream was not solely the creation of the United States but the result
of the specific historical conjuncture at the end of the Second World War.
Within a few years, the dream was universally embraced by those in power.
The dream was not seen as an easy process, however; predictably perhaps,
the obstacles perceived ahead contributed to consolidating the mission. One
of the most influential documents of the period, prepared by a group of
experts convened by the United Nations with the objective of designing
concrete policies and measures "for the economic development of underdeveloped countries," put it thus:

> There is a sense in which rapid economic progress is impossible without painful
> adjustments. Ancient philosophies have to be scrapped; old social institutions
> have to disintegrate; bonds of cast, creed and race have to burst; and large
> numbers of persons who cannot keep up with progress have to have their ex-
> pectations of a comfortable life frustrated. Very few communities are willing to
> pay the full price of economic progress. (United Nations, Department of Social
> and Economic Affairs [1951], 15)[1]

The report suggested no less than a total restructuring of "underdeveloped"
societies. The statement quoted earlier might seem to us today amazingly
ethnocentric and arrogant, at best naive; yet what has to be explained is
precisely the fact that it was uttered and that it made perfect sense. The
statement exemplified a growing will to transform drastically two-thirds of
the world in the pursuit of the goal of material prosperity and economic
progress. By the early 1950s, such a will had become hegemonic at the level
of the circles of power.

This book tells the story of this dream and how it progressively turned into
a nightmare. For instead of the kingdom of abundance promised by theorists
and politicians in the 1950s, the discourse and strategy of development produced its opposite: massive underdevelopment and impoverishment, untold
exploitation and oppression. The debt crisis, the Sahelian famine, increasing
poverty, malnutrition, and violence are only the most pathetic signs of the
failure of forty years of development. In this way, this book can be read as
the history of the loss of an illusion, in which many genuinely believed.
Above all, however, it is about how the "Third World" has been produced by
the discourses and practices of development since their inception in the
early post–World War II period.

ORIENTALISM, AFRICANISM, AND DEVELOPMENTALISM

Until the late 1970s, the central stake in discussions on Asia, Africa, and Latin America was the nature of development. As we will see, from the economic development theories of the 1950s to the "basic human needs approach" of the 1970s—which emphasized not only economic growth per se as in earlier decades but also the distribution of the benefits of growth— the main preoccupation of theorists and politicians was the kinds of development that needed to be pursued to solve the social and economic problems of these parts of the world. Even those who opposed the prevailing capitalist strategies were obliged to couch their critique in terms of the need for development, through concepts such as "another development," "participatory development," "socialist development," and the like. In short, one could criticize a given approach and propose modifications or improvements accordingly, but the fact of development itself, and the need for it, could not be doubted. Development had achieved the status of a certainty in the social imaginary.

Indeed, it seemed impossible to conceptualize social reality in other terms. Wherever one looked, one found the repetitive and omnipresent reality of development: governments designing and implementing ambitious development plans, institutions carrying out development programs in city and countryside alike, experts of all kinds studying underdevelopment and producing theories ad nauseam. The fact that most people's conditions not only did not improve but deteriorated with the passing of time did not seem to bother most experts. Reality, in sum, had been colonized by the development discourse, and those who were dissatisfied with this state of affairs had to struggle for bits and pieces of freedom within it, in the hope that in the process a different reality could be constructed.[2]

More recently, however, the development of new tools of analysis, in gestation since the late 1960s but the application of which became widespread only during the 1980s, has made possible analyses of this type of "colonization of reality" which seek to account for this very fact: how certain representations become dominant and shape indelibly the ways in which reality is imagined and acted upon. Foucault's work on the dynamics of discourse and power in the representation of social reality, in particular, has been instrumental in unveiling the mechanisms by which a certain order of discourse produces permissible modes of being and thinking while disqualifying and even making others impossible. Extensions of Foucault's insights to colonial and postcolonial situations by authors such as Edward Said, V. Y. Mudimbe, Chandra Mohanty, and Homi Bhabha, among others, have opened up new ways of thinking about representations of the Third World. Anthropology's self-critique and renewal during the 1980s have also been important in this regard.

Thinking of development in terms of discourse makes it possible to maintain the focus on domination—as earlier Marxist analyses, for instance, did—and at the same time to explore more fruitfully the conditions of possibility and the most pervasive effects of development. Discourse analysis creates the possibility of "stand[ing] detached from [the development discourse], bracketing its familiarity, in order to analyze the theoretical and practical context with which it has been associated" (Foucault 1986, 3). It gives us the possibility of singling out "development" as an encompassing cultural space and at the same time of separating ourselves from it by perceiving it in a totally new form. This is the task the present book sets out to accomplish.

To see development as a historically produced discourse entails an examination of why so many countries started to see themselves as underdeveloped in the early post–World War II period, how "to develop" became a fundamental problem for them, and how, finally, they embarked upon the task of "un-underdeveloping" themselves by subjecting their societies to increasingly systematic, detailed, and comprehensive interventions. As Western experts and politicians started to see certain conditions in Asia, Africa, and Latin America as a problem—mostly what was perceived as poverty and backwardness—a new domain of thought and experience, namely, development, came into being, resulting in a new strategy for dealing with the alleged problems. Initiated in the United States and Western Europe, this strategy became in a few years a powerful force in the Third World.

The study of development as discourse is akin to Said's study of the discourses on the Orient. "Orientalism," writes Said,

> can be discussed and analyzed as the corporate institution for dealing with the Orient—dealing with it by making statements about it, authorizing views of it, describing it, by teaching it, settling it, ruling over it: in short, Orientalism as a Western style for dominating, restructuring, and having authority over the Orient. . . . My contention is that without examining Orientalism as a discourse we cannot possibly understand the enormously systematic discipline by which European culture was able to manage—and even produce—the Orient politically, sociologically, ideologically, scientifically, and imaginatively during the post-Enlightenment period. (1979, 3)

Since its publication, *Orientalism* has sparked a number of creative studies and inquiries about representations of the Third World in various contexts, although few have dealt explicitly with the question of development. Nevertheless, the general questions some of these works raised serve as markers for the analysis of development as a regime of representation. In his excellent book *The Invention of Africa*, the African philosopher V. Y. Mudimbe, for example, states his objective thus: "To study the theme of the foundations of discourse about Africa . . . [how] African worlds have been established as realities for knowledge" (1988, xi) in Western discourse. His concern, moreover, goes beyond "the 'invention' of Africanism as a scientific discipline" (9), particularly in anthropology and philosophy, in order to investigate the "amplification" by African scholars of the work of critical European thinkers, particularly Foucault and Lévi-Strauss. Although Mudimbe finds that even in the most Afrocentric perspectives the Western epistemological order continues to be both context and referent, he nevertheless finds some works in which critical European insights are being carried even further than those works themselves anticipated. What is at stake for these latter works, Mudimbe explains, is a critical reinterpretation of African history as it has been seen from Africa's (epistemological, historical, and geographical) exteriority, indeed, a weakening of the very notion of Africa. This, for Mudimbe, implies a radical break in African anthropology, history, and ideology.

Critical work of this kind, Mudimbe believes, may open the way for "the process of refounding and reassuming an interrupted historicity within representations" (183), in other words, the process by which Africans can have greater autonomy over how they are represented and how they can construct their own social and cultural models in ways not so mediated by a Western episteme and historicity—albeit in an increasingly transnational context. This notion can be extended to the Third World as a whole, for what is at stake is the process by which, in the history of the modern West, non-European areas have been systematically organized into, and transformed according to, European constructs. Representations of Asia, Africa, and Latin America as Third World and underdeveloped are the heirs of an illustrious genealogy of Western conceptions about those parts of the world.[3]

Timothy Mitchell unveils another important mechanism at work in European representations of other societies. Like Mudimbe, Mitchell's goal is to explore "the peculiar methods of order and truth that characterise the modern West" (1988, ix) and their impact on nineteenth-century Egypt. The setting up of the world as a picture, in the model of the world exhibitions of the last century, Mitchell suggests, is at the core of these methods and their political expediency. For the modern (European) subject, this entailed that s/he would experience life as if s/he were set apart from the physical world, as if s/he were a visitor at an exhibition. The observer inevitably "enframed" external reality in order to make sense of it; this enframing took place according to European categories. What emerged was a regime of objectivism in which Europeans were subjected to a double demand: to be detached and objective, and yet to immerse themselves in local life.

This experience as participant observer was made possible by a curious trick, that of eliminating from the picture the presence of the European observer (see also Clifford 1988, 145); in more concrete terms, observing the (colonial) world as object "from a position that is invisible and set apart" (Mitchell 1988, 28). The West had come to live "as though the world were divided in this way into two: into a realm of mere representations and a realm of the 'real'; into exhibitions and an external reality; into an order of mere models, descriptions or copies, and an order of the original" (32). This regime of order and truth is a quintessential aspect of modernity and has been deepened by economics and development. It is reflected in an objectivist and empiricist stand that dictates that the Third World and its peoples exist "out there," to be known through theories and intervened upon from the outside.

The consequences of this feature of modernity have been enormous. Chandra Mohanty, for example, refers to the same feature when raising the questions of who produces knowledge about Third World women and from what spaces; she discovered that women in the Third World are represented in most feminist literature on development as having "needs" and "problems" but few choices and no freedom to act. What emerges from such modes of analysis is the image of an average Third World woman, constructed through the use of statistics and certain categories:

> This average third world woman leads an essentially truncated life based on her feminine gender (read: sexually constrained) and her being "third world" (read: ignorant, poor, uneducated, tradition-bound, domestic, family-oriented, victimized, etc.). This, I suggest, is in contrast to the (implicit) self-representation of Western women as educated, as modern, as having control over their own bodies and sexualities, and the freedom to make their own decisions. (1991b, 56)

These representations implicitly assume Western standards as the benchmark against which to measure the situation of Third World women. The result, Mohanty believes, is a paternalistic attitude on the part of Western women toward their Third World counterparts and, more generally, the perpetuation of the hegemonic idea of the West's superiority. Within this discursive regime, works about Third World women develop a certain coherence of effects that reinforces that hegemony. "It is in this process of discursive homogenization and systematization of the oppression of women in the third world," Mohanty concludes, "that power is exercised in much of recent Western feminist discourse, and this power needs to be defined and named" (54).[4]

Needless to say, Mohanty's critique applies with greater pertinence to mainstream development literature, in which there exists a veritable underdeveloped subjectivity endowed with features such as powerlessness, passivity, poverty, and ignorance, usually dark and lacking in historical agency, as if waiting for the (white) Western hand to help subjects along and not infrequently hungry, illiterate, needy, and oppressed by its own stubbornness, lack of initiative, and traditions. This image also universalizes and homogenizes Third World cultures in an ahistorical fashion. Only from a certain Western perspective does this description make sense; that it exists at all is more a sign of power over the Third World than a truth about it. It is important to highlight for now that the deployment of this discourse in a world system in which the West has a certain dominance over the Third World has profound political, economic, and cultural effects that have to be explored.

The production of discourse under conditions of unequal power is what Mohanty and others refer to as "the colonialist move." This move entails specific constructions of the colonial / Third World subject in/through discourse in ways that allow the exercise of power over it. Colonial discourse, although "the most theoretically underdeveloped form of discourse," according to Homi Bhabha, is "crucial to the binding of a range of differences and discriminations that inform the discursive and political practices of racial and cultural hierarchization" (1990, 72). Bhabha's definition of colonial discourse, although complex, is illuminating:

> [Colonial discourse] is an apparatus that turns on the recognition and disavowal of racial/cultural/historical differences. Its predominant strategic function is the creation of a space for a "subject peoples" through the production of knowledges in terms of which surveillance is exercised and a complex form of pleasure/unpleasure is incited. . . . The objective of colonial discourse is to construe the colonized as a population of degenerate types on the basis of racial origin, in order to justify conquest and to establish systems of administration and instruction. . . . I am referring to a form of governmentality that in marking out a "subject nation," appropriates, directs and dominates its various spheres of activity. (1990, 75)

Although some of the terms of this definition might be more applicable to the colonial context strictly speaking, the development discourse is governed by the same principles; it has created an extremely efficient apparatus for producing knowledge about, and the exercise of power over, the Third World. This apparatus came into existence roughly in the period 1945 to 1955 and has not since ceased to produce new arrangements of knowledge and power, new practices, theories, strategies, and so on. In sum, it has successfully deployed a regime of government over the Third World, a "space for 'subject peoples'" that ensures certain control over it.

This space is also a geopolitical space, a series of imaginative geographies, to use Said's (1979) term. The development discourse inevitably contained a geopolitical imagination that has shaped the meaning of development for more than four decades. For some, this will to spatial power is one of the most essential features of development (Slater 1993). It is implicit in expressions such as First and Third World, North and South, center and periphery. The social production of space implicit in these terms is bound with the production of differences, subjectivities, and social orders. Despite the correctives introduced to this geopolitics—the decentering of the world, the demise of the Second World, the emergence of a network of world cities, the globalization of cultural production, and so on—they continue to function imaginatively in powerful ways. There is a relation among history, geography, and modernity that resists disintegration as far as the Third World is concerned, despite the important changes that have given rise to postmodern geographies (Soja 1989).

To sum up, I propose to speak of development as a historically singular experience, the creation of a domain of thought and action, by analyzing the characteristics and interrelations of the three axes that define it: the forms of knowledge that refer to it and through which it comes into being and is elaborated into objects, concepts, theories, and the like; the system of power that regulates its practice; and the forms of subjectivity fostered by this discourse, those through which people come to recognize themselves as developed or underdeveloped. The ensemble of forms found along these axes constitutes development as a discursive formation, giving rise to an efficient apparatus that systematically relates forms of knowledge and techiques of power.[5]

The analysis will thus be couched in terms of regimes of discourse and representation. Regimes of representation can be analyzed as places of encounter where identities are constructed and also where violence is originated, symbolized, and managed. This useful hypothesis, developed by a Colombian scholar to explain nineteenth-century violence in her country, building particularly on the works of Bakhtin, Foucault, and Girard, conceives of regimes of representation as places of encounter of languages of the past and languages of the present (such as the languages of "civilization" and "barbarism" in postindependence Latin America), internal and external languages, and languages of self and other (Rojas de Ferro 1994). A similar encounter of regimes of representation took place in the late 1940s with the emergence of development, also accompanied by specific forms of modernized violence.[6]

The notion of regimes of representation is a final theoretical and methodological principle for examining the mechanisms for, and consequences of, the construction of the Third World in/through representation. Charting regimes of representation of the Third World brought about by the development discourse represents an attempt to draw the "cartographies" (Deleuze 1988) or maps of the configurations of knowledge and power that define the post–World War II period. These are also cartographies of struggle, as Mohanty (1991a) adds. Although they are geared toward an understanding of the conceptual maps that are used to locate and chart Third World people's experience, they also reveal—even if indirectly at times—the categories with which people have to struggle. This book provides a general map for orienting oneself in the discourses and practices that account for today's dominant forms of sociocultural and economic production of the Third World.

The goals of this book are precisely to examine the establishment and consolidation of this discourse and apparatus from the early post–World War II period to the present (chapter 2); analyze the construction of a notion of underdevelopment in post–World War II economic development theories (chapter 3); and demonstrate the way in which the apparatus functions through the systematic production of knowledge and power in specific fields—such as rural development, sustainable development, and women and development (chapters 4 and 5). Finally, the conclusion deals with the important question of how to imagine a postdevelopment regime of representation and how to investigate and pursue alternative practices in the context of today's social movements in the Third World.

This, one might say, is a study of developmentalism as a discursive field. Unlike Said's study of Orientalism, however, I pay closer attention to the deployment of the discourse through practices. I want to show that this discourse results in concrete practices of thinking and acting through which the Third World is produced. The example I chose for this closer investigation is the implementation of rural development, health, and nutrition programs in Latin America in the 1970s and 1980s. Another difference in relation to *Orientalism* originates in Homi Bhabha's caution that "there is always, in Said, the suggestion that colonial power is possessed entirely by the colonizer, given its intentionality and unidirectionality" (1990, 77). This is a danger I seek to avoid by considering the variety of forms with which Third World people resist development interventions and how they struggle to create alternative ways of being and doing.

Like Mudimbe's study of Africanism, I also want to unveil the foundations of an order of knowledge and a discourse about the Third World as underdeveloped. I want to map, so to say, the invention of development. Instead of focusing on anthropology and philosophy, however, I contextualize the era of development within the overall space of modernity, particularly modern economic practices. From this perspective, development can be seen as a chapter of what can be called an anthropology of modernity, that is, a general investigation of Western modernity as a culturally and historically specific phenomenon. If it is true that there is an "anthropological structure" (Foucault 1975, 198) that sustains the modern order and its human sciences, it must be investigated to what extent this structure has also given rise to the regime of development, perhaps as a specific mutation of modernity. A general direction for this anthropology of modernity has already been suggested, in the sense of rendering "exotic" the West's cultural products in order to see them for what they are: "We need to anthropologize the West: show how exotic its constitution of reality has been; emphasize those domains most taken for granted as universal (this includes epistemology and economics); make them seem as historically peculiar as possible; show how their claims to truth are linked to social practices and have hence become effective forces in the social world" (Rabinow 1986, 241).

The anthropology of modernity would rely on ethnographic approaches that look at social forms as produced by historical practices combining knowledge and power; it would seek to examine how truth claims are related to practices and symbols that produce and regulate social life. As we will see, the production of the Third World through the articulation of knowledge and power is essential to the development discourse. This does not preclude the fact that from many Third World spaces, even the most reasonable among the West's social and cultural practices might look quite peculiar, even strange. Nevertheless, even today most people in the West (and many parts of the Third World) have great difficulty thinking about Third World situations and people in terms other than those provided by the development discourse. These terms—such as overpopulation, the permanent threat of famine, poverty, illiteracy, and the like—operate as the most common signifiers, already stereotyped and burdened with development signifieds. Media images of the Third World are the clearest example of developmentalist representations. These images just do not seem to go away. This is why it is necessary to examine development in relation to the modern experiences of knowing, seeing, counting, economizing, and the like.

Deconstructing Development

The discursive analysis of development started in the late 1980s and will most likely continue into the 1990s, coupled with attempts at articulating alternative regimes of representation and practice. Few works, however, have undertaken the deconstruction of the development discourse.[7] James Ferguson's recent book on development in Lesotho (1990) is a sophisticated example of the deconstructionist approach. Ferguson provides an in-depth analysis of rural development programs implemented in the country under World Bank sponsorship. Further entrenchment of the state, the restructuring of rural social relations, the deepening of Western modernizing influences, and the depoliticization of problems are among the most important effects of the deployment of rural development in Lesotho, despite the apparent failure of the programs in terms of their stated objectives. It is at the level of these effects, Ferguson concludes, that the productivity of the apparatus has to be assessed.

Another deconstructionist approach (Sachs 1992) analyzes the central constructs or key words of the development discourse, such as market, planning, population, environment, production, equality, participation, needs, poverty, and the like. After briefly tracing the origin of each concept in European civilization, each chapter examines the uses and transformation of the concept in the development discourse from the 1950s to the present. The intent of the book is to expose the arbitrary character of the concepts, their cultural and historical specificity, and the dangers that their use represents in the context of the Third World.[8] A related, group project is conceived in terms of a "systems of knowledge" approach. Cultures, this group believes, are characterized not only by rules and values but also by ways of knowing. Development has relied exclusively on one knowledge system, namely, the modern Western one. The dominance of this knowledge system has dictated the marginalization and disqualification of non-Western knowledge systems. In these latter knowledge systems, the authors conclude, researchers and activists might find alternative rationalities to guide social action away from economistic and reductionistic ways of thinking.[9]

In the 1970s, women were discovered to have been "bypassed" by development interventions. This "discovery" resulted in the growth during the late 1970s and 1980s of a whole new field, women in development (WID), which has been analyzed by several feminist researchers as a regime of representation, most notably Adele Mueller (1986, 1987a, 1991) and Chandra Mohanty. At the core of these works is an insightful analysis of the practices of dominant development institutions in creating and managing their client populations. Similar analyses of particular development subfields—such as economics and the environment, for example—are a needed contribution to the understanding of the function of development as a discourse and will continue to appear.[10]

A group of Swedish anthropologists focus their work on how the concepts of development and modernity are used, interpreted, questioned, and reproduced in various social contexts in different parts of the world. An entire constellation of usages, modes of operation, and effects associated with these terms, which are profoundly local, is beginning to surface. Whether in a Papua New Guinean village or in a small town of Kenya or Ethiopia, local versions of development and modernity are formulated according to complex processes that include traditional cultural practices, histories of colonialism, and contemporary location within the global economy of goods and symbols (Dahl and Rabo 1992). These much-needed local ethnographies of development and modernity are also being pioneered by Pigg (1992) in her work on the introduction of health practices in Nepal. More on these works in the next chapter.

Finally, it is important to mention a few works that focus on the role of conventional disciplines within the development discourse. Irene Gendzier (1985) examines the role political science played in the conformation of theories of modernization, particularly in the 1950s, and its relation to issues of the moment such as national security and economic imperatives. Also within political science, Kathryn Sikkink (1991) has more recently taken on the emergence of developmentalism in Brazil and Argentina in the 1950s and

1960s. Her chief interest is the role of ideas in the adoption, implementation, and consolidation of developmentalism as an economic development model.[11] The Chilean Pedro Morandé (1984) analyzes how the adoption and dominance of North American sociology in the 1950s and 1960s in Latin America set the stage for a purely functional conception of development, conceived of as the transformation of "traditional" into a "modern" society and devoid of any cultural considerations. Kate Manzo (1991) makes a somewhat similar case in her analysis of the shortcomings of modernist approaches to development, such as dependency theory, and in her call for paying attention to "countermodernist" alternatives that are grounded in the practices of Third World grassroots actors. The call for a return of culture in the critical analysis of development, particularly local cultures, is also central to this book.

As this short review shows, there are already a small but relatively coherent number of works that contribute to articulating a discursive critique of development. The present work makes the most general case in this regard; it seeks to provide a general view of the historical construction of development and the Third World as a whole and exemplifies the way the discourse functions in one particular case. The goal of the analysis is to contribute to the liberation of the discursive field so that the task of imagining alternatives can be commenced (or perceived by researchers in a new light) in those spaces where the production of scholarly and expert knowledge for development purposes continues to take place. The local-level ethnographies of development mentioned earlier provide useful elements toward this end. In the conclusion, I extend the insights these works afford and attempt to elaborate a view of "the alternative" as a research question and a social practice.

ANTHROPOLOGY AND THE DEVELOPMENT ENCOUNTER

In the introduction to his well-known collection on anthropology's relation to colonialism, *Anthropology and the Colonial Encounter* (1973), Talal Asad raised the question of whether there was not still "a strange reluctance on the part of most professional anthropologists to consider seriously the power structure within which their discipline has taken shape" (5), namely, the whole problematic of colonialism and neocolonialism, their political economy and institutions. Does not development today, as colonialism did in a former epoch, make possible "the kind of human intimacy on which anthropological fieldwork is based, but insure[s] that intimacy should be one-sided and provisional" (17), even if the contemporary subjects move and talk back? In addition, if during the colonial period "the general drift of anthropological understanding did not constitute a basic challenge to the unequal world represented by the colonial system" (18), is this not also the case with the development system? In sum, can we not speak with equal pertinence of "anthropology and the development encounter"?

It is generally true that anthropology as a whole has not dealt explicitly with the fact that it takes place within the post–World War II encounter between rich and poor nations established by the development discourse. Although a number of anthropologists have opposed development interventions, particularly on behalf of indigenous people,[12] large numbers of anthropologists have been involved with development organizations such as the World Bank and the United States Agency for International Development (U.S. AID). This problematic involvement was particularly noticeable in the decade 1975–1985 and has been analyzed elsewhere (Escobar 1991). As Stacy Leigh Pigg (1992) rightly points out, anthropologists have been for the most part either inside development, as applied anthropologists, or outside development, as the champions of the authentically indigenous and "the native's point of view." Thus they overlook the ways in which development operates as an arena of cultural contestation and identity construction. A small number of anthropologists, however, have studied forms and processes of resistance to development interventions (Taussig 1980; Fals Borda 1984; Scott 1985; Ong 1987; see also Comaroff 1985 and Comaroff and Comaroff 1991 for resistance in the colonial context).

The absence of anthropologists from discussions of development as a regime of representation is regrettable because, if it is true that many aspects of colonialism have been superseded, representations of the Third World through development are no less pervasive and effective than their colonial counterparts. Perhaps even more so. It is also disturbing, as Said has pointed out, that in recent anthropological literature "there is an almost total absence of any reference to American imperial intervention as a factor affecting the theoretical discussion" (1989, 214; see also Friedman 1987; Ulin 1991). This imperial intervention takes place at many levels—economic, military, political, and cultural—which are woven together by development representations. Also disturbing, as Said proceeds to argue, is the lack of attention on the part of Western scholars to the sizable and impassioned critical literature by Third World intellectuals on colonialism, history, tradition, and domination—and, one might add, development. The number of Third World voices calling for a dismantling of the entire discourse of development is fast increasing.

The deep changes experienced in anthropology during the 1980s opened the way for examining how anthropology is bound up with "Western ways of creating the world," as Strathern (1988, 4) advises, and potentially with other possible ways of representing the interests of Third World peoples. This critical examination of anthropology's practices led to the realization that "no one can write about others any longer as if they were discrete objects or texts." A new task thus insinuated itself: that of coming up with "more subtle, concrete ways of writing and reading . . . new conceptions of culture as interactive and historical" (Clifford 1986, 25). Innovation in anthropological writing within this context was seen as "moving [ethnography] toward an unprecedentedly acute political and historical sensibility that is transforming the way cultural diversity is portrayed" (Marcus and Fischer 1986, 16).

This reimagining of anthropology, launched in the mid-1980s, has become the object of various critiques, qualifications, and extensions from within its own ranks and by feminists, political economists, Third World scholars, Third World feminists, and anti-postmodernists. Some of these critiques are more or less pointed and constructive than others, and it is not necessary to analyze them in this introduction.[13] To this extent, "the experimental moment" of the 1980s has been very fruitful and relatively rich in applications. The process of reimagining anthropology, however, is clearly still under way and will have to be deepened, perhaps by taking the debates to other arenas and in other directions. Anthropology, it is now argued, has to "reenter" the real world, after the moment of textualist critique. To do this, it has to rehistoricize its own practice and acknowledge that this practice is shaped by many forces that are well beyond the control of the ethnographer. Moreover, it must be willing to subject its most cherished notions, such as ethnography, culture, and science, to a more radical scrutiny (Fox 1991).

Strathern's call that this questioning be advanced in the context of Western social science practices and their "endorsement of certain interests in the description of social life" is of fundamental importance. At the core of this recentering of the debates within the disciplines are the limits that exist to the Western project of deconstruction and self-critique. It is becoming increasingly evident, at least for those who are struggling for different ways of having a voice, that the process of deconstructing and dismantling has to be accompanied by that of constructing new ways of seeing and acting. Needless to say, this aspect is crucial in discussions about development, because people's survival is at stake. As Mohanty (1991a) insists, both projects—deconstruction and reconstruction—have to be carried out simultaneously. As I discuss in the final chapter, this simultaneous project could focus strategically on the collective action of social movements: they struggle not only for goods and services but also for the very definition of life, economy, nature, and society. They are, in short, cultural struggles.

As Bhabha wants us to acknowledge, deconstruction and other types of critiques do not lead automatically to "an unproblematic reading of other cultural and discursive systems." They might be necessary to combat ethnocentrism, "but they cannot, of themselves, unreconstructed, represent that

otherness" (Bhabha 1990, 75). Moreover, there is the tendency in these critiques to discuss otherness principally in terms of the limits of Western
logocentricity, thus denying that cultural otherness is "implicated in specific
historical and discursive conditions, requiring constructions in different
practices of reading" (Bhabha 1990, 73). There is a similar insistence in Latin
America that the proposals of postmodernism, to be fruitful there, have to
make clear their commitment to justice and to the construction of alternative social orders.[14] These Third World correctives indicate the need for
alternative questions and strategies for the construction of anticolonialist
discourses (and the reconstruction of Third World societies in/through representations that can develop into alternative practices). Calling into question the limitations of the West's self-critique, as currently practiced in
much of contemporary theory, they make it possible to visualize the "discursive insurrection" by Third World people proposed by Mudimbe in relation
to the "sovereignty of the very European thought from which we wish to
disentangle ourselves" (quoted in Diawara 1990, 79).

The needed liberation of anthropology from the space mapped by the
development encounter (and, more generally, modernity), to be achieved
through a close examination of the ways in which it has been implicated in
it, is an important step in the direction of more autonomous regimes of representation; this is so to the extent that it might motivate anthropologists and
others to delve into the strategies people in the Third World pursue to resignify and transform their reality through their collective political practice.
This challenge may provide paths toward the radicalization of the discipline's reimagining started with enthusiasm during the 1980s.

OVERVIEW OF THE BOOK

The following chapter studies the emergence and consolidation of the discourse and strategy of development in the early post–World War II period,
as a result of the problematization of poverty that took place during those
years. It presents the major historical conditions that made such a process
possible and identifies the principal mechanisms through which development has been deployed, namely, the professionalization of development
knowledge and the institutionalization of development practices. An important aspect of this chapter is to illustrate the nature and dynamics of the
discourse, its archaeology, and its modes of operation. Central to this aspect
is the identification of the basic set of elements and relations that hold together the discourse. To speak development, one must adhere to certain
rules of statement that go back to the basic system of categories and relations. This system defines the hegemonic worldview of development, a
worldview that increasingly permeates and transforms the economic, social,

and cultural fabric of Third World cities and villages, even if the languages of development are always adapted and reworked significantly at the local level.

Chapter 3 is intended to articulate a cultural critique of economics by taking on the single most influential force shaping the development field: the discourse of development economics. To understand this discourse, one has to analyze the conditions of its coming into being: how it emerged, building upon the already existing Western economy and the economic doctrine generated by it (classical, neoclassical, Keynesian, and growth economic theories); how development economists constructed "the underdeveloped economy," embodying in their theories features of the advanced capitalist societies and culture; the political economy of the capitalist world economy linked to this construction; and finally, the planning practices that inevitably came with development economics and that became a powerful force in the production and management of development. From this privileged space, economics pervaded the entire practice of development. As the last part of the chapter shows, there is no indication that economists might consider a redefinition of their tenets and forms of analysis, although some hopeful insights for this redefinition can be found in recent works in economic anthropology. The notion of "communities of modellers" (Gudeman and Rivera 1990) is examined as a possible method to construct a cultural politics for engaging critically, and I hope neutralizing partly, the dominant economic discourse.

Chapters 4 and 5 are intended to show in detail how development works. The goal of chapter 4 is to show how a corpus of rational techniques—planning, methods of measurement and assessment, professional knowledges, institutional practices, and the like—organizes both forms of knowledge and types of power, relating one to the other, in the construction and treatment of one specific problem: malnutrition and hunger. The chapter examines the birth, rise, and decline of a set of disciplines (forms of knowledge) and strategies in nutrition, health, and rural development. Outlined initially in the early 1970s by a handful of experts in North American and British universities, the World Bank, and the United Nations, the strategy of national planning for nutrition and rural development resulted in the implementation of massive programs in Third World countries throughout the 1970s and 1980s, funded primarily by the World Bank and Third World governments. A case study of these plans in Colombia, based on my fieldwork with a group of government planners in charge of their design and implementation, is presented as an illustration of the functioning of the development apparatus. By paying close attention to the political economy of food and hunger and the discursive constructions linked to it, this chapter and the next contribute to the development of a poststructuralist-oriented political economy.

Chapter 5 extends the analysis of chapter 4 by focusing on the regimes of representation that underlie constructions of peasants, women, and the environment. In particular, the chapter exposes the links between representation and power at work in the practices of the World Bank. This institution is presented as an exemplar of development discourse, a blueprint of development. Particular attention is paid to representations of peasants, women, and the environment in recent development literature, and the contradictions and possibilities inherent in the tasks of integrated rural development, incorporating women into development, and sustainable development. The mapping of visibilities by development through the representations planners and experts utilize as they design and carry out their programs is analyzed in detail in order to show the connection between the creation of visibility in discourse, particularly through modern techniques of visuality, and the exercise of power. This chapter also contributes to theorizing the question of discursive change and transformation by explaining how discourses on peasants, women, and the environment emerge and function in similar ways within the overall space of development.

The concluding chapter tackles the question of the transformation of the development regime of representation and the articulation of alternatives. The call by a growing number of Third and First World voices to signal the end of development is reviewed and assessed. Similarly, recent work in Latin American social science, on "hybrid cultures" as a mode of cultural affirmation in the face of modernity's crisis, is used as a basis for theorizing the formulation of alternatives as a research question and a social practice. I argue that instead of searching for grand alternative models or strategies, what is needed is the investigation of alternative representations and practices in concrete local settings, particularly as they exist in contexts of hybridization, collective action, and political mobilization. This proposal is developed in the context of the ecological phase of capital and the struggles over the world's biological diversity. These struggles—between global capital and biotechnology interests, on the one hand, and local communities and organizations, on the other—constitute the most advanced stage in which the meanings of development and postdevelopment are being fought over. The fact that the struggles usually involve minority cultures in the tropical regions of the world raises unprecedented questions concerning the cultural politics around the design of social orders, technology, nature, and life itself.

The fact that the analysis, finally, is conducted in terms of tales is not meant to indicate that the said tales are mere fictions. As Donna Haraway says in her analysis of the narratives of biology (1989a, 1991), narratives are neither fictions nor opposed to "facts." Narratives are, indeed, historical textures woven of fact and fiction. Even the most neutral scientific domains are narratives in this sense. To treat science as narrative, Haraway insists, is not to be dismissive. On the contrary, it is to treat it in the most serious way, without succumbing to its mystification as "the truth" or to the ironic skepticism common to many critiques. Science and expert discourses such as development produce powerful truths, ways of creating and intervening in the world, including ourselves; they are instances "where possible worlds are constantly reinvented in the contest for very real, present worlds" (Haraway 1989a, 5). Narratives, such as the tales in this book, are always inmmersed in history and never innocent. Whether we can unmake development and perhaps even bid farewell to the Third World will equally depend on the social invention of new narratives, new ways of thinking and doing.[15]

Chapter 2

THE PROBLEMATIZATION OF POVERTY:
THE TALE OF THREE WORLDS
AND DEVELOPMENT

> The word "poverty" is, no doubt, a key word of our times,
> extensively used and abused by everyone. Huge amounts
> of money are spent in the name of the poor. Thousands of
> books and expert advice continue to offer solutions to their
> problems. Strangely enough, however, nobody, including
> the proposed "beneficiaries" of these activities, seems to
> have a clear, and commonly shared, view of poverty. For
> one reason, almost all the definitions given to the word are
> woven around the concept of "lack" or "deficiency." This
> notion reflects only the basic relativity of the concept.
> What is necessary and to whom? And who is
> qualified to define all that?"
> —Majid Rahnema, *Global Poverty:*
> *A Pauperizing Myth*, 1991

ONE OF THE many changes that occurred in the early post–World War II period was the "discovery" of mass poverty in Asia, Africa, and Latin America. Relatively inconspicuous and seemingly logical, this discovery was to provide the anchor for an important restructuring of global culture and political economy. The discourse of war was displaced onto the social domain and to a new geographical terrain: the Third World. Left behind was the struggle against fascism. In the rapid globalization of U.S. domination as a world power, the "war on poverty" in the Third World began to occupy a prominent place. Eloquent facts were adduced to justify this new war: "Over 1,500,000 million people, something like two-thirds of the world population, are living in conditions of acute hunger, defined in terms of identifiable nutritional disease. This hunger is at the same time the cause and effect of poverty, squalor, and misery in which they live" (Wilson 1953, 11).

Statements of this nature were uttered profusely throughout the late 1940s and 1950s (Orr 1953; Shonfield 1950; United Nations 1951). The new emphasis was spurred by the recognition of the chronic conditions of poverty and social unrest existing in poor countries and the threat they posed for

more developed countries. The problems of the poor areas irrupted into the
international arena. The United Nations estimated that per capita income in
the United States was $1,453 in 1949, whereas in Indonesia it barely
reached $25. This led to the realization that something had to be done before
the levels of instability in the world as a whole became intolerable. The
destinies of the rich and poor parts of the world were seen to be closely
linked. "Genuine world prosperity is indivisible," stated a panel of experts in
l948. "It cannot last in one part of the world if the other parts live under
conditions of poverty and ill health" (Milbank Memorial Fund 1948, 7; see
also Lasswell 1945).

Poverty on a global scale was a discovery of the post–World War II period. As Sachs (1990) and Rahnema (1991) have maintained, the conceptions
and treatment of poverty were quite different before 1940. In colonial times
the concern with poverty was conditioned by the belief that even if the
"natives" could be somewhat enlightened by the presence of the colonizer,
not much could be done about their poverty because their economic development was pointless. The natives' capacity for science and technology, the
basis for economic progress, was seen as nil (Adas 1989). As the same authors
point out, however, within Asian, African, and Latin or Native American
societies—as well as throughout most of European history—vernacular societies had developed ways of defining and treating poverty that accommodated visions of community, frugality, and sufficiency. Whatever these traditional ways might have been, and without idealizing them, it is true that
massive poverty in the modern sense appeared only when the spread of the
market economy broke down community ties and deprived millions of people from access to land, water, and other resources. With the consolidation
of capitalism, systemic pauperization became inevitable.

Without attempting to undertake an archaeology of poverty, as Rahnema
(1991) proposes, it is important to emphasize the break that occurred in the
conceptions and management of poverty first with the emergence of capitalism in Europe and subsequently with the advent of development in the
Third World. Rahnema describes the first break in terms of the advent in the
nineteenth century of systems for dealing with the poor based on assistance
provided by impersonal institutions. Philanthropy occupied an important
place in this transition (Donzelot 1979). The transformation of the poor into
the assisted had profound consequences. This "modernization" of poverty
signified not only the rupture of vernacular relations but also the setting in
place of new mechanisms of control. The poor increasingly appeared as a
social problem requiring new ways of intervention in society. It was, indeed,
in relation to poverty that the modern ways of thinking about the meaning
of life, the economy, rights, and social management came into place. "Pauperism, political economy, and the discovery of society were closely inter-
woven" (Polanyi 1957a, 84).

The treatment of poverty allowed society to conquer new domains. More perhaps than on industrial and technological might, the nascent order of capitalism and modernity relied on a politics of poverty the aim of which was not only to create consumers but to transform society by turning the poor into objects of knowledge and management. What was involved in this operation was "a techno-discursive instrument that made possible the conquest of pauperism and the invention of a politics of poverty" (Procacci 1991, 157). Pauperism, Procacci explains, was associated, rightly or wrongly, with features such as mobility, vagrancy, independence, frugality, promiscuity, ignorance, and the refusal to accept social duties, to work, and to submit to the logic of the expansion of "needs." Concomitantly, the management of poverty called for interventions in education, health, hygiene, morality, and employment and the instillment of good habits of association, savings, child rearing, and so on. The result was a panoply of interventions that accounted for the creation of a domain that several researchers have termed "the social" (Donzelot 1979, 1988, 1991; Burchell, Gordon, and Miller 1991).

As a domain of knowledge and intervention, the social became prominent in the nineteenth century, culminating in the twentieth century in the consolidation of the welfare state and the ensemble of techniques encompassed under the rubric of social work. Not only poverty but health, education, hygiene, employment, and the poor quality of life in towns and cities were constructed as social problems, requiring extensive knowledge about the population and appropriate modes of social planning (Escobar 1992a). The "government of the social" took on a status that, as the conceptualization of the economy, was soon taken for granted. A "separate class of the 'poor'" (Williams 1973, 104) was created. Yet the most significant aspect of this phenomenon was the setting into place of apparatuses of knowledge and power that took it upon themselves to optimize life by producing it under modern, "scientific" conditions. The history of modernity, in this way, is not only the history of knowledge and the economy, it is also, more revealingly, the history of the social.[1]

As we will see, the history of development implies the continuation in other places of this history of the social. This is the second break in the archaeology of poverty proposed by Rahnema: the globalization of poverty entailed by the construction of two-thirds of the world as poor after 1945. If within market societies the poor were defined as lacking what the rich had in terms of money and material possessions, poor countries came to be similarly defined in relation to the standards of wealth of the more economically advantaged nations. This economic conception of poverty found an ideal yardstick in the annual per capita income. The perception of poverty on a global scale "was nothing more than the result of a comparative statistical operation, the first of which was carried out only in 1940" (Sachs 1990, 9). Almost by fiat, two-thirds of the world's peoples were transformed into poor subjects in 1948 when the World Bank defined as poor those countries with an annual per capita income below $100. And if the problem was one of insufficient income, the solution was clearly economic growth.

Thus poverty became an organizing concept and the object of a new problematization. As in the case of any problematization (Foucault 1986), that of poverty brought into existence new discourses and practices that shaped the reality to which they referred. That the essential trait of the Third World was its poverty and that the solution was economic growth and development became self-evident, necessary, and universal truths. This chapter analyzes the multiple processes that made possible this particular historical event. It accounts for the 'developmentalization' of the Third World, its progressive insertion into a regime of thought and practice in which certain interventions for the eradication of poverty became central to the world order. This chapter can also be seen as an account of the production of the tale of three worlds and the contest over the development of the third. The tale of three worlds was, and continues to be despite the demise of the second, a way of bringing about a political order "that works by the negotiation of boundaries achieved through ordering differences" (Haraway 1989a, 10). It was and is a narrative in which culture, race, gender, nation, and class are deeply and inextricably intertwined. The political and economic order coded by the tale of three worlds and development rests on a traffic of meanings that mapped new domains of being and understanding, the same domains that are increasingly being challenged and displaced by people in the Third World today.

THE INVENTION OF DEVELOPMENT

The Emergence of the New Strategy

From July 11 to November 5, 1949, an economic mission, organized by the International Bank for Reconstruction and Development, visited Colombia with the purpose of formulating a general development program for the country. It was the first mission of this kind sent out by the International Bank to an underdeveloped country. The mission included fourteen international advisers in the following fields: foreign exchange; transportation; industry, fuel, and power; highways and waterways; community facilities; agriculture; health and welfare; financing and banking; economics; national accounts; railroads; and petroleum refineries. Working closely with the mission was a similar group of Colombian advisers and experts.

Here is how the mission saw its task and, consequently, the character of the program proposed:

> We have interpreted our terms of reference as calling for a comprehensive and internally consistent program. . . . The relationships among various sectors of

Colombian economy are very complex, and intensive analysis of these relationships has been necessary to develop a consistent picture. . . . This, then, is the reason and justification for an overall program of development. Piecemeal and sporadic efforts are apt to make little impression on the general picture. Only through a generalized attack throughout the whole economy on education, health, housing, food and productivity can the vicious circle of poverty, ignorance, ill health and low productivity be decisively broken. But once the break is made, the process of economic development can become self-generating. (International Bank 1950, xv)

The program called for a "multitude of improvements and reforms" covering all important areas of the economy. It constituted a radically new representation of, and approach to, a country's social and economic reality. One of the features most emphasized in the approach was its comprehensive and integrated character. Its comprehensive nature demanded programs in all social and economic aspects of importance, whereas careful planning, organization, and allocation of resources ensured the integrated character of the programs and their successful implementation. The report also furnished a detailed set of prescriptions, including goals and quantifiable targets, investment needs, design criteria, methodologies, and time sequences.

It is instructive to quote at length the last paragraph of the report, because it reveals several key features of the approach that was then emerging:

One cannot escape the conclusion that reliance on natural forces has not produced the most happy results. Equally inescapable is the conclusion that with knowledge of the underlying facts and economic processes, good planning in setting objectives and allocating resources, and determination in carrying out a program for improvements and reforms, a great deal can be done to improve the economic environment by shaping economic policies to meet scientifically ascertained social requirements. . . . Colombia is presented with an opportunity unique in its long history. Its rich natural resources can be made tremendously productive through the application of modern techniques and efficient practices. Its favorable international debt and trade position enables it to obtain modern equipment and techniques from abroad. International and foreign national organizations have been established to aid underdeveloped areas technically and financially. All that is needed to usher a period of rapid and widespread development is a determined effort by the Colombian people themselves. In making such an effort, Colombia would not only accomplish its own salvation but would at the same time furnish an inspiring example to all other underdeveloped areas of the world. (International Bank 1950, 615)

The messianic feeling and the quasi-religious fervor expressed in the notion of salvation are noticeable. In this representation, "salvation" entails the conviction that there is one right way, namely, development; only through development will Colombia become an "inspiring example" for the rest of the underdeveloped world. Nevertheless, the task of salvation/development is complex. Fortunately, adequate tools (science, technology, planning, and international organizations) have already been created for such a task, the value of which has already been proved by their successful application in the West. Moreover, these tools are neutral, desirable, and universally applicable. Before development, there was nothing: only "reliance on natural forces," which did not produce "the most happy results." Development brings the light, that is, the possibility to meet "scientifically ascertained social requirements." The country must thus awaken from its lethargic past and follow the one way to salvation, which is, undoubtedly, "an opportunity unique in its long history" (of darkness, one might add).

This is the system of representation that the report upholds. Yet, although couched in terms of humanitarian goals and the preservation of freedom, the new strategy sought to provide a new hold on countries and their resources. A type of development was promoted which conformed to the ideas and expectations of the affluent West, to what the Western countries judged to be a normal course of evolution and progress. As we will see, by conceptualizing progress in such terms, this development strategy became a powerful instrument for normalizing the world. The 1949 World Bank mission to Colombia was one of the first concrete expressions of this new state of affairs.

Precursors and Antecedents of the Development Discourse

As we will see in the next section, the development discourse exemplified by the 1949 World Bank mission to Colombia emerged in the context of a complex historical conjunction. Its invention signaled a significant shift in the historical relations between Europe and the United States, on the one hand, and most countries in Asia, Africa, and Latin America, on the other. It also brought into existence a new regime of representation of these latter parts of the world in Euramerican culture. But "the birth" of the discourse must be briefly qualified; there were, indeed, important precursors that presaged its appearance in full regalia after World War II.

The slow preparation for the launching of development was perhaps most clear in Africa, where, a number of recent studies suggest (Cooper 1991; Page 1991), there was an important connection between the decline of the colonial order and the rise of development. In the interwar period, the ground was prepared for the institution of development as a strategy to remake the colonial world and restructure the relations between colonies and metropoles. As Cooper (1991) has pointed out, the British Development Act of the 1940s—the first great materialization of the development idea—was a response to challenges to imperial power in the 1930s and must thus be seen as an attempt to reinvigorate the empire. This was particularly clear in the settler states in southern Africa, where preoccupations with questions of labor and food supplies led to strategies for the modernization of segments of the African population, often, as Page (1991) argues, at the expense of Afrocentric views of food and community defended by women. These early attempts were to crystallize in community development schemes in the 1950s. The role of the League of Nations in negotiating decolonization through the system of mandates was also important in many cases in Asia and Africa. After the Second World War, this system was extended to a generalized decolonization and the promotion of development by the new system of international organizations (Murphy and Augelli 1993).

Generally speaking, the period between 1920 and 1950 is still ill understood from the vantage point of the overlap of colonial and developmentalist regimes of representation. Some aspects that have received attention in the context of north and/or sub-Saharan Africa include the constitution of a labor force and a modernized class of farmers marked by class, gender, and race, including the displacement of African self-sufficient systems of food and cultural production; the role of the state as architect, for instance, in the "detribalization" of wage labor, the escalation of gender competition, and the struggle over education; the ways in which discourses and practices of agricultural experts, health professionals, urban planners, and educators were deployed in the colonial context, their relation to metropolitan discourses and interests, and the metaphors furnished by them for the reorganization of the colonies; the modification of these discourses and practices in the context of the colonial encounter, their imbrication with local forms of knowledge, and their effect on the latter; and the manifold forms of resistance to the colonial power/knowledge apparatuses (see, for instance, Cooper and Stoler 1989; Stoler 1989; Packard 1989; Page 1991; Rabinow 1989; Comaroff 1985; Comaroff and Comaroff 1991; Rau 1991).

The Latin American case is quite different from the African, although the question of precursors of development must also be investigated there. As is well known, most Latin American countries achieved political independence in the early decades of the nineteenth century, even if on many levels they continued to be under the sway of European economies and cultures. By the beginning of the twentieth century, the ascendancy of the United States was felt in the entire region. United States–Latin American relations took on a double-edged significance early in the century. If on the one hand those in power perceived that opportunities for fair exchange existed, on the other hand the United States felt increasingly justified in intervening in Latin American affairs. From the interventionist big stick policy of the early part of the century to the good neighbor principle of the 1930s, these two tendencies coexisted in U.S. foreign policy toward Latin America, the latter having much more important repercussions than the former.

Robert Bacon, former U.S. secretary of state, exemplified the "fair exchange" position. "The day has gone,"he stated in his 1916 report of a trip to South America, "when the majority of these countries, laboriously building up a governmental structure under tremendous difficulties, were unstable, tottering and likely to fall from one month to another. . . . They 'have passed,' to use the words of Mr. Root, 'out of the condition of militarism, out of the condition of revolution, into the condition of industrialism, into the path of successful commerce, and are becoming great and powerful nations'" (Bacon 1916, 20). Elihu Root, whom Bacon mentioned in a positive light, actually represented the side of active interventionism. A prominent statesman and an expert in international law, Root was a major force in shaping U.S. foreign policy and took active part in the interventionist policy of the earlier part of the century, when the U.S. military occupied most Central American countries. Root, who was awarded the Nobel Peace Prize in 1912, played a very active role in the separation of Colombia from Panama. "With or without the consent of Colombia," he wrote on that occasion, "we will dig the canal, not for selfish reasons, not for greed or gain, but for the world's commerce, benefiting Colombia most of all. . . . We shall unite our Atlantic and Pacific coasts, we shall render inestimable service to mankind, and we shall grow in greatness and honor and in the strength that comes from difficult tasks accomplished and from the exercise of the power that strives in the nature of a great constructive people" (Root 1916, 190).

Root's position embodied the conception of international relations then prevailing in the United States.[2] The readiness for military intervention in the pursuit of U.S. strategic self-interest was tempered from Wilson to Hoover. With Wilson, intervention was accompanied by the goal of promoting "republican" democracies, meaning elite, aristocratic regimes. Often these attempts were fueled by ethnocentric and racist positions. Attitudes of superiority "convinced the United States it had the right and ability to intervene politically in weaker, darker, poorer countries" (Drake 1991, 7). For Wilson, the promotion of democracy was the moral duty of the U.S. and of "good men" in Latin America. "I am going to teach the South American republics to elect good men," he summed up (quoted in Drake 1991, 13). As Latin American nationalism mounted after World War I, the United States reduced open interventionism and proclaimed instead the principles of the open door and the good neighbor, especially after the mid-twenties. Attempts were made to provide some assistance, particularly regarding financial institutions, the infrastructure, and sanitation. During this period the Rockefeller Foundation became active for the first time in the region (Brown 1976). On the whole, however, the 1912–1932 period was ruled by a desire on the part of the United States to achieve "ideological as well as military and economic hegemony and conformity, without having to pay the price of permanent conquest" (Drake 1991, 34).

Although this state of relations revealed an increasing U.S. interest in Latin America, it did not constitute an explicit, overall strategy for dealing with Latin American countries. This situation was profoundly altered during the subsequent decades and especially after the Second World War. Three inter-American conferences—held at Chapultepec in Mexico (February 21–March 8, 1945), Rio de Janeiro (August 1947), and Bogotá (March 30–April 30, 1948)—were crucial in articulating new rules of the game. As the terrain for the cold war was being fertilized, however, these conferences made evident the serious divergence of interests between Latin America and the United States, marking the demise of the good neighbor policy. For while the United States insisted on its military and security objectives, Latin American countries emphasized more than ever economic and social goals (López Maya 1993).[3]

At Chapultepec, several Latin American presidents made clear the importance of industrialization in the consolidation of democracy and asked the United States to help with a program of economic transition from war production of raw materials to industrial production. The United States, however, insisted on questions of hemispheric defense, reducing economic policy to a warning to Latin American countries to abandon "economic nationalism." These disagreements grew at the Rio Conference on Peace and Security. Like the Bogotá conference of 1948—which marked the birth of the Organization of American States—the Rio conference was dominated by the growing anti-Communist crusade. As U.S. foreign policy became more militarized, the need for appropriate economic policies, including the protection of the nascent industries, became more and more central to the Latin American agenda. The United States to some extent finally acknowledged this agenda in Bogotá. Yet then secretary of state General Marshall also made clear that Latin America could in no way expect something similar to the Marshall Plan for Europe (López Maya 1993).

In contrast, the United States insisted on its open door policy of free access of resources to all countries and on the encouragement of private enterprise and the "fair" treatment of foreign capital. U.S. experts on the area completely misread the Latin American situation. A student of U.S. foreign policy toward Latin America during the late 1940s put it thus:

> Latin America was closest to the United States and of far greater economic importance than any other Third World region, but senior U.S. officials increasingly dismissed it as an aberrant, benighted area inhabited by helpless, essentially childish peoples. When George Kennan [head of State Department policy planning] was sent to review what he described as the "unhappy and hopeless" background there, he penned the most acerbic dispatch of his entire career. Not even the Communists seem viable "because their Latin American character inclines them to individualism [and] to undiscipline." . . . Pursuing the motif of

the "childish" nature of the area, he condescendingly argued that if the United States treated the Latin Americans like adults, then perhaps they would have to behave like them (Kolko 1988, 39, 40).[4]

Like Currie's image of "salvation," the representation of the Third World as a child in need of adult guidance was not an uncommon metaphor and lent itself perfectly to the development discourse. The infantilization of the Third World was integral to development as a "secular theory of salvation" (Nandy 1987).

It must be pointed out that the economic demands Latin American countries made were the reflection of changes that had been taking place for several decades and that also prepared the ground for development—for instance, the beginning of industrialization in some countries and the perceived need to expand domestic markets; urbanization and the rise of professional classes; the secularization of political institutions and the modernization of the state; the growth of organized labor and social movements, which disputed and shared the industrialization process; increased attention to positivist sciences; and various types of modernist movements. Some of these factors were becoming salient in the 1920s and accelerated after 1930.[5] But it was not until the World War II years that they began to coalesce into a clearer momentum for national economic models. In Colombia, talk of industrial development and, occasionally, the economic development of the country appeared in the early to mid-1940s, linked to a perceived threat by the popular classes. State interventionism became more noticeable, even if within a general model of economic liberalism, as an increase in production began to be seen as the necessary route to social progress. This awareness was accompanied by a medicalization of the political gaze, to the extent that the popular classes began to be perceived not in racial terms, as until recently, but as diseased, underfed, uneducated, and physiologically weak masses, thus calling for unprecedented social action (Pécaut 1987, 273–352).[6]

Despite the importance of these historical processes, it is possible to speak of the invention of development in the early post–World War II period. In the climate of the great postwar transformations, and in scarcely one decade, relations between rich and poor countries underwent a drastic change. The conceptualization of these relations, the form they took, the scope they acquired, the mechanisms by which they operated, all of these were subject to a substantial mutation. Within the span of a few years, an entirely new strategy for dealing with the problems of the poorer countries emerged and took definite shape. All that was important in the cultural, social, economic, and political life of these countries—their population, the cultural character of their people, their processes of capital accumulation, their agriculture and trade, and so on—entered into this new strategy. In the next section, we look in detail at the set of historical conditions that made the creation of development possible, and then I undertake an analysis of the discourse itself, that is, of the nexus of power, knowledge, and domination which defines it.

HISTORICAL CONDITIONS, 1945–1955

If during World War II the dominant image of what was to become the Third World was shaped by strategic considerations and access to its raw materials, the integration of these parts of the world into the economic and political structure that emerged at the end of the war grew more complicated. From the founding conference of the United Nations held in San Francisco in 1945 and throughout the late 1940s, the fate of the nonindustrialized world was the subject of intense negotiations. Moreover, the notions of underdevelopment and Third World were the discursive products of the post–World War II climate. These concepts did not exist before 1945. They emerged as working principles within the process by which the West—and, in different ways, the East—redefined itself and the rest of the world. By the early 1950s, the notion of three worlds—the free industrialized nations, the Communist industrialized nations, and the poor, nonindustrialized nations, constituting the First, Second, and Third World respectively—was firmly in place. Even after the demise of the Second, the notions of First and Third worlds (and North and South) continue to articulate a regime of geopolitical representation.[7]

For the United States, the dominant concern was the reconstruction of Europe. This entailed the defense of the colonial systems, because the continued access by European powers to the raw materials of their colonies was seen as crucial to their recovery. Struggles for national independence in Asia and Africa were on the increase; these struggles led to the leftist nationalism of the Bandung Conference of 1955 and the strategy of nonalignment. During the late 1940s, in other words, the United States supported European efforts to maintain control of the colonies, although with an eye to increasing its influence over the resources of the colonial areas, most clearly perhaps in the case of Middle East oil.[8]

As far as Latin America was concerned, the major force to contend with for the United States was growing nationalism. Since the Great Depression a number of Latin American countries had begun efforts to build their national economies in a more autonomous fashion than ever before, through state-sponsored industrialization. Middle-class participation in social and political life was on the rise, organized labor was also entering political life, and even the Communist Left had made important gains. In general terms, democracy was emerging as a fundamental component of national life in the sense of a recognized need for the wider participation of popular classes, particularly the working class, and a growing sense of the importance of social justice and the strengthening of the domestic economies. In fact, in the period 1945–1947 many democracies seemed to be in the process of consolidation, and previously dictatorial regimes were undergoing transitions to democracy (Bethell 1991). As already mentioned, the United States completely misread this situation.

Besides the anticolonial struggles in Asia and Africa and growing nationalism in Latin America, other factors shaped the development discourse; these included the cold war, the need to find new markets, the fear of communism and overpopulation, and faith in science and technology.

Finding New Markets and Safe Battlefields

In the fall of 1939, the Inter-American Conference of Foreign Ministers, which met in Panama, proclaimed the neutrality of the American republics. The U.S. government recognized, however, that if this continental unity was to endure, it would have to apply special economic measures to help Latin American nations face the period of distress that was expected to follow the loss of peacetime markets. The first step in this direction was the establishment of the Inter-American Development Commission, set up in January 1940 to encourage Latin American production geared toward the U.S. market. Although financial assistance to Latin America was relatively modest during the war period, nevertheless it was of some significance. The two main sources of assistance, the Export-Import Bank and the Reconstruction Finance Corporation, funded programs for the production and procurement of strategic materials. These activities often involved large-scale technical aid and the mobilization of capital resources to Latin America. The character of these relations also served to focus attention on the need to help the Latin American economies in a more systematic manner.[9]

The year 1945 marked a profound transformation in world affairs. It brought the United States to an undisputable position of economic and military preeminence, placing under its tutelage the whole Western system. This privileged position did not go unchallenged. There was the rising influence of socialist regimes in Eastern Europe and the successful march of Chinese Communists to power. Old colonies in Asia and Africa were claiming independence. The old colonial systems of exploitation and control were no longer tenable. In sum, a reorganization of the structure of world power was taking place.

The period 1945–1955, then, saw the consolidation of U.S. hegemony in the world capitalist system. The need to expand and deepen the market for U.S. products abroad, as well as the need to find new sites for the investment of U.S. surplus capital, became pressing during these years. The expansion óf the U.S. economy also required access to cheap raw materials to support the growing capacity of its industries, especially of the nascent multinational corporations. One economic factor that became more noticeable during the period was the change in the relation of industrial production to the production of foods and raw materials, to the detriment of the latter, which pointed toward the need for an effective program to foster primary production in underdeveloped areas. Yet the fundamental preoccupation of the period was the revitalization of the European economy. A massive program of economic aid to Western Europe was established, which culminated in the formulation of the Marshall Plan in 1948.[10]

The Marshall Plan can be seen as "an exceptional event of historical importance" (Bataille 1991, 173). As Georges Bataille, following French economist François Perroux's 1948 analysis of the plan argued, with the Marshall Plan, and for the first time in the history of capitalism, the general interest of society seemed to have taken primacy over the interest of particular investors or nations. It was, Bataille writes borrowing Perroux's expression, "an investment in the [Western?] world's interest" (177). The mobilization of capital that accompanied the plan ($19 billion in U.S. foreign assistance to Western Europe in the period 1945–1950) was exempt from the law of profit, in what constituted, according to Bataille, a clear reversal of the principles of classical economics. It was "the only way to transfer to Europe the products without which the world's fever would rise" (175). For a short time at least, the United States gave up "the rule on which the capitalist world was based. It was necessary to deliver the goods without payment. It was necessary to *give away* the product of labor" (175).[11]

The Third World was not deserving of the same treatment. Compared with the $19 billion received by Europe, less than 2 percent of total U.S. aid, for instance, went to Latin America during the same period (Bethell 1991, 58); only $150 million for the Third World as a whole were spent in 1953 under the Point Four Program (Kolko 1988, 42). The Third World was instructed to look at private capital, both domestic and foreign, which meant that the "right climate" had to be created, including a commitment to capitalist development; the curbing of nationalism; and the control of the Left, the working class, and the peasantry. The creation of the International Bank for Reconstruction and Development (most commonly known as the World Bank) and the International Monetary Fund did not represent a departure from this law. To this extent, "the inadequacy of the International Bank and the Monetary Fund presented a negative version of the Marshall Plan's positive initiative" (Bataille 1991, 177). Development, in this way, fell short from the outset. The fate of the Third World was seen as part of the "general interest" of humankind only in a very a limited manner.[12]

The cold war was undoubtedly one of the single most important factors at play in the conformation of the strategy of development. The historical roots of development and those of East-West politics lie in one and the same process: the political rearrangements that occurred after World War II. In the late 1940s, the real struggle between East and West had already moved to the Third World, and development became the grand strategy for advancing such rivalry and, at the same time, the designs of industrial civilization. The confrontation between the United States and the Soviet Union thus lent legitimacy to the enterprise of modernization and development; to extend the sphere of political and cultural influence became an end in itself.

The relationship between military concerns and the origins of development has scarcely been studied. Pacts of military assistance, for example, were signed at the Rio conference of 1947 between the United States and all Latin American countries (Varas 1985). In time, they would give way to doctrines of national security intimately linked to development strategies. It is no coincidence that the vast majority of the approximately 150 wars of the last four decades were fought in the Third World, many of them with the direct or indirect participation of powers external to the Third World (Soedjatmoko 1985). The Third World, far from being peripheral, was central to superpower rivalry and the possibility of nuclear confrontation. The system that generates conflict and instability and the system that generates underdevelopment are inextricably bound. Although the end of the cold war and the rise of the New World Order have changed the configuration of power, the Third World is still the most important arena of confrontation (as the Gulf War, the bombing of Libya, and the invasions of Grenada and Panama indicate). Although increasingly differentiated, the South is still, perhaps more clearly than ever, the opposite camp to a growingly unified North, despite the latter's localized ethnic wars.

Anti-Fascist sentiment easily gave way to anti-Communist crusades after the war. The fear of communism became one of the most compelling arguments for development. It was commonly accepted in the early 1950s that if poor countries were not rescued from their poverty, they would succumb to communism. To a greater or lesser extent, most early writings on development reflect this preoccupation. The espousal of economic development as a means of combating communism was not confined to military or academic circles. It found an even more welcoming niche in the offices of the U.S. government, in numerous smaller organizations, and among the American public. The control of communism, the ambivalent acceptance of the independence of former European colonies as a concession to preventing their falling into the Soviet camp, and the continued access to crucial Third World raw materials, on which the U.S. economy was growing increasingly dependent, were part of the United States's reassessment of the Third World in the period that ended with the Korean War.

Poor and Ignorant Masses

The war on poverty was justified on additional grounds, particularly the urgency believed to characterize the "population problem." Statements and positions regarding population began to proliferate. In many instances, a crude form of empiricism was followed, making Malthusian views and prescriptions inevitable, although economists and demographers made serious attempts to conceptualize the effect of demographic factors on development.[13] Models and theories were formulated seeking to relate the various variables and to provide a basis for policy and program formulation. As the experience of the West suggested, it was hoped that growth rates would begin to fall as the countries developed; but, as many warned, countries could not wait for this process to occur and should speed up the reduction of fertility by more direct means.[14]

To be sure, this preoccupation with population had existed for several decades, especially in relation to Asia.[15] It was a central topic in discussions on race and racism. But the scale and form that the discussion took were new. As one author stated, "It is probable that in the last five years more copies have been published of discussions related to population than in all the previous centuries" (Pendell 1951, 377). The discussions held in academic circles or in the ambit of the nascent international organizations also had a new tone; they focused on topics such as the relationship between economic growth and population growth; between population, resources, and output; between cultural factors and birth control. They also took on topics such as the demographic experience of the rich countries and its possible extrapolation to the poor ones; the factors affecting human fertility and mortality; population trends and projections for the future; the conditions necessary for successful population control programs; and so on. In other words, in much the same way that was happening with race and racism during the same period[16]—and in spite of the persistence of blatant racist views—the discourses on population were being redeployed within the "scientific" realm provided by demography, public health, and population biology. A new view of population, and of scientific and technological instruments to manage it, was taking shape.[17]

The Promise of Science and Technology

The faith in science and technology, invigorated by the new sciences arising from the war effort, such as nuclear physics and operations research, played an important role in the elaboration and justification of the new discourse of development. In 1948, a well-known UN official expressed this faith in the following way: "I still think that human progress depends on the development and application of the greatest possible extent of scientific research. . . . The development of a country depends primarily on a material factor: first, the knowledge, and then the exploitation of all its natural resources" (Laugier 1948, 256).

Science and technology had been the markers of civilization par excellence since the nineteenth century, when machines became the index of civilization, "the measure of men" (Adas 1989). This modern trait was rekindled with the advent of the development age. By 1949, the Marshall Plan was showing great success in the restoration of the European economy, and increasingly attention was shifted to the longer-range problems of assistance for economic development in underdeveloped areas. Out of this shift of attention came the famous Point Four Program of President Truman, with which I opened this book. The Point Four Program involved the application to the poor areas of the world what were considered to be two vital forces: modern technology and capital. However, it relied much more heavily on technical assistance than on capital, in the belief that the former would provide progress at a lower price. An Act for International Development was approved by Congress in May 1950, which provided authority to finance and carry out a variety of international technical cooperation activities. In October of the same year, the Technical Cooperation Administration (TCA) was established within the Department of State with the task of implementing the new policies. By 1952, these agencies were conducting operations in nearly every country in Latin America, as well as in several countries in Asia and Africa (Brown and Opie 1953).

Technology, it was believed, would not only amplify material progress, it would also confer upon it a sense of direction and significance. In the vast literature on the sociology of modernization, technology was theorized as a sort of moral force that would operate by creating an ethics of innovation, yield, and result. Technology thus contributed to the planetary extension of modernist ideals. The concept of the transfer of technology in time would become an important component of development projects. It was never realized that such a transfer would depend not merely on technical elements but on social and cultural factors as well. Technology was seen as neutral and inevitably beneficial, not as an instrument for the creation of cultural and social orders (Morandé 1984; García de la Huerta 1992).

The new awareness of the importance of the Third World in global economy and politics, coupled with the beginning of field activities in the Third World, brought with it a recognition of the need to obtain more accurate knowledge about the Third World. Nowhere was this need perceived more acutely than in the case of Latin America. As a prominent Latin Americanist put it, "The war years witnessed a remarkable growth of interest in Latin America. What once had been an area which only diplomats and pioneering scholars ventured to explore, became almost overnight the center of attraction to government officials, as well as to scholars and teachers" (Burgin [1947] 1967, 466). This called for "detailed knowledge of the economic potential of Latin America as well as of the geographic, social and political environment in which that potential was to be realized" (466). Only in "history, literature and ethnology" was the status of knowledge considered adequate. What was needed now was the kind of precise knowledge that could be obtained through the application of the new "scientific" social sciences that were experiencing remarkable growth on U.S. campuses (such as Parsonian sociology, Keynesian macroeconomics, systems analysis and operations research, demography, and statistics). In 1949, an illustrious Peruvian scholar described the "mission of Latin American Studies" as, "through study and research, [to] provide a background which will assist in interpreting and evaluating objectively the problems and events of the day from the perspective of history, geography, economics, sociology, anthropology, social psychology and political science" (Basadre [1949] 1967, 434).

Basadre's was a progressive call for social change as well, even if it became captive to the development mode. The earlier model for the generation of knowledge, organized around the classical professions according to nineteenth-century usage, was replaced by the North American model. Sociology and economics were the disciplines most affected by this change, which involved most natural and social sciences. Development had to rely on the production of knowledge that could provide a scientific picture of a country's social and economic problems and resources. This entailed the establishment of institutions capable of generating such a knowledge. The "tree of research" of the North was transplanted to the South, and Latin America thus became part of a transnational system of research. As some maintain, although this transformation created new knowledge capabilities, it also implied a further loss of autonomy and the blocking of different modes of knowing (Fuenzalida 1983; Morandé 1984; Escobar 1989).

Gone were the days, so most scholars thought in the wake of empirical social science, when science was contaminated by prejudice and error. The new objectivity ensured accuracy and fairness of representation. Little by little, older ways of thinking would yield to the new spirit. Economists were quick to join this wave of enthusiasm. Latin America was suddenly discovered to be "a *tabula rasa* to the economic historian" (Burgin [1947] 1967, 474), and economic thinking in Latin America was found to be devoid of any connection with local conditions, a mere appendage of European classical economics. The new scholars realized that "the starting point of research must be the area itself, for it is only in terms of its historical development and objectives that the organization and functioning of the economy can be fully understood" (469). The terrain was prepared for the emergence of economic development as a legitimate theoretical endeavor.

The better and more widespread understanding of the workings of the economic system strengthened the hope of bringing material prosperity to the rest of the world. The unquestioned desirability of economic growth was, in this way, closely linked to the revitalized faith in science and technology. Economic growth presupposed the existence of a continuum stretching from poor to rich countries, which would allow for the replication in the poor countries of those conditions characteristic of mature capitalist ones (including industrialization, urbanization, agricultural modernization, infrastructure, increased provision of social services, and high levels of literacy). Development was seen as the process of transition from one situation to the other. This notion conferred upon the processes of accumulation and development a progressive, orderly, and stable character that would culminate, in the late 1950s and early 1960s, in modernization and "stages of economic growth" theories (Rostow 1960).[18]

Finally, there was another factor that influenced the formation of the new strategy of development: the increased experience with public intervention in the economy. Although the desirability of this intervention, as opposed to a more laissez-faire approach, was still a matter of controversy,[19] the recognition of the need for some sort of planning or government action was becoming generalized. The experience of social planning during the New Deal, legitimized by Keynesianism, as well as the "planned communities" envisaged and partly implemented in Native American communities and Japanese American internment camps in the United States (James 1984), represented significant approaches to social intervention in this regard; so were the statutory corporations and public utility companies established in industrialized countries by government enterprise—for instance, the British Broadcasting Commission (BBC) and the Tennessee Valley Authority (TVA). Following the TVA model, a number of regional development corporations were set up in Latin America and other parts of the Third World.[20] Models for national, regional, and sectoral planning became essential for the spread and functioning of development.

These, very broadly stated, were the most important conditions that made possible and shaped the new discourse of development. There was a reorganization of power at the world level, the final result of which was still far from clear; important changes had occurred in the structure of production, which had to be brought to fit the requirements of expansion of a capitalist system in which the underdeveloped countries played an increasingly important role, if yet not thoroughly defined. These countries could forge alliances with any pole of power. In the light of expanding communism, the steady deterioration of living conditions, and the alarming increase in their populations, the direction in which they would decide to go would largely depend on a type of action of an urgent nature and unprecedented level.

Rich countries, however, were believed to have the financial and technological capacity to secure progress the world over. A look at their own past
instilled in them the firm conviction that this was not only possible—let
alone desirable—but perhaps even inevitable. Sooner or later the poor
countries would become rich, and the underdeveloped world would be developed. A new type of economic knowledge and an enriched experience
with the design and management of social systems made this goal look even
more plausible. Now it was a matter of an appropriate strategy to do it, of
setting in motion the right forces to ensure progress and world happiness.

Behind the humanitarian concern and the positive outlook of the new
strategy, new forms of power and control, more subtle and refined, were put
in operation. Poor people's ability to define and take care of their own lives
was eroded in a deeper manner than perhaps ever before. The poor became
the target of more sophisticated practices, of a variety of programs that
seemed inescapable. From the new institutions of power in the United
States and Europe; from the offices of the International Bank for Reconstruction and Development and the United Nations; from North American
and European campuses, research centers, and foundations; and from the
new planning offices in the big capitals of the underdeveloped world, this
was the type of development that was actively promoted and that in a few
years was to extend its reach to all aspects of society. Let us now see how this
set of historical factors resulted in the new discourse of development.

THE DISCOURSE OF DEVELOPMENT

The Space of Development

What does it mean to say that development started to function as a discourse, that is, that it created a space in which only certain things could be
said and even imagined? If discourse is the process through which social
reality comes into being—if it is the articulation of knowledge and power, of
the visible and the expressible—how can the development discourse be individualized and related to ongoing technical, political, and economic
events? How did development become a space for the systematic creation of
concepts, theories, and practices?

An entry point for this inquiry on the nature of development as discourse
is its basic premises as they were formulated in the 1940s and 1950s. The
organizing premise was the belief in the role of modernization as the only
force capable of destroying archaic superstitions and relations, at whatever
social, cultural, and political cost. Industrialization and urbanization were
seen as the inevitable and necessarily progressive routes to modernization.
Only through material advancement could social, cultural, and political

progress be achieved. This view determined the belief that capital investment was the most important ingredient in economic growth and development. The advance of poor countries was thus seen from the outset as
depending on ample supplies of capital to provide for infrastructure, industrialization, and the overall modernization of society. Where was this capital
to come from? One possible answer was domestic savings. But these countries were seen as trapped in a "vicious circle" of poverty and lack of capital,
so that a good part of the "badly needed" capital would have to come from
abroad (see chapter 3). Moreover, it was absolutely necessary that governments and international organizations take an active role in promoting and
orchestrating the necessary efforts to overcome general backwardness and
economic underdevelopment.

What, then, were the most important elements that went into the formulation of development theory, as gleaned from the earlier description? There
was the process of capital formation, and the various factors associated with
it: technology, population and resources, monetary and fiscal policies, industrialization and agricultural development, commerce and trade. There were
also a series of factors linked to cultural considerations, such as education
and the need to foster modern cultural values. Finally, there was the need
to create adequate institutions for carrying out the complex task ahead: international organizations (such as the World Bank and the International
Monetary Fund, created in 1944, and most of the United Nations technical
agencies, also a product of the mid- 1940s); national planning agencies
(which proliferated in Latin America, especially after the inauguration of the
Alliance for Progress in the early 1960s); and technical agencies of various
kinds.

Development was not merely the result of the combination, study, or
gradual elaboration of these elements (some of these topics had existed for
some time); nor the product of the introduction of new ideas (some of which
were already appearing or perhaps were bound to appear); nor the effect of
the new international organizations or financial institutions (which had some
predecessors, such as the League of Nations). It was rather the result of the
establishment of a set of relations among these elements, institutions, and
practices and of the systematization of these relations to form a whole. The
development discourse was constituted not by the array of possible objects
under its domain but by the way in which, thanks to this set of relations, it
was able to form systematically the objects of which it spoke, to group them
and arrange them in certain ways, and to give them a unity of their own.[21]

To understand development as a discourse, one must look not at the elements themselves but at the system of relations established among them. It
is this system that allows the systematic creation of objects, concepts, and
strategies; it determines what can be thought and said. These relations—
established between institutions, socioeconomic processes, forms of knowl-

edge, technological factors, and so on—define the conditions under which objects, concepts, theories, and strategies can be incorporated into the discourse. In sum, the system of relations establishes a discursive practice that sets the rules of the game: who can speak, from what points of view, with what authority, and according to what criteria of expertise; it sets the rules that must be followed for this or that problem, theory, or object to emerge and be named, analyzed, and eventually transformed into a policy or a plan.

The objects with which development began to deal after 1945 were numerous and varied. Some of them stood out clearly (poverty, insufficient technology and capital, rapid population growth, inadequate public services, archaic agricultural practices, and so on), whereas others were introduced with more caution or even in surreptitious ways (such as cultural attitudes and values and the existence of racial, religious, geographic, or ethnic factors believed to be associated with backwardness). These elements emerged from a multiplicity of points: the newly formed international organizations, government offices in distant capitals, old and new institutions, universities and research centers in developed countries, and, increasingly with the passing of time, institutions in the Third World. Everything was subjected to the eye of the new experts: the poor dwellings of the rural masses, the vast agricultural fields, cities, households, factories, hospitals, schools, public offices, towns and regions, and, in the last instance, the world as a whole. The vast surface over which the discourse moved at ease practically covered the entire cultural, economic, and political geography of the Third World.

However, not all the actors distributed throughout this surface could identify objects to be studied and have their problems considered. Some clear principles of authority were in operation. They concerned the role of experts, from whom certain criteria of knowledge and competence were asked; institutions such as the United Nations, which had the moral, professional, and legal authority to name subjects and define strategies; and the international lending organizations, which carried the symbols of capital and power. These principles of authority also concerned the governments of poor countries, which commanded the legal political authority over the lives of their subjects, and the position of leadership of the rich countries, who had the power, knowledge, and experience to decide on what was to be done.

Economists, demographers, educators, and experts in agriculture, public health, and nutrition elaborated their theories, made their assessments and observations, and designed their programs from these institutional sites. Problems were continually identified, and client categories brought into existence. Development proceeded by creating "abnormalities" (such as the "illiterate," the "underdeveloped," the "malnourished," "small farmers," or "landless peasants"), which it would later treat and reform. Approaches that could have had positive effects in terms of easing material constraints became, linked to this type of rationality, instruments of power and control. As time went by, new problems were progressively and selectively incorporated; once a problem was incorporated into the discourse, it had to be categorized and further specified. Some problems were specified at a given level (such as local or regional), or at various of these levels (for instance, a nutritional deficiency identified at the level of the household could be further specified as a regional production shortage or as affecting a given population group), or in relation to a particular institution. But these refined specifications did not seek so much to illuminate possible solutions as to give "problems" a visible reality amenable to particular treatments.

This seemingly endless specification of problems required detailed observations in villages, regions, and countries in the Third World. Complete dossiers of countries were elaborated, and techniques of information were designed and constantly refined. This feature of the discourse allowed for the mapping of the economic and social life of countries, constituting a true political anatomy of the Third World.[22] The end result was the creation of a space of thought and action the expansion of which was dictated in advance by the very same rules introduced during its formative stages. The development discourse defined a perceptual field structured by grids of observation, modes of inquiry and registration of problems, and forms of intervention; in short, it brought into existence a space defined not so much by the ensemble of objects with which it dealt but by a set of relations and a discursive practice that systematically produced interrelated objects, concepts, theories, strategies, and the like.

To be sure, new objects have been included, new modes of operation introduced, and a number of variables modified (for instance, in relation to strategies to combat hunger, knowledge about nutritional requirements, the types of crops given priority, and the choices of technology have changed); yet the same set of relations among these elements continues to be established by the discursive practices of the institutions involved. Moreover, seemingly opposed options can easily coexist within the same discursive field (for instance, in development economics, the structuralist school and the monetarist school seem to be in open contradiction; yet they belong to the same discursive formation and originate in the same set of relations, as will be shown in the next chapter; it can also be shown that agrarian reform, green revolution, and integrated rural development are strategies through which the same unity, "hunger," is constructed, as I will do in chapter 4). In other words, although the discourse has gone through a series of structural changes, the architecture of the discursive formation laid down in the period 1945–1955 has remained unchanged, allowing the discourse to adapt to new conditions. The result has been the succession of development strategies and substrategies up to the present, always within the confines of the same discursive space.

It is also clear that other historical discourses influenced particular representations of development. The discourse of communism, for instance, influenced the promotion of those choices which emphasized the role of the individual in society and, in particular, those approaches which relied on private initiative and private property. So much emphasis on this issue in the context of development, so strong a moralizing attitude probably would not have existed without the persistent anti-Communist preaching that originated in the cold war. Similarly, the fact that economic development relied so much on the need for foreign exchange influenced the promotion of cash crops for export, to the detriment of food crops for domestic consumption. Yet the ways in which the discourse organized these elements cannot be reduced to causal relations, as I will show in later chapters.

In a similar vein, patriarchy and ethnocentrism influenced the form development took. Indigenous populations had to be "modernized," where modernization meant the adoption of the "right" values, namely, those held by the white minority or a mestizo majority and, in general, those embodied in the ideal of the cultivated European; programs for industrialization and agricultural development, however, not only have made women invisible in their role as producers but also have tended to perpetuate their subordination (see chapter 5). Forms of power in terms of class, gender, race, and nationality thus found their way into development theory and practice. The former do not determine the latter in a direct causal relation; rather they are the development discourse's formative elements.

The examination of any given object should be done within the context of the discourse as a whole. The emphasis on capital accumulation, for instance, emerged as part of a complex set of relations in which technology, new financial institutions, systems of classification (GNP per capita), decision-making systems (such as new mechanisms for national accounting and the allocation of public resources), modes of knowledge, and international factors all played a role. What made development economists privileged figures was their position in this complex system. Options privileged or excluded must also be seen in light of the dynamics of the entire discourse— why, for instance, the discourse privileged the promotion of cash crops (to secure foreign exchange, according to capital and technological imperatives) and not food crops; centralized planning (to satisfy economic and knowledge requirements) but not participatory and decentralized approaches; agricultural development based on large mechanized farms and the use of chemical inputs but not alternative agricultural systems, based on smaller farms, ecological considerations, and integrated cropping and pest management; rapid economic growth but not the articulation of internal markets to satisfy the needs of the majority of the people; and capital-intensive but not labor-intensive solutions. With the deepening of the crisis, some of the previously excluded choices are being considered, although most often within a developmentalist perspective, as in the case of the sustainable development strategy, to be discussed in later chapters.

Finally, what is included as legitimate development issues may depend on specific relations established in the midst of the discourse; relations, for instance, between what experts say and what international politics allows as feasible (this may determine, for instance, what an international organization may prescribe out of the recommendation of a group of experts); between one power segment and another (say, industry versus agriculture); or between two or more forms of authority (for instance, the balance between nutritionists and public health specialists, on the one hand, and the medical profession, on the other, which may determine the adoption of particular approaches to rural health care). Other types of relations to be considered are those between sites from which objects appear (for instance, between rural and urban areas); between procedures of assessment of needs (such as the use of "empirical data" by World Bank missions) and the position of authority of those carrying the assessment (this may determine the proposals made and the possibility of their implementation).

Relations of this type regulate development practice. Although this practice is not static, it continues to reproduce the same relations between the elements with which it deals. It was this systematization of relations that conferred upon development its great dynamic quality: its immanent adaptability to changing conditions, which allowed it to survive, indeed to thrive, up to the present. By 1955 a discourse had emerged which was characterized not by a unified object but by the formation of a vast number of objects and strategies; not by new knowledge but by the systematic inclusion of new objects under its domain. The most important exclusion, however, was and continues to be what development was supposed to be all about: people. Development was—and continues to be for the most part—a top-down, ethnocentric, and technocratic approach, which treated people and cultures as abstract concepts, statistical figures to be moved up and down in the charts of "progress." Development was conceived not as a cultural process (culture was a residual variable, to disappear with the advance of modernization) but instead as a system of more or less universally applicable technical interventions intended to deliver some "badly needed" goods to a "target" population. It comes as no surprise that development became a force so destructive to Third World cultures, ironically in the name of people's interests.

The Professionalization and Institutionalization of Development

Development was a response to the problematization of poverty that took place in the years following World War II and not a natural process of knowledge that gradually uncovered problems and dealt with them; as such, it must be seen as a historical construct that provides a space in which poor countries are known, specified, and intervened upon. To speak of development as a historical construct requires an analysis of the mechanisms through which it becomes an active, real force. These mechanisms are structured by forms of knowledge and power and can be studied in terms of processes of institutionalization and professionalization.

The concept of professionalization refers mainly to the process that brings the Third World into the politics of expert knowledge and Western science in general. This is accomplished through a set of techniques, strategies, and disciplinary practices that organize the generation, validation, and diffusion of development knowledge, including the academic disciplines, methods of research and teaching, criteria of expertise, and manifold professional practices; in other words, those mechanisms through which a politics of truth is created and maintained, through which certain forms of knowledge are given the status of truth. This professionalization was effected through the proliferation of development sciences and subdisciplines. It made possible the progressive incorporation of problems into the space of development, bringing problems to light in ways congruent with the established system of knowledge and power.

The professionalization of development also made it possible to remove all problems from the political and cultural realms and to recast them in terms of the apparently more neutral realm of science. It resulted in the establishment of development studies programs in most major universities in the developed world and conditioned the creation or restructuring of Third World universities to suit the needs of development. The empirical social sciences, on the rise since the late 1940s, especially in the United States and England, were instrumental in this regard. So were the area studies programs, which became fashionable after the war in academic and policy-making circles. As already mentioned, the increasingly professionalized character of development caused a radical reorganization of knowledge institutions in Latin America and other parts of the Third World. Professionalized development required the production of knowledge that could allow experts and planners "scientifically [to] ascertain social requirements," to recall Currie's words (Fuenzalida 1983, 1987).[23]

An unprecedented will to know everything about the Third World flourished unhindered, growing like a virus. Like the landing of the Allies in Normandy, the Third World witnessed a massive landing of experts, each in charge of investigating, measuring, and theorizing about this or that little aspect of Third World societies.[24] The policies and programs that originated from this vast field of knowledge inevitably carried with them strong normalizing components. At stake was a politics of knowledge that allowed experts to classify problems and formulate policies, to pass judgment on entire social groups and forecast their future—to produce, in short, a regime of truth and norms about them. The consequences for these groups and countries cannot be emphasized enough.

Another important consequence of the professionalization of development was the inevitable translation of Third World people and their interests into research data within Western capitalist paradigms. There is a further paradox in this situation. As an African scholar put it, "Our own history, culture and practices, good or bad, are discovered and translated in the journals of the North and come back to us re-conceptualized, couched in languages and paradigms which make it all sound new and novel" (Namuddu 1989, 28; quoted in Mueller 1991, 5). The magnitude and consequences of this apparently neutral but profoundly ideological operation is fully explored in subsequent chapters.

The invention of development necessarily involved the creation of an institutional field from which discourses are produced, recorded, stabilized, modified, and put into circulation. This field is intimately imbricated with processes of professionalization; together they constitute an apparatus that organizes the production of forms of knowledge and the deployment of forms of power, relating one to the other. The institutionalization of development took place at all levels, from the international organizations and national planning agencies in the Third World to local development agencies, community development committees, private voluntary agencies, and nongovernmental organizations. Starting in the mid-1940s with the creation of the great international organizations, this process has not ceased to spread, resulting in the consolidation of an effective network of power. It is through the action of this network that people and communities are bound to specific cycles of cultural and economic production and through which certain behaviors and rationalities are promoted. This field of intervention relies on myriad local centers of power, in turn supported by forms of knowledge that circulate at the local level.

The knowledge produced about the Third World is utilized and circulated by these institutions through applied programs, conferences, international consultant services, local extension practices, and so on. A corollary of this process is the establishment of an ever-expanding development business; as John Kenneth Galbraith wrote, referring to the climate in U.S. universities in the early 1950s, "No economic subject more quickly captured the attention of so many as the rescue of the people of the poor countries from their poverty" (1979, 29). Poverty, illiteracy, and even hunger became the basis of a lucrative industry for planners, experts, and civil servants (Rahnema 1986). This is not to deny that the work of these institutions might have benefited people at times. It is to emphasize that the work of development institutions has not been an innocent effort on behalf of the poor. Rather, development has been successful to the extent that it has been able to integrate, manage, and control countries and populations in increasingly detailed and encompassing ways. If it has failed to solve the basic problems of underdevelopment, it can be said—perhaps with greater pertinence—that it has succeeded well in creating a type of underdevelopment that has been, for the most part, politically and technically manageable. The discord between institutionalized development and the situation of popular groups in the Third World has only grown with each development decade, as popular groups themselves are becoming apt at demonstrating.

THE INVENTION OF "THE VILLAGE": DEVELOPMENT AT THE LOCAL LEVEL

James Ferguson (1990) has shown that the construction in development literature of Third World societies as less developed countries—similar to the World Bank mission's construction of Colombia as underdeveloped in 1949—is an essential feature of the development apparatus. In the case of Lesotho, for instance, this construction relied on three main features: portraying the country as an aboriginal economy, cut off from world markets; picturing its population as peasant and its agricultural production as traditional; and assuming that the country is a national economy and that it is the task of the national government to develop the country. Tropes such as "less developed country" repeat themselves in an endless number of situations and with many variations. Mitchell's (1991) analysis of the portrayal of Egypt in terms of the trope "the overcrowded Nile River valley" is another case in point. As he points out, development reports on Egypt invariably start with a description of 98 percent of the population crammed onto 4 percent of the land along the Nile River. The result of this description is an understanding of "the problem" in terms of natural limits, topography, physical space, and social reproduction, calling for solutions such as improved management, new technologies, and population control.

Mitchell's deconstruction of this simple but powerful trope starts by recognizing that "objects of analysis do not occur as natural phenomena, but are partly constructed by the discourse that describes them. The more natural the object appears, the less obvious this discursive construction is. . . . The naturalness of the topographic image sets up the object of development as just that—an object, out there, not a part of the study but external to it" (1991, 19). Moreover, a more subtle ideological operation is at play:

> Development discourse wishes to present itself as a detached center of rationality and intelligence. The relationship between West and non-West will be constructed in these terms. The West possesses the expertise, technology and management skills that the non-West is lacking. This lack is what has caused the

problems of the non-West. Questions of power and inequality . . . will nowhere be discussed. To remain silent on such questions, in which its own existence is involved, development discourse needs an object that appears to stand outside itself. What more natural object could there be, for such a purpose, than the image of a narrow river valley, hemmed in by the desert, crowded with rapidly multiplying millions of inhabitants? (1991, 33)

The tropes of the discourse repeat themselves at all levels, even if few studies exist to date of the effect and modes of operation of development discourses at the local level. There are already indications, however, of how development images and languages circulate at the local level, for instance, in Malaysian villages where educated villagers and party officials have become adept at using the language of development promoted by the national and regional governments (Ong 1987). A rich texture of resistance to the practices and symbols of development technologies, such as the green revolution, has also been highlighted (Taussig 1980; Fals Borda 1984; Scott 1985). Yet local-level ethnographic studies that focus on development discourses and practices—how they are introduced in community settings, their modes of operation, the ways in which they are transformed or utilized, their effects on community identity formation and structures, and so on— are just beginning to be conducted.

Stacy Leigh Pigg's excellent study of the introduction of images of development in communities in Nepal is perhaps the first study of this kind. Pigg (1992) centers her analysis on the construction of another trope, "the village," as an effect of the introduction of the development discourse. Her interest is to show how ideologies of modernization and development become effective in local culture, even if, as she warns, the process cannot be reduced to simple assimilation or appropriation of Western models. On the contrary, a complex Nepalization of development concepts occurs, peculiar to Nepal's history and culture. The Nepalized concept of development (*bikas*) becomes an important social organizing force through a variety of means, including its participation in scales of social progress structured according to place of residence (rural versus urban), mode of livelihood (from nomadic herding to office work), religion (Buddhist to more orthodox Hindu), and race (Central Asian to Aryan). In these scales, bikas pertains more to one pole than to the other, as villagers incorporate the ideology of modernization into local social identity to become bikasi.

Bikas thus transforms what it means to be a villager. This effect is a result of how the village is constructed by the bikas discourse. As in the case of the trope of the "less developed country," a generic village is produced by the discourse:

It follows that the generic village should be inhabited by generic villagers. . . . People in development planning "know" that villagers have certain habits, goals, motivations and beliefs. . . . The "ignorance" of villagers is not an absence of knowledge. Quite the contrary. It is the presence of too much locally-instilled belief. . . . The problem, people working in development will tell each other and a foreign visitor, is that villagers "don't understand things." To speak of "people who don't understand" is a way of identifying people as "villagers." As long as development aims to transform people's thinking, the villager must be someone who doesn't understand. (Pigg 1992, 17, 20)

More often than not, Nepalese development workers understand the discord between the attitudes and habits they are supposed to promote and those that exist in the villages; they are aware of the diversity of local situations in opposition to the homogenized village. Yet because what they know about real villages cannot be translated upward into the language of development, they fall back into the construct of "villagers" who "don't understand things." Pigg, however, states that social categories of development are not simply imposed; they circulate at the village level in complex ways, changing the way villagers orient themselves in local and national society. Places are arranged according to how much bikas they have achieved (water pipes, electricity, new breeds of goats, health posts, roads, videos, bus stops); and although people know that bikas comes from the outside, they endorse bikas thinking as a way to become bikasi. People thus move between two systems for framing local identity: one marked by local distinctions in terms of age, caste/ethnicity, gender, patronage, and the like; and the other the national society, with its centers, peripheries, and degrees of development.

As the bikas apparatus becomes more important in terms of providing jobs and other means of social wealth and power, more and more people want a piece of the bikas pie. Indeed, it is not so much to be a beneficiary of development programs that people want—they know they do not get much out of these programs—but to become a salaried worker in the implementation of bikas. Pigg, in sum, shows how the culture of development works within and through local cultures. The development encounter, she adds, should be seen not so much as the clash of two cultural systems but as an intersection that creates situations in which people come to see each other in certain ways. In the process, social differences come to be represented in new ways, even if the prevailing forms (in terms of caste, class, and gender, for instance) do not disappear; they are given new meaning, and new forms of social positioning appear.

The general question this case study raises is the circulation and effects of languages of development and modernity in different parts of the Third World. The answer to this question is specific to each locality—its history of immersion in the world economy, colonial heritage, patterns of insertion into development, and the like. Three additional brief examples will bring this point home. What is bikas in Nepalese villages is kamap ("coming up") in Gapun, a small village in Papua New Guinea in which the quest for development has become a way of life. In Gapun, the reservoir of images of development comes form the village's history, marked by the steady influence of Catholic missionaries, Australian colonial administrators, and Japanese and American soldiers. It is also shaped by cargo cults, particularly the villagers' belief that their ancestors will return from the dead, bringing with them all the cargo that white people had. With the advent of cash crops, the symbols of development have multiplied as people's economic activities diversified. Today, prestige foods like packaged white rice and Nescafé top the list as signs of development. As in Nepal, lack of development is identified with features such as the persistence of traditional ways and carrying heavy loads. Children now go to school to learn about white people and their ways.

Yet this does not mean that Gapun is just becoming "modernized." In fact, much of the cash obtained is spent in traditional ways such as feasts, although to the customary yams and pigs are added rice and Nescafé for festive occasions. And although *kamap* signifies a transformation of the Gapuners' ways of existence into those beyond their shores, "coming up" "is not envisaged so much as a process, but rather as a sudden metamorphosis, a miraculous transformation—of their houses into corrugated iron, of their swampy land into a tarred web of highways, or their food into rice and *tinpis* [canned mackerel] and Nescafé, and of their skins, most significantly, into white" (Kulick 1992, 23). This metamorphosis is religious in nature rather than a scientific or economic enterprise. Development in Gapun is, in fact, a sort of sophisticated cargo cult; literacy, schooling, and politics are evaluated in terms of cargo, even as the vernacular language is displaced by the introduction of schooling in the 1960s. Gapuners, in short, have a clear idea about what development means and where it leads, even if couched in a strikingly different language and different cultural practices.

Another study of the nature of development at the local level concerns women's notions of development and modernity in the town of Lamu, Kenya. In this community, the models of development are even more diversified; besides the Western sources, they include Islamic movements (revivalist or revisionist), cultural productions brought by migrants returning from affluent Arab states, and Indian music, films, and soap operas transmitted through videocassettes and the mass media. The crux of the matter is women's evolving understanding of what it means to be developed and modern while retaining their identity as Muslim. Female identity is at the center of this process, including questions such as whether to use the veil, schooling for girls, acccess to modern commodities, greater mobility, and the like. As young women wish to achieve *maisha mazuri* (the good life), they look to European and other foreign products for sources of change and seek to take distance from traditional practices such as veiling, which they nevertheless see not as a sign of inferior status or of control but as impractical or unmodern (Fuglesang 1992).

Fashion, Indian popular films, and access to modern appliances constitute some of the most important indicators of modernity and the avenues toward crafting new identities and conceptions of womanhood. Again, the process is not a simple modernization, although this is clearly happening as well. Pictures of Indian film stars might appear on the walls of women's rooms together with pictures of Michael Jackson and Khomeini. The call of the muezzin frequently means freezing the image in the latest video brought from Saudi Arabia or Dubai by returning migrant workers so that five or ten minutes of prayer can take place. Life and gender relations are definitely changing—women no longer want to be "ghosts"; yet what they mean by modern womanhood does not equate with the language of liberation of the West.

Technical knowledge often becomes an important marker of development, as the recent introduction of rural development schemes in the Pacific Coast region of Colombia indicates. Afro-Colombian peasants of this rainforest region, recently introduced by government extension agents into the world of accounting, farm planning methodologies, commercialization cooperatives, and the use of modern inputs such as pesticides, almost invariably list the acquisition of *conocimiento técnico* (technical knowledge) as an important transformation in the quality of their lives. Technical knowledge is imparted to most farmers on location, although a handful of them are regularly flown to cities of the interior to be *capacitados* (trained) in new farming and planning practices. The chosen farmers tend to become ardent advocates of development.

These farmers, moreover, begin to interpret their lives before the program as filled with ignorance and apathy. Before the program, they say, they knew nothing about why their crops died; now they know that the coconut trees are killed by a particular pest that can be combated with chemicals. They also learned that it is better to dedicate the family labor to one plot and plan well the activities to be performed on it day by day and month by month, instead of simultaneously working two or three plots that are often several hours' walking distance from each other, as they used to do. That was not really work, they now say. They have adapted, in sum, the vocabulary of "efficiency." Yet, as in the other examples already discussed, the farmers retain many of the beliefs and practices from former times. Next to the language of efficiency, for instance, one hears them say that the land needs to be "caressed" and "spoken to," and they still devote some time to the distant, "untechnified" plots. In short, they have developed a hybrid model of sorts, ruled neither by the logic of modern farming nor by traditional practices. I will return to the notion of hybrid models in the concluding chapter.[25]

The impact of development representations is thus profound at the local level. At this level, the concepts of development and modernity are resisted, hybridized with local forms, transformed, or what have you; they have, in short, a cultural productivity that needs to be better understood. More research on the languages of development at the local level needs to be done if our understanding of the discourse's modes of operation is to be satisfactory. This project requires in-depth ethnographies of development situations such as those exemplified earlier. For the anthropologists, Pigg concludes, the task is to trace the contours and cultural effects of development without endorsing or replicating its terms. I will come back to this principle in my discussion of Third World cultures as hybrid products of modern and traditional cultural practices and the many forms in between.

CONCLUSION

The crucial threshold and transformation that took place in the early post–World War II period discussed in this chapter were the result not of a radical epistemological or political breakthrough but of the reorganization of a number of factors that allowed the Third World to display a new visibility and to irrupt into a new realm of language. This new space was carved out of the vast and dense surface of the Third World, placing it in a field of power. Underdevelopment became the subject of political technologies that sought to erase it from the face of the Earth but that ended up, instead, multiplying it to infinity.

Development fostered a way of conceiving of social life as a technical problem, as a matter of rational decision and management to be entrusted to that group of people—the development professionals—whose specialized knowledge allegedly qualified them for the task. Instead of seeing change as a process rooted in the interpretation of each society's history and cultural tradition—as a number of intellectuals in various parts of the Third World had attempted to do in the 1920s and 1930s (Gandhi being the best known of them)—these professionals sought to devise mechanisms and procedures to make societies fit a preexisting model that embodied the structures and functions of modernity. Like sorcerers' apprentices, the development professionals awakened once again the dream of reason that, in their hands, as in earlier instances, produced a troubling reality.

At times, development grew to be so important for Third World countries that it became acceptable for their rulers to subject their populations to an infinite variety of interventions, to more encompassing forms of power and systems of control; so important that First and Third World elites accepted the price of massive impoverishment, of selling Third World resources to the most convenient bidder, of degrading their physical and human ecologies, of killing and torturing, of condemning their indigenous populations to near extinction; so important that many in the Third World began to think of themselves as inferior, underdeveloped, and ignorant and to doubt the value of their own culture, deciding instead to pledge allegiance to the banners of reason and progress; so important, finally, that the achievement of development clouded the awareness of the impossibility of fulfilling the promises that development seemed to be making.

After four decades of this discourse, most forms of understanding and representing the Third World are still dictated by the same basic tenets. The forms of power that have appeared act not so much by repression but by normalization; not by ignorance but by controlled knowledge; not by humanitarian concern but by the bureaucratization of social action. As the conditions that gave rise to development became more pressing, it could only increase its hold, refine its methods, and extend its reach even further. That the materiality of these conditions is not conjured up by an "objective" body of knowledge but is charted out by the rational discourses of economists, politicians, and development experts of all types should already be clear. What has been achieved is a specific configuration of factors and forces in which the new language of development finds support. As a discourse, development is thus a very real historical formation, albeit articulated around an artificial construct (underdevelopment) and upon a certain materiality (the conditions baptized as underdevelopment), which must be conceptualized in different ways if the power of the development discourse is to be challenged or displaced.

To be sure, there is a situation of economic exploitation that must be recognized and dealt with. Power is too cynical at the level of exploitation and should be resisted on its own terms. There is also a certain materiality of life conditions that is extremely preoccupying and that requires great effort and attention. But those seeking to understand the Third World through development have long lost sight of this materiality by building upon it a reality that like a castle in the air has haunted us for decades. Understanding the history of the investment of the Third World by Western forms of knowledge and power is a way to shift the ground somewhat so that we can start to look at that materiality with different eyes and in different categories.

The coherence of effects that the development discourse achieved is the key to its success as a hegemonic form of representation: the construction of the poor and underdeveloped as universal, preconstituted subjects, based on the privilege of the representers; the exercise of power over the Third World made possible by this discursive homogenization (which entails the erasure of the complexity and diversity of Third World peoples, so that a squatter in Mexico City, a Nepalese peasant, and a Tuareg nomad become equivalent to each other as poor and underdeveloped); and the colonization and domination of the natural and human ecologies and economies of the Third World.[26]

Development assumes a teleology to the extent that it proposes that the "natives" will sooner or later be reformed; at the same time, however, it reproduces endlessly the separation between reformers and those to be reformed by keeping alive the premise of the Third World as different and inferior, as having a limited humanity in relation to the accomplished European. Development relies on this perpetual recognition and disavowal of difference, a feature identified by Bhabha (1990) as inherent to discrimination. The signifiers of "poverty", "illiteracy," "hunger," and so forth have already achieved a fixity as signifieds of "underdevelopment" which seems impossible to sunder. Perhaps no other factor has contributed to cementing the association of "poverty" with "underdevelopment" as the discourse of economists. To them I dedicate the coming chapter.

Chapter 3

ECONOMICS AND THE
SPACE OF DEVELOPMENT:
TALES OF GROWTH AND CAPITAL

All types of societies are limited by economic factors.
Nineteenth century civilization alone was economic in a
different and distinctive sense, for it chose to base itself in
a motive rarely acknowledged as valid in the history of
human societies, and certainly never before raised to the
level of a justification of action and behavior in everyday
life, namely, gain. The self-regulating market system was
uniquely derived from this principle. The mechanism
which the motive of gain set in motion was comparable in
effectiveness only to the most violent outburst of religious
fervor in history. Within a generation the whole human
world was subjected to its undiluted influence.
—Karl Polanyi, *The Great Transformation*, 1944

The Arrival of Development Economics

Lauchlin Currie, a former Harvard economist and official in the Roosevelt
administration, evoked in the following way, at a testimonial dinner party in
Bogotá in 1979, the first World Bank mission, which thirty years earlier had
taken him to that same country:

> I don't know where in my conservative Canadian background I acquired a
> reformer's zeal, but I must admit that I had it. I just happen to be one of those
> tiresome people who can't encounter a problem without wanting to do some-
> thing about it. So you can imagine how Colombia affected me. Such a marvel-
> ous number of practically insoluble problems! Truly an economic missionary's
> paradise. I had no idea before I came what the problems were but that did not
> dull for a moment my enthusiasm nor shake my conviction that if only the Bank
> and the country would listen to me I could come up with a solution of sorts to
> most. I had my baptism of fire in the Great Depression. I had played some role
> in working out the economic recovery program in the New Deal for the worst
> depression the United States had ever experienced. I had been very active in
> government during the Second World War. (Quoted in Meier 1984, 130)

This candid recollection reveals a number of features that are at the root of many enterprises undertaken by North Americans in colonial and post-colonial contexts: the "reformer's zeal" and the drive toward reform and pedagogy; the utopian posture that finds a "missionary's paradise" in those lands riddled with "a marvelous number of practically insoluble problems"; the belief that all wrongs can be corrected and all manifestations of human conflict eradicated. In Currie's case, these traits had been rekindled by the recovery from the Great Depression and the reconstruction of Europe; the same traits were shared by many of the "pioneers of development"—economists like Currie, who later became a leading figure in the field—who disembarked in the Third World some time after the war full of good intentions, armed with the tools of their profession, sometimes even with a progressive agenda, and invigorated by the fact that their science had just been subjected to the fine-tuning of the Keynesian mind.

But we are getting somewhat ahead in the story, for at the time of Currie's arrival in Colombia, there was nothing resembling development economics. Let us listen to an earlier recollection of his, again referring to the Colombia mission discussed in chapter 2:

> When, in 1949, I was asked to organize and direct the first study mission of the World Bank there were no precedents for a mission of this sort and indeed nothing called development economics. I just assumed that it was a case of applying various branches of economics to the problems of a specific country, and accordingly I recruited a group of specialists in public finance, foreign exchange, transport, agriculture, and so on. I did, however, include some engineers and public health technicians. What emerged was a series of recommendations in a variety of fields. I was at pains to entitle it "the basis of a program" rather than a socioeconomic plan. (Currie 1967, 31; quoted in Meier 1984, 131)

Currie's remembrance also reminds us of one of the quintessential aspects of modernity: the need to compose the world as a picture. If upon his arrival in Colombia all he could perceive was problems, darkness, and chaos, it was because Colombia refused to compose itself as a picture he could read. Development relies on setting up the world as a picture, so that the whole can be grasped in some orderly fashion as forming a structure or system. In the case of the economist, the picture is provided by economic theory. Currie's ensemble of experts needed to compose Colombia as a picture; paradoxically, all they were left with was another representation, Colombia's "underdeveloped" economy, while the "real" Colombia forever receded into the background. The need to compose the world as a picture is central to all theories of economic development.[1]

The lack of economic theories specific to development commented on by Currie gave way to a proliferation of theories in the 1950s. Writing in 1979, John Kenneth Galbraith captured well the remarkable character of this transformation. When, in 1949, he began instruction "in the economics of poverty and economic development" at Harvard University, he was confronted with the fact that

> as a different field of study, the special economics of the poor countries was held not to exist. In the next fifteen years in the United States these attitudes were decisively reversed. . . . Over a somewhat longer period, the Ford Foundation contributed well over a billion dollars between 1950 and 1975, and the Rockefeller, Carnegie, and some CIA-supported foundations added smaller amounts. . . . Intellectual interest in the problem of mass poverty had also greatly expanded. Seminars and courses on economic development had proliferated in universities and colleges across the land. . . . *No economic subject more quickly captured the attention of so many as the rescue of the poor countries from their poverty.* . . . To be involved with the poor countries provided the scholar with a foothold in the field of study that would assuredly expand and endure. (1979, 26, 30; emphasis added).

As we will see, the 1980s saw a number of encompassing analyses on the origins and evolution of development economics by its leading pioneer figures, who, almost forty years later, looked at their record with a critical eye. From their entrenched positions in prestigious institutions, these now-senior economists declared the demise of the old field. "Development economics is dead. May it rest in peace. It was quite exciting while it lasted, and—in spite of the many serious problems that remain to be solved—it fared reasonably well in the real world. Let us now be more realistic about our expectations, recognize the limits of our discipline, and leave behind the naive dreams of solving the world's problems once and for all. Let us turn to the theory that we already know well." These are the sentences that like a nostalgic epitaph seem to emerge from the recent books of the pioneers of the field.

The death and recasting of development economics are undoubtedly linked to the demise of neo-Keynesianism and the rise of neoliberalism. At issue are the draconian economic reforms introduced in the Third World during the 1980s under pressure from the International Monetary Fund, particularly monetary and exchange controls, privatization of public enterprises and government services, reduction of imports, and opening to world markets. The same approach underwrites the strategy of "market friendly development" hailed by the World Bank in its 1991 *World Development Report* as the leading theme for the 1990s. This occurrence symbolizes the return of neoliberal orthodoxy in development economics, paralleling the advance of the free market in Eastern Europe. Never mind that as a supposedly temporary casualty of the necessary adjustment people's living standards have fallen to unprecedented levels. "The essential is to press on with structural reforms," or so the litany goes. People's welfare can be bracketed for a while, even if hundreds of thousands might die. Hail the market.

The discourse of development economics gave us successive promises of affluence for the Third World through active intervention in the economy in the 1950s and 1960s, planning throughout the development era, stabilization and adjustment policies in the 1980s, and anti-interventionist "market friendly development" for the 1990s. This chapter examines how this discourse could have taken place within the order of economic discourse as a whole; how it was articulated upon a domain of institutions, economic processes, and social relations; how the historical problematization of poverty gave rise to this peculiar discourse, which developed its own kind of historicity; how, finally, development economics effected development through the techniques of planning to which it gave rise. The aim of the chapter is not to decide whether the early development economists were right or wrong, but to develop a historical, epistemological, and cultural awareness of the conditions under which they made their choices. Even if the economists operated in a domain of discourse that had been created not as a result of individual acts of cognition but through the active participation of many in a historical context, the choices they made embodied commitments that had social and cultural consequences.

The first part of the chapter suggests an approach to examining both the economy and its science as cultural constructions, a task for which few guideposts exist at this time.[2] The second part looks at some of the notions central to the articulation of classical and neoclassical economic discourse before the advent of development, particularly those notions which provided the building blocks of development economics. The third section analyzes in detail the elaboration of economic development theories in the 1940s, 1950s, and 1960s; it also addresses the rise of planning as the practical side of development economics. The fourth section builds upon recent literature on economic anthropology that posits the existence of marginal models of the economy harbored in the practice of popular groups in the Third World today; it discusses the need for a cultural politics that takes seriously the existence of both mainstream economics as a dominant discourse and the manifold local models implicitly maintained by Third World groups. The chapter concludes by suggesting ways of shifting economic discourse within the context of global political economy as a strategy to pursue alternatives to economics and development.

ECONOMICS AS CULTURE

Needless to say, economists do not see their science as a cultural discourse. In their long and illustrious realist tradition, their knowledge is taken to be a neutral representation of the world and a truth about it. Theirs is not, as

Patricia Williams writes referring to the law in ways that are equally applicable to economics, "an imposition of an order—the ironclad imposition of a world view" (1991, 28). "At issue," Williams continues, *"is a structure in which a cultural code has been inscribed"* (1991, 19; my emphasis). This inscription of the economic onto the cultural took a long time to develop, as the philosopher Charles Taylor explains:

> There are certain regularities which attend our economic behaviour, and which change only very slowly. . . . But it took a vast development of civilization before the culture developed in which people do so behave, in which it became a cultural possibility to act like this; and in which the discipline involved in so acting became widespread enough for this behaviour to be generalized. . . . Economics can aspire to the status of a science, and sometimes appear to approach it, because there has developed a culture in which a certain form of rationality is a (if not the) dominant value. (Taylor 1985, 103).

What is the cultural code that has been inscribed into the structure of economics? What vast development of civilization resulted in the present conception and practice of the economy? The answer to this question is complex and can only be hinted at here. Indeed, the development and consolidation of a dominant view and practice of the economy in European history is one of the most fundamental chapters in the history of modernity. An anthropology of modernity centered on the economy leads us to question the tales of the market, production, and labor which are at the root of what might be called the Western economy. These tales are rarely questioned; they are taken as normal and natural ways of seeing life, "the way things are." Yet the notions of economy, market, and production are historical contingencies. Their histories can be traced, their genealogies demarcated, and their mechanisms of truth and power revealed. In short, the Western economy can be anthropologized and shown to be made up of a peculiar set of discourses and practices—very peculiar at that in the history of cultures.

The Western economy is generally thought of as a production system. From the perspective of the anthropology of modernity, however, the Western economy must be seen as an institution composed of systems of production, power, and signification. The three systems, which coalesced at the end of the eighteenth century, are inextricably linked to the development of capitalism and modernity. They should be seen as cultural forms through which human beings are made into producing subjects. The economy is not only, or even principally, a material entity. It is above all a cultural production, a way of producing human subjects and social orders of a certain kind. Although at the level of production the history of the Western economy is well known—the rise of the market, changes in the productive forces and the social relations of production, demographic changes, the transformation of everyday material life, and the commodification of land, labor, and money—analyses of power and signification have been incorporated much less into the cultural history of the Western economy.

How does power enter into the history of the economy? Very briefly, the institutionalization of the market system in the eigtheenth and nineteenth centuries also required a transformation at the level of the individual—the production of what Foucault (1979) has called docile bodies—and the regulation of populations in ways consistent with the movements of capital. People did not go into the factories gladly and of their own accord; an entire regime of discipline and normalization was necessary. Besides the expulsion of peasants and serfs from the land and the creation of a proletarian class, the modern economy necessitated a profound restructuring of bodies, individuals, and social forms. This restructuring of the individual and society was achieved through manifold forms of discipline, on the one hand, and through the set of interventions that made up the domain of the social, to which I have alluded, on the other. The result of this process—*Homo oeconomicus*—was a normalized subject that produces under certain physical and cultural conditions. To accumulate capital, spread education and health, and regulate the movement of people and wealth required no less than the establishment of a disciplinary society (Foucault 1979).[3]

At the level of signification, the first important historical aspect to consider is the invention of the economy as an autonomous domain. It is well known that one of the quintessential aspects of modernity is the separation of social life into functional spheres (the economy, the polity, society, culture, and the like), each with laws of its own. This is, strictly speaking, a modern development. As a separate domain, the economy had to be given expression by a proper science; this science, which emerged at the end of the eighteenth century, was called political economy. In its classical formulation by Smith, Ricardo, and Marx, political economy was structured around the notions of production and labor. In addition to rationalizing capitalist production, however, political economy succeeded in imposing production and labor as a code of signification on social life as a whole. Simply put, modern people came to see life in general through the lens of production. Many aspects of life became increasingly economized, including human biology, the nonhuman natural world, relations among people, and relations between people and nature. The languages of everyday life became entirely pervaded by the discourses of production and the market.

The fact that Marx borrowed the language of political economy he was criticizing, some argue (Reddy 1987; Baudrillard 1975), defeated his ultimate purpose of doing away with it. Yet the achievements of historical materialism cannot be overlooked: the formulation of an anthropology of use value in lieu of the abstraction of exchange value; the displacement of the notion of absolute surplus by that of surplus value and, consequently, the replacement of the notion of progress based on the increase of surplus by that based on the appropriation of surplus value by the bourgeoisie (exploitation); the emphasis on the social character of knowledge, as opposed to the dominant epistemology, which placed truth on the side of the individual's mind; the contrast between a unilinear conception of history, in which the individual is the all-powerful actor, and a materialist one, in which social classes appear as the motor of history; a denunciation of the natural character of the market economy and a conceptualization, instead, of the capitalist mode of production, in which the market appears as the product of history; and finally the crucial insight of commodity fetishism as a paradigmatic feature of capitalist society.

Marx's philosophy, however, faced limits at the level of the code.[4] The hegemony of the code of signification of political economy is the underside of the hegemony of the market as a social model and a model of thought. Market culture elicits commitments not only from economists but also from all those living with prices and commodities. "Economic" men and women are positioned in civil societes in ways that are inevitably mediated, at the symbolic level, by the constructs of markets, production, and commodities. People and nature are separated into parts (individuals and resources), to be recombined into market commodities and objects of exchange and knowledge. Hence the call by critical analysts of market culture to remove political economy from the centrality that it has been accorded in the history of modernity and to supersede the market as a generalized frame of reference by developing a wider frame of reference to which the market itself might be referred (Polanyi 1957b, 270; Procacci 1991, 151; Reddy 1987).[5] I suggest that this wider frame of reference should be the anthropology of modernity.

Anthropologists have been complicit with the rationalization of modern economics, to the extent that they have contributed to naturalizing the constructs of economy, politics, religion, kinship, and the like as the fundamental building blocks of all societies. The existence of these domains as presocial and universal must be rejected. Instead, "we must ask what symbolic and social processes make these domains appear self-evident, and perhaps even 'natural,' fields of activity in any society" (Yanagisako and Collier 1989, 41). The analysis of economics as culture must thus start by subjecting to scrutiny the apparent organization of societies into seemingly natural domains. It must reverse the "spontaneous impulse to look in every society for 'economic' institutions and relations separate from other social relations, comparable to those of Western capitalist society" (Godelier 1986, 18).

This task of cultural critique must begin with the clear recognition that economics is a discourse that constructs a particular picture of the economy. To use Stephen Gudeman's metaphor (1986; Gudeman and Rivera 1990),

what we usually recognize as economics is only one "conversation" among
many regarding the economy; this conversation became dominant throughout the centuries, thanks to the historical processes already sketched. Gudeman's unveiling of the use in anthropology of allegedly universal economic
models is instructive:

> Those who construct universal models . . . propose that within ethnographic
> data there exists an objectively given reality which may be captured and ex-
> plained by an observer's formal model. They utilize a "reconstructive" method-
> ology by which observed economic practices and beliefs are first restated in the
> formal language and then deduced or assessed with respect to core criteria such
> as utility, labor or exploitation. Although the particular theories used in eco-
> nomic anthropology are quite diverse, they share the assumption that one or
> another universal model exists and can be used to explain a given field data.
> According to this perspective, a local model usually is a rationalization, mystifi-
> cation or ideology; at most, it only represents the underlying reality to which
> the observer has privileged access. (1986, 28)

Any model, however, whether local or universal, is a construction of the
world and not an indisputable, objective truth about it. This is the basic
insight guiding the analysis of economics as culture. The coming into dominance of modern economics meant that many other existing conversations or
models were appropriated, suppressed, or overlooked. At the margins of the
capitalist world economy, Gudeman and Rivera insist, there existed and
continue to exist other models of the economy, other conversations, no less
scientific because they are not couched in equations or produced by Nobel
laureates. In the Latin American countryside, for instance, these models are
still alive, the result of overlapping conversations that have been carried out
for a long time. I will come back to the notion of local models in the last
section of the chapter.

There is, then, an orientalism in economics that has to be unveiled—that
is, a hegemonic effect achieved through representations that enshrine one
view of the economy while suppressing others. The critique of economics as
culture, finally, must be distinguished from the better-known analysis of
economics as "rhetoric" advocated by McCloskey (1985). McCloskey's work
is intended to show the literary character of economic science and the price
economics has paid for its blind adherence to the scientistic attitude of modernism. This author shows how literary devices systematically and inevitably
pervade the science of economics. His aim is to improve economics by
bringing it into the realm of rhetoric. The aim of this chapter is quite different. Although some rhetorical analysis is used, particularly in the reading of
the economic development theories of the 1950s and 1960s, the analysis of
economics as culture goes well beyond the formal aspect of the rethoric of

economics. How did particular constructions of the economy come to exist? How do they operate as cultural forces? What practices do these constructions create, and what are the resulting cultural orders? What are the consequences of seeing life in terms of such constructions?

THE WORLD OF ECONOMICS AND THE ECONOMICS OF THE WORLD: THEORETICAL AND PRACTICAL ANTECEDENTS OF DEVELOPMENT ECONOMICS

"The Static Interlude" and the World of Economics

The opening paragraph of what was perhaps the most celebrated article on economic development, written in 1954, entitled "Economic Development with Unlimited Supplies of Labour," and authored by W. Arthur Lewis, reads as follows:

> This essay is written in the classical tradition, making the classical assumption, and asking the classical question. The classics, from Smith to Marx, all assumed, or argued, that an unlimited supply of labour was available at subsistence wages. They then enquired how production grows through time. They found the answer in capital accumulation, which they explained in terms of their analysis of the distribution of income. Classical systems thus determined simultaneously income distribution and income growth, with the relative prices of commodities as a minor by-product. (Lewis [1954] 1958 , 400)

Let us pause for a moment to recall some of the pertinent aspects of the "classical tradition." The cornerstone of the classical theory of growth was capital accumulation (understood in its "bourgeois" sense, that is, not as a dialectical process), associated with an increasingly specialized labor force. Changes in capital and labor productivity were considered of paramount importance, whereas natural resources and institutions were regarded as constant and technical change as an exogenous variable (treated as such by all classical economists except Marx). Classical economists also believed that natural resources are limited; scarcity became an inescapable imperative. The corollaries of this premise were progressive impoverishment, the stunting of growth (the theory of diminishing returns), and the possibility of reaching a stationary state.[6] This retarding effect could be offset only by technical progress. According to the classical theory, the economy would reach a point at which wages would rise above the subsistence minimum, thus squeezing profits down to a point where investment would stop; average wages would then drop again, technological progress would make labor more productive, and growth would resume, only to be once again subjected to forces that pulled it toward a stationary state, and so forth.[7]

For Ricardo, the laws that regulate the distribution of the national product among rents, profits, and wages was the main problem of political economy. The level of profits was crucial, because it determined the level of capital accumulation and economic growth. His economic theory thus consisted of a theory of rent, a subsistence theory of wages, an explanation of the impact of diminishing returns in agriculture on the profit rate, and a labor theory of value. One of the most important contributions of the Ricardian formulation was precisely this theory of value. Labor became a unit common to all merchandise and the source of value because it embodied the producing activity (Dobb 1973). Labor, in fact, appeared as a transcendental that made possible the objective knowledge of the laws of production. The economy became a system of successive productions based on labor (the product of labor of one process went into another). This economic concept fostered a view of accumulation according to temporal sequences and, generally speaking, made possible the articulation of economics with history. Production and accumulation began to shape indelibly the modern notion and experience of history (Foucault 1973).[8]

The notion that labor is the basis of all value did not survive for long. The "marginal revolution" of the 1870s sought to debunk the Ricardian formulation by introducing a different theory of value and distribution. Interestingly, the search for an absolute determinant of value was abandoned. "Prevailing opinions make labor rather than utility the origin of value," wrote Jevons, the father of the conceptual revolution. "Repeated reflection and inquiry have led me to the somewhat novel opinion, that value depends entirely upon utility" (quoted in Dobb 1973, 168). Jevons defined utility as "the abstract quality whereby an object serves our purposes, and becomes entitled to rank as a commodity," and the problem of the economy as the satisfaction of "our wants to the utmost with the least effort . . . to maximize comfort and pleasure." As the supply of a given commodity is increased, its utility starts to decrease until "satisfaction or satiety" is approached (Dobb 1973, 166–210).[9]

A whole new sphere of economic analysis—usually referred to as neoclassical economics—was built on this peculiar law. The idea that the economy could reach a state of general equilibrium became the centerpiece of economic theory. This idea was originally postulated by the French economist Leon Walras as a series of simultaneous equations relating a number of economic variables (prices and quantities of goods and services, either products or factors of production to be bought by households and firms). According to this theory, the free play of forces of supply and demand would tend to establish, under competitive conditions, an equilibrium pattern in the prices of commodities in such a way that all markets would be "cleared." This is so because there is a "concatenation and mutual dependence" of economic acts among all producers and consumers, a certain "circular flow of economic life." Schumpeter (1934, 8) defines this circular flow of the self-regulating market in a revealing manner:

> Hence it follows that somewhere in the economic system a demand is, so to say, ready awaiting every supply, and nowhere in the system are there commodities without complements, that is other commodities in the possession of people who will exchange them under empirically determined conditions for the former goods. It follows, again from the fact that all goods find a market, that the circular flow of economic life is closed, in other words that the sellers of all commodities appear again as buyers in sufficient measure to acquire those goods which will maintain their consumption and their productive equipment in the next economic period at the level so far attained, and vice versa.[10]

It was an extremely harmonious view of the economy, without politics, power, or history; an utterly rational world, made even more abstract with the passing of time by the increasing use of mathematical tools. Why did the neoclassical economists abandon classical concerns such as growth and distribution? A commonsense explanation is usually put forward: Because capitalism became consolidated in the second half of the nineteenth century—having achieved remarkable rates of economic growth, elevated the living standards of the masses, and dispelled the old fears of getting to a point where growth would no longer be possible—the analytical preoccupation with growth seemed superfluous. The turn in analysis toward static and short-term theoretical interests, such as the optimization of resource allocation and the decision behavior of individuals and firms, was a logical step to follow.[11] Once capitalism was decidedly working, the interest of economists shifted to the fine-tuning of the operations of the system, including the rationalization of decisions and the coordinated performance of markets toward an optimum equilibrium. The dynamic aspects of the economy thus gave way to static considerations. It was what a development economist aptly called the static interlude (Meier 1984, 125–28).

Progress had not been without vicissitudes, especially toward the end of the century (falling prices, unemployment, business losses, class struggles, and workers' organizations); but these problems would fade away as the process of continued growth was not in doubt. And in spite of the fact that by the end of the century the faith in the virtues of laissez-faire had been shaken (especially in relation to the need to control business monopoly), in 1870 most observers believed that universal and perfect trade would reign unhindered. It was as if, the economy having achieved some degree of apparent stability, economists busied themselves with the more mundane but theoretically exciting realm of the quotidian. This confidence was to be torn to pieces with the Great Depression. But by the time this happened, the

great "neoclassical edifice," built in the 1870s and furnished with impecca-
ble precision in the next one hundred years, was firmly in place, shaping the
discursive firmament of the discipline.

For Schumpeter (1954, 891–909), however, the neoclassical revolution
left untouched many of the elements of the classical theory, including "its
sociological framework." The general vision of the economic process was
still pretty much the same as in Mill's time. In short, despite its rejection of
the labor theory of value, neoclassical economics inherited, and functioned
within, the basic discursive organization laid down during the classical period. The emphasis on individual satisfaction reinforced the atomistic bias of
the discipline; more than in classical thought, the economic system was irremediably identified with the market, and economic inquiry with market conditions (especially prices) under which exchange takes place. The problem
of distribution was removed completely from the sphere of politics and social relations and reduced to the pricing of inputs and outputs (the marginal
productivity theory of distribution). By further isolating the economic system, questions of class and property relations fell outside the scope of economic analysis; analytical efforts were directed instead to the question of
optimization (Dobb 1973, 172–83). The focus on particular static equilibri-
ums, finally, militated against the analysis of macro relations and questions
of economic development from a more holistic (for example, Marxist or
Schumpeterian) perspective.

The great "neoclassical edifice" rested on two basic assumptions: perfect
competition and perfect rationality. Perfect and universal knowledge ensured that existing resources would be optimally utilized, guaranteeing full
employment. "Economic man" could go about his business in peace because
he could be confident that there was a corpus of theory, namely, marginal
utility and general equilibrium, which, because it had recourse to a perfect
knowledge of things, would provide him with the information he needed to
maximize the use of his scarce resources. The underlying picture of the
neoclassical world was that of order and tranquillity, of a self-regulating,
self-optimizing economic system, a view undoubtedly related to the pom-
posity of the Pax Britannica then prevailing.

This was, then, the neoclassical world at the turn of the century. A world,
it was believed, where theory resembled the real economy as a clock re-
sembles time; where the fundamental "niggardliness of nature" was held
at bay by those rugged individuals who were able to extract from nature
the most precious products; where the invisible hand that ensured the
smooth operation of the economy and the welfare of the majority had not
yet been burdened with the cumbersome strings of protectionism. The crisis that hit the capitalist world economy from 1914 to about 1948 was to
add a number of important components to that edifice. Among them was a
new interest in growth. It might be worth recalling these events in some

detail, because it was this situation that development economists found at their doorstep when, with great excitement, they decided to build a home for themselves.

"The Years of High Theory" and the Economics of the World

We have seen how classical political economy underwent a significant change with the marginalist revolution. After almost one century of Pax Britannica, the capitalist world economy entered a period of deep crisis, which motivated a second important transformation in economic discourse. Let us summarize the argument to be developed in this regard. Between the First and Second World wars, a new social system began to take shape. It rested on the dissolution of the old distinction between the state and the economy (so dear to the neoclassical economists), the development of unprecedented institutional arrangements, and an important reformulation of the neoclassical understanding of the economy. Historians argue that in the 1920s there occurred a recasting of bourgeois Europe through the development of corporatist forms of control of the polity and the economy and a restructuring of the relationship between private and public power. A recentering of the world economy also took place, shifting the center of the capitalist system to the United States. The styles and forms of intervention in the economy developed during this period were retained and extended during the 1930s, 1940s, and 1950s, before blossoming during the development era.

Keynesianism and a revitalized growth economics provided the understanding and rationalization of these processes. All these changes not only prepared the ground for a new scale of integration of the peripheral countries (those parts of the world later known as the Third World) under Pax Americana but provided the building blocks of a theory of economic development which guided and justified such integration. Classical theories of growth, improved upon by a new macroeconomics and a new mathematics of growth, were ready to provide the fundamental elements of the new discourse. So were the new forms of management and planning developed in the 1920s. After 1945, the underdeveloped world acquired a position of importance in the capitalist world economy it had never had before. Neither had there ever existed a discourse so refined to deal with it.

The depth of the economic and social transformation that started to take place in the first decade of the twentieth century—which saw not only the collapse of nineteenth-century economic organization but also unprecedented wars and fascism—has been most forcefully and insightfully discussed by Karl Polanyi (1957a). Polanyi finds the origins of this transformation "in the utopian endeavor of economic liberalism to set up a self-regulating system" (1957a, 29). The demise of the assumption of the self-regulating market was thus the first victim of the changes. The First World

War opened the way for new methods of management and planning of economic and social affairs. Out of the smoke and destruction of the battlefield emerged forms of organization of industry and labor that provided the foundations for a new economy after the war. This new economy was based on the belief that the economic process could not be left to the private market alone; the division between economic and political power became blurred. As the state's influence on the control of prices, labor, and resources became greater, new mechanisms of administration and bargaining were developed. In some countries (France, Germany, and Italy) the various interests (industry, agriculture, labor, and the military) became organized into corporate forms (Maier 1975)

A technocratic vision of the economy emerged out of the offices of the new engineers and professional businessmen. Taylorism, Americanism, and Fordism took deeper roots as scientific management extended its reach in its attempt to make the use of labor and capital ever more efficient. The introduction of all of these techniques cannot be underestimated. Gramsci characterized the transformation that Americanism and Fordism fostered "the biggest collective effort to date to create, with unprecedented speed, and with a consciousness of purpose unmatched in history, a new type of worker and a new type of man" (quoted in Harvey 1989, 126). This was achieved in the span of several decades, despite resistance by workers to Fordist and Taylorist work practices in the early years. The Left's demands for democratization in the factory became entangled with the Right's emphasis on rationalization through scientific management. In sum, the twilight of the nineteenth-century order saw, after the dark night of the war, the birth of a new order in which, despite many a great transformation, the old one still breathed at ease. "Rescuing bourgeois Europe meant recasting bourgeois Europe: dealing with unions (or creating pseudo-unions as in Italy), giving state agencies control over the market, building interest-group spokesmen into the structure of the state" (Maier 1975, 594).[12]

With the demise of the self-regulating market, the assumption of perfect knowledge was also discarded, especially in the late 1920s and early 1930s, when economic theory "had to come to terms with the restless anarchy of the world of fact." "Until the 1930s," wrote a student of the economic theory of the period, "economics was the science of coping with basic scarcity. After the 1930s, it was the account of how men cope with scarcity and uncertainty. This was by far the greatest of the achievements of the 1930s in economic theory" (Shackle 1967, 7). Pax Britannica had instilled in many people the sense of a natural, irrefutable order. To continue with Shackle's account:

> "There was," as John Maynard Keynes says, "nothing to be afraid of." . . . The
> most essential and powerful difference between this world and the world of the
> 1930s was the loss of tranquility itself. Problems of "the price of a cup of tea" as
> Professor Joan Robinson put it, no longer counted much against the problem of

unemployment arising, so Keynes explained, from the failure of the incentive to invest, which failure itself was due to the sudden oppression of business minds by the world's incalculable uncertainties. There was no longer equilibrium in fact, and there could no longer be equilibrium in theory. (1967, 289)

Keynes was the hero of the new revolution. He demonstrated that there could be equilibrium at levels lower than full employment—indeed, at any level of output and employment. The theories of employment and growth produced during "the years of high theory" (1926 to 1939, by economists such as Keynes, Kahn, Robinson, Harrod, Myrdal, Hicks, Kalecky, Samuelson, and Kaldor) arose from the realization of the fundamental lack of information that decision makers had to confront. Perfect competition became imperfect (writing in 1926, Piero Sraffa demonstrated the existence of factors internal to the firm, called economies of scale, which made the assumption of perfect competition illusory); perfect knowledge became muddled, giving way to uncertainty; and the empty space left by the disappearance of the concern with static conditions was soon filled by inquiry into the dynamics of growth, now enshrined in the altar of theory. Because of the limitations of knowledge, the tools to manage reality had to be sharpened; hence a new emphasis on public policy and planning arose to fill the need for mechanisms of order and control.

The innovations in question reflected closely the events of the period: deflation, wage reductions, and unemployment in the 1920s, economic crisis and aggravated unemployment in the 1930s. Keynes's prescription was for government to propend for full employment through appropriate state spending and through investment, fiscal, and budgetary policy. Economists consider the theoretical achievements of this period extremely important. For Dobb (1973, 211–27), however, the new theory did not challenge the neoclassical theory of value; it moved within its general framework (Keynes considered the neoclassical theory a "special case" of his General Theory). Its radical challenge to existing views was restricted to the assumption of a unique position of static equilibrium, which in turn entailed full employment of resources. Yet it must be admitted that Keynes's disruption of the terribly rational and smooth neoclassical world was important. Keynes's successors, however, soon summoned to their aid rationality and the mathematization of economics, thus overlooking what could have been the most radical lessons of Keynes's work (Gutman 1994).[13]

Growth economics lent credence to this mode of theory construction according to conventional rationality and model building. In the late 1930s, and in the wake of Keynes's General Theory, a number of economists (Harrod in 1939 and Domar in 1946) focused their attention on the rates of growth of output (national production) and income as the fundamental variables to be explained by a truly dynamic theory. The mood set in for elaborating a theory of growth that was as abstract and general in application as

that of general equilibrium. The key to such a theory was the relation between investment and general output—how the pace of investment governs
the level of general output, and how the acceleration of general output in
turn affects the pace of investment. Investment, it was noted, not only accel-
erates income but also generates increased productive capacity. A net addition to the capital stock brings about a corresponding increase in national
output (gross national product, or GNP); this correspondence is expressed
by what economists of the period called the capital-output ratio, which Harrod defined as the value of capital goods required for the production of a unit
increment of output.

Capital for new investment must come from somewhere, and the answer
was savings. Part of the national income must be saved to replace worn-out
capital goods (equipment, buildings, materials, and so on) and to create new
ones. What mattered then was to establish the necessary "savings ratio"
(proportion of national output to be saved), which, coupled with a given
capital-output ratio, would produce the desired rate of growth of GNP.
Every economy would have a "natural rate of growth," defined as the maximum rate allowed by the increase of population, capital accumulation, and
technological progress; because these variables could not be controlled ac-
curately, the process of growth was seen as necessarily unstable. This theory
was thus clearly consistent not only with the "classical question" and "the
classical assumption" but also with the Keynesian innovation, which related
the expansion or contraction of the economy to savings and investment. Although significant variations were introduced to the original Harrod-Domar
theory, this formulation shaped the nascent development economics. The
consequences of the adoption of this theory, as we will see in the next section, were enormous.

Let us return for a moment to the economics of the world. The stability
allegedly achieved in the most powerful countries in the late 1920s and,
again, in the late 1930s was not without its contradictions. As a distinctive
regime of accumulation, Fordism did not reach maturity until after 1945,
when it became the basis for the postwar boom that lasted until the early
1970s. By the time Fordism started to decline, it had already become "less
a mere system of mass production and more a total way of life" (Harvey 1989,
135). It had introduced not only a new culture of work and consumption but
a new aesthetic, which built upon and contributed to the aesthetic of modernism, with its concern with functionality and efficiency.

Let us see how Marxist-inspired political economists explain the capitalist
dynamics of the period. Fordist accumulation determined the incorporation
of the periphery in novel ways.[14] The horizontal (geographic) integration of
the capitalist world economy had been largely completed by 1910, and a
process of vertical integration—for the periphery, an increase in the rate of
extraction of surplus value through means other than geographic expan-

sion—began to take place. By 1913, the major core nations (England, the United States, France, and Germany) owned about 85 percent of all capital invested in the semiperiphery (at that point composed of Spain, Portugal, Russia, Japan, Australia, and parts of Eastern Europe) and the periphery (most of Latin America, Asia, and Africa). However, certain factors created instability: increased competition from the semiperiphery (especially Russia and Japan); increased anticore ideologies and social movements in the periphery (as the pace of foreign investment and direct military intervention augmented); internal changes in the class structure of the core nations; and competition among the core nations for control of the increasingly important natural resources of the periphery.[15]

The growing importance of the United States in the capitalist world economy had important repercussions for the periphery. In the case of Latin America, trade with the United States increased dramatically, and so did direct U.S. investment. A large borrowing program, mainly from U.S. bankers, was initiated, especially during the 1920s. The 1920s marked the first decade of "modernization" of the Latin American continent, and the period in general (1910–1930) saw an important transition in the social and economic structure of the larger countries of the region. The Great Depression hit hard the Latin American economies. Imports by core nations from Latin America were severely reduced. The large debt obligations that many countries contracted during the 1920s became an unbearable burden (a situation not unlike that of the 1980s) and, indeed, by 1935 most of the debt was in default. The euphoric mood the boom of the 1920s created turned somber, out of which came the need either to adapt to depressed international conditions in the best possible way (the course of action most countries of the region took) or to proceed with the industrialization process through a strategy of import substitution—that is, to produce at home what was previously imported (the larger countries, such as Brazil, Argentina, Mexico, and Colombia, took this route). The countries of the periphery were obliged to abandon the old liberalism and implement active state policies to protect and develop their national economies.[16]

The free enterprise system was in peril after the Second World War. To save such a system, the United States was faced with various imperatives: to keep the existing core nations of the capitalist system together and going, which required continuous expansion and efforts to avoid the spread of communism; to find ways to invest U.S. surplus capital that had accumulated during the war (particularly abroad, where the largest profits could be made); to find markets overseas for American goods, given that the productive capacity of American industry had doubled during the war; to secure control over the sources of raw materials in order to meet world competition; and to establish a global network of unchallenged military power as a way to secure access to raw materials, markets, and consumers (Amin 1976;

Borrego 1981; Murphy and Augelli 1993). The pact signed at Bretton Woods, establishing the International Monetary Fund and the World Bank, inaugurated the new era. Keynesian theory provided guidelines to strengthen the private sector, expand domestic and foreign markets, and revitalize international trade under the aegis of multinational corporations. The production process of the core states was thus newly integrated with their political apparatuses as well as with the emerging international financial organizations.

"The Great Transformation," so admirably described by Polanyi, thus marked the collapse of some of the most cherished economic principles of the nineteenth century. Laissez-faire and old-fashioned liberalism gave way to more efficient ways of managing economies and populations, more pervasive perhaps if only because they were carried out under the legitimizing wing of science and increasingly (especially with the development of welfare economics in the 1950s) for the "good of the people." The "static interlude" was over, but the new economics did little to alter the boundaries of classical and neoclassical discourse. Theoretical refinements and sophisticated mathematical techniques—such as Leontieff's input-ouput analysis, in gestation since the 1930s—were developed, but they did not depart significantly from the basic discursive organization of classical economics. The imperatives the United States faced at the end of the war placed Latin America and the rest of the periphery in a well-demarcated space within the capitalist world economy.

To conclude this section, let us return to the introduction of the chapter. I referred to a certain reformist ethos in the attitude of the pioneers of development. This ethos was partly linked to the experience of the Great Depression. Indeed, as the progressive Harvard economist Stephen Marglin maintains, this experience changed economics for a generation, both in terms of the people it attracted and the problems it sought to address. Between 1935 and 1960, some economists even thought that the end of capitalism was a possibility. Scholars such as Galbraith, Kuznets, Currie, and, at the tail end of the period, Marglin acquired a political disposition toward their subject matter and the problems they wished to confront. (One also thinks of Latin American economists such as Raúl Prebisch, Antonio García, Celso Furtado, and Fernando Henrique Cardoso in a similar way). Macroeconomic theory of the period also arose in the context of decolonization, which for these economists meant the final destruction of empires. Although the needs of empire were to bring the colonized into the market, the well-being of the people suggested that they would be better off if left alone.[17]

For a moment then there was a contradiction in the mind of some economists between the welfare of the people and interventionist policies. Only after the Second World War would welfare and development join ranks as compatible goals. But, Marglin insists, many of the early development economists espoused a progressive agenda in the beginning years of their work. Without disputing this perception, it is important to emphasize, as this section has shown, that it was the whole movement of many decades that prepared the ground for the final arrival of development economics. Fueled by this momentum, development economists arrived in the Third World full of hopes and aspirations, eager to apply the best of their knowledge to a complex but exciting task. Their discourse, discussed in the next section, was extremely influential; it continues to be an important chapter in the cultural history of the Third World.

THE DEVELOPMENT OF DEVELOPMENT ECONOMICS

The Early Theories: Structuring the Discourse

The ten years between 1948 and 1958 saw the rise and consolidation of development economics as a practice concerned with certain questions, performed by particular individuals, and entrusted with given social tasks. During those years, development economics constructed its object, the "underdeveloped economy," out of the historical and theoretical processes reviewed in the previous section. How this construction actually happened needs to be analyzed in detail for our analysis of the politics of discourse and regimes of representation.

There were important precursors to the post–World War II concept of economic development. As Arndt (1978, 1981) has noted, when the term *development* was used before the 1930s, it was usually understood in a naturalistic sense, as the emergence of something over time. Two exceptions were Schumpeter, whose work on economic development, to be discussed later, was published in German in 1911, and a number of historians of the British Empire. A third exception was Marx, who derived his concept of development from the inexorable Hegelian dialectics. The clearest forerunner of the current use, mentioned in chapter 2, was the 1929 British Colonial Development Act. In the colonial context, economic development was not an inevitable historical process but an activity that had to be fostered by the government. The economic system did not develop; resources had to be developed. "Economic development in Marx's sense derives from the intransitive verb, in [the colonial] sense from the transitive verb" (Arndt 1981, 460).

Arndt traces the use of economic development in the transitive sense to Australia and to a lesser extent Canada, where economic development did not happen spontaneously. He also mentions in passing a 1922 study by Sun Yat-sen, a Chinese nationalist leader, proposing a massive program for the economic development of China. But not until the middle of the 1940s was the term applied to the economic development of "underdeveloped areas."

The Depression and World War II had brought to the fore the questions of full employment and growth. There was, as Arndt (1978) put it in his study of the rise and fall of the concept of economic growth, a "return to scarcity" and to the "general problem of poverty." Growth started to be seen as a remedy for poverty and unemployment rather than as an end in itself.

The classical concern with capital accumulation became central, via contemporary growth theories, to the first attempts at applying known tools of economic analysis to poor countries. The emphasis on investment implied a focus on savings and opened the way for foreign aid and foreign investment, because it was soon recognized that poor countries seldom possessed sufficient amounts of capital to meet the investment required for rapid growth. This conclusion was reinforced by the consideration that the growth of GNP had to be greater than the growth of population, which was relatively high in most countries. Moreover, a privileged arena for investment, one in which the benefits of capital accumulation would be larger than in any other realm, was discovered: industrialization. Industrialization would pave the way for the modernization of the backward economies and for spreading among the natives the proper rationality—"training labour and accustoming it to factory discipline," as W. Arthur Lewis wrote in 1946 referring to Jamaica's industrialization (quoted in Meier 1984, 143); it would also be the most efficient way of putting to productive use the large pool of the unemployed and underemployed who inhabited the countryside.

Similarly, industrialization would be the only way in which the poor countries could undo the structural disadvantage that they faced in the domain of international trade as predominantly primary producers confronted with the higher prices and productivity of goods coming from industrialized countries. Through industrialization, poor countries would stop producing "the wrong things" and start producing items with a higher exchange value. That industrialization was the key to development was as "clear as daylight," to quote again from Lewis's report on Jamaica (in Meier 1984, 143). The actual way in which industrialization was to take place constituted the core of most development models of the 1950s. It was clear that industrialization was not going to happen spontaneously. Deliberate efforts were required if the perceived obstacles to industrialization were going to be overcome. This called for a type of planning that ensured the right allocation of scarce resources, corrected market prices, maximized savings, oriented foreign investment in the right direction, and in general orchestrated the economy in terms of a well-balanced program. Development planning was thus from the outset the twin of development economics; this was already clear at the time of the 1949 World Bank mission to Colombia.

In sum, the major ingredients of the economic development strategy commonly advocated in the 1950s were these: (1) capital accumulation; (2) deliberate industrialization; (3) development planning; and (4) external aid. The underdeveloped economies, however, were thought to be characterized by a number of features that set them apart from the economies studied by orthodox economics, which then called for modifying existing theory—what Hirschman calls the rejection of the "monoeconomic claim" (1981). Among these features were high levels of rural underemployment, a low level of industrialization, a set of obstacles to industrial development, and a disadvantage in international trade. The first three of these captured the attention of most theorists building their models. Initially, attention focused on the "obstacles" that lay in the way of development, as well as in the "missing components" that would have to be supplied to make the models work. The models proposed characterized the effort that would have to be made to remove obstacles and provide missing components in such a manner that industrialization would take off with vigor and celerity.[18]

Classical and neoclassical theories of growth provided the building blocks for these models. The milestones of classical growth theory, let us remember, were capital accumulation, greater division of labor, technological progress, and trade. As we saw, postwar growth theory was influenced as well by Keynes's analysis of the interaction of savings and investments. It is useful to recall the thrust of the growth argument as postulated by Harrod and Domar. In order to grow, economies must save and invest a certain proportion of their gross national product. Given a specific level of savings and investment, the actual rate of growth will depend on how productive the new investment is; and the productivity of investment can be measured by the capital-output ratio. Investment creates new capacity to produce, which must be matched, in turn, by new demand. Income thus must rise by an equivalent proportion to ensure no idle capacity of capital goods.

The model assumed a number of features that held reasonably well for industrialized countries but not for underdeveloped economies. It assumed a constant capital-output ratio, did not analyze the effect of price changes (they were models in real terms), and presupposed constant terms of trade. But the underdeveloped economies were found to be characterized by deteriorating terms of trade for their primary products (vis-à-vis manufactured products from the industrialized countries), they were seen in need of rapid technological change, and their prices changed continually due to the inflationary bias of their economies. They also had a much lower level of savings. The main obstacle to development was thus low capital availability; moreover, although domestic savings could be increased, there would still be a "savings gap," which had to be filled with foreign aid, loans, or private foreign investment. Despite these differences, growth theories that had developed in the context of industrialized economies shaped economic development models to a significant extent.

Let us look in detail at some of the most important models. Rosenstein-Rodan, coming from his experience with relatively depressed Eastern European economies in the 1920s and 1930s, argued for a "big push" in investment to mobilize the rural underemployed for the task of industrialization.

For this author, industrialization required a large, carefully planned initial effort in order to be successful; small, isolated efforts were very likely to fail.[19] Other models had the same thrust: either a "critical minimum effort" was needed (Liebenstein 1957), or countries were seen as caught in a "low-level equilibrium trap," out which only an effort of a certain magnitude would get them (Richard Nelson). Rostow's historicoeconomic model (1960, 1952), which assumed that all countries went through a linear path of stages in their transition to modernity, with one of these stages being the "take-off" into self-sustained growth, became well known in the late 1950s and early 1960s. So did Nurkse's "balanced growth" conception—which predicted that a country would escape the "vicious circle of poverty" only through a concerted application of capital to a wide range of industries—and Hirschman's (1958) notion of "backward and forward linkages" for rationalizing the industrialization process. All of these conceptions soon found their way into the voluminous literature coming out of the United Nations and international lending organizations, and in the poor countries themselves, either because theorists visited the Third World—often for long periods of time—or through the education of Third World students in North American and British universities, a practice that became widespread in the 1960s.[20]

The models Nurkse and Lewis developed in the early 1950s were among the most influential, and it is appropriate to examine them briefly, not from the point of view of their economic rationality, but as cultural constructs and central pieces in the politics of the development discourse. Nurkse's book (1953), written in 1952 and based on a series of lectures delivered by the author in Rio de Janeiro a year earlier, is dedicated to analyzing the factors associated with "the vicious circle of poverty" and the possible ways to "break the deadlock" of such a circle. In his conception, poverty is produced by a circular constellation of forces that links lack of food and ill health with low work capacity, low income, and back to lack of food. This vicious circle is paralleled by a circular relationship in the realm of the economy.

> A circular relationship exists on both sides of the problems of capital formation in the poverty-ridden areas of the world. On the supply side, there is the small capacity to save, resulting from the low level of real income. The low real income is a reflection of low productivity, which in turn is due largely to the lack of capital. The lack of capital is a result of the small capacity to save, and so the circle is complete. On the demand side, the inducement to invest may be low because of the small buying power of the people, which is due to their small real income, which again is due to low productivity. The low level of productivity, however, is a result of the small amount of capital used in production, which in its turn may be caused at least partly by the small inducement to invest. (Nurkse 1953, 5)

Behind this "vicious" economic circle lies implicitly the "proper" circular view that was held to underlie a sound economy. The goal of balanced

growth was innocuously stated as "enlarging the size of the market and creating inducements to invest," for which capital was obviously essential. To
increase production of one commodity (shoes is the example Nurkse uses)
was not enough; the increase had to take place simultaneously in a wide
range of consumer goods if demand was to be sufficiently augmented. Commercial policy should then seek to direct properly the additional savings and
external sources of capital in order to expand the domestic market to the
degree needed for the takeoff into self-sustained development.

Interestingly, for Nurkse the problem of capital formation was not restricted to low savings capacity; it was also due to small inducement to invest. In this he was closer to Schumpeter, whom he explicitly invoked. But
neither Nurkse nor any other development economist adopted a Schumpeterian view; the reasons for this are revealing in terms of the politics of
discourse. Schumpeter's *Theory of Economic Development* had been available in English since 1934. This book, as most of Schumpeter's works, is
tight and unifying, with an emphasis on processual aspects. ("The argument
of the book forms one connected whole," he writes in the introduction.) The
surprisingly small influence of this book on postwar development thinking
may have been due to several factors. To begin with, Western economists
saw this book as a theory of business cycles, not as a theory of development;
moreover, Schumpeter's emphasis on the role of the private entrepreneur
seemed to rule out its application to poor countries, where entrepreneurship was thought to be almost nonexistent, in spite of some allegations to the
contrary (Bauer and Yamey 1957). The alleged lack of entrepreneurship was
influenced by the perception of Third World people as backward and even
lazy.

Schumpeter's theory seemed pertinent to the concerns of the early development economists. He was concerned not with small changes in economic
life but precisely with those revolutionary changes cherished by development economists with their "big push" and "takeoff" theories. To adhere to Schumpeter's framework, however, would have required taking seriously a number of aspects that would have posed uncomfortable problems to
most economists of the period—for instance, the fact that for Schumpeter
mere growth was not development but just "changes in data," or that "the
economic state of a people does not emerge simply from the preceding economic conditions, but only from the preceding total situation" (Schumpeter
1934, 58). How could these views be translated into manageable models
and planning schemes?[21]

W. Arthur Lewis's model of the dual economy, as influential as Nurkse's
model, if not more so, was originally published in 1954. The pivotal discursive operation of this model was the division of a country's economy and
social life into two sectors: one modern, the other traditional. Development
would consist of the progressive encroachment of the modern upon the traditional, the steady extension of the money economy on the vast world of

subsistence or near subsistence. This assumption pervaded the development view of most economists and international organizations for several decades (witness, for instance, the quotation that opens the first chapter of this book, excerpted from a report prepared by a committee of which Lewis was one of five participants). From the point of view of a discursive economy, the consequences of such a dualistic construction are enormous. To begin with, Lewis's construction equates tradition with backwardness, a burden to be disposed of as quickly as possible and a part of the economy with nothing to contribute to the process of development. Had a nondualistic view of the underdeveloped economy been adopted (Braudelian, Schumpeterian, or Marxist, not to mention one based on non-Western traditions), the consequences would have been quite different, for development would have had to involve all sectors of social life.

There is another mechanism at work in the modern-traditional dichotomy. This split distances one pole from the other, making remote the second term of the division. This feature of discourse is by no means restricted to economics. It is deeply embedded in the social sciences and in Western culture in general. In his analysis of the use of time in anthropology, Johannes Fabian (1983) found this feature, which he calls denial of coevalness, to be central to the writings about other cultures. In spite of the fact that the ethnographer or researcher/economist is mandated to share the time of the other—the "native," the "underdeveloped"—in the fieldwork experiences or in the economists' missions, this other is nevertheless represented as belonging to another time period (even to the Stone Age in some texts); thus time is used to construct the object of anthropology, or economics, in such a way that a specific power relation is created. By constructing the other as living in another time period, these scientists avoid having to take into account the other seriously; a monologue from the height of power results. These features are borne in Lewis's depiction of the dual economy:

> We find a few industries highly capitalized, such as mining or electric power, side by side with the most primitive techniques. . . . We find the same contrast also outside their economic life. There are one or two modern towns, with the finest architecture, water supplies, communications, and the like, into which people drift from other towns and villages which might almost belong to another planet. There is the same contrast even within people; between the few highly westernized, trousered, natives, educated in western universities, speaking western languages, and glorifying Beethoven, Mills, Marx or Einstein, and the great mass of their countrymen which live in quite other worlds. . . . Inevitably what one gets are very heavily developed patches of the economy, surrounded by economic darkness. (Lewis [1954] 1958, 408)

In this discourse, the traditional segment is a world of economic darkness, where new ideas are impossible, architecture is inadequate (despite the fact that it seems adequate for its dwellers), and there are no communications (because only the airplane, the automobile, and television count as communications)—in short, another planet. It does not matter that those aliens are human beings as well (although those who belong to the modern sector are apparently more human, because they speak prestigious languages, listen to Beethoven, have memorized Einstein's equations, and have mastered Samuelson, Friedman, or Marx) or that they constitute about 80 percent of the world. Their existence can be brushed aside, because they live in quite another age bound to be swept away by the fruits of the Enlightenment and the travails of economists. The rightness of the actions of the harbingers of modernity is corroborated by the fact that the native elite cherishes the modern world—even if their native side might pop up from time to time, for instance, when they become "corrupt" or "uncooperative."

The economic development conception that comes out of this view is its logical extension. "The central problem in the theory of economic development," writes Lewis, "is how to understand the process by which a community which was previously saving and investing 4 or 5 per cent of its national income or less, converts itself into an economy where voluntary saving is running at about 12 to 15% of national income or more" (Lewis [1954] 1958, 416). "This is the central problem because the central fact of economic development is rapid capital accumulation (including knowledge and skills with capital)," he adds (416). The means to achieve this feat also follows: to use the traditional sector to fuel the modern one. This would require moving "the rural underemployed," who, because of their large numbers, can be removed from the countryside without reducing agricultural output (in the economist's jargon, this can be done because the marginal productivity of labor in agriculture is negligible or zero). This "surplus labor" would be hired at near-subsistence wages by the new industries set up with additional savings and foreign capital. Both the historical "record," as well as economic rationality, attests to the fact that people will move as long as they can be secured higher wages in the modern sector.

What happened to rural people (never mind what they thought) did not matter. From an economic perspective, these people simply did not count.

We are interested not in the people in general, but only say in the 10 per cent of them with the largest incomes, who in countries with surplus labor receive up to 40 per cent of the national income. . . . The remaining 90 per cent of the people never manage to save a significant fraction of their income. The important question is why does the top 10 per cent save more? . . . The explanation is . . . likely to be that saving increases relatively to national income because the incomes of the savers increase relatively to the national income. The central fact of economic development is that the distribution of incomes is altered in favour of the saving class. (Lewis [1954] 1958, 416, 417)

Not surprisingly, theories of this type led to regressive distributions of income that reached embarrassing proportions. Not until the early 1970s did economists fully realize this fact, especially with Albert Fishlow's empirical findings that the "Brazilian miracle" of the late 1960s and early 1970s (growth rates of more than 10 percent per year maintained for a number of years) had not only produced a more unequal distribution of income but left low-income groups worse off in absolute terms. The second important aspect that should be noted is that unemployment was not eased in most cases, nor did wages and living standards rise significantly, as theory predicted; instead a permanent condition of surplus labor was produced, which fitted nicely the needs of multinational corporations. Poverty and unemployment inevitably increased, parallel to increases in the growth of GNP. These "undesirable" consequences, these "painful realizations"—as economists often euphemistically call them when they look at the "development record"— were by no means peripheral to the models used but belonged to their inner architecture.[22]

A third model of economic development, which achieved significant influence, especially in Latin America, was propounded in the late 1940s and 1950s by a group of Latin American economists working within the newly established Economic Commission for Latin America (CEPAL) in Santiago. CEPAL economists based their approach on the empirical demonstration of the historical deterioration of the terms of trade against primary goods from the countries of the periphery. The terms *center* and *periphery* (radicalized into a theory of dependency in the 1960s) were coined by CEPAL as elements of their explanation for this phenomenon. The deterioration of the terms of trade was seen as a reflection of the fact that the advances in technical progress were concentrated in the industrialized center. CEPAL's doctrine was not unrelated to Lewis's. Because output per worker was lower in the periphery, and given surplus labor, the conclusion for CEPAL economists was lower capacity for capital accumulation in the periphery. Ergo, a specific industrialization policy was needed. The lack of industrialization severely curtailed access to foreign exchange—the crucial component for economic growth because it determined the capacity to import capital goods. The answer thus lay in programs of domestic industrialization that would allow countries to manufacture at home goods that were previously imported. Hence the name given to this strategy, "import substitution industrialization," one of CEPAL's trademarks.[23]

CEPAL theorists also paid attention to other salient issues, such as inflation, and to structural obstacles to development, particularly the sluggishness of the agricultural sector and the lack of coordination among sectors of the economy. The assessment of CEPAL theories remains a matter of controversy in Latin America to this date.[24] Albert Fishlow (1985), for instance, has rightly observed the paradoxical fact that CEPAL's strategy of import substitution industrialization aggravated precisely those factors it sought to correct: it increased the foreign-exchange vulnerability, magnified certain aspects of sectoral disequilibriums, and exacerbated the inflationary bias of the growth process. Yet it is undeniable that CEPAL economists challenged a number of tenets of orthodox economic theory (particularly the theory of international trade), provided a more complex view of development, which included structural considerations, and showed greater concern for the standard of living of the masses. Despite these differences, economic development remained in essence, in the eyes of these economists, a process of capital accumulation and technical progress. In short, as Cardoso (1977) pointedly put it, CEPAL thinking constituted "the originality of a copy."

This is to say that CEPAL's proposals were easily assimilated into the established views, to the extent that they lent themselves to a modernization process that international experts and national elites were eager to undertake. Its fate was to be absorbed into the power grid of the dominant discourse. One may say generally that at the level of discursive regularities, the CEPAL doctrine did not constitute a radical challenge. This does not mean, however, that it did not have important effects. From the point of view of the history of ideas, one should acknowledge, with Sikkink (1991), the impressive contribution of the Latin American economists who articulated a particular view of developmentalism as a model in the 1940s and 1950s. The fact that CEPAL-type developmentalism was adopted among several possible models reflects, for Sikkink, the resourcefulness of Latin American economists and policymakers of the period in the face of rapidly changing international and domestic opportunities and constraints.

Marxist or neo-Marxist theories of development, finally, did not achieve significant visibility until the 1960s, through theories of dependency, peripheral capitalism, and unequal exchange (Cardoso and Faletto 1979; Amin 1976; Emmanuel 1972). Paul Baran's influential article of 1952 and canon-setting book of 1957 was the starting point for most Marxist formulations. His 1952 article (see Baran 1958), entitled "On the Political Economy of Backwardness," contained a diatribe against Western capitalism and the middle and upper classes of the backward countries for having failed to develop these countries. For Baran, the eradication of the feudal order of backward countries and its replacement with market rationality would have been an indication of progress. At this level he was close to the dominant discourse. Nevertheless, his dialectical approach gave him the foresight to denounce the inappropriateness of the policies then being proposed and to pinpoint the need for structural changes in the political framework and the prevailing class alliances.

To what extent did Marxist or neo-Marxist views become circumvented, appropriated, or subverted by the dominant discourse? Many of the concepts these theories used can be described according to the conceptual basis of classical political economy. Even if concepts such as dependency and unequal exchange were new, the discursive space in which they operated was not. Nevertheless, because they functioned within a system that had a different set of rules (that of Marxist political economy, in which concepts such as profit and capital establish a different discursive practice), they are—at the level of discursive strategies—a challenge to the dominant frameworks. In sum, although they did not constitute an alternative to development, they amounted to a different view of development and an important critique of bourgeois development economics.[25]

Cheryl Payer (1991) has offered a powerful indictment of the early theories of development economics from a contemporary angle, the debt crisis. Payer finds the origins of the debt crisis precisely in these early models. The early theories assumed that developing countries were "natural importers of capital" and that only a flow of external capital could guarantee their development. This myth was based on a number of fallacious assumptions: (1) that foreign capital would always be an addition to domestic savings (in many instances this was not the case: it made more sense to use grants and low-interest loans for investment and divert domestic savings to politically oriented social programs); (2) that external markets would always be available, so that Third World countries could use the foreign exchange earned from exports to pay off loans (more often than not, center countries levied high tariffs against Third World products); (3) that the industrialization that would occur due to added investment would reduce the need for imports (this was hardly the case: countries became more dependent on imports of capital goods—machinery—to produce locally what they previously imported, thus worsening balance-of-payment problems); and (4) that foreign capital would necessarily activate growth (as the historical experience of countries like Norway and Australia shows, the opposite can be the case).

The main factor economists forgot, Payer strongly states, was that loans have to be repaid. The way they solved this predicament was to assume that loans would always be available to pay past debt, ad infinitum, or to overlook completely the problem of servicing the debt. Payer refers to this as the Ponzi scheme, a scheme in which original investors are paid off with money supplied by later investors. The underlying premise was that loans would be invested properly and have high rates of return, thus making payment possible. This did not happen in many cases, for reasons such as those cited earlier. It was also assumed that there were balance-of-payments stages—again, as read from the economic history of the U.S. and the U.K.: nations would move from being young debtors (like Third World countries in the 1950s) to mature debtors (when aid is no longer required, countries having developed the capacity to use efficiently commercial loans) to new creditors to, finally, mature creditors (net exporters of capital). For this theory to work, mature creditors would have had to accept imports from debtors at a scale they never did, thus worsening the debt problem.

The main factor these models overlooked, however, was that the historical context of the Third World after World War II and that of the U.S. and England a century earlier were completely different. Although countries of the center became industrialized at a time when they could dictate the rules of the game and extract surpluses from their colonies (albeit not always and not in every colonial possession), Third World countries in the postwar period had to borrow under the opposite conditions: deterioration of the terms of trade against the periphery, extraction of surplus by center countries, and a position of subordination in terms of policy formulation. Said bluntly, whereas Europe was feeding off its colonies in the nineteenth century, the First World today feeds off the Third World, as attested by the fact that Latin America in the 1980s paid an average of $30 billion more each year than it received in new lending.

To sum up: The pioneers of development economics conceived of development as something to be achieved by the more or less straightforward application of savings, investment, and productivity increases. Their notion of development was not, for the most part, structural or dialectical—not one in which development could be seen as the result of the dialectical interaction of socioeconomic, cultural, and political factors seen as a totality. As Antonio García, a prominent Latin American economist, pointed out, the notion of underdevelopment that these economists assumed was necessarily mechanistic and fragmentary:

> It is mechanistic because it is based on the theoretical assumption that development is an effect induced by certain technological innovations and by certain mechanisms that accelerate the equation savings/investment. It is compartmentalizing because it is built on a view of social life as the arithmetic sum of compartments (economic, political, cultural, ethical) that can be isolated at will and treated accordingly. (1972, 16, 17)

The early models had an implicit standard (the prosperous, developed countries), and development was to be measured by the yardstick of Western progress. Their notion of underdevelopment occupied the discursive space in such a manner that it precluded the possibility of alternative discourses. By constructing the underdeveloped economy as characterized by a vicious circle of low productivity, lack of capital, and inadequate industrialization, development economists contributed to a view of reality in which the only things that counted were increased savings, growth rates, attracting foreign capital, developing industrial capacity, and so on. This excluded the possibility of articulating a view of social change as a project that could be conceived of not only in economic terms but as a whole life project, in which the material aspects would be not the goal and the limit but a space of possibilities for broader individual and collective endeavors, culturally defined.

It has often been said that classical political economy was the rationalization of certain hegemonic class interests: those of a capitalist world economy centered in England and its bourgeoisie. The same can be said of development economics in relation to the project of capitalist modernization launched by the core nations after the Second World War. Indeed, the set of imperatives the United States faced after the war—the five imperatives mentioned earlier: to consolidate the core, find higher rates of profit abroad, secure control of raw materials, expand overseas markets for American products, and deploy a system of military tutelage—shaped the constitution of development economics. Yet development economics should not be seen as the ideological or superstructural reflection of this set of imperatives. This interpretation would only relate a certain descriptive discourse (a set of assertions about a given economy: the five imperatives) to another discourse enunciated in the form of theoretical propositions (namely, development economics). That is, one should avoid falling back into the division between the "ideal" (the theory) and the "real" (the economy); instead one should investigate the epistemological and cultural conditions of the production of discourses that command the power of truth, and the specific mode of articulation of these discourses upon a given historical situation.

From this perspective, the emergence of development economics was not due to theoretical, institutional, or methodological advances. It was due to the fact that a certain historical conjuncture transformed the mode of existence of economic discourse, thus making possible the elaboration of new objects, concepts, and methodologies. Economics was called upon to reform societies perceived as underdeveloped, based on a new grid for theoretical interpretation (Keynesian and growth economics) and new technologies for social management (planning and programming). Said differently, the fact that the economic, political, and institutional changes of the period shaped the consciousness and perceptions of the economists was true in a number of ways—for instance, the need for economic expansion influenced the economists' concern with growth; the rising tide of multinational corporations influenced the economists' attention to capital accumulation via industrialization; and so on. Those changes, however, exerted their effect on economic discourse through other mechanisms as well: by opening new fields for the construction of economic objects; by conferring a new status on economists and their science; and by multiplying the sites from which the discourse could be produced and from which its associated practices could be set into motion.

Development economics made possible the elaboration of historical events into objects of economic discourse. What we called the economics of the world (the 1914–1948 crisis, the ensuing post–World War II situation, and the imperatives of the world economy) influenced the making up of the world of economics. The interests and struggles that made up those events found their way into the discourse and deployed their strategy in it. Throughout this period, then, a fundamental structure was laid down which united a theoretical corpus, forms of diffusing it and controlling it, a body of practices—such as planning, discussed in the next section—international organizations (in whose ambit negotiations were conducted for the establishment of a new relation between international capital and the peripheral economies), and decision-making centers in the Third World eager to drink from the cup of economic knowledge so that they could elevate their peoples, once and for all, to the surface of civilization. Beyond the models themselves, it is this system that can be properly called development economics.

The development economist played a special role in this new universe of discourse. To him (he was almost invariably a male)[26] belonged the expertise that was most avidly sought; it was he who knew what was needed, he who decided on the most efficient way to allocate scarce resources, he who presided over the table at which—as if they were his personal entourage—demographers, educators, urban planners, nutritionists, agricultural experts, and so many other development practitioners sat in order to mend the world. Within this configuration, the economist retained for himself the less mundane role of giving overall directions, because it was his truth that circumscribed the task and gave it legitimacy in the name of science, progress, and freedom. To the latter were reserved the daily chores of social supervision and intervention, the detailed programs and projects through which development was carried out. The system as a whole rested on the economist's shoulders; sooner or later, the Third World would yield its secrets to the gaze of the economist; and this gaze, in keeping with the best Cartesian tradition, was undeniably objective and unprejudiced.

As the discourse of development economics became consolidated, so did its associated institutions and practices: economic institutes and faculties and, more important, the planning institutions. The next section introduces briefly the discusion of planning, although a more detailed analysis of its functioning as a field of knowledge and technique of power must await subsequent chapters.

Managing Social Change:
The Constitution of Development Planning

During the 1960s, economic-growth theories occupied "an exalted position" (Arndt 1978, 55). The challenge that growth not be equated with development was still a decade away. The widespread belief that growth could be planned for contributed to solidifying the growth approach. Planning had ceased to be an affair of the socialist Left and the Soviet world. Even in countries like England and France the need for some sort of long-term planning to orchestrate economic growth was recognized. But planning was not just the application of theoretical knowledge; it was the instrument through which economics became useful, linked in a direct fashion to policy and the state. At the practical level of planning, truth spoke for itself, because it had been previously summoned by the discourse of the economist. What for the planner was a field of application and experimentation, for the economist was the locus of a systematic truth he was obliged to find and bring to everybody's attention.

The first loan the World Bank made to an underdeveloped country was to Chile, in 1948. A World Bank official called Chile's initial loan application, a seven-page proposal, "a completely undigested list of projects." For World Bank economists, this was a clear indication of how far they would have to go to bring Latin American social scientists and government officials to the point where they could prepare a satisfactory project proposal. One of the early World Bank economists put it thus:

> We began to discover the problem with our first mission which went to Chile in 1947 to examine a proposal that we finance a power project there. The presentation of this proposal had been made in a book handsomely bound in black Morocco leather. . . . But when we opened the book, we found that what we had really was more of an idea about a project, not a project sufficiently prepared that its needs for finance, equipment, and manpower resources could be accurately forecast. . . . Before the loan was finally made, members of the Bank staff had made suggestions about the financial plan, had contributed to the economic analysis of the scheme, had advised on changes of engineering, and had helped study measures for improving the organization of the company which was to carry out the scheme. When we finally made the loan, the project had been modified and improved, the borrowing organization had been strengthened, and the foundation had been laid for a power expansion program in Chile which has been proceeding steadily ever since. (Quoted in Meier 1984, 25)

This telling anecdote, which Meier cites as an example of the evolving "efforts" of the World Bank and other agencies, reveals "a power expansion program," although not primarily of electric power. It reveals the pressures that Latin American social scientists and government officials faced to transform radically the style and scope of their activities to fit the needs of the development apparatus. Latin American social scientists did not know what World Bank officials meant by *project*, nor were they conversant with the new techniques (such as surveys and statistical analyses) that were becoming part of the empirical social sciences in vogue in the United States. The anecdote also highlights the importance of project preparation and planning in general in the expansion of the development apparatus. More important, it calls attention to the need to form cadres of social technicians who could invent and manage the discourses, practices, and symbols of modernity (Rabinow 1989), this time in the context of the development apparatus.

The case of Colombia exemplifies the route followed by those countries which embraced planning without much reservation. *The Basis of a Devel-*

opment Program for Colombia, the report of the World Bank mission to Co-lombia headed by Lauchlin Currie in 1949, was the first of a long list of plans produced in the country during the last forty years. Since the late 1950s, every national administration has formulated a development plan for the country. The constitutional reform of 1945 introduced for the first time the notion of planning, making possible its institutional development. With the Currie mission, the nascent preoccupation with planning became more vis-ible, and technical organisms for planning were established. The chronology of planning institutions includes the Consejo Nacional de Planeación and the Comité de Desarrollo Económico, established in 1950; the Oficina de Planeación (1951); the Comité Nacional de Planeación (1954); the Consejo Nacional de Política Económica y Planeación and the Departamento Ad-ministrativo de Planeación y Servicios Técnicos (1958); the Consejo Nacional de Política Económica y Social and the Departamento Nacional de Planeación (1966). It also includes the creation of a Ministerio de Desarrollo and of planning units within most of the other ministries (agriculture, health, education, and so on).[27]

Planning activities during the 1950s, however, were modest, due to a se-ries of social and political factors that affected the country during that de-cade and that ended with the signing of the National Front Pact in 1958. The task of the Comité de Desarrollo Económico (September 1950–September 1951), for instance, was to advise the government regarding the recommen-dations of the Currie report, including provisions for external financing. The lack of qualified Colombian personnel was reflected in the fact that the first development plan was prepared by a foreign mission and that foreign ex-perts advised the planning organisms of the country during the first two decades of the "age of planning," the 1950s and 1960s (L. Currie and A. Hirschman in the early 1950s; Lebret in 1957, 1958; Watterson, from the World Bank, in 1963–1964; a Harvard mission, 1960–1970; a CEPAL mission, 1959–1962; a World Bank mission, 1970; and an International Labour Organization mission, 1970). Besides the resort to foreign experts and advice, Colombian students were sent to university centers, especially in the United States, where they could develop the knowledge of the new planning techniques and the spirit and frame of mind required for the new enterprise.

Short-term external assistance was also regularly practiced beginning in the early 1950s, sometimes financed by external sources. This type of as-sistance was not always restricted to national planning advice but often involved the design of specific projects. One such instance was the devel-opment of the Autonomous Regional Development Corporation of the Cauca Valley (Corporación Regional Autónoma del Cauca, CVC). An ex-amination of the role that external assistance played in this case reveals a number of practices of advising and planning introduced in the context of development.

In October 1954 the government of Colombia approved the creation of the CVC, following a set of initiatives taken by local industrialists and agricultural entrepreneurs of the Cauca Valley region. The Departmental Planning Commission had been set up a year earlier with the objective of formulating a development plan for the region. In early 1954, David Lilienthal, former chairman of the Tennessee Valley Authority (TVA), visited Colombia on an official invitation. His report of the visit, which reflected closely the TVA's experience, was instrumental in shaping the conception of the CVC, the statutes of which were finally approved in July 1955. In addition, the CVC requested the assistance of the International Bank for Reconstruction and Development (IBRD, better known as the World Bank) in defining the corporation's tasks and in delineating the technical and financial procedures for their implementation.

The IBRD mission, composed of six members, arrived in Colombia in February 1955 and remained there for two months. The chief of the mission returned to Colombia in September of the same year to discuss with CVC officials the contents of the report drafted in Washington. The report (International Bank for Reconstruction and Development 1955) addressed a whole range of technical issues (flood control, electric power, irrigation, present and potential agricultural activities, agricultural programs, transportation, minerals, industry, financial considerations, and so on). It also included provisions for future external technical assistance. Ever since, the CVC became the most important factor in the capitalist transformation of the fertile Cauca River Valley region, to such an extent that it became an international showcase of regional development planning.

The establishment of the CVC exemplifies well the interests and practices of the World Bank and other international lending organizations during the 1950s. The overall goal was dictated by development economics: to promote growth through certain types of investment projects, resorting to foreign financing when possible or necessary. This goal required the rationalization of the productive apparatus, according to the methods developed in industrialized nations—the well-reputed TVA in this case, which served as a model for similar programs in various parts of the Third World, often, as in Colombia, with Lilienthal's direct involvement. This could be done only through new practices concerning the everyday actions of an ever larger number of development technicians and institutions. The importance of these micro practices—replicated by hundreds of technicians at all levels— cannot be overemphasized, because it is through them that development is constituted and advanced.

The new practices concerned many activities and domains, including, among others, technical assessments; institutional arrangements; forms of advice; the generation, transmission, and diffusion of knowledge; the training of personnel; the routine preparation of reports; and the structuring of bureaucracies. It is through these practices that development is effected, as I will show in the detailed discussion of food and nutrition planning that follows this chapter. Although the state plays a crucial role in this process, it is not through a uniform form of intervention but through a multiplicity of sites of intervention in the economy (economic planning, planning in agriculture, health, education, family planning, and project design and implementation in many arenas). Nevertheless, the progressive encroachment of what was to become the great edifice of planning in the late 1960s cannot be divorced from the emergence of a politics of development as a national problem. Once the basic organization of the discourses of planning and development economics was in place in the early 1950s, it increasingly determined the nature of social policy and thinking—even if it did not become consolidated until a decade later, especially with most Latin American governments' commitment to planning, agrarian reform, and the Alliance for Progress at the Punta del Este meeting in 1961.

Older styles of knowledge and assistance progressively disappeared as development economics and planning became consolidated. Pre–World War II economic inquiry could not fulfill the demands for model building and empirical research placed by the new science (Escobar 1989). Politically, what was at stake was a way of treating poverty and underdevelopment in a new fashion. After 1945, the task of governments was to make poverty useful by fixing it to the apparatus of production that planning sought to deploy. A completely utilitarian and functional conception of poverty emerged, linked inextricably to questions of labor and production. The new institutions of planning were replicated at the level of cities, departments, towns, and rural areas in relation to minute economic and welfare concerns. Through this network of power, the "poor," the "underdeveloped," the "malnourished," and the "illiterate" were brought into the domain of development; it was in them that the political technologies of development were inscribed. Beyond the requirements of capital, development technologies became a mechanism of social production of unprecedented reach. As we will see, the development apparatus succeeded only partly in this task.

SHIFTING ECONOMIC DISCOURSE: LOCAL MODELS AND THE GLOBAL ECONOMY

The 1980s: The Lost Decade and the Return to Realism

The intellectual and political climate that saw the birth of development economics started to change in the 1960s. A number of important changes have taken place within the discipline since then—the abandonment of the early *dirigisme* and the overconcern with growth, and the successive appearance, within the non-Marxist camp, of "growth-plus-distribution" strategies, export-led growth, international monetarism, neostructuralism, and neoliberalism. A certain degree of innovation and structural mutations has occurred, although always within the confines of established economic discourse, whose laws of formation have not changed. In the mid-1980s, a prominent analyst saw Latin American economics as dominated by pragmatic adaptations: neither a return to laissez-faire nor an invigoration of dirigisme but a sort of eclectic practice dictated by the consideration of special problems—particularly the debt, inflation, and the role of the state—which recombined rather than reinvented theoretical perspectives (Fishlow 1985).

The most drastic contextual changes took place in the 1980s, when large parts of Asia, Africa, and Latin America saw, according to observers of many persuasions, their worst crisis in the century. In Latin America, the 1980s are known as the lost decade. In 1982, Mexico's announcement that it could not meet its debt service obligations unleashed the infamous debt crisis. What followed is well known by now: repeated attempts at economic stabilization and adjustment; austerity measures that translated into rapidly declining living standards for the popular and middle classes; industrial decline in many countries in the wake of strong neoliberal and free market economic policies, even negative growth rates in some countries; in sum, a reversal of development (Portes and Kincaid 1989; Dietz and James 1990). The social and political implications of these changes were equally onerous and menacing. Social exclusion and violence increased significantly. What were perceived as transitions to democracy during the first half of the decade became difficult to consolidate as the decade progressed. Even nature seemed to take issue with the region, as tornadoes, erupting volcanoes, earthquakes, and, more recently, the resurgence of cholera brought to the region more than its usual share of nature-related but socially aggravated hardships.

These changes fostered a significant reassessment of development economics. In the first half of the decade, a number of articles by leading development economists appeared which tried to assess the experience of the last four decades in the field.[28] "Few subject areas," read the opening paragraph of one of them, "have undergone so many twists and transformations as has development economics during the past thirty years" (Livingstone 1982, 3). Although a number of initial errors were recognized, the 1980s' assessments emphasized considerable learning at the level of types of empirical research, concreteness and specificity, and theoretical advances in a number of subfields. Moreover, a number of competing paradigms (neoclassical, structuralist, and neo-Marxist) were thought to have come into existence.

Trenchant critiques, however, also appeared. One of the most poignant was penned by Raúl Prebisch, CEPAL's first director and originator of the center-periphery conception, in referring to the application of the neoclassical economic theories to the Third World:

In their striving after rigorous consistency . . . these [neoclassical] theories shelved important aspects of social, political and cultural reality, as well as of the historical background of collectivities. In making a tenacious effort at doctrinal asepsis, they evolved their arguments in the void, outside time and space. . . . If the neoclassical economists were to confine themselves with building their castles in the air, without claiming that they represent reality, that would be a respectable intellectual pastime, apt at times to arouse admiration for the virtuosity of some of its eminent exponents overseas. But the position is very different when an attempt is made in these peripheral countries to explain development without taking account of the social structure, of the time-lag in peripheral development, of the surplus, and of all the characteristics of peripheral capitalism. . . . It is worth while to recall this at the present time, when such vigorous offshoots are springing up in some of the Latin American countries. (Prebisch 1979, 168)

It must be borne in mind that those "vigorous offshoots" to which Prebisch referred in 1979 were the neoliberal experiments of the authoritarian regimes of the Southern Cone countries (particularly Chile and Argentina), which were to become the standard approach all over Latin America by the end of the 1980s.[29] A similar critique was put forth by P. T. Bauer from an entirely different position. For Bauer, the development economists of the early 1950s completely misread a number of factors that characterized the economies of the less developed countries (the problem of trade, the alleged lack of capital and entrepreneurship, the vicious circle of poverty, and stagnation). Based on these misreadings, a series of ideas developed which became the core of economic development literature. "Even when some of the elements of the core have disappeared from most academic writings," he concluded, "they have continued to dominate political and public discourse, an instance of the lingering effect of discarded ideas" (1984, 1).

For Dudley Seers, the fact that the early theories allowed economists and policymakers to concentrate on technical issues, leaving aside important social and political questions, contributed to their rapid adoption. An additional factor in this regard were "the professional convenience and career interests especially in the 'developed' countries, where most of the theoretical advances in the field originated" (1979, 709). Albert Hirschman (1981) analyzed the early years of the discipline from a different angle. In its initial stages, according to him, development economics was fueled with "unreasonable hopes," a reflection of the ethnocentric behavior that has characterized Western societies' attempts to deal with other cultures. In his words,

The Western economists who looked at [Asia, Africa, and Latin America] at the end of World War II were convinced that these countries were not at all that complicated: their major problems would be solved if only their income per capita could be raised adequately. . . . With the new doctrine of economic growth, contempt took a more sophisticated form: suddenly it was taken for granted that progress of these countries would be smoothly linear if only they adopted the right kind of integrated development program! Given what was seen as their overwhelming problem of poverty, the underdeveloped countries were expected to perform as wind-up toys and to "lumber through" the various stages of development single-mindedly. (1981, 24)

These reflections were accompanied by concrete proposals in some cases. Seers (1979), for instance, advocated the incorporation of development economics into a broader field of development studies so that it could deal seriously with social, political, and cultural aspects of development. For Meier, development economics needed to move "beyond neo-classical economics." It is difficult to see what he meant by this, because he—as most economists—continued to uphold the belief that "the laws of logic are the same in Malawi as anywhere else. But the economic problems of Malawi may still be quite different in empirical content from those in another country" (Meier 1984, 208). This same "logic" led him to assert that "the population problem arouses more alarm than any other aspect of development" (211). One might be tempted to read these assertions in the following manner: "The laws of logic that must rule for the type of capitalist development embodied in neoclassical economics have to be the same in Malawi as in the United States. Only then would the problems of population, unemployment, and so on, be solved." Logic, for Meier, is an ahistorical fact. This is why in his discourse the economist is much more "the guardian of rationality" than "the trustee of the poor"; he argues that economists have to balance both roles.

Hollis Chenery, a leading development economist at the World Bank, held that development economics could be recast without significant reformulation. For him, "the neo-classical model has proven to be a useful starting point even though it seems to require more extensive adaptation to fit the developing countries" (1983, 859). His prescription was to adapt the model better by conducting more empirical studies and constructing "computable general equilibrium models" and more complex algorithms (859). Chenery's call for more empirical studies was mandated by the theoretical framework within which such studies would be conducted; they could only reinforce that framework. The hope was that by conducting more empirical studies, economists would finally get it right, avoiding the question of whether the framework itself was adequate. After all, economists such as Prebisch, Seers, and some neo-Marxists had shown that neoclassical economics was an inadequate theoretical apparatus for understanding the situation of poor countries.

A fundamental assumption that persisted in all of these proposals was that there is a reality of underdevelopment that a carefully conducted economic science can grasp progressively, pretty much following the model of the natural sciences. In this view, economic theory was built out of a vast bloc of preexisting reality that is independent of the theorist's observations. This assumption has fueled the sense of progression and growth of economic theory in general and of development economics in particular. In economic theory, this sense has been further legitimized by the canonization of the most important developments—such as the innovations of the 1870s and 1930s—as veritable scientific revolutions. As a prominent economic historian put it, "Appeal to paradigmatic reasoning has quickly become a regular feature in controversies in economics and 'paradigm' is now the by-word of every historian of economic thought" (Blaug 1976, 149; see Hunt 1986 for paradigms in development economics).[30]

In Latin America and most of the Third World (as in the United States and the United Kingdom), a mixture of approaches under the overall label neoliberal economics became dominant at the level of the elite as the 1980s unfolded. Statist and redistributive approaches gave way to the liberalization of trade and investment regimes, the privatization of state-owned enterprises, and policies of restructuring and stabilizing under the control of the ominous International Monetary Fund (IMF). There was, indeed, a noticeable policy reversal. Reagan's "magic of the market" speech, delivered at the North-South conference in Cancún in 1981, publicly announced this turn. A certain reading of the experience of the "newly industrializing countries" of East Asia in terms of the advantages of liberal exchange regimes (opening up to the world economy), as well as the influential Berg Report for Africa (World Bank 1981), plus rational choice critiques of the distortional effects of government intervention, all contributed to the dismantling of the economic development approaches that prevailed until the 1970s (Biersteker 1991). The World Bank's "market friendly development" (1991), the institution's strategy for the 1990s, was the final crystallization of the return of neoliberalism. Most economists see these changes as a return to realism.

Within economics, even the approaches to sustainable development have been permeated by the neoliberal turn. As the 1991 World Bank Annual Conference on Development Economics put it (Summers and Shah 1991), the achievement of "sustainable economic growth" is seen as dependent on the existence of "an undistorted, competitive, and well-functioning market" (358). As before, the allegedly improved economic theory is produced by a small elite of economists entrenched in prestigious universities and backed by the World Bank and the IMF. In Latin America, timid attempts at proposing a certain "neo-structuralism" (Sunkel 1990) have not found much support, even if a number of countries (such as Colombia) continued to make efforts throughout the 1980s to maintain a type of mixed economic policy, only partly committed to neoliberalism and the free market. In the Colombian case, as in most of Latin America, any resistence to neoliberalism that could have existed had disappeared by the beginning of the 1990s. The total opening of the economy—coupled with a new round of privatization of services and the so-called modernization of the state—has become the order of the day. The policies of *apertura económica*, as the new approach is anachronistically known, is opposed from a number of fronts; yet for now the global elites seem committed to it.[31]

The assessments of development economics conducted during the 1980s, in short, did not lead to a significant recasting of the discipline. What we seem to be witnessing is its progressive dissolution. A break in economic development theory may come not, as the authors of the assessments reviewed here assumed, from the field of economics (for example, from the introduction of new concepts, better models, and algorithms) but from a wider critique of the field of development. Conversely, any strategy to modify development theory and practice will have to consider current economic thought and practices. This process of critique is yet to be done. Recent works in anthropology and political economy provide elements toward a more creative reformulation of economic inquiry than the recasting attempted in the 1980s.

The Cultural Politics of Economic Discourse: Local Models in Global Contexts

It should be clear by now that development economics, far from being the objective universal science its practitioners assumed it was, is, as "any model, local or universal, a construction of the world" (Gudeman 1986, 28). This chapter has shown in detail the nature of this construction. It is now time to explore the consequences of this analysis in terms of its relation to other possible constructions. If there are other constructions, how are these to be made visible? What is their relation to dominant models? How can this relation be modified, given the global political economy of discourses and power that rules the interaction between the various models and their sociocultural matrices?

Economic historians and anthropologists have investigated different economic models, either in antiquity or in "primitive" societies. Frequently, these efforts have been marred by the epistemological traps and ethnocentricity denounced by Polanyi, Godelier, Gudeman, and others with which we started our discussion of economics as culture. Succinctly stated, universal models—whether neoclassical, substantivist, or Marxist—"continuously reproduce and discover their own assumptions in the exotic materials" (Gudeman 1986, 34). In the process, they deny the capacity of people

to model their own behavior and reproduce forms of discourse that contribute to the social and cultural domination effected through forms of
representation.

One way to detect and investigate local constructions is to focus on popular groups' forms of resistance to the introduction of capitalist practices. This
was the route followed by the ethnographies of resistance of the 1980s, such
as those by Nash (1979), Taussig (1980), Scott (1985), and Ong (1987). One
of the most unambiguous expressions of the cultural basis of resistance was
given by Taussig in his analysis of the spread of capitalist agriculture in the
Cauca River Valley in southwest Colombia. The spread of sugarcane was
met by fierce opposition by the mostly Afro-Colombian peasants of the region. There was much more at stake than material resistance. In Taussig's
words,

> Peasants represent as vividly unnatural, even as evil, practices that most of us
> in commodity-based societies have come to accept as natural in the everyday
> workings of our economy, and therefore of the world in general. This represen-
> tation occurs only when they are proletarianized and refers only to the way of
> life that is organized by capitalist relations of production. It neither occurs nor
> refers to peasant ways of life. (1980, 3).

Taussig invites us to see in this type of resistance a response by people "to
what they see as an evil and destructive way of ordering economic life" (17).
Other authors in disparate contexts derive similar lessons—for instance,
Fals Borda (1984) in his analysis of the introduction of barbed wire and other
technologies in northern Colombia at the turn of the century; and Scott
(1985) in his study of the fate of green revolution technologies in Malaysia.
The works of the 1980s, however, used resistance to illuminate practices of
power more than the logic of the subaltern. Several authors have paid more
attention to this latter aspect in recent years, introducing new ways of thinking about it (Guha 1988; Scott 1990; Comaroff and Comaroff 1991). In their
discussion of the colonial encounter in southern Africa, for example, Comaroff and Comaroff emphatically assert that the colonized "did not equate
exchange with incorporation, or the learning of new techniques with subordination" (1991, 309); instead, they read their own significance into the colo-
nizers' practices and sought to neutralize their disciplines. Although Africans were certainly transformed by the encounter, the lesson derived by this
more subaltern actor–oriented view of resistance is that hegemony is more
unstable, vulnerable, and contested than previously thought.

Ranajit Guha has also called on historians to see the history of the subaltern "from another and historicaly antagonistic universe" (1989, 220). There
is a counterappropriation of history by the subaltern that cannot be reduced
to something else, such as the logic of capital or modernity. It has to be
explained in its own terms. Turning back to local models of the economy, do

they exist in "another and historically antagonistic universe"? One thing is certain in this regard: local models exist not in a pure state but in complex hybridizations with dominant models. This is not to deny, however, that people do model their realities in specific ways; local models are constitutive of a people's world, which means that they cannot be readily observed by objectifying positivist science.

I already introduced Gudeman and Rivera's (1990) notion of local models as conversations that take place in the context of dominant conversations. Indeed, what counts most from the perspective of these authors is to investigate the articulation of local and "centric" (dominant) conversations, including the relationship between inscriptions from the past and practices of the present, between centric text and marginal voices, between the "corporation" in the center and the "house" in the margins. Center and periphery thus emerge not as fixed points in space, external to each other, but as a continuously moving zone in which practices of doing conversations and economies get intermingled, always shifting their relative position. Marginality becomes an effect of this dynamic. Gudeman's earlier work (see especially 1986) provides a view of the importance and coherence of local models of the economy in Panama, a view further refined through work in Colombia. For these anthropologists, the peasant model that exists today in the Colombian Andes "is the outcome of an extensive conversation"—from Aristotle to Smith and Marx—"that occurred over several thousand years and continues to take place in many lands" (1990, 14). These conversations are incorporated into local social practice, producing a local model of the economy.[32]

At the basis of the peasant model is the notion that the Earth "gives" based on its "strength." Humans, however, must "help" the land to give its products through work. There is a relation of give and take between humans and the earth, modeled in terms of reciprocity and ultimately validated by Providence (God). The land may produce abundance or scarcity; most people agree that the land gives less now, and that there is more scarcity. Scarcity is thus not given a metaphysical character (the way things are) but linked to what happens to the land, the house, and the market. If scarcity persists, it is because the Earth needs more help, although peasants know that chemical products—as opposed to organic manure—"burn the earth" and "take away" its force. Food crops draw their strength from the land; humans, in turn, gain their energy and force from food crops and animal products, and this strength, when applied as work on the land, yields more force. Work, construed as concrete physical activity, is the final "using up" of the land's strength.

> This construction brings the model full circle. There is a flow of strength from the land to crops to food to humans to work that helps the land give more force.

Strength is secured from the earth and used up as humans gather more. Control over this process is established through the house, for by using resources of the house to sustain their work the people gain control over the results of their efforts. (Gudeman and Rivera 1990, 30)

The house has two main purposes: to reproduce itself and to increase its "base" (its stock of land, savings, and implements). The house is not purely a market participant; indeed, peasants in this part of the world try to minimize their interaction with the market, which they see as a concrete place rather than as an abstract mechanism. Peasants, however, are aware that they are being increasingly pushed into the market; they interpret this fact as a diminishing margin for maneuvering. The house model persists at the margins, where the model of the corporation (which epitomizes the market economy) has not become dominant. House and corporation are in a contrapuntal relation, the latter always trying to incorporate the contents of the former.[33] The house economy is based on livelihood; the corporation's, on acquisition. Peasants are aware that they participate in both types of economy. They also have a theory of how they are being drained by those who control the market.

The local model thus includes a view of the circularity and equilibrium of economic life, albeit very different from the classical and neoclassical view. The peasant model can be seen as closer to the land-based model of the Physiocrats, and the use of "force" can be related to the Marxist notion of labor force, although "force" is applied equally to work, land, and food. Beyond these differences, there is a crucial distinction between both models, arising from the fact that the house model is based on daily practice. Local models are experiments in living; the house model "is developed through use . . . it has to do with land, foodstuffs, and everyday life" (Gudeman and Rivera 1990, 14, 15). This does not contradict the assertion that the peasant model is the product of past and present conversations and their adaptation through practice.

More than the house model, in Latin America what one increasingly finds is the house business. As the site of conjunction of forms, "dynamic and multicultural yet fragile and unstable in identity" (Gudeman 1992, 144), the house business can be interpreted in terms of metaphors of "bricolage" (de Certeau 1984; Comaroff and Comaroff 1991) or hybridization (García Canclini 1990). It is composed of partly overlapping domains of practices that must be studied ethnographically. Gudeman and Rivera believe that this general dynamic also marked the development of modern economics, even if the latter became more and more technical with the development of capitalism.[34] The implications of this view are enormous. Not only does the idea of a universal model of the economy have to be abandoned, it becomes necessary to recognize that forms of production are not independent from the representations (the "models") of social life in which they exist. The remaking of development must thus start by examining local constructions, to the extent that they are the life and history of a people, that is, the conditions of and for change. This brings into consideration the relation between models and power. Gudeman and Rivera advocate a process based on "communities of modelers," in which local and dominant models are accorded a say. But who is to belong to and organize these communities of modelers? Again, what we have here is a confrontation of local and global power, popular and scientific knowledge. At issue is the distribution of global power and its relation to the economy of discourses.

There are then two levels, two vectors, that must be considered in rethinking development from the perspective of the economy. The first refers to the need to make explicit the existence of a plurality of models of the economy. This entails placing oneself in the space of local constructions. But this by itself will not make it. Even if communities of modelers are brought into existence as part of the process of designing development (not inconceivably by the World Bank itself!), the process of inscription will not stop. A second level of concern must be added. One must have a theory of the forces that drive this inscription and that keep the inscribing systems in place. What needs to be studied at these levels is the mechanisms by which local cultural knowledge and economic resources are appropriated by larger forces (mechanisms such as unequal exchange and surplus extraction between center and periphery, country and city, classes, genders, and ethnic groups) and, conversely, the ways in which local innovations and gains can be preserved as part of local economic and cultural power.

Part of this inquiry has been advanced within political economy—particularly theories of imperialism, unequal exchange, world systems, and peripheral capitalism. Yet these theories fall short of the task, especially because they do not deal with the cultural dynamics of the incorporation of local forms by a global system of economic and cultural production. A more adequate political economy must bring to the fore the mediations effected by local cultures on translocal forms of capital. Seen from the local perspective, this means investigating how external forces—capital and modernity, generally speaking—are processed, expressed, and refashioned by local communities. Local-level ethnographies of development (such as those discussed in chapter 1) and theories of hybrid cultures (analyzed in the conclusion) are a step in this direction, although they tend to fall short in their analysis of the capitalist dynamics that circumscribe the local cultural constructions.

A political economy of global economic and cultural production must thus explain both the new forms of capital accumulation and the local discourses and practices through which the global forms are necessarily deployed; it must explain, briefly put, "the production of cultural difference within a structured system of global political economy" (Pred and Watts 1992, 18).

Local communities bring their material and cultural resources to bear in their encounter with development and modernity. The persistence of local and hybrid models of the economy, for instance, reflects cultural contestations that take place as capital attempts to transform the life of communities. Cultural difference partly becomes, indeed, an effect of forms of connectedness that are structured by global systems of economic, cultural, and political production. They are part of what Arjun Appadurai (1991) calls global ethnoscapes.

In fact, global capital—as a global machine, a "worldwide axiomatic" (Deleuze and Guattari 1987)—relies today not so much on homogenization of an exterior Third World as on its ability to consolidate diverse, heterogenous social forms. According to these authors, in the post-Fordist age capital requires a certain "peripheral polymorphy" (436) because it actively repeals its own limit. Here we find an expression of Gudeman and Rivera's dialectic of folk voice and centric text. Although the centric texts of the global economy steadily exert their influence on manifold folk voices, the latter do not necessarily join in a harmonious Western polyphony. Some of the peripheral forms take on this dissonant role because of their inadequacy in relation to their own national markets. This does not mean that they are less organized by capital. At this level, capital's task is different: to organize "conjunctions of decoded flows as such" (451). The minority social organizations of the tropical rain-forest areas, for instance, are not entirely coded or territorialized by capital (as are the formal urban economies). Yet to the extent that the economy constitutes a worldwide axiomatic, even these minor forms are the target of social subjections. The global economy must thus be understood as a decentered system with manifold apparatuses of capture—symbolic, economic, and political. It matters to investigate the particular ways in which each local group participates in this complex machinelike process, and how it can avoid the most exploitative mechanisms of capture of the capitalist megamachines.

Let us now see if the contributions of the political economy of development can still provide useful criteria for the two-edged process we envision, that of making visible local constructions side by side with an analysis of global forces. Samir Amin (1976, 1985, 1990), perhaps more eloquently than others, has sought to provide general criteria for constructing alternative development orders within the capitalist world economy. For Amin, the primary criterion for reaching this goal is to encourage autocentric accumulation, defined as an economic model in which external relations to the world markets are subordinated to the needs of internal capital accumulation. Autocentric development supposes a radically different economic, social, and political order. It has a series of requirements which is not the point to analyze here—such as the equalization of income between rural and urban areas and between modern and traditional sectors; priority for agriculture in many countries; control of production by popular organizations and social movements; a new role for the state; innovations in technology to meet a new demand structure; and significant restrictions or partial delinking in relation to international markets. The obstacles to this type of restructuring of peripheral countries into autocentric economies are, needless to say, enormous. In Amin's vision, some of them might be overcome through new forms of South-South cooperation, including the formation of regional blocs of several countries along socialist lines.[35]

Amin's notions of polycentrism and autocentric accumulation can serve as useful principles for guiding action at the macroeconomic and political levels. It is necessary to emphasize, however, that Amin's prescriptions are written in a universalistic mode and a realist epistemology, precisely the kinds of thinking criticized here. Nevertheless, as a description of the world that seeks to explain a hegemonic order and that relies on a dominant language, realist political economy cannot be overlooked in the imagining of alternatives to that world and that language. Yet it is necessary to insist that if the analysis in terms of political economy needs to be summoned in this context, it must also be continuously destabilized. It has to be accompanied by a strategic repositioning in the domain of representation. Forms of production and forms of representation can be distinguished only for analytical purposes. Modifying political economies involves both material and semiotic resistance, and material and semiotic strengthening of local systems.

To be sure, although the social projection of subaltern languages rests largely with social movements, it calls for strategies to modify local, regional, and international political economies. The primary goal of this modification, however, should be not healthier regimes of accumulation and development, as in Amin's case,but to provide conditions that are more conducive to local and regional experiments based on autonomous (hybrid) models. Moreover, the analysis of political economy must be conducted from the perspective of its integration with local forms, as discussed earlier. It should also contribute to shifting the political economy of discourse production and the multiplication of the centers of discourse. From the classical political economists to today's neoliberals at the World Bank, economists have monopolized the power of speech. The effects of this hegemony and the damaging centrality of economics need to be exposed in novel ways. Making other models visible is a way of advancing this task. "Mediating this communication [among modelers] or formulating a conversational community across cultures is an important project of anthropology" (Gudeman 1992, 152). It is, indeed,one must add,a political project of importance.

The suggestion that we take into account people's own models is not only a politically correct position. On the contrary, it constitutes a sound philosophical and political alternative. Philosophically, it follows the mandate of interpretive social science (Rabinow and Sullivan 1987; Taylor 1985) that we take subjects as agents of self-definition whose practice is shaped by their self-understanding. This self-understanding may be grasped by the researcher or activist through ethnographic methods. This does not mean that the researcher or activist has to adopt the subjects' view or that the subjects' view is always right. Cultural relativists have often fallen into this double trap. It means that the interpretive social scientist has to take into account people's own descriptions as the starting point of theory, that is, of what has to be explained.[36]

What I have been talking about in this chapter is a kind of social power linked to the economy of goods and discourses. At the level of regimes of representation, this power goes on for the most part unchallenged explicitly, although it is often resisted at various levels. Social power of this kind has an insidious way of encroaching upon the most recondite corners of social life, even if in inconspicuous ways. This is no less true in those arenas in which life itself is at stake, such as in the arena of food and hunger, as the next chapter will show. I will examine in detail how today's practices in nutrition, rural development, and health care came into existence not as a result of improved consciousness, scientific progress, or technological refinements but rather as effects of power brought about by the problematization of hunger in the context of the pervasive economization of subsistence.

Chapter 4

THE DISPERSION OF POWER:
TALES OF FOOD AND HUNGER

> Since disease can be cured only if others intervene with
> their knowledge, their resources, their pity, since a patient
> can be cured only in society, it is just that the illness of
> some should be transformed into the experience of
> others. . . . What is benevolence towards the poor is
> transformed into knowledge that is applicable
> to the rich.
> —Michel Foucault, *The Birth of the Clinic*, 1975

THE LANGUAGE OF HUNGER AND THE HUNGER OF LANGUAGE

NO ASPECT of development appears to be as straightforward as hunger. When people are hungry, is not the provision of food the logical answer? Policy would be a matter of ensuring that enough food reaches those in need on a sustained basis. The symbolism of hunger, however, has proven powerful throughout the ages. From famine in prehistoric times to the food riots in Latin America during the 1980s and early 1990s, hunger has been a potent social and political force. From the Bible to Knut Hamsun, Dickens, Orwell, Steinbeck, and, in twentieth-century Latin America, Ciro Alegría, Jorge Icaza, and Graciliano Ramos writers of many countries have been moved by the individual or collective experience of hunger. Images of hunger have also been portrayed in the cinema, never as powerfully as in the early years of Brazil's Cinema Novo during the first half of the 1960s. "From *Arruanda* to *Barren Lives*," Glauber Rocha, one of the founders of this movement, nakedly stated, "Cinema Novo has narrated, described, poeticized, discussed, analyzed, and stimulated the themes of hunger: characters eating dirt and roots, characters stealing to eat, characters killing to eat, characters fleeing to eat" (1982, 68); a veritable "aesthetics of hunger," as Rocha entitled his manifesto, the only one appropriate to an insurrectionist cinema in the context of neocolonialism in the Third World at the time.

The liberties accorded to creative writing and cinema have not been granted to society at large. Indeed, as Josué de Castro, the Brazilian physician and first director of the United Nations Food and Agricultural Organization (FAO), put it at the dawn of the development era,

Because of its explosive political and social implications, the subject [of hunger] until very recently has been one of the taboos of our civilization. . . . Hunger has unquestionably been the most potent source of social misfortunes, but our civilization has kept its eyes averted, afraid to face the sad reality. War has always been loudly discussed. Hymns and poems have been written to celebrate its glorious virtues as an agent of selection. . . . Thus, while war became a leitmotiv of Western thought, hunger remained only a vulgar sensation, the repercussions of which were not supposed to emerge from the realm of the subconscious. The conscious mind, with ostentatious disdain, denied its existence. ([1952] 1977, 51)

This obscurity of hunger changed dramatically after World War II, when hunger entered irremediably the politics of scientific knowledge. Famines in the 1960s and 1970s (Biafra, Bangladesh, the Sahel)brought massive hunger to public awareness. Yet the more intractable aspects of persistent malnutrition and hunger entered the scientific world a decade earlier. From the 1950s to today, an army of scientists—nutritionists, health experts, demographers, agriculturalists, planners, and so on—has been busy studying every single aspect of hunger. This hunger of (scientific) language has resulted in manifold strategies that have succeeded each other throughout the development era; from food fortification and supplementation, nutrition education, and food aid in the 1950s and 1960s to land reform, the green revolution, integrated rural development, and comprehensive national food and nutrition planning since the late 1960s, the languages of hunger have grown increasingly inclusive and detailed. Whether "the nutrition problem" was thought to be due to insufficient protein intake, lack of calories, lack of nutrition education, inadequate food intake combined with poor sanitation and health, low incomes, or inefficient agricultural practices—or to a combination of many of these factors—a battery of experts was always on call to design strategies and programs on behalf of the hungry and malnourished people of the Third World.

To be blunt, one could say that the body of the malnourished—the starving "African" portrayed on so many covers of Western magazines, or the lethargic South American child to be "adopted" for $16 a month portrayed in the advertisements of the same magazines—is the most striking symbol of the power of the First World over the Third. A whole economy of discourse and unequal power relations is encoded in that body. We may say, following Teresa de Lauretis (1987), that there is a violence of representation at play here. This violence, moreover, is extreme; scientific representations of hunger and "overpopulation" (they often go together) are most dehumanizing and objectifying. After all, what we are talking about when we refer to hunger or population is people, human life itself; but it all becomes, for Western science and media, helpless and formless (dark) masses, items to be counted and measured by demographers and nutritionists, or systems with feedback mechanisms in the model of the body espoused by physiologists and biochemists. The language of hunger and the hunger of language join forces not only to maintain a certain social order but to exert a kind of symbolic violence that sanitizes the discussion of the hungry and the malnourished. It is thus that we come to consume hunger in the West; in the process our sensitivity to suffering and pain becomes numbed by the distancing effect that the language of academics and experts achieved. To restore vividness and political efficacy to the language becomes almost an impossible task (Scheper-Hughes 1992).

The situation is even more paradoxical when one considers that the strategies implemented to deal with the problems of hunger and food supply, far from solving them, have led to their aggravation. Susan George (1986) best captured the cynicism of these strategies with the title "More Food, More Hunger." Countries that were self-sufficient in food crops at the end of World War II—many of them even exported food to industrialized nations—became net food importers throughout the development era. Hunger similarly grew as the capacity of countries to produce the food necessary to feed themselves contracted under the pressure to produce cash crops, accept cheap food from the West, and conform to agricultural markets dominated by the multinational merchants of grain. Although agricultural output per capita grew in most countries, this increase was not translated into increased food availability for most people. Inhabitants of Third World cities in particular became increasingly dependent on food their countries did not produce.

How can one account for this cynicism of power? This brings us again to the question of how discourse works, how it produces "domains of objects and rituals of truth" (Foucault 1979, 194). The discourse of development is not merely an "ideology" that has little to do with the "real world"; nor is it an apparatus produced by those in power in order to hide another, more basic truth, namely, the crude reality of the dollar sign. The development discourse has crystallized in practices that contribute to regulating the everyday goings and comings of people in the Third World. How is its power exercised in the daily social and economic life of countries and communities? How does it produce its effect on the way people think and act, on how life is felt and lived?

So far I have said little about what developers actually do in their day-to-day work. I still have to show how the discourse of development gets dispersed in or through a field of practices; how it relates to concrete interventions that organize the production of types of knowledge and forms of power, relating one to the other. It is necessary to scrutinize the specific practices through which international lending agencies and Third World governments carry out their task, bringing together bureaucrats and experts of all kinds with their Third World "beneficiaries"—peasants, poor women, urban marginals, and the like. This will be the task of this chapter; it examines in detail the deployment of development.

The chapter investigates the concrete forms that the mechanisms of professionalization and institutionalization take in the domain of malnutrition and hunger. In particular, the chapter reviews the strategy of comprehensive national Food and Nutrition Policy and Planning (FNPP), created by the World Bank and a handful of universities and institutions in the developed countries in the early 1970s and implemented in a number of Third World countries throughout the 1970s and 1980s. FNPP grew out of the realization that the complex problems of malnutrition and hunger could not be dealt with through isolated programs but that a comprehensive, multisectoral strategy of planning at the national level was needed. Based on this realization, a body of theory was produced in the above institutions, and national food and nutrition plans were designed and implemented which included ambitious programs that covered all areas related to food, such as food production and consumption, health care, nutrition education, food technology, and so on. After examining the production of FNPP theory, we will look closely at the implementation of such a strategy in Colombia during the period 1975–1990.

In order to analyze the practices of development, we have to analyze what development institutions actually do. Institutional practices are crucial not so much because they account for most of what is earmarked as development, but mostly because they contribute to producing and formalizing social relations, divisions of labor, and cultural forms. Thus illustrating how development functions, the aim of this chapter, is not a simple task. It requires that we investigate the production of discourses about the problem in question; that we show the articulation of these discourses with socioeconomic and technological conditions that they, in turn, help produce; and, finally and more importantly, that we examine the actual work practices of institutions involved with these problems. Discourse, political economy, and institutional ethnography should be woven in order to provide an adequate understanding of how development works.

The daily practices of institutions are not just rational or neutral ways of doing. In fact, much of an institution's effectiveness in producing power relations is the result of practices that are often invisible, precisely because they are seen as rational. It is then necessary to develop tools of analysis to unveil and understand those practices. I do this in the first part of this chapter, by explaining the notion of institutional ethnography. The second part reconstructs the birth, life, and death of FNPP, focusing on the view of hunger that this strategy produced and the practices that actualized it. In the third part, I summarize the political economy of the agrarian crisis in Latin America in the period 1950–1990 and examine the response that the Colombian government and the international development establishment gave to this crisis. I focus especially on the so-called Integrated Rural Development strategy, produced by the World Bank in the early 1970s and implemented in Colombia from the mid-1970s to the early 1990s, with the cooperation of the World Bank and other international agencies. Finally, in the fourth section I propose an interpretation of FNPP as a paradigmatic case in the deployment of development.

The underlying premise of this investigation is that as long as institutions and professionals are successfully reproducing themselves materially, culturally, and ideologically, certain relations of domination will prevail; and to the extent that this is the case, development will continue to be greatly conceptualized by those in power. By focusing on the practices that structure the daily work of institutions, on one hand, I hope to illustrate how power works, namely, how it is effected by institutional and documentary processes. The emphasis on discourse, on the other hand, is intended to show how a certain subjectivity is privileged and at the same time marginalizes the subjectivity of those who are supposed to be the recipients of progress. It will become clear that this marginalization produced by a given regime of representation is an integral component of institutionalized power relations.

INSTITUTIONAL ETHNOGRAPHY: THE BUREAUCRATIZATION OF
KNOWLEDGE ABOUT THE THIRD WORLD

More than three-quarters of the population of the Third World lived in rural areas at the time of the inception of development. That this proportion is now reduced to less than 30 percent in many Latin American countries is a striking feature in its own right, as if the alleviation of the peasants' suffering, malnutrition, and hunger had required not the improvement of living standards in the countryside, as most programs avowedly purported, but the peasants' elimination as a cultural, social, and producing group. Nevertheless, peasants have not disappeared completely with the development of capitalism, as both Marxist and bourgeois economists ineluctably predicted, a fact already hinted at in my brief account of resistance in the previous chapter.

The constitution of the peasantry as a persistent client category for development programs was associated with a broad range of economic, political, cultural, and discursive processes. It rested on the ability of the development apparatus systematically to create client categories such as the "malnourished," "small farmers," "landless laborers," "lactating women," and the like which allow institutions to distribute socially individuals and populations in ways consistent with the creation and reproduction of modern capitalist relations. Discourses of hunger and rural development mediate and organize the constitution of the peasantry as producers or as elements to be displaced in the order of things. Unlike standard anthropological works on development, which take as their primary object of study the people to be "developed," understanding the discursive and institutional construction of client categories requires that attention be shifted to the institutional apparatus that is doing the "developing" (Ferguson 1990, xiv). Turning the apparatus itself into an anthropological object involves an institutional ethnography that moves from the textual and work practices of institutions to the effects of those practices in the world, that is, to how they contribute to structuring the conditions under which people think and live their lives. The work of institutions is one of the most powerful forces in the creation of the world in which we live. Institutional ethnography is intended to bring to light this sociocultural production.

One may note first, in following this line of analysis, that peasants are socially constructed prior to the agent's (planner, researcher, development expert) interaction with them. *Socially constructed* here means that the relation between client and agent is structured by bureaucratic and textual mechanisms that are anterior to their interaction. This does not deter the agent or institution from presenting the results of the interaction as "facts," that is, as true discoveries of the real situation characterizing the client. The institution possesses schemata and structuring procedures, embedded in the institution's routine work practices, that organize the actuality of a given situation and present it as facts, the way things are. These structuring procedures must be made invisible for the operation to be successful, in the same way that in cinema all marks of enunciation (the director's work, the acting, the point of view of the camera, and so on) must be effaced to create the impression of reality that characterizes it (Metz 1982).

Canadian feminist sociologist Dorothy Smith has pioneered the analysis of institutions from this perspective (Smith 1974, 1984, 1986, 1987, 1990). Smith's point of departure is the observation that professional discourses provide the categories with which "facts" can be named and analyzed and thus have an important role in constituting the phenomena that the organization knows and describes. Facts are presented in standardized ways, so that they can be retold if necessary. In this sense, facts must be seen as an aspect of social organization, a practice of knowing that, through the use of ready-made categories, constructs an object as external to the knower and independent of him or her. Because often decisions are made by centralized organizations headed by representatives of ruling groups, the whole work of organizations is biased in relation to those in power. "Our relation to others in our society and beyond is mediated by the social organization of its ruling. Our 'knowledge' is thus ideological in the sense that this social organization preserves conceptions and means of description which represent the world as it is for those who rule it, rather than as it is for those who are ruled" (Smith 1974, 267).

This has far-reaching consequences, because we are constantly implicated and active in this process. But how does the institutional production of social reality work? A basic feature of this operation is its reliance on textual and documentary forms as a means of representing and preserving a given reality. Inevitably, texts are detached from the local historical context of the reality that they supposedly represent.

> For bureaucracy is *par excellence* that mode of governing that separates the performance of ruling from particular individuals, and makes organization independent of particular persons and local settings. . . . Today, large-scale organization inscribes its processes into documentary modes as a continuous feature of its functioning. . . . This [produces] a form of social consciousness that is the property of organizations rather than of the meeting of individuals in local historical settings. (Smith 1984, 62)

Institutions and conventional sociology see all this "a system of rational action." Ethnomethodologists have pointed out that organizational texts cannot be taken as "objective" records of external reality but are to be understood in relation to organizational uses and goals and in the context of their production and interpretation (Garfinkel 1967). Instead of a system of rational action, the documentary basis of an organization is but a means to objectify knowledge; it produces forms of social consciousness that are more the property of organizations than of individuals trying to understand their problems. This objectification and transcendence of local historicity are achieved in the process of inscription, to use the term given to it by Latour and Woolgar (1979), namely, the translation of an event or object into a textual form. In this process, the organization's perception and ordering of events is preordained by its discursive scheme, and the locally historical is greatly determined by nonlocal practices of institutions, embedded in turn in textual practices. I quote again from Smith to sum up this point:

> Discourse creates forms of social consciousness that are extra-local and externalized *vis-à-vis* the local subject. . . . Discourse develops the ideological currency of society, providing schemata and methods that transpose local actualities into standardized conceptual and categorical forms. . . . This movement between the locally historical and textually mediated discourse is characteristic of many contemporary social forms. (1984, 63)

Documentary practices are thus by no means innocuous. They are embedded in external social relations and deeply implicated in mechanisms of ruling. Through them, as we will see in detail, the internal processes of organizations are linked to external social relations involving governments, international organizations, corporations, and communities in the Third World. They are active in directing and ordering the relations among these various groups and must then be regarded as important constituents of social relations, even if the text is apparently detached from the social relations it helps to organize (the text is removed from the social context by the work of the professional). Documentary procedures, in sum, represent a significant dimension of those practices through which power is exercised in today's world—even if a dimension that has been for the most part neglected in critical analyses.

From the perspective of institutional ethnography, a local situation is less a case study than an entry point to the study of institutional and discursive forces and how these are related to larger socioeconomic processes. What is important is to describe the actual practices organizing people's everyday experience, "to disclose the non-local determinations of locally historic or lived orderliness" (Smith 1986, 9). In the case of institutions, it is necessary to investigate how professional training provides the categories and concepts that dictate the practices of the institution's members and how local courses of action are articulated by institutional functions; in other words, how a textually mediated discourse substitutes for the actual relations and practices of the "beneficiaries," burying the latter's experience in the matrix that organizes the institution's representation. Going back to my example, what must be analyzed is how the peasant's world is organized by a set of institutional processes. One must also investigate how the institutional practices and professional discourses coordinate and interpenetrate different levels of social relations; that is, how the relations between different actors (peasants, mothers and children, planners, international agencies, agribusiness corporations, and so on) are rendered accountable only through a set of categories that originated in professional discourse; and, finally, how the latter implicate other types of relations, such as class and gender.

Special mention should be made of labeling as a fundamental feature of organizations. I already alluded to the pervasive use of labels by the development discourse in the form of client categories and "target groups," such as "small farmers," "pregnant women," "landless laborers," "slum dwellers," and the like. These labels are essential to the functioning of institutions dealing with problems in the Third World ("Third World" itself is a label). Labels are by no means neutral; they embody concrete relationships of power and influence the categories with which we think and act. Geof Wood has insightfully summarized the rationale for labeling:

> Thus the validity of labels becomes not a matter of substantive objectivity but of the ability to use labels effectively in action as designations which define parameters for thought and behavior, which render environments stable, and which establish spheres of competence and areas of responsibility. In this way

labelling through these sorts of designations is part of the process of creating social structure. It is people making history by making rules for themselves and others to follow. . . . So the issue is not *whether* we label people, but *which* labels are created, and *whose* labels prevail to define a whole situation or policy area, under what conditions and with what effects? . . . Labels reveal more about the process of authoritative designation, agenda setting and so on than about the characteristics of the labelled. . . . In that sense, labels do in effect reveal this relationship of power between the given and the bearer of the label. (1985, 349)

Labels determine access to resources, so that people must adjust to such categorization to be successful in their dealings with the institution. A key mechanism at work here is that the whole reality of a person's life is reduced to a single feature or trait (access to land, for instance; or inability to read and write); in other words, the person is turned into a "case." That this case is more the reflection of how the institution constructs "the problem" is rarely noticed, so that the whole dynamics of rural poverty is reduced to solving a number of "cases" with apparently no connection to structural determinants, much less to the shared experiences of rural people. Explanations are thus dissociated from the nonpoor and "easily explained as deriving from characteristics internal to the poor" (Wood 1985, 357); this is achieved by focusing on a narrow target and usually involves pathologies or lacks that can be isolated and treated through some sort of technological fix. This type of labeling implies not only abstraction from social practice but the action of professional monopolies that share the interest of ruling classes. An entire politics of needs interpretation, mediated by expert discourses, is at stake, as Nancy Fraser (1989) has demonstrated in the context of the U.S. women's movement. Experts become brokers of sorts mediating the relations between communities, the state, and—in some cases—social movements.

Labels are invented and maintained by institutions on an ongoing basis, as part of an apparently rational process that is essentially political. Although the whole process has at times devastating effects on the labeled groups— through stereotyping, normalizing, fragmentation of people's experience, disorganization of the poor—it also implies the possibility of counterlabeling ("nonaligned nations," for instance, was a counterlabel to "underdeveloped nations"), as part of a process of democratization and debureaucratization of institutions and knowledge. To realize this possibility it is necessary to analyze closely how labels function as mechanisms of power in concrete institutional instances and to counteract individuating and imposed labeling processes with collective political practices.

There are other important practices, besides the documentary practices and labeling already discussed, that institutions employ and that institutional ethnographies should take into account. Organizations involved with planning, for instance, follow a planning model based on certain practices that allow them not only to construct problems in ways they can handle but also to avoid responsibility for the plan's implementation altogether. Themes, agendas, "sectors," "subdisciplines," and so on, are created by planning institutions according to procedures presented as rational and "common-sense." The commonsense model of planning, as Clay and Shaffer (1984) have called this feature in their helpful analysis of public policy practices, is one major way in which policy is depoliticized and bureaucratized. These authors unveil a whole realm, "bureaucratics," in which politics and bureaucratic processes are linked to ensure the maintenance of given ways of seeing and doing. The commonsense planning model will be analyzed in detail when we examine the National Food and Nutrition Plan of Colombia.

It is crucial to unveil these aspects of discourse and organization by investigating the documentary practices of development institutions. We must analyze how peasants are constituted by the work practices of development professionals; that is, how the former's concrete experience is elaborated upon by the professional discourse of the latter, separated from the context in which the peasants' problems arise and shifted to that in which institutions speak and act. This work of abstraction is a necessary condition for development to work in the process of describing, inquiring into, interpreting, and designing treatment for their clients or beneficiaries. Although most times this process of abstraction and structuring—which goes on in large part unconsciously—takes place at the top (international or national levels), it inevitably works its way down to the local situation, where most of the work is done. The local level must reproduce the world as the top sees it, so to speak.

In the case of hunger, local situations are subsumed under the professional discourses of agricultural economists, planners, nutritionists, extension workers, health workers, and so on. Only certain kinds of knowledge, those held by experts such as World Bank officials and developing country experts trained in the Western tradition, are considered suitable to the task of dealing with malnutrition and hunger, and all knowledge is geared to making the client knowable to development institutions. The interaction of local field personnel (extension workers, health workers) with their clients is conditioned by this need and automatically structured by the bureaucratic operations already in place.[1] Similarly, the interaction of national-level planners with officials from, say, the World Bank is conditioned by the need to obtain funding and structured by World Bank routines. Needless to say, one never finds in these accounts consideration given to peasants' struggle and oppression, nor accounts of how the peasants' world may contain a different way of seeing problems and life. What emerges instead is a view of the "malnourished" or "illiterate peasant" as a problem to be rid of through effective development. This problem is presupposed regardless of the actual

practices of the beneficiaries; the whole process not only affects the consciousness of all the actors but contributes to maintaining certain relations of
domination. These implicit operations must be made explicit.

Specific programs must thus be seen as the result of interactions between
international organizations, universities, and research centers in both the
First and Third World, professional organizations in the Third World, and
expert discourses of various types. This interaction is reflected in and organized by documentary practices—the elaboration of program descriptions,
evaluation reports, research reports, meeting documents, scholarly papers,
and so on—that ceaselessly take place as part of a process that is largely
self-referential, to the extent that these documents are written not to illuminate a given problem but to ensure their insertion into the ongoing flow of
organizational texts. Building on Dorothy Smith's work, Adele Mueller, who
studied the bureaucratic organization of knowledge about Third World
women, summarized this problematic succinctly:

> Women in development texts do not, as they claim, describe the situation of
> Third World women, but rather the situation of their own production. The
> depiction of "Third World Women" which results is one of poor women, living
> in hovels, having too many children, illiterate, and either dependent on a man
> for economic survival or impoverished because they have none. The important
> issue here is not whether this is a more or less accurate description of women,
> but who has the power to create it and make claims that it is, if not accurate,
> then the best available approximation. . . . The Women in Development discur-
> sive regime is not an account of the interests, needs, concerns, dreams of poor
> women, but a set of strategies for managing the problem which women repre-
> sent to the functioning of development agencies in the Third World. (1987b, 4)

For forty years, discourses and strategies to combat hunger have succeeded one another. This striking versatility, especially when seen in relation to the persistence and aggravation of the problems they are supposed to
eradicate, must be accounted for. The general questions in this regard can
be posed as follows: Why, and by what processes, did the experience of
hunger become successively land reform, green revolution, single-cell protein, integrated rural development, comprehensive food and nutrition planning, nutrition education, and so on? Why such a host of applied food and
nutrition programs, of nutritional, agricultural, and economic sciences devoted to this problem? What has been their impact? In response to what
local objectives did these strategies arise, and what forms of knowledge did
they produce, relating them to what types of power? We should try to identify how the system of formation that resulted in these strategies was set in
place; how all these strategies share a common space; and how they have
transformed into one another. In other words, we should describe "the system of transformation that constitutes change" (Foucault 1972, 173).

Hunger, it can be stated, is constituted by all of the discourses that refer to it; it is made visible by the existence of those grandiose strategies that, through their very appearance, give the illusion of progress and change. We should examine how strategies such as FNPP produce a specific organization of the discursive field, and how this field is held in place by institutional processes that determine specific courses of action, contribute to knitting social relations, and take part in organizing a division of labor marked by cultural, geographic, class, and gender factors. This type of analysis moves from the specific to the general and from concrete practices to forms of power that account for the functioning of development.

The purpose of institutional ethnography is to unpack the work of institutions and bureaucracies, to train ourselves to see what culturally we have been taught to overlook, namely, the participation of institutional practices in the making of the world. Institutional ethnography equips us to discern how we inevitably live and even produce ourselves within the conceptual and social spaces woven, as ever-so-fine spiderwebs, by the unglamorous but effective tasks that all types of institutions perform daily. This type of ethnographic endeavor attempts to explain the production of culture by institutions that are, themselves, the product of a certain culture.

BIRTH, LIFE, AND DEATH OF
FOOD AND NUTRITION POLICY AND PLANNING

The Birth of a Discipline:
Knowledge and the Bureaucratization of Policy Practice

In 1971, experts from various fields and planning officials from fifty-five countries gathered at the Massachusetts Institute of Technology (MIT) for the first International Conference on Nutrition, National Development, and Planning. Most of the experts came from universities, research centers, and foundations located in developed countries, whereas most of the planners came from the Third World. A gathering of this kind was not new. Experts and officials from all over the world had been meeting to discuss and assess scientific and practical progress in agriculture, health, and nutrition for at least two decades, usually under the auspices of one or another international or bilateral organization or foundation, such as the United Nations Food and Agricultural Organization (FAO), the Rockefeller Foundation, the United States Agency for International Development (U.S. AID), or the World Health Organization (WHO). What was new was the scope of the topic to be discussed: nutrition, national development, and planning. The meeting, indeed, gave official birth to a new discipline: food and nutrition policy and planning.

The field of international nutrition (conceived broadly as the study of problems of malnutrition and hunger in the Third World and ways to deal with them) had been until then the province of scientists and technical experts—medical doctors, biologists, agronomists, plant geneticists, food technologists, statisticians, nutritionists, and the like—who, by the very nature of their expertise, maintained the problem within the bounds of strict scientific discourse. Laboratory and clinical research had dominated the health and biochemical aspects of nutrition, and agronomy and plant and food science had covered the field of food production and processing. Nutrition interventions per se were relatively modest until the late 1960s, being restricted for the most part to supplementary child feeding, nutrition education, clinical treatment of severe malnutrition, and fortification of certain foods with vitamins, minerals, or amino acids. On the food production side, two strategies had been pursued: land reform and the so-called green revolution. This latter strategy had promised to free humankind from the scourge of hunger through the application of the latest scientific and technological breakthroughs in plant sciences and agronomy. Its failure to do so was already becoming evident in the early to mid-1970s.

Until then, there was nothing that called for seeing nutrition as part of national development. Nutrition and health were still under the firm control of the medical profession. None of the strategies that medical experts proposed, however, seemed to make significant inroads on the prevalence of malnutrition and hunger, in spite of improved knowledge in food science and in the physiology and biochemistry of nutrition. Although the food supply had increased steadily during the 1950s and 1960s, even keeping abreast of population growth in most countries, and although a number of countries had achieved remarkable rates of economic growth in the same period, the dream of attaining a basic level of needs satisfaction for all seemed to be receding. During the 1960s, however, a number of nutritionists and economists had been experimenting with nutrition programs that were broader in conception and scope, especially in India and some South American countries, where the governments themselves, confronted with the appalling reality of increasing malnutrition, were trying to come up with newer visions. These professionals, most of whom were there either working for U.S. AID or other major international organizations or were funded by them, were instrumental in shaping a new approach to the problems of food and hunger.[2]

A number of these forces converged with the creation, in the fall of 1972, of the International Nutrition Planning Program at MIT. The program, initiated with a grant from the Rockefeller Foundation and later supplemented by funds from U.S. AID, was conceived as a joint multidisciplinary undertaking of the Department of Nutrition and Food Science and the Center for International Studies at MIT, thus including in its ambit not only nutritionists and food science and medical experts but also economists, demographers, political scientists, engineers, anthropologists, and urban studies experts. The program was reinforced in 1977 by its association with the United Nations University's World Hunger Program and the Harvard School of

Public Health. The Harvard/MIT International Food and Nutrition Program became the main training institute—along with Cornell University's International Nutrition Program—for scores of foreign students coming to the program for advanced training in the new field of international food science and nutrition under the sponsorship of their governments or international organizations.[3]

The new approach to the problems of malnutrition and hunger in the Third World was being developed simultaneously at a few universities and research centers, especially in the United States and England (with the participation of some Third World health and nutrition experts associated with the pilot projects mentioned earlier). The work of this relatively small number of scholars and institutions coalesced in and was given impetus by the publication of two volumes in 1973. One of these volumes, edited by key participants in the new field (Berg, Scrimshaw, and Call 1973), grew out of the 1971 MIT conference.[4] The second volume, Alan Berg's *The Nutrition Factor* (1973), was to play a central role in the constitution of food and nutrition policy and planning. Indeed, it is possible to identify the textual origin of the new strategy with the publication of this book, in which the author argued forcibly that nutrition had to be regarded as an essential factor in national development policy and planning. The limited and fragmented interventions of previous decades, he maintained, were no longer sufficient in the face of the severity of the problems affecting the Third World. "Comprehensive nutrition planning and analysis are sorely needed," Berg insisted (1973, 200).

The new approach was christened Nutrition Planning, or, in subsequent versions, Food and Nutrition Policy and Planning (FNPP). How this strategy arose in the early 1970s, flourished, and was eclipsed a decade later, originating a whole body of knowledge, endless programs, and new institutions in many Third World countries, constitutes a prime example of how development works. "The response to malnutrition in most countries is modest, fragmented and lacking in operational orientation," wrote Berg of well-accepted nutrition programs of the period, such as institutional child feeding, nutrition education, production of protein-rich foods, pediatric nutrition in hospitals and health centers, and food aid. "For nutrition to attain a place in development, attention must be directed to the form and scope of nutrition planning and programming. . . . All require radical change" (1973, 198, 200). Moreover,

> Today in other fields there are accepted planning approaches that can and should be adapted for nutrition purposes. . . . Malnutrition's close relationship to socioeconomic forces argues for a comprehensive and systematic approach to planning analysis. . . . Strong leadership in nutrition programming and a vigorous, goal-oriented organization with a clear mandate are essential. (1973, 200, 202)

The new professional was to be sharply distinguished from the scientific-oriented expert, who until then had reigned uncontested over the field of nutrition:

> In a successful nutrition activity . . . the issues move beyond the clinic, the laboratory, and experimental field project. Concern shifts to operations, communications, logistics, administration, and economics, and the need shifts to professional planners, programmers, and managers. . . . This all suggests a role for a new discipline or nutrition sub-discipline including professionals with planning and project design capabilities. Nutrition programmers, or "macro-nutritionists," are needed to convert the findings of the scientific community into large-scale action programs. (Berg 1973, 206, 207)

The new discipline purported to be a systematic and multidisciplinary approach that would enable nutrition planners to design comprehensive and multisectoral plans capable of playing a leading role in development planning. The pillars of the subdiscipline were, on one hand, the elaboration of complex models of the factors regulating the nutritional status of a particular population and, on the other, a series of sophisticated methodologies that would allow planners successfully to design and implement food and nutrition plans. The core of this methodology was a nutrition planning sequence, initially summarized by Berg and Muscatt in the following way:

> The nutrition planning sequence starts with a definition of the nature, scope, and trends of the nutrition problem, leading to a preliminary statement of broad objectives. It then moves through a description of the system in which the nutritional condition arises. In the process of tracing causes, the planner begins to sense which programs and policies are relevant to the objectives. Next comes a comparison of the alternatives, which in turn leads to constructing an inter-related nutrition program. Final selection of objectives, programs and projects emerge after a budgetary and political process in which programs to attack malnutrition are pitted against other competing claims on resources and, if necessary, redesigned within actual budget allocations. The last step is evaluation of the actions put forth, feeding the conclusions back into subsequent rounds of the planning process. (Berg and Muscatt 1973, 249)

Berg and Muscatt also offered detailed prescriptions of how to go about carrying out the planning sequence: how to identify "the problem," determine the "target group," set objectives, analyze causes and alternative courses of action, and so on. In keeping with the planning spirit of the period, they claimed to follow a systems approach to problem identification and solution. In other words, they not only sought to identify and combat immediate causes but recognized the systemic nature of malnutrition and the need to mount a concerted attack on the many factors involved in its causation. All of the methodologies that followed the Berg and Muscatt model in the period 1973–1982 claimed to pursue a systems approach. It is not my intent to discuss here the various models proposed, their differences, and comparative virtues or shortcomings, which other authors have done in a competent manner.[5] Instead my intent is to discuss FNPP as a discursive field and analyze the policy practices that it involves and their effect on the construction of hunger.

Food and Nutrition Policy and Planning thus emerged as a subdiscipline in the early 1970s. The demarcation of fields and their assignment to experts is not new; it is a significant feature of the rise and consolidation of the modern state. What usually goes unnoticed is how a new subdiscipline introduces a set of practices that allows institutions to structure policy themes, enforce exclusions, and modify social relations. Even long-hailed panaceas such as the green revolution, still very much alive at this time, were tactically branded as failures or insufficient as part of the process of opening a space for FNPP, without a thorough examination of why they failed or what they produced. Needless to say, the green revolution was not dismantled but subsumed into the new strategy. The view of hunger that emerged from FNPP was even more aseptic and harmless, because it was couched in the language of planning and supported by unprecedented amounts of data obtained with ever more sophisticated methodologies.

By the beginning of the 1980s, numerous international seminars and volumes had been devoted to FNPP, and nutrition and rural development plans were being implemented in many countries of Latin America and Asia.[6] The United Nations technical agencies with competence in food and hunger (the Food and Agricultural Organization, and the World Health Organization) had sanctified the new approach in a joint technical report (FAO/WHO 1976) and were active, along with the World Bank and a host of international development agencies, in advising and financing the new programs. Once again, as so many times in the past, the "international nutrition/development community" held the cherished belief that the control of malnutrition and hunger was in sight. Once again, to almost nobody's surprise, this realization was to be deferred, for by the middle of the decade most of the plans produced under the spell of FNPP were being dismantled.[7]

It would be too easy to explain this paradoxical situation—the persistence of the problems of malnutrition and hunger in the face of myriad programs carried out in their name—as a reflection of a necessary "learning process" that institutions must go through as part of the "development effort." But one begins to suspect that what is at stake is not really the eradication of hunger (even if the planners wholeheartedly desired so) but its multiplication and dispersion into an ever finer web, a play of mobile visibilities which is hard to hold in one's sight. As Ferguson makes clear in his study of development in Lesotho, the failure of development projects nevertheless has powerful effects. And because failure is more the norm than the exception, it is of central importance to examine at what levels and in what ways projects like nutrition, health, and rural development programs produce their effects. This question takes us deeper into the dynamics of the creation and implementation of these strategies.

FNPP in Latin America:
The Hidden Practices of Commonsense Planning

The early 1970s were years of gestation for Food and Nutrition Policy and Planning in various parts of the world. Interest in the formulation of national food and nutrition policies began to grow in Latin America in 1970 among health and agriculture ministries and among the resident representatives of international organizations, who were aware of the new tendencies. As a response to this growing interest, in 1971 several United Nations agencies (FAO, WHO, the Panamerican Health Organization [PAHO], the United Nations Children's Fund[UNICEF], the Economic Commission for Latin America [ECLA], and the United Nations Organization for Education, Science and Culture [UNESCO]) created the Inter-Agency Project for the Promotion of National Food and Nutrition Policies (PIA/PNAN). This project, based in Santiago de Chile, was instrumental in spreading the new orthodoxy concerning food and nutrition planning in Latin America.

The first task the PIA/PNAN accomplished was the elaboration of a Methodological Guide for the Planning of Integrated National Food and Nutrition Policies (PIA/PNAN 1973a). In March 1973 a meeting was convened in Santiago to discuss the guide with a group of international and Latin American experts, most of whom were working with national governments or with United Nations agencies. The purpose of the ten-day meeting was to agree on the most acceptable planning methodology to be disseminated by the PIA/PNAN among Latin American governments, based on the premise that the food and nutrition problem had "its roots in a series of economic, social, cultural, environmental and health factors which are closely interconnected," and that consequently, "a multisectoral approach [was] necessary" (PIA/PNAN 1975a, 1).[8] The Inter-Agency Project defined its approach as follows:

> By food and nutrition policy we understand a coherent set of principles, objectives, priorities and decisions adopted by the state and carried out by its institutions with the aim of providing all of the country's population with the amount of food and other social, cultural and economic elements which are indispensable for adequate food and nutrition welfare. This policy should be an integral component of the country's national development plan, and each country should strive to realize the content of this definition according to its own capabilities, resources and stage of development. (PIA/PNAN 1973b, 6)

The Methodological Guide, accompanied by elegant flow charts, contained a description of the planning process as well as detailed prescriptions of how to go about it. The emphasis of the document was on overall food and nutrition strategy and policy analysis, with the ultimate purpose of formulating a national food and nutrition plan. The PIA/PNAN adhered to a type of analysis in which the nutritional status of a given population was seen as the product of a series of factors grouped under three rubrics: food supply, food demand, and biological utilization of food, including the following elements:

1. Food supply: food production (according to the resource base of the country, types of crop, conditions of cultivation, food policy, institutional support, and so on); food-trade balance (import and export, foreign exchange, international prices, commodity agreements, food aid); commercialization of food (marketing, roads, storage infrastructure, prices, food processing).

2. Food demand: demographic factors (population size and growth rate, age structure, spatial distribution, migration); cultural factors (general educational level, nutrition education, cultural values and food habits, weaning and child-feeding practices, housing and cooking facilities); economic conditions (employment and wages, income distribution, access to means of production, rural versus urban location); and consumption factors (diet composition, food subsidies).

3. Biological utilization of food: health factors (health services, prevention and control of contagious diseases, immunization, health education); environmental factors (water supply, sanitation, sewage systems, food quality control).

The basis of the PIA/PNAN model is a representation of the way in which the various elements pertaining to the three spheres are interrelated in the causation of malnutrition. The "explicative model of the process of malnutrition in Latin America," as the PIA/PNAN termed its approach, "describes how these forces are interconnected in the generation of the high degree of malnutrition that affects a great segment of the Latin American population" (1975b, 1). Armed with this theory, the PIA/PNAN went about establishing a presence in most Latin American countries. The first step—following a planning sequence similar to Berg's—was the collection of information with the aim of preparing a diagnosis of the food and nutrition situation of the country in question. Information was collected on all factors related to the supply, demand, and biological utilization of food, whether from existing data or through specially devised surveys. The instruments more commonly used in this regard were the national food-balance sheet, which contains estimates of the availability of different foods within the country, translated into calories and nutrients and, after comparison with recommended standards, into aggregate "nutritional gaps"; consumer expenditure surveys;

food consumption surveys by households; and medical and anthropometric surveys, especially to assess the nutritional status of children. In addition, information was collected on health, sanitation, employment, agriculture, and demographic factors. These data were used to identify food deficits, nutritional problems, and the adequacy of services. The result was an idea of "the nutrition problem" in the country in question.

A second step was to establish projections of food supply and demand. These projections were needed in order to identify aggregate production gaps by crop, which would be the basis of agricultural production policy. Projections were estimated according to standard statistical and economet- ric routines (production and demand functions, budget constraints, and so on), taking into account economic and demographic factors (growth of GNP, population growth rate, productivity increases, income distribution trends, income elasticity of demand for different foodstuffs, and so on). Once projec- tions are done,

> the next step is to consider the policies necessary to satisfy such projections. To this effect, the Guide introduces all the policies relevant to food production, commercialization and international trade; those of population, income, educa- tion and food aid; and those of sanitation, health and nutrition. After these are examined in the light of the problem diagnosis and the objectives already estab- lished, there comes the technical and political process of selecting the most appropriate policies and programs given the conditions and possibilities of the country. This is the time at which priorities must be decided upon and re- sources should be assigned. Responsibility for implementation is agreed upon, and a time frame is chosen. International technical and financial cooperation must also be decided upon. . . . Programs should be evaluated periodically after their implementation has proceeded for some time. (PIA/PNAN 1973b, 3, 4)

The Inter-Agency Project recommended the establishment of a special nu- trition planning unit within the national planning office to carry out the design. This unit, also recommended by Berg (1973) and Joy and Payne (1975), would report to a national food and nutrition council, staffed by the highest government officials (the president and the pertinent members of the cabinet or their representatives). Universities, research institutes, spe- cialized government agencies such as nutrition institutes, and, it goes with- out saying, international consultants would provide technical support.

How did the PIA/PNAN go about spreading its credo in Latin America? The first move, facilitated by its status as a United Nations project, was to contact pertinent agencies in each country and make them cognizant of the project's existence. Then followed a meeting with representatives from the agencies—including the national planning office, the ministries of health, agriculture, education, economics, and development, and the national nutri- tion institute—in which the project's framework and methodology were presented and discussed. An important step at this point was the promotion and creation of the special Nutrition Planing Unit, to which the PIA/PNAN was to give financial and technical support for the task of beginning the process of formulating a national nutrition policy. This support was supplemented in some countries with funds and technical assistance from other agencies, particularly FAO and U.S. AID. Negotiations and advising were maintained until the country launched its first national nutrition plan. Once the plan was under way, the project's involvement was restricted in most cases to supporting the evaluation component of the plan; this closed the cycle of PIA/PNAN involvement.[9]

By 1975, the PIA/PNAN was conducting activities in approximately fifteen countries in Latin America and the Caribbean, including Colombia (similar schemes were introduced in several Asian countries, including the Philippines and Sri Lanka). Before I discuss the role of the PIA/PNAN in the formulation of the Colombian National Food and Nutrition Plan, however, it is worth pausing to examine some of the underlying assumptions of this kind of planning discourse. The basis of the approach is the definition of the nutrition problem. The first question to be raised in this regard is "whether there is an objective world of problems outside the problems with which the practices of policy claim to be concerning themselves" (Shaffer 1985, 375). In other words, planners take their practice as a true description of reality, uninfluenced by their own relation to that reality. Planners do not entertain the idea that the characterization of the food and nutrition system in terms of three spheres (supply, demand, and biological utilization) might be a specific representation with political, social, and cultural consequences. In practice, however, "policy constructs those sorts of agendas of problems which can be handled. It then labels the items of these agendas as problems in particular ways. For example, people are referred to as categories of target groups to whom items of services can be delivered" (Shaffer 1985, 375).

Even within this type of positivist thinking, the assessment of the prevalence of malnutrition and hunger has been riddled with problems. Estimates of malnutrition worldwide have ranged from two-thirds of the population to only 10–15 percent. Policy options are influenced by the kind of estimate chosen; in fact, the setting of norms (standards and requirements of nutritional adequacy) and degrees of incidence of malnutrition is an area of active scientific-political struggle.[10] For instance, although the difficulties of calculating aggregate deficits have been amply demonstrated, emphasis at both the international and national level is still on aggregate figures, in spite of the fact that alternatives have been proposed. One such alternative suggests starting with limited data and stories of how concrete individuals got to be malnourished and then constructing a functional classification of groups of people that relates malnutrition to the particular ecological, social, and economic factors that condition it (Joy and Payne 1975; Pacey and Payne 1985).

This approach would call for interventions that are localized and, as the proponents of this methodology recommended, participatory. This runs counter to an institution like the World Bank, which operates on the basis of the identification of large food-production deficits; aggregates of this sort can be tackled with macro policies that incorporate the agricultural interests that figure prominently in the Bank's thinking.

There are other practices that shape inquiry. Strategies such as rural development and nutrition planning are seen "as if [they] were exogenous to the social and political situations which, nevertheless, are held to necessitate [them]" (Apthorpe 1984, 138). In other words, interventions are thought of as a beneficent medicine placed by the hand of government or the international community on a sore spot that is perceived as external. Planners are notorious for not seeing themselves as part of the system for which they plan. They give all of their attention to the allegedly rational techniques of policy and planning (such as surveys, forecasting, maximizing algorithms, and cost-benefit analyses), which, as we know, bypass local situations and concrete historical forces. These considerations hold true despite the fact that, as many planners know, standard methodologies are never followed rigidly. Appeal to the method is used to avoid discussing where, when, and what decisions were made and by whom. As Shaffer points out, this avoidance of responsibility is an essential feature of public policy practice. Predictably, policy practitioners are sheltered by the very institutional mechanisms they employ. Accountability becomes impossible to enforce. Planning, in a sense, exists without concrete social actors.

Shaffer refers to models such as the PIA/PNAN's as the mainstream or "common-sense" view of planning. This view sees policy and planning as a systematic, information-based process composed of fixed stages (problem definition; identification and assessment of alternatives; policy formulation; program implementation; and evaluation). The model gives the impression that policy is the result of discrete, voluntaristic acts, not the process of coming to terms with conflicting interests in the process of which choices are made and exclusions effected. How the new policy and accompanying technologies are decided upon is completely overlooked. In this way, agendas and decisions appear natural; decisions are seen as following automatically from analysis, and it never seems that a different decision could have been reached. Decisions are, in fact, foregone conclusions, the genesis of which is almost impossible to identify, because the choices and debates are hidden by the model. Further inquiry into what alternatives could have been followed is precluded when policy is seen as the result of a rational ends-means process.

Another consequence of the view of planning as composed of linear stages is the assumption that policy-making and implementation are distinct, as if implementation were a problem for someone else (the implementing agencies), independent of policy. This separation is often utilized in the evaluation of policy performance: the policy failed, or was ineffective, because "politics" got in the way, or because the implementation agencies did not do their job properly, or because of lack of funds or of trained personnel, or due to a long list of "obstacles to implementation" which are never related to how policy was shaped in the first place. Escape hatches such as these are used continually to explain program failures and to call for new inputs into the planning process. The reification of data contributes to this feature. As Hacking (1991) has shown, along with particular data come administrative measures and categorizations of people that make people conform to the bureaucracy's discursive and practical universe. This is more so when a situation of scarcity of resources and/or services is supposed to exist. Another escape hatch is the assumption that it is possible to identify what is a more or less rational alternative, independent of politics. Rationality is reinforced by the use of physicalist discourse (Apthorpe 1984), that is, a type of discourse that emphasizes physical aspects (production factors, prices, medical considerations). Even when social issues are taken into account, they are reduced to the language of probability or other technical devices, such as in discussions about income distribution.

In sum, the very existence of models such as the PIA/PNAN's allows governments and organizations to structure policy and construct problems in such a way that the construction is made invisible. Conventional analyses focus on what went wrong with the model, or whether the model is adequate or not. They overlook more important questions: What did institutions do under the rubric of planning, and how did these practices relate to policy outcomes? In other words, policy has to be seen as a practice that involves theories about policy decisions, types of knowledge and administrative skills, and processes of bureaucratization, all of which are deeply political. This deconstruction of planning leads us to conclude that only by problematizing these hidden practices—that is, by exposing the arbitrariness of policies, habits, and data interpretation and by suggesting other possible readings and outcomes—can the play of power be made explicit in the allegedly neutral deployment of development (Escobar 1992a).

AGRARIAN CRISIS AND ITS CONTAINMENT THROUGH PLANNING IN COLOMBIA, 1972–1992

The Road to Nutrition Planning

The first contact between the PIA/PNAN and the Colombian government took place in 1971, when Colombia agreed to participate in the PIA/PNAN project.[11] A key Colombian participant in these early events recorded the importance of the PIA/PNAN as follows:

Of special importance was the commitment made by the Colombian government to participate in the U.N. Inter-Agency Project for the Promotion of National Food and Nutrition Policy (PIA/PNAN), based in Santiago. This activity
was of great importance not only because it generated an increased interest
in food and nutrition on the part of the government, but also because it contributed technical assistance, methodological approaches and, along with
UNICEF, limited but timely funding for some of the key activities carried out
by the National Committee on Food and Nutrition Policy. (Varela 1979, 38)[12]

The National Committee on Food and Nutrition Policy had been created
by the government in July 1972 with the purpose of making recommendations to the government regarding food and nutrition. These developments
were not solely the result of the PIA/PNAN's influence. A major event that
had made its debut in the sad theater of hunger during those years was the
world food crisis, which led to the famous World Food Conference of November 1974. In this conference, held in Rome under the auspices of the
UN's Food and Agricultural Organization, all the countries of the world
committed themselves to ending hunger, and major guidelines were issued
to this end, including planning approaches (see, for instance, FAO 1974a,
1974b). The conference was extremely important in motivating planners to
imagine actions of unprecedented proportions. The documents of this conference found their way to the desks of planning officials in many parts of the
Third World.[13]

Let us return to the account of the antecedents of the Colombian National
Food and Nutrition Plan found in the recollection quoted earlier:

[The Plan was] the culmination of a long process of knowledge, experience and
institutional development that spans three decades. . . . The first step goes back
to 1942, when a group of Colombian professionals began their graduate work at
Harvard University. There began thus a lasting and beneficial relationship with
this university, which was to include at a later date advising by Harvard experts
and even the realization of joint projects. (Varela 1979, 31)

One of those projects had been a longitudinal study on the relationship
between malnutrition and psychological development, carried out jointly in
Bogotá by Colombian, North American, and West German scientists with
funds from the Ford Foundation. A similar study was carried out in Cali
during the 1970s, with the involvement of two Northwestern University
psychologists and funding from the Rockefeller Foundation and the U.S.
National Science Foundation (see McKay, McKay, and Sinisterra 1979).
The rationale for the projects on malnutrition and mental development—as
well as that of projects on malnutrition and work capacity, also in vogue
during the 1970s—was that governments would be more inclined to act
vigorously if it could be proven scientifically that malnutrition led to im-

paired mental development in children and decreased work capacity in adults. Besides these projects, several other research projects and pilot programs were under way by then in the regions surrounding Bogotá and Cali, with active participation of U.S. and European scientists and foundations, on topics such as primary health care, rural development, and maternal and child nutrition.

These projects created a public space for discussing the nutrition problem, always within the confines of science.[14] Although the Rockefeller Foundation had been active in public health activities in many countries of Latin America since the late 1910s,[15] nutrition research per se did not start in Colombia until the founding of the Nutrition Institute in 1947 within the Ministry of Hygiene (now Public Health Ministry). Nutrition activities achieved a much greater scope with the beginning in 1954 of food supplementation programs that utilized existing health and educational institutions to distribute foods donated by international agencies (CARE and CARITAS initially, joined in the 1960s by U.S. AID and the World Food Program). The first attempt to coordinate and integrate nutrition activities (food supplementation and nutrition education) with health and agricultural projects (extension services, school and family gardens, technology transfer) was the Integrated Programs of Applied Nutrition, started in the mid-1960s with considerable support from international organizations and voluntary agencies. Numerous nutrition surveys, health projects, and food-technology research were also carried out on a limited scale throughout the 1960s (Grueso n.d.).

In spite of all of these activities, there was no overall food and nutrition policy. Most nutrition programs were linked to international food aid, the origin of which, as is well known, was the need of the United States to dispose of its agricultural surplus by donating it to friendly Third World nations (Lappé, Collins, and Kinley 1980). When the PIA/PNAN arrived in the country, and in the wake of the world food crisis of the early 1970s, conditions were ripe for a more encompassing and integrated strategy. Perhaps more important than this slow institutional buildup in making possible the new strategies were changes that had taken place in the rural sector since about 1950, which reached a climax in the late 1960s with unprecedented peasant political activism and a deep crisis in agricultural production. Out of this situation, which Colombia shared with many other Latin American countries, the new strategies emerged.

To make sense of Colombia's food and nutrition policy of the 1970s and 1980s, it is necessary to analyze the broader politicoeconomic conditions that characterized the Colombian countryside. These conditions both favored and required a new arrangement of the social, political, and economic landscape of rural Colombia. The new strategies of nutrition and rural development played a primary role in effecting this arrangement. In the next

section, I summarize briefly the major features of the agrarian crisis in Colombia up to the early 1970s, before proceeding to my account and analysis
of the Colombian National Food and Nutrition Plan.

The Political Economy of Food and Nutrition, 1950–1972

In 1950, about two-thirds of the Colombian population lived in rural areas,
and agriculture provided close to 40 percent of the gross domestic product (GDP). By 1972 these numbers had declined to less than 50 percent and
26 percent respectively (in 1985, the percentage of people living in rural
areas was estimated at 30 percent). Conversely, the largest cities grew at an
annual rate of 7 percent or more, and the manufacturing sector also grew
rapidly as economic diversification continued and the country shifted from
a rural- to an urban-oriented economy. The decline of agriculture, however,
was not an even process. A closer look reveals stagnation tendencies, particularly among crops cultivated by peasants, and fast growth rates in crops
cultivated by capitalist farmers under modern conditions. It also reveals significant social and cultural changes and massive impoverishment among
peasants. These aspects—stagnation of peasant production, impoverishment
of the peasantry, and associated social and cultural changes—formed the
background of the health, nutrition, and rural development strategies of the
1970s and 1980s.

One of the most striking features of agrarian change in the period 1950–
1972 was the rapid growth of crops cultivated under modern capitalist conditions—namely, the use of a high degree of mechanization and of chemical
inputs and technology—such as cotton, sugarcane, rice, and soybeans. As a
group, these commercial crops grew at a rate of 8.2 percent per annum for
the twenty-two years under consideration, almost five times faster than more
traditional crops—such as beans, cassava, and plantains—and about three
times faster than other crops under mixed (capitalist and traditional) conditions of cultivation, including corn, coffee, potatoes, wheat, tobacco, cocoa,
and bananas. Initially, commercial agriculture based its rapid growth on the
dynamism of the domestic market arising from increasing industrial demand
for agricultural products and from some increase in family income (the result
of urbanization and industrialization). Once this demand was satisfied, it
continued its expansion primarily through export markets and thanks to the
continual replacement of traditional products by those produced mostly for
urban consumption by the growing food-processing industry. Traditional
crops, however, lay at the other end of the growth scale. If commercial crops
experienced spectacular growth rates, traditional crops became almost stagnant. This is the first feature of Colombian (and most Latin American) agriculture during the first two decades of development: spectacular growth of
the modern sector and stagnation of the traditional one.[16]

Let us look at how Marxist political economists explain this pattern of uneven agricultural development. Part of the answer, in this line of analysis, lies in the class basis of agricultural production (Crouch and de Janvry 1980). So-called traditional foods are produced and consumed primarily by peasants, although some of them are also part of the urban diet (this is the case of beans in Colombia). Commercial crops, however, are produced by capitalist farmers and are intended for either urban consumption (in the case of wage goods such as rice and sugar, rice being the staple of the urban working class), industrial or luxury consumption (soybeans, cotton, beef, mushrooms), or export (flowers, bananas, or coffee, which now is produced mostly on farms between ten and one hundred hectares or larger). Social class is thus a major determinant of production and consumption. Rice, produced by capitalists, has had the highest growth rate in a number of Latin American countries, whereas peasant foods have systematically had the lowest rates of growth, with a number of crops falling somewhere in between.

This, in turn, is a reflection of a series of historical, political, and agro-economic determinants. On the political side, capitalist farmers have more political influence than peasant farmers. Traditionally powerful in Colombia, the landed elite have been able to retain an important degree of control over the state apparatus, in spite of the fact that the government has put pressure on them to modernize their methods of production. In fact, the land reform initiated by the government in the early 1960s had the primary objective of compelling landowners with large plots to adopt more efficient forms of cultivation. Political influence was reflected at the time in public policy instances, such as protectionist measures for commercial crops and privileged access to services, research, technology, credit, and irrigation. For instance, rice benefited from research in the best centers, was protected from cheaper imports, and enjoyed access to credit and support prices; at the same time, the production of wheat—a peasant crop in Colombia—stagnated due to cheaper imports allowed by the government via food aid. In Mexico, by , contrast, wheat, a capitalist crop, enjoyed measures similar to those of rice in Colombia. It is not a coincidence that wheat in Mexico and rice in Colombia were the miracle stories of the green revolution. Among the agro-economic determinants, differential responsiveness to inputs and irrigation, geographical conditions, labor intensity, and demand conditions influenced why crops went capitalist or remained traditional (Crouch and de Janvry 1980; de Janvry 1981).

Increasing the production of food grains in Latin America—political economists continue in their explanation—was seen as necessary in the face of decreasing shipments of U.S. surplus grain and in order to quell what was seen as teeming social unrest in the countryside. Development theory had already shifted its emphasis toward agricultural modernization. The initial result of this shift was the in/famous green revolution, called upon to neu-

tralize social upheaval, demobilize politicized peasantries, and increase production while providing an exportable surplus. Another factor that motivated the rapid expansion of the green revolution was the interest of multinational companies producing inputs (fertilizers, pesticides, and improved
seeds) in expanding their markets.[17] De Janvry has summarized this set of
factors and the concomitant responses:

> By the mid-1960s, the export of P.L. 480 foods to Latin America was on the
> decline. Stagnation of domestic food production did not permit the food deficit
> countries to compensate for decreasing concessional imports, and the industri-
> alization strategy based on cheap food was compromised. The development of
> food production in commercial agriculture became the center of reformism.
> This was sought via the transfer of capital and technology to Latin America; a
> massive increase in research expenditures on food crops (the Green Revolu-
> tion); the strengthening of extension programs; greater availability of agricul-
> tural credit; and the entry of multinational firms into agricultural production,
> the manufacturing of inputs, and the processing and distribution of products.
> Agricultural research expenditures doubled in real terms between 1962 and
> 1968 while expenditures in agricultural extension services more than doubled.
> International agricultural research centers were created for wheat and corn
> (CIMMYT in 1966 in Mexico), tropical food crops and cattle (CIAT in 1968 in
> Colombia), and potatoes (CIP in 1972 in Peru). World Bank loans for agricul-
> tural projects—principally large irrigation works—increased substantially to
> some 23 percent of total lending. And in the land reforms of this period, the
> dominant objective became economic: to increase production, principally by
> inducing (through threats of expropriation) modernization of the nonreformed
> sector. (De Janvry 1981, 199, 200)

What was the "industrialization strategy based on cheap food," and what
was its relevance? According to de Janvry, industrialization in the world's
periphery depends on the availability of cheap labor, which is maintained
chiefly through the provision of cheap food and the exploitation of the peasantry and urban working class. The requirement of cheap labor is imposed
by the "laws of motion" of capital globally and its contradictions, in ways that
is not the point to analyze here. The result is a structural situation in which
a "modern" sector—based on a combination of multinational, state, and local
capital—coexists with a "backward," or traditional, sector, the chief function
of which is to provide cheap labor and cheap food for the former (what de
Janvry calls functional dualism). Because the dynamic sectors of the economy produce for export or for the modern sector, there is no real need for
consolidating an internal market that would encompass most of the population. Productivity is raised and profits are maintained without a concomitant
rise in wages; hence the "logic" of cheap labor. The social articulation that
exists in the center countries regulating wages, profits, consumption, pro-

duction, and the size of the internal market does not exist in the periphery. And because development in the periphery proceeds so unevenly among sectors, it can be said that the periphery is not only socially but also sectorally disarticulated.

What is the relation between disarticulation and the agrarian crisis? The production of cheap food has been increasingly entrusted to the modern sector, through both land-saving and labor-saving technologies. This was the main objective of the green revolution. This move, however, was riddled with contradictions. Disarticulated accumulation supposes two pressing and competing needs: on the one hand, the need to maintain cheap food and cheap labor required to make investment profitable; on the other hand, the need to generate foreign exchange to import the technology and capital goods required for the industrialization process. In this struggle between food for domestic consumption and industrialization, on the one hand, and foreign-exchange generating activities (that is, export agriculture), on the other, the latter has benefited most from public resources. The result has been the stagnation of peasant foods and the inability of the capitalist sector to compensate for decreasing peasant production, due to biases against agriculture in general and to the preference granted to agriculture for export and for industry or luxury consumption. Governments in Latin America and other parts of the Third World have resorted to other means to maintain the price of food low, including a variety of cheap food policies, such as price controls and subsidies. These policies have acted as disincentives to peasant agriculture and food production in general. In some cases, however, the development of capitalism has been quite successful, such as rice in Colombia. Fostering the development of agribusiness was another route followed, especially the multinational kind, which was supposed to contribute to generating foreign exchange; as it is now known, this rarely happened (Burbach and Flynn 1980; Feder 1977).

These negative tendencies notwithstanding, in most of Latin America a great percentage of food crops is still produced by peasants. In Colombia, for instance, an estimated 55 percent of all food produced for direct consumption in the country at the time of the inception of the Integrated Rural Development Program (1976) was still grown by what is known as the traditional sector (DNP/DRI 1979). Yet peasants are unable to accumulate capital and are progressively drained; those who remain in production do so increasingly only to feed themselves, and the majority are displaced from their lands and turned into proletarian (the landless) or semiproletarian labor (those who still have access to some land but not enough to survive).[18] Peasants are then pulled in opposite directions by divergent forces: they have to serve as a source of cheap labor yet keep producing cheap food at the same time; and they tend to become semiproletarians while a tendency for full proletarianization nevertheless exists. And in spite of the fact that peasants in many communities have been able to resist the intrusion of commercial capitalism or maneuver around it while maintaining viable small family farms, the overall tendency, most argue, seems to be toward proletarianization—although the persistence of the family farm has been important in some regions of Colombia, as Reinhardt shows (1988).

In the midst of all this, and to take account of these contradictions, integrated rural development programs emerged in the early 1970s. Increased displacement of the peasantry from their land, and semiproletarianization or full proletarianization of rural people dictated by the logic of cheap labor, increased exploitation of the peasants' physical and human ecologies (degradation of the resource base and increased exploitation of women and children) and produced widespread hunger and malnutrition. In this way, according to de Janvry, the agrarian crisis and the strategies to solve it have to be seen as integral components of disarticulated development. Designed to rationalize the situation of food production following the logic of cheap food, the green revolution failed to deliver what it promised, aggravating not only the food situation but also its social manifestations.

Up to this point I have recounted the most widely accepted explanation of the political economy of agrarian change in Latin America. This explanation is useful only up to a point. It must be subjected, however, to the analysis of economics as culture advanced in the previous chapter. De Janvry's functionalism reduces social life to a reflection of the "contradictions" of capital accumulation; despite a certain dialectical analysis, the realist (never interpretive) epistemology that this brand of analysis espouses subjects understanding of social life to some "really real" force, namely, the "laws" of motion of capital, encoded in the main contradiction between production and circulation, the concomitant tendency for the rate of profit to fall, and repeated realization crises. From a poststructuralist perspective, however, there cannot be a materialist analysis that is not at the same time a discursive analysis. Everything I have said so far in this book suggests that representations are not a reflection of "reality" but constitutive of it. There is no materiality that is not mediated by discourse, as there is no discourse that is unrelated to materialities. From this perspective, the making of food and labor and the making of narratives about them must be seen in the same light. To put it simply, the attempt at articulating a political economy of food and health must start with the construction of objects such as nature, peasants, food, and the body as an epistemological, cultural, and political process.

The discursive nature of capital is evident in various ways—for instance, in the resignification of nature as resources; in the construction of poverty as lack of development, of peasants as merely food producers, and of hunger as lack of food requiring rural development; and in the representation of capital and technology as agents of transformation. As we will see shortly and in the next chapter, the requirements that political economists discovered rest upon the ability of the development apparatus to create discourses that allow institutions to distribute individuals and populations in ways consistent with capitalist relations. The logic of capital, whatever it is, cannot explain fully why a given group of rural people were made the targets of the interventions we are discussing. Such a logic could equally have dictated another fate for the same group, including its total disappearance in order to give way to triumphant capital, which has not occurred. Analyses in terms of political economy, finally, are too quick to impute purely economic functions to development projects; they reduce the reason for these projects to sets of interests to be unveiled by analysis. They also believe that the discourses (such as integrated rural development) are just ideologies or misrepresentations of what developers are "really" up to (Ferguson 1990). Without denying their value, this amounts to a simplification that is no longer satisfactory.

By the early 1970s, the contradictions of the green revolution had become evident and the international development community—that self-appointed group of experts and bankers always eager to renew their good intentions, despite the catastrophic results of their previous magic formulas—was ready to provide a new solution. The realization suddenly dawned on them—as if fallen from the sky, a new revelation from a prophet none other than the discourse of development itself—that the peasants ("small farmers" in their eyes) were not so unimportant after all; that given the appropriate level of attention, they too could be turned into productive citizens and that, who knows, perhaps they could be made to increase their production capacity so as to maintain the levels of cheap food required to maintain the levels of cheap labor required for multinational corporations to continue reaping their huge profits, which, in any case, are only their rightful retribution for contributing so much to the development of those poor lands and peoples. And directly from the U.S. Department of Defense, after having reorganized the Pentagon and participated in the management of the Vietnam war, there came to the World Bank a new president to lead the fight against the world's "absolute poverty," with rural development as his favorite weapon: Robert McNamara. And, always willing to be the first guinea pig for the experiments of the international development community, Colombia started in the mid-1970s to implement the first nationwide integrated rural development program in the Third World. In the next section I sketch broadly the major components of this program.

The Colombian National Food and Nutrition Plan

We have already become acquainted with the major features of FNPP and its progressive presence in the international scene: its appearance in the august and authoritative quarters of North American and British campuses, its spread through the United Nations system (including the World Bank), and finally its safe arrival in Latin America on the wings of the PIA/PNAN. It is worthwhile at this point to take a finer look at the process of dispersion of this strategy in Colombia; in other words, to visualize how the Colombian countryside, conceived by the apparatus in terms of traditional peasant communities and a modern capitalist sector, was mapped by FNPP producing a system of dispersion and controls through the activities of a variety of institutions.

A National Committee for Food and Nutrition Policy, let it be recalled, had been formed in July 1972 at the highest levels of government. Early in 1973, the committee entrusted a small technical group within the Department of National Planning (DNP) with the task of formulating a national food and nutrition policy. This Coordinating Group was headed by a Colombian sociologist with a graduate degree in medical sociology from Berkeley and staffed by two economists, one agricultural economist, one education expert, and one international adviser, provided by the United Nations Development Programme (UNDP). The first meetings of this group—housed within the DNP's Division of Population and Nutrition, in turn part of the larger Unit of Social Development—convinced its members that the first step to take was the construction of a multicausal systems diagnosis that paid special attention to social and economic factors, until then largely neglected.

The first few months of intense work by the Coordinating Group saw its fruits with the publication of its first document in July 1973, entitled *Basis for a Food and Nutrition Policy in Colombia* (DNP/UDS 1973). This document summarized and assessed the known information about the food and nutrition situation of the country, proposing guidelines for the work ahead. At the nutrition level, the major problems were found to be protein-calorie malnutrition (from mild to severe, affecting perhaps two-thirds of all children in the country),[19] adult chronic undernutrition, and a series of specific nutritional deficiencies (especially iron-deficiency anemia and vitamin A deficiency). Nutritional deficiencies were identified as one of the main factors contributing to infant mortality. At the level of food production, national food-balance sheets showed overall production to be sufficient to feed adequately the entire population of the country. A disaggregated analysis, however, revealed ample disparities, with people in lower income categories presenting the most serious nutrient gaps.

The Coordinating Group lucidly identified the skewed income distribution of the country as the single major factor responsible for the high incidence of malnutrition, thus opening the door for a host of social questions. Whereas the lowest 50 percent of the population received only 20 percent of the country's income, almost 45 percent of it went to the top 10 percent of the population. In simple terms, people just did not have enough income to feed themselves adequately. A recent study had shown that 40 percent of

Colombians would not be able to afford a "minimum cost diet" even if they devoted all of their income to food. Nevertheless, this situation was not all due to income disparities. High margins of commercialization were found to increase the cost of food dramatically, especially for urban consumers; another factor influencing nutritional status, according to the Coordinating Group's diagnosis, was ignorance of the nutritive value of foods and negative food habits.

Adhering to PIA/PNAN style, the group convened a National Intersectoral Conference on Food and Nutrition in December 1973 at the fancy headquarters of the International Center of Tropical Agriculture (CIAT).[20] The conference had the following objectives: (1) To bring to the country's attention the magnitude of the nutritional problems; (2) To support the thesis that malnutrition is not only a medical problem but also an economic, technological, agricultural, and social problem; and (3) To convince the leading political and technical groups of the country of the possibility of mounting a food and nutrition strategy capable of revitalizing the country's economy as a whole (Varela 1979, 39)

The conference, funded by UNICEF, was attended by all relevant Colombian institutions—including the government, universities, and private interests—and by representatives of United Nations agencies, U.S. AID, and the World Bank. The thrust of the conference was to demonstrate the relationship between nutrition and agricultural production, and the role that a planning strategy that integrated both of these aspects could have in the solution of the "nutrition problem." Even the medical profession complied with the new vision, although not without resistance.[21] Planners, economists, agronomists, and the medical profession were eager to capitalize on the unprecedented expansion of state intervention in food and nutrition entailed by the proposed strategy. Work in the following months was dedicated to refining the initial diagnosis, to putting together a number of working groups involving the various agencies that were to carry out the different programs, and to the actual design of the plan and its programs. Objectives were set, a number of food crops were selected to be included in the plan, and negotiations were started with the World Bank and other funding agencies.[22]

Negotiations with the World Bank included furnishing the Bank (as it is usually known) with detailed information on every step taken and the visit to the country of at least four Bank missions before the first agreement was signed.[23] It was also a period of training and advising; a number of Colombians, for instance, were sent to Mexico to study experimental integrated rural development programs, of which there were several in Colombia as well. This experience was influential in the formulation of the Colombian strategy. Activities peaked with the publication and approval by the highest authorities of the *Plan Nacional de Alimentación y Nutrición* (PAN) in March

1975 (DNP 1975a). The overall development plan for the 1974–1978 administrative period, modestly entitled *Para Cerrar la Brecha* (To close the gap) (DNP 1975b), hailed PAN and DRI (Programa de Desarrollo Rural Integrado) as the milestones of the government's social policy. By the time the PAN was published, however, all critical consideration of income distribution had already been dropped.[24] The government, it was argued, had other programs that were supposed to increase the income of the poor.

Para Cerrar la Brecha purported to raise the living standard of the poorest 50 percent of the population. To meet this guideline, and as a necessary step toward ensuring adequate targeting and evaluation of PAN and DRI, and also responding to World Bank requirements, the PAN/DRI national group carried out a "regionalization exercise," which aimed at identifying the poorest 30 percent in the country. The national group wanted to draw a national poverty map; to this end, data on one hundred different socioeconomic and demographic variables were collected in each of the 930 municipalities of the country and aggregated under three overall indicators (mean family income, educational level, and access to services). The weighted index permitted the ranking of rural and marginal urban areas so that a cutoff point could be drawn separating the 30 percent poorest to benefit directly from the government's social programs. In 1979, the regionalization exercise was adjusted and improved by a private firm under PAN contract, with the use of new data and sophisticated statistical and computerized models (DNP/PAN 1975a, 1976a; Instituto SER 1980a).

The regionalization exercise was without precedent in the country. In the early 1970s, the French government had provided technical assistance to the Department of National Statistics (DANE) on models for the collection and use of social indicators, at a time when the DNP was becoming interested in regional information systems to rationalize its development plan. However, in keeping with accepted development doctrine of the time—disseminated at the highest level by Lauchlin Currie, who in 1970, already a Colombian national, was the chief economic adviser to then-president Misael Pastrana Borrero—these efforts were geared toward making visible the "poles of development" (regions of actual or potential high degree of development), rather than "the 30% poorest." The PAN/DRI regionalization, then, signified a tactical reversal: the machines of visibility were turned on the poor, as the poor were becoming more and more visible.

The National Food and Nutrition Plan had two major components: the Integrated Rural Development Program (Programa de Desarrollo Rural Integrado, DRI), which consisted of a series of programs to increase production and the productivity of small farmers; and a set of nutrition and health programs intended to improve food consumption and the biological utilization of food (in keeping with DNP usage, I reserve the acronym PAN to refer to these latter, that is, not including DRI). Although the two strategies were conceptually a unit, their implementation was divided geographically for operational reasons. In this way, PAN's first phase was implemented in about half of the *departamentos* (provinces) of the country, those with a higher concentration of landless and semiproletarian laborers, and DRI was implemented in the remaining departamentos, those with a higher concentration of small to medium-size peasants. The explicit objectives of PAN were to decrease protein-calorie malnutrition, especially in the target population (pregnant and lactating women and children under five) and to contribute to the reduction of child mortality and morbidity in general. To achieve these objectives, the plan considered three principal types of interventions:[25]

Programs to Increase the Availability of Foods

Subsidized food production and distribution. This program consisted of two major subprograms: a food stamp program and direct food distribution. In the first, mothers were asked to come to health centers to collect food coupons that could be used as partial payment for the acquisition of certain foods. The second program was a replacement for the external food aid programs that were being phased out. The main product distributed was an enriched flour mix produced in the country from a plant obtained through U.S. AID. The product is still distributed today by the Colombian Institute for Family Welfare.

Production incentives for small, part-time farmers (PANCOGER). This program was intended for semiproletarians who derived most of their income from wage labor but who still had access to some land. Extension, credit, and technical assistance were provided to peasants with very small plots (usually 0.5–3.0 hectares) to encourage them to produce crops to help fulfill the family's nutritional needs. Nutrition education and subsidized inputs were also provided.

Programs to Improve the Biological Utilization of Food

Programs intended to improve the biological utilization of food concerned sanitation and health. The cornerstone of the strategy was the program of primary health care (PHC), a preexisting program that consisted of a decentralized, referral health system articulated around local health centers and the use of paramedical personnel. Water supply and sanitation facilities were also to be constructed through this program. Primary health care strategies had been in ascendance in various parts of the Third World since the late 1960s (usually in the form of pilot projects) before becoming canonized by the United Nations at the famous conference convened in 1978 in Alma Ata by the World Health Organization. As in the case of FNPP, the setting

up of an institutional apparatus at the highest international levels acted as a
potent incentive for governments to embark upon ambitious projects for
restructuring the mostly urban and hospital-based health delivery structures, the cost of which they could no longer maintain. In Colombia, a novel
national health system, designed along PHC lines, had been introduced in
1976; it included a community participation component.[26]

Nutrition and Health Education Programs

Nutrition and health education programs included mass media campaigns,
interpersonal education, professional training, and school gardens. Mass
media campaigns focused on certain items, such as the use of water, the
treatment of diarrhea, and breast-feeding. Interpersonal education relied on
paraprofessionals to train communities on these and other pertinent issues,
such as the home storage of food, food habits, and weaning practices. The
professional component provided resources for training Colombian professionals both in the country and abroad.[27] With PAN support, a graduate
program in nutrition planning was established at the Jesuit university in
Bogotá in the early 1980s, closely patterned after MIT's. Finally, the school
garden program purported to teach rural children about the growth and
consumption of nutritious foods.

Smaller programs were geared toward supporting the production of
highly nutritious, low-cost processed foods (such as texturized-vegetable-
protein products and enriched flours, pasta, and cookies) through research
and credit to agro-industrial firms. Some of these products were distributed
through the food stamps program. Finally, PAN developed a significant
evaluation program based on the design of an information system to monitor
the plan's progress. This component was suggested by the World Bank.

It is not easy to assess the results of these programs in relation to their
stated objectives (the reduction of malnutrition and hunger by 50 percent among the target population). PAN evaluations relied on increasingly
complex and expensive surveys.[28] The results of the "definitive" National
Household Survey, carried out in 1981, became available only in 1984, when
PAN was, for most practical purposes, being phased out. As a former head of
PAN's evaluation unit put it in 1986, "A significant and overall impact evaluation of the Plan has not been done, and probably never will be" (Uribe
1986, 58). One may wonder whether a significant percentage of PAN's
budget, for which poor Colombians had to pay, did not go down the drain.
The delivery of basic health services through PHC centers was generally
deficient. Figures of numbers of people covered by PHC tended to be in-
flated; in some cases, a community was counted as covered by the program
if a census had been taken by the health promoter. Problems in the training
of paramedical personnel, resistance on the part of the medical profession to

the delegation of responsibility, inadequate stocking of supplies for the centers, and skyrocketing operating costs as the number of centers multiplied are cited as factors in the poor performance of the PHC strategy.[29]

In financial terms, PAN's budget was close to $250 million for the period 1976–1981, and DRI's approached $300 million. DRI's external financing (about 45 percent of the total) was considerably greater than PAN's. PAN's external financing for the period came from the World Bank ($25 million), U.S. AID ($6 million), and UNICEF, and DRI's originated in loans from the Inter-American Development Bank ($65 million), the World Bank ($52 million), and the Canadian International Development Agency ($13.5 million). By a curious twist in the style of government financing, part of the government's portion of the budget came from external sources as well (the Chemical Bank). About 60 percent of DRI's first-phase budget went to production component programs. This reflected the central priority of the program— to increase production. External financing for DRI continued to be high throughout the 1980s.

The Integrated Rural Development Program (DRI)

Let us now turn our attention to the second central component of the food and nutrition strategy, the more controversial DRI program. As we will see in the next chapter, the philosophy of integrated rural development was largely developed by the World Bank and taken simultaneously to many countries in the Third World, although in this case also, as in the case of nutrition planning, a number of pilot projects carried out in the 1960s in various parts of the Third World (with a lesser or greater degree of foreign funding, but always with important indigenous participation) were also influential.[30] In both intention and design, Colombia's Integrated Rural Development Program remained in its first phase (1976–1981) close to the World Bank blueprint. Its "target population" was the sector "composed of small units of production, conventionally known as the traditional or backward sub-sector and, more recently, as the peasant economy" (DNP/DRI 1979). DRI's primary objective was to increase food production among this group by rationalizing the sector's insertion in the market economy. Capital, technology, training, and infrastructure—the "missing" factors accounting for the backwardness of small-peasant production—were to be provided as a package through a strategy unprecedented in both scope and style. The intent was to bring the green revolution to the small farmers so as to turn them into entrepreneurs in the fashion of commercial farmers, only on a smaller scale.

Who were these small producers who constituted the "peasant economy"? DRI identified its intended beneficiaries according to two criteria: size of landholding and amount of income derived from farm sources. The upper ceiling for farm size was set at 20 hectares; farms included in the program ranged from 5 to 20 hectares. Farmers within this range were thought to have the capacity to respond to the program's inputs and to take off as independent entrepreneurs as a result of the program. These farmers constituted a sort of buffer group or "minimal agrarian petty bourgeoisie" (de Janvry 1981). In terms of income, only those farmers who derived at least 70 percent of their family income from farming activities were considered; these were "true" farmers. A survey of the entire rural population of the country, coupled with complex regionalization models, allowed DRI planners to identify this population group and to select ninety-two thousand families (20 percent of those with farms of less than 20 hectares) in several regions to be included in the first phase of the program (1976–1981); a second phase, to start in 1982, would reach most of the country. By 1993 (the end of third phase), more than 600 municipalities, out of close to 1,000 in the country, were to be covered.

The strategy (DNP/DRI 1975a, 1975b, 1976a, 1976b) was articulated around three main components: production, social programs, and infrastructure, with the following programs:

Production Component

Program of Technology Development. The aim of this program was the development and transfer of technologies appropriate to the traditional subsector as a means of increasing production and productivity, raising family income, and ensuring a more intense use of family labor.

Credit Program. The credit program sought to finance the new costs of production of DRI participants. The rationale was to secure sufficient capital to obtain in a short time sizable surpluses for regional and national markets.

Organization and Training Program. This program trained DRI participants in organizational and entrepreneurial techniques necessary to implementing DRI's integrated approach. Central to this effort was the training of peasants in integrated farm planning, which included the technical programming of all aspects of the production process. All farmers had to become conversant with these techniques as a prerequisite for entering the program; farmers also had to participate in local DRI committees, from the date the program was introduced in the area to its completion.

Natural Resources Program. DRI considered that a lasting improvement of production would depend on "the rational exploitation of soil and water resources," including measures such as reforestation, soil conservation, and aquaculture. The objective of this subprogram was to provide financial and technical assistance for projects intended to protect and manage the environment and—as in the case of aquaculture—provide protein alternatives to the diet.

Marketing and Commercialization Program. DRI anticipated that as farmers became more tied to the market economy as a result of the program, their financial risks would also increase due to price fluctuations, decreased control over marketing conditions, transportation costs, and so on. DRI planners sought to control these risks by providing credit and technical assistance to marketing peasant associations. This program was also intended to lower the price of foods for the urban consumer by decreasing the commercialization margins.

Social Program Component

The social program component included a series of education and health programs to raise living standards in the countryside, similar to those PAN had introduced in its project areas. In principle, PAN and PHC programs would be available to DRI participating communities, so that strategies conceived in terms of food production, consumption, and biological utilization would have a synergistic effect.

Infrastructure Component

The infrastructure component included three subprograms: rural roads, rural electrification, and water supply. They were conceived as necessary to the improvement of living standards and commercialization networks, linking rural producers more efficiently to the market.

One of DRI's most innovative aspects was the integration of the different strategies at the local level. Farmers were carefully selected and followed step by step, chiefly through the so-called integrated farm planning methodology, which each farmer had to follow under the guidance of DRI technicians. Local-level committees were instrumental in extending and deepening the reach of the various programs. These committees were headed by the DRI representative to the Agrarian Bank, in turn the most important agrarian lending institution in the country. Coordination of the various strategies was ensured at the regional and national levels. This was of tremendous importance, as DRI relied in its first phase on thirteen different government institutions for the implementation of its various programs, the actions of which had to be coordinated at all levels of the planning process. Indeed, it is usually pointed out that perhaps the most important achievement of PAN and DRI was to make all these agencies work together for the first time in the country, as this was seen as a great step toward rendering state planning and intervention more rational and effective.[31]

The Integrated Rural Development Program went through a series of significant changes, conceptually and institutionally, from the end of the first phase until the launching of the third phase in 1989. The first step at the end

of phase one (1981) was to integrate PAN and DRI administratively, only to
see the death of PAN, which took the form of a slow financial strangling
due to a lack of interest on the part of the new administration (that of President Belisario Betancour, 1982–1986). This was the last attempt to adhere to
the initial conceptual framework of FNPP, within which rural development
was seen as a component of the overall nutrition strategy. Indeed, the very
name of the strategy was inverted, from PAN-DRI to DRI-PAN, because the
new administration saw DRI as a more appropriate response to agrarian
problems.

DRI's orientation changed significantly after 1982. During the second
phase (DRI two: 1982–1989), the focus shifted to regions of greater potential
for small farm production and to advancing a successful strategy of commercialization of peasant food crops. Improved commercialization and marketing, identified as critical bottlenecks, became the surrogate for land redistribution.[32] At the level of overall agrarian policy, and in the wake of the
post-1982 debt crisis and the beginning of structural adjustment programs
under the aegis of the International Monetary Fund, the discussion ran once
again in terms of protectionism versus free market neoliberalism, with the
organized commercial groups—the cotton, coffee, rice, sugarcane, and livestock growers' associations, representing capitalist farmers—playing a leading role, broadly in favor of export promotion measures.[33] Because of these
changes in the macroeconomic environment, fewer and fewer resources
were available for programs during this period, so that DRI's scale of operations was reduced drastically. In the early 1990s, as the process of economic
opening to world markets deepened, most of the agricultural sector suffered
greatly.

The advent of Virgilio Barco's administration (1986–1990) brought DRI-
PAN once again to the forefront as one of two key components of the government's overall strategy of "Fight[ing] against Absolute Poverty" (the other
being the National Rehabilitation Plan [PNR], to be implemented in zones
of intense guerrilla activity as part of the peace process initiated by Betancur). DRI-PAN continued to be "the fundamental policy element used by
the state to face and solve the peasant question . . . without addressing the
issue of land ownership" (Fajardo, Errázuriz, and Balcázar 1991, 155). The
state continued to perceive the peasant problem as one of the key areas of
social conflict in the country, along with drug trafficking and guerrilla activity. Some additional small programs were also introduced in 1985, such as
the Program for the Development of Peasant Women, although female planners described the amount allocated to this program as "laughable." More on
this program in the next chapter.

The Technological Development Program, one of the key interventions in
DRI two, took the form of setting up model farms in various regions of the

country, which varied according to the region's socioeconomic and ecological context (Fondo DRI 1989b). Peasant farmers' adoption of technological packages was found to be hampered by a number of constraints, such as the high cost of inputs compared with the low price and inadequate marketing conditions for peasant products, insufficient size of landholdings, low levels of education, and "cultural backwardness" (Fondo DRI 1989a). In addition, by the end of the 1980s planners were becoming aware that the technological packages were unduly geared toward the maximization of the biological productivity of crops (through the use of fertilizers, improved seeds, and the like) and that they did not pay attention to potential increases in the productivity of natural resources, investment capacity, and the economic profitability of the peasant economy. These factors were taken into account in the launching of DRI three as a central component of the Plan of Integral Peasant Development (1988–1993) of the Barco administration, which saw technological change as the keystone of an invigorated production strategy (DNP/UEA 1988; Fondo DRI 1989a, 1989b). What was at stake, as always, was the modernization of peasant practices through its economic and symbolic capitalization.

As mentioned before, DRI had included a participatory component since its inception. Nevertheless, the decision making and the control of resources remained at the national level, thus rendering local participation insignificant. Up to this point, DRI's participation scheme had been more an intelligent and utilitarian imposition than a strategy of empowerment for local communities. Not only that, it assumed that participation could be learned and effected through management techniques infused with academic concepts. As most other development institutions, DRI understood participation as a bureaucratic problem to be solved by the institution, not as a process circumscribed by complex political, cultural, and epistemological questions. Indeed, the rhetoric of participation must be seen as a counterproposal to increased peasant mobilization; this was clearly the case in Colombia, where peasant demands and militancy reached an all-time high in the late 1960s and early 1970s (Zamocs 1986).

Toward the end of the 1980s, however, the opening up of spaces for peasant participation in policies such as DRI—fostered by the government's new commitment to decentralization at all levels—was beginning to generate social processes of some relevance. In particular, the promotion of self-managed development schemes, through a combination of community organizing efforts at the village, municipal, and district levels, produced what planners referred to as an organizational opening, which made possible a more significant peasant participation in the diagnosis, planning, and allocation of resources for the concrete projects contemplated by the program. In theory, within DRI three the municipality and the community of beneficiaries constituted the basic unit for the planning of rural development (DNP/UEA 1988). Yet it is also clear that the government's goal in decentralizing the state apparatus is not really to promote the autonomy of local and regional communities but rather, as Fajardo, Errázuriz, and Balcázar put it, to open up "new spaces for capital, a solution to the fiscal crisis, and the creation of new conditions for the management of the social and political conflicts generated by the pattern of development" (1991, 240).

The decentralization processes that the government started as a result of macroeconomic, institutional, and popular pressures—extended by the Constitutional Reform of 1991, which considers unpredecented local, regional, and cultural autonomies—cannot be seen solely as an attempt at cooptation. Indeed, they raise the complex question of the assessment of policies such as PAN and DRI and, in general, of the analysis of the real effects of development projects and strategies, to the extent that both rely on and unleash socioeconomic and cultural processes that go well beyond their intended scope and rationality. I now turn to this aspect in order to conclude my analysis of the deployment of development.

THE EVALUATION EXERCISE: EXPERT KNOWLEDGE AND THE CONTEST OVER THE NATURE OF SOCIAL CHANGE

If the efficacy of strategies such as PAN and DRI is difficult to evaluate even on their own terms and in relation to their own objectives, there is another aspect of the assessment of development interventions that has remained highly intractable and has been seldom addressed. What are strategies such as PAN and DRI really about? What happens when they are introduced in a given social setting? How do they occupy social spaces, and what processes—alteration of sensibilities, transformations in ways of seeing and living life, of relating to one another—do they set in motion? In sum, to what extent do these political technologies contribute to creating society and culture?

These questions should be posed and answered at many levels. As we will see, DRI planners have moved from the straightforward evaluation exercises of the earlier years regarding the performance of the program in terms of amounts spent, increases in production, and so on, to a more ambitious self-reflection on the nature and rationality of the strategy. These debates, which take place in the context of concrete struggles over the instruments of public policy, should be considered in order to make sense of the question, what is DRI really about? The analysis, however, cannot remain there. There is another level of reflection on the social and cultural productivity of development strategies based on the dynamics of discourse and power within the history and culture of modernity. Let us start with this second angle.

The Instrument-Effects of Development Projects

In his study of the development apparatus in Lesotho, James Ferguson (1990, 251–77) retakes Foucault's question of the "instrument-effects" of political technologies such as the prison or, in our case, rural development. Ferguson's basic contention is that even if rural development projects in Lesotho were for the most part a failure, their side effects—or, better, instrument-effects—nevertheless had far-reaching consequences for the communities involved. Like the prison in Foucault's case—which fails in terms of its explicit objective of reforming the criminal and yet succeeds in producing a normalized, disciplined society—the development apparatus shows remarkable productivity: not only does it contribute to the further entrenchment of the state, it also depoliticizes the problems of poverty that it is supposed to solve.

> It may be that what is most important about a "development" project is not so much what it fails to do but what it does do. . . . The "instrument-effect," then, is two-fold: alongside the institutional effect of expanding bureaucratic state power is the conceptual or ideological effect of depoliticizing both poverty and the state. . . . If the "instrument-effects" of a "development" project end up forming any kind of strategically coherent or intelligible whole, this is it: the anti-politics machine. (Ferguson 1990, 256)

The provision of government services is not culturally and politically innocent. Services, as Ferguson adds, "serve to govern" (253). Aihwa Ong points at a more profound effect of DRI-like strategies in her analysis of rural development projects in Malaysia. What is at stake in these strategies, she ventures, is an entire biopolitics: a set of policies regulating a plurality of problems such as health, nutrition, family planning, education, and the like which inevitably introduce not only given conceptions of food, the body, and so on, but a particular ordering of society itself. "In the specified spheres of social welfare, sexuality, and education, to name only a few, the everyday lives of village Malays are being reconstituted according to new concepts, language, and procedures" (Ong 1987, 55). In nineteenth-century Europe, biopolitics took the form of the invention of the social alluded to in chapter 2; in important respects, the biopolitics of development continues the deployment of modernity and the governmentalization of social life in the Third World. Let us see how this worked in Colombia's DRI strategy.

As already mentioned, DRI subjected peasants to a set of well-coordinated and integrated programs that sought to transform them into rational, business-minded entrepreneurs. Thirteen different institutions (the number grew with DRI two) acted on the chosen peasants, all of them in charge of a specific aspect: credit, technical assistance, natural-resource management, health, education, organizational skills, women, commercialization, and sanitation. New practices were introduced: the integrated farm management methodology that DRI and other agents utilized to make farmers accept and follow a strict set of prescriptions; the preparation of a *ficha técnica* (technical register), which contained detailed information on family life, production, and health; and individualized assistance, which also required close coordination of most of the participating agencies. Peasants appeared as never before under the gaze of power.

DRI's farm system conception (Cobos and Góngora 1977) was a normalizing mechanism: farmers had to adopt a "technological package" (improved seeds, herbicides, chemical pest control), specialize in the production of certain crops (usually, not more than three in a given subregion; often only one or two), follow a rigid layout of the fields, adhere to preset cultivation routines, prepare detailed production plans, maintain records with periodic entries, and organize for marketing by crop. These practices were very different from those which peasants in many regions were accustomed to follow and which included the use of organic fertilizers and pest control, unspecialized production (traditional plots had a mixture of cash crops, food crops, fruit trees, and small animal species), production primarily for self-consumption, and less intense use of family labor and more intense use of farm resources (for instance, the use of animal manure and the leaves of the trees for compost). Studies published in Colombia (Taussig 1978; Reinhardt 1988) and elsewhere (Richards 1984; Carney and Watts 1991) attest to this change. As Reinhardt has shown in her in-depth study of a peasant community in Colombia, DRI farmers increasingly had to abide by the rules of capitalist production and use their relative behavioral or technological advantages to this end as they tried to deal with the new practices.

Rosemary Galli summarized well this aspect of DRI in her study of the Colombian program.

> Thus the DRI peasant was surrounded by technicians and advisors. Communication was generally through the [local committees]; however, in the case of ICA, SENA, the Caja, and CECORA, communication was direct. Each DRI family was in their special care since each family was considered a potential leader in the village. Yet the superficiality of this communication was symbolized by the fact that ICA was in the process of gathering minute details about each family's life without the family knowing it so that DRI might design programs to improve the quality of home life. The so-called *ficha* was filled out by the home improvement staff from their direct observations; it contained such data as the amount of protein consumed weekly, the kinds of clothes worn, family illnesses, hygiene, and patterns of recreation. The *ficha* was symbolic of the paternalism of the program. (1981, 68)

One might rightly doubt the efficacy of these operations, yet it is necessary to recognize that on some level a sort of policing of families (Donzelot 1979) was going on. There was nothing paternalistic about this, really, but rather a power effect, to the extent that the translation of local situations into organizational terms is a sine qua non of institutional functioning. Galli also wondered whether whatever benefits might have accrued to peasants could amount to anything but "sweetening the bitter pill" of peasant poverty. Regardless of the results in terms of increased income and production, DRI introduced new mechanisms of social production and control. DRI was not only about DRI farmers; it also concerned the creation of semiproletarians and proletarians, the articulation of peasant production with commercial agriculture and of the agrarian sector as a whole with the rest of the economy, particularly the foreign-exchange-generating sector. One must also acknowledge, however, that when the pill is already bitter, running water, health posts, and the like may mean real improvements in people's living conditions. This should be recognized, while realizing at the same time that these changes enter into an ongoing situation of power and resistance.

In a similar vein, rural development cannot be seen as the mere instrument of social differentiation in terms of two classes. It creates a spectrum of social and cultural strata and operates on the basis of the strata it creates. In contrast to the extreme heterogeneity of peasant reality, DRI-type interventions tend to create relatively homogeneous strata through the imposition of certain practices. Even the characterization of people in terms of proletarians, semiproletarians, small farmers, and capitalist farmers is a simplification. As these social strata change, other power configurations change as well: domestic relations, gender relations, and cultural relations. New ways of individuation are brought into play as the existing division of labor is transformed, but also new forms of resistance appear.

Finally, it must be emphasized that bureaucratic control is an essential component of the deployment of development. Rural development is about a bureaucratics that seeks to manage and transform how rural life is conceived and organized. Like FNPP, DRI functions as a productive technique that through its very functioning relates certain entities in specific ways (capital, technology, and resources), reproduces long-established cultural fabrications (for example, the market), and redistributes forces with a significant impact on people, visibilities, and social relations. The organization of factors that development achieved contributes to the disciplining of labor, the extraction of surplus value, and the reorientation of consciousness. As we will see in the next chapter, these strategies inevitably bypassesd peasants' culturally based conceptions. Beyond the economic goals, World Bank–style integrated rural development sought a radical cultural reconversion of rural life.

The instrument-effects of the deployment of the development discourse in cases such as PAN and DRI do not presume any kind of conspiracy; on the contrary, they are the result of a certain economy of discourses. This economy of discourses dictates that interventions such as integrated rural development show a significant degree of uniformity worldwide; these strategies rely on a relatively undifferentiated and context-independent body of knowledge and expertise; they are part of a relatively standard discursive practice, a sort of "devspeak" and "devthink"; at a general level, they produce similar results, particularly in terms of governmentalizing social life (Ferguson 1990, 258–60). Colombia is a typical case of this dynamics in some repects. However, the Colombian case presents a feature rarely analyzed in the development context, namely, the high level of debate about the policies maintained by national planners, intellectuals, and experts of various types. This debate suggests that we need to qualify the development encounter by looking carefully at the participation of planners in the adaptation and re-creation of the strategies.

From Documentary Reality to the Politics of Policy Reform

Like the Agrarian Reform Program of the 1960s, the implementation of PAN and especially DRI generated heated debates within the intellectual and policy-making community in the country. It is perhaps improper to speak of a community here, given the variety of perspectives involved in the discussions; yet a certain discursive community has been created as a result of the debates over the nature and implementation of DRI, even more so than in the case of the Agrarian Reform Program, when positions were extremely polarized along political lines. Indeed, planners and intellectuals of various political and epistemological persuasions not infrequently circulate in the same spaces. DRI's national planning unit has been effective in channeling debates on the "peasant question" and its relation to the state, a question that has a rich history of scholarly and political activity in the country. These debates have been advanced through the celebration of well-attended national and international meetings with the participation of planners and government staff, as well as conservative, liberal, and dissenting intellectuals,[34] and by incorporating intellectuals from various universities of the country in the program's evaluation exercises.

Institutional practices, let it be remembered, rely on the creation of what Dorothy Smith calls a documentary reality. The materiality of the planners' practice is intimately tied to the crafting of documents. In the case of PAN and DRI, this was and is particularly true at the national level, where the preparation, writing, and follow-up of documents occupy a very significant part of the planners' day. Although established categories and professional discourses are generally reproduced through these documentary processes, there is also a subtle and slow displacement of entrenched categories that is not without effects, as we will see shortly.

I should say a few words about the planning staff before continuing with this aspect of the discussion. During the first phase (1976–1981), PAN's staff consisted of sixty to seventy highly qualified people, men and women roughly equally divided, whereas DRI's was around ninety (this does not include the staff of the implementing agencies participating in the programs); about half of the staff were in the national headquarters in Bogotá, and the other half in regional offices. Let us see how a high-level PAN planner saw her role and that of her peers:

> Though the original design of the Plan had been made by economists, a broad range of professions were needed to implement its different components. Teachers, communicators, physicians, nutritionists, administrators, anthropologists, sociologists and agronomists had joined PAN since 1976. Hard working and highly motivated, they all shared the illusion of doing something meaningful for the country and its poorest population. But this was bound to be true only in the long-run, if the plan had persevered through the years and extended sufficiently to become a meaningful source of support to much of the poor population of Colombia. Traditional politicians, however, were wary of PAN and its technical outlook was sometimes seen as bearing the mask of an imported, technocratic perspective. No regional leader praised PAN any longer than was strictly needed to insure budget approval. (Uribe 1986, 58)

This statement coincides with my observations: PAN and DRI planners were "hard working and highly motivated," although their level of political awareness varied greatly, from the very naive about the rationality of state intervention to the savvy and the cynical. The fact that politicians saw in PAN an "imported, technocratic perspective" is not surprising; it was, despite the role of national planners, in the design of the plan. The National Planning Department (DNP) itself is known to be a highly technocratic establishment, and its effect on the country's development has been quite noticeable. Most professionals, however, know that the life span of any strategy is short, seldom more than the four years of a president's term (DRI's continuity to this date is quite exceptional in this respect). To expect effects only in the long run, then—as much as to blame politicians for program failure—begs the question of the conditions in which policy practice takes place.

As perhaps at no other time, the work ethic of PAN and DRI planners became apparent immediately before and during the visit of World Bank missions. One would hate to think that the hard and competent work of the Colombian planners served as a (one more) subsidy for the World Bank, an additional mechanism through which this institution dispersed its blueprint and accumulated symbolic capital, but some of this clearly happened. This realization, however, has to be accompanied by the consideration that many of those planners would reorient their activities in a more political fashion if the conditions for doing so existed. Actually, upon leaving the DNP, some of them, women and men, seem to take this step by returning to universities, research centers, or activist organizations.

   The micropolitics surrounding the production, circulation, and utilization
of development knowledge is still poorly understood. At one level, one must
consider the whole issue of the instrument-effects and the dispersion of
power that accompanies the development apparatus. But this cannot be
seen only synchronically, because the changes that policies such as DRI
undergo throughout the years must be accounted for. Strategies are modified, undermined, added on. Third World planners manifest great inventive-
ness in this regard, depending on many factors, including the stability and
permanence of the interventions (including their own jobs). Some of the
components of PAN and DRI were originally thought out in Latin America
or other parts of the Third World—through the pilot projects of the 1960s
and 1970s already mentioned—and then adapted and standardized by the
World Bank and other organizations. This was the case particularly with the
primary health care strategy.

   It would be too simple to see this process as mere appropriation, although
this undoubtedly takes place continually; it would be equally simplistic to
see the knowledge process as a mere imposition of strategies on the Third
World on the part of First World interests. The conventional view of knowledge as produced in one place (the center) and applied in another (the periphery) must be reformulated. In the contemporary world, as Clifford
(1989) has suggested, theory production and use take place in a discontinuous terrain, with ongoing and complex processes of appropriations and contestations in various directions. That both theories and theorists travel in a
socially and epistemologically discontinuous terrain is clear in the case of
the development apparatus. At the same time, however, there are also clear
centers of power and systemic instrument-effects that cannot be overlooked.

   To conclude, let us look briefly at the relevance of DRI's learning process
to our discussion of the politics of discourse. During the first phase, evaluation studies carried out internally or independently by Colombian scholars
showed uneven results: a relatively high degree of program success in some
regions, little or no success in others.[35] This led to the policy reformulation
for DRI two already described: to focus on the regions having the right
concentration of the right peasants (in terms of productive potential) and to
address certain bottlenecks, particularly commercialization and marketing.
Subsequent evaluations related the success or failure of specific program
components to structural constraints, such as those reflected in insufficient
capital and size of holdings, the conceptualization of technological packages,
pressures toward proletarianization, increased exploitation of the soil, and
precarious links to markets. As the complexity of the evaluations grew, programs became more carefully conceived and targeted.

   Generally speaking, it was found throughout the 1980s that the performance of specific components and of the program as a whole varied greatly,
given the regional, cultural, and historical heterogeneity of the peasant

economy, thus calling for greater flexibility in policy and program design. The search for a classification of peasant economies in terms of the mechanisms responsible for regional differentiation resulted in the formulation of four major types, corresponding respectively to (1) zones where the traditional peasant economy predominates; (2) zones where low-intensity cattle ranching in large holdings predominates; (3) zones characterized by the rapid penetration of capitalist agriculture; and (4) zones of recent colonization. The benefits of the program were found to be significant in type 1 regions, relatively insignificant in those of type 2 (chiefly because of marked restrictions in the access to land), and generally detrimental to peasant farms in zones where capitalist agriculture is dominant. In type 4 zones there were no DRI programs.

Among the more noticeable changes evidenced in those regions with the larger peasant presence were the following: a trend toward specialization in production, that is, the substitution of crop arrangements characterized by high profitability for those traditionally practiced, with concomitant improvements in productivity and income;[36] the adoption of technological innovations, although not always of those initially pushed by the agencies in charge, which tended to be capital and energy intensive; increases in production capacity thanks to the availability of credit; increased use of family labor on the farm itself; higher margins of commercialization of peasant crops; and better links to the market.

To what extent these changes entail a deeper transformation in terms of the adoption by peasants of a capitalist rationality is still an open question, requiring a type of ethnographic fieldwork, unavailable at this point, similar to that of Gudeman and Rivera (1990) but conceived explicitly in the context of the programs. Some observers believe that the logic of peasant production in the Colombian Andes continues to be significantly different from that of capitalist production. It is still ruled by the overall goal of subsistence and reproduction of the farm base, thus coinciding with the observations of Gudeman and Rivera mentioned earlier. This does not mean, however, that under certain conditions peasants are uninterested in intensifying production or generating surpluses. They certainly are, as DRI evaluations show, although it is the logic of maintenance of the family farm that characterizes the adoption of new practices and the allocation of resources. In this respect, peasants are extremely pragmatic, always proceeding by trial and error. I will return to the meaning of these changes for peasant culture in the next chapter.

As mentioned, debates over the nature of the peasantry have motivated the creation of a loosely bound discursive or epistemic community in which ideas and experiences are shared and debated across professional, ideological, and political positions. Although neoclassical economists predominate within DNP, the debate is by no means restricted to neoclassical terms.[37]

Even important groups of social scientists who work generally within neo-classical paradigms practice a kind of eclecticism that makes possible a dialogue with, say, Marxist-inspired political economists.[38] This rich dialogue has fueled a significant learning process, translated into policy debates, scholarly studies, and concrete recommendations for alternative interventions. The best of this learning process is perhaps reflected in the work of anthropologist and historian Darío Fajardo, who moved in the late 1970s from the National University in Bogotá to head PAN's evaluation unit for several years, to return again to the university in the mid-1980s (a cycle not uncommon in Colombian planning and intellectual circles), moving finally to head an ecological foundation in the early 1990s without severing completely his links to the university, social movements, and the state. As insider first and critical intellectual thereafter, Fajardo's sustained effort of reflection on DRI and peasant issues (Fajardo 1983, 1984, 1987; Fajardo 1991; Fajardo, Errázuriz, and Balcázar 1991) has pushed the limits of the debates on the relation between capital, the state, and the peasant economy to levels that could not have been anticipated by the integrated rural development discourse of the 1970s.

A number of themes regarding the meaning of government policy emerge clearly from Fajardo's work. In the first place, he emphasizes that the majority of peasants and rural workers in Colombia continue to be poor and subjected to "backward relations of domination"; these relations of domination hold back the modernization of the peasant economy. Government efforts such as DRI are not changing significantly this state of affairs, to the extent that the bulk of financial, technological, and intellectual resources devoted to agrarian policy is still geared toward the modern capitalist sector. This ambiguity on the part of the government—at the same time arguably committed to rural development, yet making this policy subordinate to the needs of commercial agriculture—accounts for the uneven and reduced results DRI achieved so far. Indeed, agrarian policy is generally detrimental to peasant interests. Politically, DRI seeks to improve peasant living and production conditions without touching the terribly skewed land tenure systems still existing in the country;[39] or, to put it in the context of World Bank discourse, the problem is thought to be characterized by exclusion from markets and state policy, not by exploitation within the market and the state, as Fajardo believes is the case.

This somewhat schizophrenic situation, continuing with Fajardo's analysis, is related to DRI's reliance on outside loans, the subordination of government social policy to macroeconomic policy, and the effect of these two factors on the allocation of resources to the agrarian sector, particularly the peasant subsector. Despite recent efforts at decentralization, government policy has failed to control the power of the capitalist sector, articulate the various components of the regional economies, and reduce the drain of surplus from the peasant economy by the capitalist sector and of the agrarian sector as a whole by urban industrial interests. A number of tasks thus become fundamental to a new, truly peasant-centered development, including the following: (1) a new agrarian reform, "because there cannot be DRI without land" (Fajardo 1987, 220); (2) more explicit organizational and participatory processes so that communities themselves can identify the goals of regional development and the means to carry them out; (3) a policy of technological research and development in support of autonomous peasant production systems; and (4) more substantial resources for credit, commercialization, and integral agrarian reform programs, according to the logic of the peasant economy.

This proposal entails an autonomous peasant development strategy, not unlike that proposed by Amin, already discussed, and generated by peasant communities through their participation in the planning process. This would allow peasants to obtain significant leverage in relation to the state and the capitalist sector, so as to modify the social relations of production in their favor, even if the peasant economy would have to articulate with other regional and urban actors of importance. As another analyst put it, a strategy such as this would conceive of the peasantry in terms of not lacks but possibilities, that is, as a social actor in its own right; this in turn requires an effective respect for peasants in terms of establishing new rules of the game to satisfy peasant demands (Bejarano 1987). All this implies the strengthening of peasant organizations so that peasants can create spaces to modify the existing balance of power.

This proposal can have a correcting effect in relation to the depoliticizing and bureaucratizing pressures of the development apparatus. It opens spaces of struggle within which peasants might defend not only their economic systems but their way of life. The strategic effects of the changes Fajardo and others envisioned—one might call them specific intellectuals, in Foucault's sense of the term (1980c)—cannot be overlooked, even if the proposal is in principle as modernizing as DRI. In the process of contributing to the affirmation of the peasants' world, new possibilities for struggle and for destabilizing the development apparatus might emerge. In fact, the proposals are produced with clear political criteria; some of its suggestions seem to be slowly finding their way into DRI's machinery, generating social processes the outcome of which is difficult to foresee. In this way, even what today goes under the rubric of integrated rural development is not the same as what the World Bank started to promote in the mid-1970s all over the Third World. A more satisfactory theorization of the relevance of this difference, however, is still missing.

The proposal does not challenge explicitly the basic tenets of the development discourse. Particularly, it accepts a relatively conventional view of the "peasantry," which is problematic, as we will see in the next chapter when

I introduce a cultural analysis absent from all discussions of rural development. This type of analysis is adumbrated by another critical intellectual with links to DRI, Alejandro Sanz de Santamaría, who headed a team of university researchers contracted out by DRI to evaluate the program's performance in one region.

One of the most significant insights derived from the work of this researcher (Sanz de Santamaría 1987; Sanz de Santamaría and Fonseca 1985) is that any conventional evaluation process relies on the separation in time and space between knowledge producers (the researchers), knowledge users (DRI planners), and the investigated community; this separation makes practically impossible the production of sound knowledge on which to base policy recommendations, let alone the production of knowledge about the community. Not only do conventional evaluations fall into "the indecency of speaking for others"[40] by necessarily abstracting from the local reality through the use of a social science framework, but the choice of interpretive framework is largely arbitrary. For knowledge to be useful, it must start with the peasants' self-understanding, and then proceed to build a system of communication involving peasants, DRI functionaries, and researchers. This entails, on the one hand, the integration of knowledge production, circulation, and use and, on the other hand, the increasing constitution of the local community into a subject of its own collective action. Sanz de Santamaría sees this political project, which exposes the totalitarian character ingrained in conventional knowledge-producing processes, as an inevitable component of a radical transformation of development policy. The concrete proposals that emerged from his exercise, which met some response from DRI, seem to indicate that there is hope for some of this to happen, although the local elites' violent reaction to the political process generated by the exercise points to the difficulties in doing so.[41]

This brings us full circle. I started with a discussion of some features of institutions that, although apparently rational and neutral, are nevertheless part of the exercise of power in the modern world. The development apparatus inevitably relies on such practices and thus contributes to the domination of Third World people such as Colombian peasants. At the end of chapter 3, and again at the end of this chapter, I identified the need for a cultural politics that builds upon local cultures and that, engaging strategically with the conditions of regional, national, and international political economy, seeks to contribute to the affirmation of Third World groups and the displacement of the development imaginary. In this chapter, I tentatively concluded that one way of advancing this politics of cultural affirmation might be to free up spaces within, and in spite of, existing programs such as DRI. But this widening of spaces must be pursued from the vantage point of the cultural imposition and instrument-effects of the development apparatus, not only in terms of political economy, as it has been until now. Only then will dissenting strategies have a clearer chance for life.

In his politico-artistic manifesto "An Aesthetic of Hunger," written in 1965, Glauber Rocha wrote the following angry words:

> Thus, while Latin America laments its general misery, the foreign onlooker cultivates the taste of that misery, not as a tragic *symptom*, but merely as an aesthetic object within his field of interest. . . . We [Cinema Novo filmmakers] understand the hunger that the European and the majority of Brazilians have not understood. . . . We know—since we made these sad, ugly films, these screaming, desperate films where reason does not always prevail—that this hunger will not be cured by moderate governmental reforms and that the cloak of technicolor cannot hide, but only aggravates, its tumors. Therefore, only a culture of hunger, weakening its own structures, can surpass itself qualitatively; the most noble cultural manifestation of hunger is violence. (Rocha 1982, 70)

As Michael Taussig (1987, 135) said, "From the represented shall come that which overturns the representation." He continues, commenting on the absence of the narratives of South American indigenous peoples from most representations about them, "It is the ultimate anthropological conceit, anthropology in its highest, indeed redemptive, moment, rescuing the 'voice' of the Indian from the obscurity of pain and time" (135).

This is to say that as much as the plain exclusion of the peasant's voice in rural development discourse, this conceit to "speak for the others," perhaps even to rescue their voice, as Taussig says, must be avoided. The fact that violence is a cultural manifestation of hunger applies not only to hunger's physical aspects but to the violence of representation. The development discourse has turned its representations of hunger into an act of consumption of images and feelings by the well nourished, an act of cannibalism, as Cinema Novo artists would have it. This consumption is a feature of modernity, we are reminded by Foucault (1975, 84) ("It is just that the illness of some should be transformed into the experience of others"). But the regimes of representation that produce this violence are not easily neutralized, as the next chapter will show.

Chapter 5

POWER AND VISIBILITY:
TALES OF PEASANTS, WOMEN,
AND THE ENVIRONMENT

We can only deplore the mechanism which favors the
transfer to Africa of problems and their solutions, of certain
institutions which result from a purely Western historical
process. Organizations for the promotion of women's
rights tend naturally to extend identical activities into
Africa, and, in so doing, to assimilate us into a strictly
European mentality and historical experience. Hardly
anything has been written about African women that has
not presented them as minor elements.
—Proceedings from the meeting the Civilization of the
Woman in African Tradition, Abidjan, Ivory Coast,
quoted in Trinh T. Minh-ha, *Woman,*
Native, Other, 1989

DISCOURSE AND VISUALITY

THE HISTORY of development is seen in conventional analyses in terms of the
evolution of theories and ideas, or as the succession of more or less effective
interventions. For political economists, the same history reflects different
ideological responses to allegedly deeper contradictions, dictated by capital
accumulation and circulation. This history, however, can also be seen from
the perspective of the changes and transformations in the discursive regime,
even if these changes, as should be clear by now, are circumscribed by discursive practices tied to political economies, knowledge traditions, and institutions of ruling.

In chapter 2, I argued that the development discourse is a rule-governed
system held together by a set of statements that the discursive practice continues to reproduce—whether such practice refers to industrialization, agriculture, peasants, or women and the environment, as we will see shortly.
Although it is true that the discursive practice has remained largely unchanged, significant changes have occurred within the discursive formation
of development. What is the meaning of these changes, particularly in terms
of creating conditions for types of transformation that might take us into

other discursive orders? Should the proliferation of new areas of inquiry and intervention be understood merely as the discourse's conquest of new domains? Even if this is the case, does this process not inevitably create new possibilities for struggle and resistance, for advancing alternative cultural possibilities?

For example, intergrated rural development was conceived by experts as a strategy to correct the biases of the green gevolution. Did the inclusion of a new client category, small farmers, modify in any significant way the development discourse? How were peasants represented? What were the consequences for them? It is worth examining in detail the specific representations that "packaged" the peasantry for the development apparatus. The inclusion of the peasantry was the first instance in which a new client group was created en masse for the apparatus, in which the economizing and technologizing gaze of the apparatus was turned on a new subject. From the late 1970s until today, another client group of even larger proportions has been brought into the space of visibility of development: women. It was thus that the women in development (WID) discourse achieved a certain preeminence. Finally, in the 1980s, the objectifying gaze was turned not to people but to nature—or, rather, the environment—resulting in the by now in/famous discourse of sustainable development.

This chapter follows the displacement of the development gaze across the terrains in which these three social actors move. The gaze turned peasants, women, and the environment into spectacles. Let us remember that the apparatus (the *dispositif*) is an abstract machine that links statements and visibilities, the visible and the expressible (Deleuze 1988). Modernity introduced an objectifying regime of visuality—a scopic regime, as it has been called (Jay 1988)—that, as we will see, dictated the manner in which peasants, women, and the environment were apprehended. New client categories were brought into the field of vision though a process of enframing that turned them into spectacles. The "developmentalization" of peasants, women, and the environment took place in similar ways in the three domains, a reflection of the existence of discursive regularities at work. The production of new discourses, however, is not a one-sided process; it might create conditions for resistance. This can be gleaned in the discourse of some peasants, feminists, and environmentalists; it is reflected in new practices of vision and knowledge, even if these resistances take place within the modes of the development discourse.

Why emphasize vision? The phrase *panoptic gaze*—the gaze of the guard who, in his tower, can watch over all the prisoners in the building without being seen—has become synonymous with apparatuses of social control. But the role of vision extends far beyond technologies of control to encompass many modern means for the production of the social. The birth of science itself was marked by an alliance that almost two centuries ago "was forged between words and things, enabling one *to see* and *to say*" (Foucault 1975, xii). This alliance was enacted by the empirical clinician upon opening the corpse for the first time "to really see" what was inside. The spatialization and verbalization of the pathological inaugurated regimes of visuality that are still with us. From the analysis of tissues in nineteenth-century medicine through the microscope and the camera to satellite surveillance, sonography, and space photography the importance of vision has only grown:

> The eyes have been used to signify a perverse capacity—honed to perfection in the history of science tied to militarism, capitalism, colonialism, and male supremacy—to distance the knowing subject from everybody and everything in the interest of unfettered power. . . . The visualization technologies are without apparent limit. . . . Vision in this technological feast becomes unregulated gluttony; all seems not just mythically about the god trick of seeing everything from nowhere, but to have put the myth into ordinary practice. (Haraway 1988, 581)

This affirmation about visualization technologies applies to the politics of discourse in more than metaphorical ways. To bring people into discourse— as in the case of development—is similarly to consign them to fields of vision. It is also about exercising "the god trick of seeing everything from nowhere." As we will see, this assertion describes well the work style of the World Bank. The development discourse maps people into certain coordinates of control. The aim is not simply to discipline individuals but to transform the conditions under which they live into a productive, normalized social environment: in short, to create modernity. Let us see in detail what this means, how it is achieved, and what it entails in terms of the possibility of shifting visibilities.

THE DISCOVERY OF "SMALL FARMERS": FROM GREEN REVOLUTION IMPERIALISM TO RURAL DEVELOPMENT POPULISM

The Mapping of Visibilities

In one of the most celebrated technical papers prepared by DRI in its initial years on the traditional or small production subsector, one finds the following statement on the potential effects of the program on various types of peasant farmers:

> The articulation of small production units to the market, be it through the market for products, inputs, labor or capital (especially credit), fosters continuous transformation of the sub-sector's internal organization and its position within the national economy. . . . Two situations may happen: a) the small producer may be able to technify his productive process, which entails his becoming an

agrarian entrepreneur; and b) the small producer is not prepared to assume such level of competitiveness, in which case he will be displaced from the market and perhaps even from production in that area altogether. (DNP/DRI 1979, 47)

In other words, produce or perish. Only those farmers who accomplished successfully their "graduation into small entrepreneurs," as the transformation was commonly referred to at DRI, would survive. This statement was in accordance with DRI's overall objective—to increase production and income in the traditional subsector by rationalizing its insertion into the market economy—also explicit, as we will see in the next section, in the World Bank's rural development theory.

In those cases in which the program's performance did not fulfill these objectives, it was, as an influential DRI evaluation study put it on the eve of phase two, "due to structural factors such as the precarious availability of land, deficient soil quality and the strong resistance of rural communities to produce for the market. As it was already pointed out," the document continued, "DRI does not intend to provide solutions for this type of problems." In conlusion, "DRI's effectiveness as a rural development strategy is demonstrated only when it has to deal with the following factors: lack of capital for production, unskilled labor and backward production practices, lack of community organization, and insufficient physical infrastructure, especially roads" (DNP/UEA 1982a, 10).

At stake was a redistribution of the economy of visibilities articulated around the dualism of tradition and modernity. This dualism was already present in the original development map; but the positions then occupied by the main actors were quite different: before the productive potential of the small farmer was discovered, peasants figured in development discourse only as a somewhat bothersome and undifferentiated mass with an invisible face; they were part of the amorphous "surplus population," which sooner or latter would be absorbed by a blooming urban economy. As their face became more present and unpleasant, and as their muted voice became more audible, a tactical reshuffling of forces began to occur. Another aspect of the rural face started to engulf the city: thousands of migrants putting new demands on the city, coupled with a countryside that could no longer produce enough food. The dynamics of the discourse (its "machinic" processes) dictated a reorganization of visibilities, linking state support, international institutions, class conflict, existing food politics, and the like into a new strategy: integrated rural development (IRD).

Not surprisingly, the representation of peasants deployed in this strategy was—and continues to be—essentially economistic. Since the mid-1960s, economists studying small farmers had not ceased to emphasize that the same backward peasants they had discounted in previous decades would behave like good and decent capitalist farmers if they were provided with the necessary conditions for doing so. Economists discovered, to their pleasant surprise and with the help of economic anthropologists, that peasants behaved rationally; given their constraints, they optimized their options, minimized risks, and utilized resources efficiently. This called for "investing in human resources" (Schultz 1964). These conceptions went into the making of rural development strategies; predictably, the failure of farmers to behave as theory predicted was construed as the peasants' inability to respond adequately to the programs' inputs. Occasionally one finds in DRI evaluation documents mention of peasant "resistance to produce for the market," but without any further explanation.

This understanding of peasants is intimately linked to certain views of food, agriculture, the land, development, and nature. Although it would be impossible to trace these connections here, it is worth mentioning those which came to shape the core of the IRD discourse. Integrated rural development was conceived as a way of bringing the green revolution to small farmers, and it was in this latter strategy that many of the constructs of the former originated. Let us listen attentively to how green revolution experts built their arguments, how they carried themselves in the realm of statements. For Norman Borlaug, the father of the green revolution, in "provoking rapid economic and social changes . . . [the green revolution] was generating enthusiasm and new hope for a better life . . . displacing an attitude of despair and apathy that permeated the entire social fabric of these countries only a few years ago." Moreover,

> In the awakening there is a growing demand for more and better schools, better housing, more warehouses, improved rural roads and transportation, more electricity to drive the motors and wells and to light the houses. . . . As the entire activity of the country [continues] to increase in tempo . . . many millions of rural people, who formerly lived outside the general economy of the country—at a subsistence level—are becoming active participants in the economy. Millions of others desire to enter. If they are denied this opportunity, then the new upsurge will lead to increasing political unrest and political upheaval. (Quoted in Bird 1984, 5)

We already encountered the trope of economic darkness in Lewis's description of the dual economy. Borlaug adds a realm of social darkness, apathy, and despair so pervasive that it will recede only before the avalanche of progress. But people have first to be awakened to the new possibilities; they have to be taken by the hand into the new, exciting road. Millions desire to enter. It would be the task of the white fathers to introduce the good but backward Third World people into the temple of progress. Otherwise, a violent future might be in store, and they might revert to their marginal past with its tendency toward apathy and despair—not discounting savagery.

This representation speaks "of fathers and sons and younger brothers with the vague feminized threats of engulfment and return to irrationality."[1] It is also about disallowing anything that is outside the market economy, especially the activities of subsistence and local reciprocity and exchange, so many times crucial to peasants, women, and indigenous people; it is, finally, about a definition of progress that is taken as universally valid, not as marked by culture and history.

Let us listen to the defense of the the the so-called green revolution offered by another of its leading advocates, Lester Brown (now master of ceremonies at the World Watch Institute, where the "facts" about the state of the world are produced annually):

> The "Green Revolution" has . . . already made major contributions to the well-being of millions of people in many countries and thus bears witness to the fact that careful evaluation, sound scientific and economic planning, and sustained effort can overcome the pathology of chronic under-production and gradually bring about rapidly increasing economic advance. A formula for success can be designed for any area that has available the new adapted plant varieties and the other inputs and accelerators that must be applied in logical fashion. (Quoted in Bird 1984, 7)

In other words, the change that must happen requires unprecedented action carefully guided by the experts of the West. Because the Third Worlders do not have this knowledge—but instead are caught in a chronic pathological condition—the scientist, like a good doctor, has the moral obligation to intervene in order to cure the diseased (social) body. Moreover, the formula for success is available to anybody, meaning any country that is willing to accept the call of the new savior and be led into the salvation that only modern science and technology can offer. In short, as Elizabeth Bird succinctly put it,

> The messages [in the green revolution literature] are, first, that these development planners know what "the people" in the "developing countries" want; that what they want is what "we" have; third, that "they" are not yet advanced enough to be able to fully indulge themselves without repercussions; and fourth, that discipline, prudence and forebearance are some of the qualities necessary to success. (1984, 23)

The green revolution literature is full of cultural asumptions regarding science, progress, and the economy, in which one can discern the authorial stances of a father/savior talking with selfless condescension to the child/native. It is also full of statements about the dangers of many "monsters," particularly the "population monster," the "spectre of hunger," and "political upheaval." Did the new preoccupation with the small farmer temper the dreams of massive solutions that would work once and for all? Did it in any

way shake the universals embodied in the discourse of the green revolution?
To answer these questions, we may start with another founder of discourse,
the father of IRD and the basic human needs (BHN) approach, the president
of the World Bank at the time, Robert McNamara.

McNamara presented the basis of the IRD strategy in his famous Nairobi
speech of September 1973, delivered at the annual meeting of the board of
governors of the World Bank Group. The problem, he stated, is a serious
one: more than 100 million families with holdings of land too small and
conditions of cultivation too unproductive to contribute significantly to agricultural production. "The question," he remarked after having introduced
"the problem" without spelling out whose problem or by whose standard, "is
what can the developing countries do to increase the productivity of the
small farmer. How can they duplicate the conditions which have led to very
rapid agricultural growth in a few experimental areas and in a few countries
so as to stimulate agricultural growth and combat rural poverty on a broad
scale?" The few experimental areas were the pilot IRD projects in Mexico,
Colombia, and other places; the "few countries" were Japan and, to some
extent, China. What, then, would be the goal?

> I suggest that the goal be to increase production on small farms so that by 1985
> their output will be growing at the rate of 5% per year. If the goal is met, and
> small holders maintain that momentum, they can double their annual output
> between 1985 and the end of the century. Clearly, this is an ambitious objective
> . . . But if Japan in 1970 could produce 6,720 kilograms of rice per hectare on
> very small farms, then Africa with its 1,270 kilograms per hectare, Asia with
> 1,750 and Latin America with 2,060 have an enormous potential for expanding
> productivity. Thus I believe the goal is feasible. (McNamara 1975, 90, 91)

We begin to recognize here many of the traits already analyzed; for instance, the use of physicalist and probabilistic discourse, based on a purely
instrumental conception of nature and work; the setting of goals according
to statistical calculations that bear no relation to actual social conditions; and
the reliance on a model (Japan), without recognizing any historical specificity. The principle of authority is clear: "I believe the goal to be feasible,"
when the "I" is uttered as representative of all bankers investing in development. Qualifying this principle of authority only makes authority stronger:
"Neither we at the Bank, nor anyone else, have very clear answers on how
to bring the improved technology and other inputs to other 100 million small
farmers. . . . But we do understand enough to get started. Admittedly, we
will have to take some risks. We will have to improvise and experiment. And
if some of the experiments fail, we will have to learn from them and start
anew (McNamara 1975, 91).

If "the Bank" does not have clear answers, nobody else does. Being "the
Bank," however, it can take some risks, and if "some of the experiments fail,"

they will bow to the difficulties of life (in the Third World) and humbly start all over again. Quite a comfortable position, especially if we consider that it is not they who have to suffer the consequences of failure, because the loans are paid back by Third World people. This position allows the World Bank to maintain all options open; it certainly will not be driven out of business by repeated failure. But McNamara's address was only the announcement of a strategy to be spelled out in a series of ensuing "sector policy papers." The first discursive operation was to explain the rationale for the new strategy; this was done in one of the most celebrated sector policy papers:

> Past strategies in most developing countries have tended to emphasize economic growth without specifically considering the manner in which the benefits of growth are to be redistributed. . . . Although, in the long run, economic development for the growing rural population will depend on expansion of the modern sector and on nonagricultural pursuits, too strong an emphasis on the modern sector is apt to neglect the growth potential of the rural areas. Failure to recognize this has been a major reason why rural growth has been slow and rural poverty has been increasing. (World Bank 1975, 16)

In this type of statement—invariably without subject—the World Bank did not see itself as part of those somewhat misguided past strategies. Its response was unmistakable: growth was the right answer, yet there was growth potential in the rural areas as well. Moreover, with this move the World Bank appeared as the champion of justice, because the new strategy spoke of redistribution. This begged the question on two counts: not only did it assume that the Bank's proposal for redistribution would actually redistribute in the right direction, that is, toward greater income equality (which was and is almost never the case); it intelligently hid the role of the Bank and growth strategies in creating inequality in the first place.

Given this rationale, let us now see how the new approach was formulated:

> Rural development is a strategy designed to improve the economic and social life of a specific group of people—the rural poor. It involves extending the benefits of development to the poorest among those who seek a livelihood in rural areas. The group involves small-scale farmers, tenants and the landless. A strategy for rural development must recognize three points. Firstly, the rate of transfer of people out of low productivity agriculture and related activities into more rewarding pursuits has been slow. . . . Secondly, the mass of people in the rural areas of developing countries face varying degrees of poverty; their position is likely to get worse if population expands at unprecedented rates while limitations continue to be imposed by available resources, technology, and institutions and organizations. Thirdly, rural areas have labor, land and at least some capital which, if mobilized, could reduce poverty and improve the quality of life. (World Bank 1975, 3)

"Extending the benefits of development" to rural areas overlooked the fact that a majority of the people in the modern sector—the poor urban classes—did not enjoy the fruits of development. Peasants were seen in purely economic terms, as "seeking a livelihood in the rural areas," not as trying to make viable a whole way of life. They were talked about as a group whose "rate of transfer" into "more rewarding activities" had to be accelerated, pretty much in the same way as cows are moved from low-productivity ranches to tightly packed commercial livestock farms where they are fed concentrates. Their "labor" had to be "mobilized" if they were to be taken out of the pit of their poverty—as if subsistence, "low-productivity" farming did not involve labor. Having too many babies naturally was a curse they imposed upon themselves.

Imbued with the major tenets of economistic, reductionistic, and Malthusian thinking, it is not surprising that the World Bank defined rural development as a strategy "concerned with the modernization and monetization of rural society, and with its transition from traditional isolation to integration with the national economy . . . [it] implies greater interaction between the modern and traditional sectors" (1975, 3). These experts would not entertain the idea that too much interaction with the modern sector was the source of peasants' problems. Nor would they give up the belief that modern-sector and macroeconomic policies continued to be the most important for development theory (16), even if a few sentences earlier too much concern with growth had been blamed for rural poverty!

This imperialism in representation reflects structural and institutionalized power relations; it is a mechanism of truth production more than of repression. The rural development discourse repeats the same relations that has defined development discourse since its emergence: the fact that development is about growth, about capital, about technology, about becoming modern. Nothing else. "Traditional peasants need to be modernized; they need to be given access to capital, technology, and adequate assistance. Only in this way can production and productivity be increased." These statements were uttered pretty much in the same way in 1949 (World Bank mission to Colombia) as in 1960 (the Alliance for Progress) and in 1973 (McNamara's speech), and today they are still repeated ad nauseam in many quarters. Such a poverty of the imagination, one may think. The persistence of such a monotonous discourse is precisely what is most puzzling.

This persistence, especially in light of the unassuaged intensity of the problems these programs are supposed to solve, cannot be explained in any way but by acknowledging a remarkable productivity in terms of power relations. What the IRD discourse achieves is the integration of those statements which reproduce, as it were, the world we know: a world of production and markets, of good and bad, of developed and underdeveloped, of aid, of investment by multinational corporations, of science and technology, of progress and happiness, of individuality and economics. This curve of integration of statements influences our perceptions greatly; the orderings, prioritizations, and serializations in which it relies circumscribe the Third World, fragment and recompose the countryside and its people, manipulate visibilities, act on imperfections or deficiencies (of capital, of technology, of knowledge, perhaps even of the right skin color), make projects happen; in short, they ensure a certain functioning of power.

Integrated rural development differentiates tradition and modernity, making them distinct by creating strata that encompass both. As a regime of statements and a field of visibilities, in short, as a discourse, IRD is summoned by and at the same time constitutes and reproduces the apparatus of development. And it does so even if between the statements that it produces and the visibilities it organizes there exists a noticeable gap; for, are not the statements about the improvement of people's conditions? And are not visibilities about practices of discipline and control, about managing social relations? This disjunction between statements and visibilities is a characteristic feature of discourse (Deleuze 1988). At this level, the green revolution and IRD are the same thing, even if they define different fields of statements and visibilities.

It is important to keep in mind that the entire debate is primarily about food production. What is involved in agricultural strategies such as IRD is the further expansion of the type of agriculture responsible for the emergence of modern food (fully commodified and industrially produced food products of remarkable uniformity, perhaps best exemplified in sliced white bread as a standard of modern life), with the concomitant effect of generalizing the culturally accepted transformation of natural products, which in our days accounts for genetically improved corn, tomatoes, or milk—instances of nature "improved upon" by culture (Goodman, Sorj, and Wilkinson 1987). The process, however, has not been successful; food production has not increased sufficiently, and where it has food has not reached those who need it; consequently, the levels of poverty and malnutrition have become staggering. This is the political economy that goes with the economy of statements and visibilities organized by the development discourse. The World Bank, master strategist in the game of linking the economies of discourse and production, has been the chief champion and agent of this process. It is worth taking a brief look at the practices of this institution.

The World Bank: An Exemplar of Development

The World Bank is by far the largest international development agency. What this institution stands for and its style of development are well expressed by an anthropologist doing research on local languages of development in Nepal. Her observation concerns an encounter with World Bank

staff in a family planning program, who tried to get her to contribute data on
local life in the countryside:

> Naively, I hadn't realized that health in Nepal's development mostly means
> family planning. I was rather shocked, in fact, to see how much money goes into
> trying to get these folks not to reproduce. And all this seems so incongruous in
> relation to the joy and delight Nepalis find in children. I went back for a week
> to visit the people I'd lived with, and their pleasure in children was the thing I
> most noticed. . . . Which goes only to show how pathetically narrow the World
> Bank's vision is, if it can be a radically new idea to understand what happens at
> the local level. . . . Thus I learned something very important about the World
> Bank in Nepal. To work there you cannot set foot in the real Nepal. Literally.
> Being in the World Bank office assumes you live in a house with running water
> and that you have a driver to take you from door to door.[2]

This is the tip of the iceberg of what Ernest Feder (1983) has called perverse development. The World Bank, however, continues to be the official
policy guide in the development world. In Africa, the World Bank has been
the major foreign donor and the most powerful external force in economic
policy-making; these policies, some argue (Rau 1991; Gran 1986), are largely
responsible for the Sahelian famines of the last three decades. "That most
policy makers in North and South continue to sanction the same institutions,
values, analytic approaches and programs, thus insuring continued starva-
tion, merits comment," writes Guy Gran in his study of the role of development knowledge in the creation of African famines (1986, 275). The comment that needs to be made is how the World Bank achieves this feat.

The importance of the World Bank in the Third World derives in part
from the volume of lending but is greatly amplified through a series of practices, critically analyzed by Cheryl Payer (1982, 1991). Cofinancing with
other funding agencies is one such practice; it relies on the World Bank's
persuading other funding agencies to participate in projects that have been
already appraised by the Bank. The World Bank also engages in mutual-
assistance agreements with UN agencies, particularly FAO, whose professional staff have helped the World Bank prepare agriculture and rural development projects. The World Bank also coordinates the so-called donor
clubs, which determine external financing of a select group of Third World
countries. Colombia is one of those selected countries. Since 1963, Colombia's Consultative Group has been meeting periodically in Paris (Bogotá is
clearly not fancy enough for these international financiers, including their
Colombian counterparts), with the World Bank coordinating the donor
group, which includes private banks and official development agencies from
the United States, United Kingdom, Germany, Japan, Holland, France,
Italy, Canada, and a few other European countries. In the 1979 Paris meeting, for instance, Colombian government economists negotiated loans for

about $1.5 billion a year for the period 1979–1983, mostly from private banks (including $600 million from the Chemical Bank of New York). One of those loans went to DRI (Banco de la República 1979).

Most of the loans the World Bank disbursed correspond to projects subjected to international bidding. Needless to say, most often the contracts go to multinational companies, which reap the profits of this multibillion-dollar market (a cumulative $80 billion at the end of 1980, of which about 80 percent had been allocated through "international competitive bidding," mostly awarded to multinationals and experts from the First World). This is how the World Bank maintains intellectual and financial hegemony in development: it channels the largest amount of funds; it opens new regions to investment through transportation, electrification, and telecommunications projects; it contributes to the spread of MNCs through contracts; it deepens dependence on international markets by insisting on production for exports; it refuses to lend to "unfriendly governments" (such as Chile under Allende); it opposes protectionist measures of local industries; it fosters the loss of control of resources by local people by insisting on large projects that benefit national elites and MNCs; it responds closely to the interests of international capitalism in general and U.S. foreign policy in particular (the United States controls about 21 percent of the voting power, with the top five—the United States, United Kingdom, Germany, France, and Japan—controlling almost 45 percent); and it collaborates with and helps maintain in power corrupt and undemocratic regimes throughout the Third World (Brazil, Mexico, Indonesia, South Korea, Turkey, Colombia, and the Philippines had been the major borrowers, in that order, until 1981) (Payer 1982).

The World Bank, on the other hand, exercises a bureaucratics that ensures the institution against responsibility thorugh a series of practices. Its field missions usually rely on official contacts in capital cities and are programmed according to what Robert Chambers rightly called "rural and urban development tourism" (which refers not so much to the mission members' traveling first class and staying at the best hotels, which they invariably do, but rather to their style of work); its learning about a country's problems is achieved through the lens of neoclassical economics, which is the only one compatible with its predetermined model (about 70 percent of the World Bank's professional staff are economists; a good portion of the remaining 30 percent are engineers); and it never discusses in any significant way the underlying causes of the problems it deals with—for instance, the lengthy appraisal report for PAN's loan devoted one paragraph to discussing "the causes of malnutrition" and another to "the consequences of malnutrition," whereas most of the report was devoted to technical and economic discussions, including cost-benefit analysis (World Bank 1977). It is then not surprising that A. W. Clausen, who came to the World Bank to succeed Mc-Namara from his post as president of Bank of America, could say that "the

heart of Africa's economic crisis is the low rate of return on its capital investment" (quoted in Gran 1986, 279), in spite of well-known studies that show
the African famines to be the result of complex socioeconomic and historical
processes (Watts 1983).

Gran concludes:

> The World Bank generates knowledge and transforms it into policy and prac-
> tice by means of a remarkably closed, insular and elitist process. Neo-classical
> economists in Washington rather than African peasants define both the prob-
> lem and the solution for African rural development. . . . The current situation is
> a dialogue of elites. . . . The absence of peasant participation matters. (1986,
> 277, 278)

As a pacesetter in the development industry, the World Bank influences
decisively the fate of the nearly $60-billion-a-year offical aid to the South. As
already mentioned, up to 80 percent of that aid is spent in donor countries
on the contracts and salaries of staff and consultants, representing a not
insignificant subsidy to the domestic economies of the First World, paid for
mostly by its working people. Indeed, thousands of domestic jobs in the
First World depend on development aid. This aid also contributes to spreading the commercial interests of First World corporations. Of the fifty largest
customers of U.S. commodity corporations (Cargill, Monsanto, General
Foods, and so on), thirty are developing countries, and of these thirty the
majority are or were major recipients of Food for Peace (P.L. 480) aid (Hancock 1989). This is not a coincidence; it makes patently clear the role of
development aid in creating business opportunities for First World elite
interests. Finally, the fact that the higher echelons of development organizations—particularly the World Bank and the IMF—earn extremely high salaries even by First World standards and enjoy substantial fringe benefits does
not seem to produce moral qualms in the minds of these lords of poverty and
aristocrats of mercy, as Hancock calls international bureaucrats in his study
of development aid (1989). Hancock rightly denounces this situation as an
indecency of major proportions built on the backs of working people in the
Third and First worlds.

Finally, the impact of World Bank financing on a single country can be
immense, even in cases where this influence does not take the form of overt
meddling in matters of internal policy and overall development approach, as
in Colombia. With the exception of one year (1957), the World Bank has
extended loans to Colombia in every year since 1949. These loans have been
negotiated for the most part at the annual Paris meeting, out of a list of
projects prepared jointly by the World Bank and the Department of National Planning. In terms of dollars per capita, Colombia ranks first among
World Bank loan recipients. The influence of this volume of lending has
been felt primarily in areas such as the cycle of capital formation (acting as

a disincentive to domestic financing of public investment), sector policy development (contributing to sectoral disarticulation, because of its concentration on industrial schemes, roads, and electricity), and institutional buildup (strengthening the cutting-edge technocractic and modernizing institutions). Although electricity generation has been given high priority, the World Bank has been extremely reluctant to support water-supply projects (Londoño and Perry 1985). This reveals not only the capitalist modernizing bent of the institution but also its lack of concern for the welfare of poor people in the Third World.

Even if national planners admit that there are internal errors in policy formulation, the Colombian experience unmistakably shows the influence of international lending institutions. Between 1968 and 1985, external credit financed between 25 percent and 38 percent of total public investment. This financing is actually more critical, because the government gives central importance to projects that have external funds. Indeed, as Londoño and Perry conclude in their study of the presence of the World Bank in Colombia, "There has not been any important public investment projects without some external financing" (1985, 213). This presence became more decisive after 1985, when the World Bank and the IMF forced a conventional stabilization program on the government which contradicted the recommendation of national planners and only worsened the balance-of-payments problem (Londoño and Perry 1985). As Payer (1991) rightly affirms in her study of the Latin American debt, these institutions act more like arsonists than fire fighters, to the extent that their maneuvers contribute to creating or worsening the debt problem. After reading Payer's elaborate argument, it is difficult not to entertain seriously the thought that "the Fund and the Bank must be considered among the major perpetrators of the debt crisis" (82).

The impact of the World Bank goes well beyond the economic aspects. This institution should be seen as an agent of economic and cultural imperialism at the service of the global elite. As perhaps no other institution, the World Bank embodies the development apparatus. It deploys development with tremendous efficiency, establishing multiplicities in all corners of the Third World, from which the discourse extends and renews itself.

Decolonizing Representation: The Politics of Cultural Affirmation

Studies of peasant struggles in the context of strategies such as rural development generally focus on the politics of land tenure and the open revolts to take over or recapture land. Despite the crucial importance of this issue, it is necessary to keep in mind that peasant resistance reflects more than the struggle for land and living conditions; it is above all a struggle over symbols and meanings, a cultural struggle. Scott's vivid description of the struggle against the combine harvester introduced by the green revolution in rural

Malaysia, for instance, illustrates well the contest over views of history and the ways of life the new technologies foster (1985, 154–64). Studies of resistance, however, only hint at the cultures from which resistance springs. The forms of resistance and the concept itself are usually theorized in relation to the cultures of the West. It is more difficult for the researcher to learn to habitate the inner interpretive architecture of the resisting culture, which would be the prerequisite for a representation that does not depend so much on Western knowledge practices (Strathern 1988).

In his study of peasant transformation in southwestern Colombia in the 1970s, Michael Taussig concluded that the effect of the introduction of the green revolution and integrated rural development had to be examined in terms of two clashing cultural possibilities: one based on use-value—a peasant economy geared toward the satisfaction of needs defined qualitatively; and another based on exchange value, with its drive toward accumulation and profit and its quantitative rationality. Confronted with the new way of ordering economic life that DRI and similar programs introduced, the black peasant communities of this part of the country gave a series of responses (such as the devil contracts) with which they sought to counteract the imposition of commodity production on their customary ways (Taussig 1980).

Similarly, Gudeman and Rivera (1990, 1993) demonstrate the coexistence of two different economies in the Latin American countryside: one based on livelihood, the other on acquisition. As mentioned, peasant and market economies encompass aspects of both types, although the economy of livelihood still predominates in the peasant world. The livelihood economy is not ruled by the rationality laws of the market system. Peasants, for instance, keep accounts of only those activities which are fully monetized. They continually innovate and attune their practices through trial and error, in a manner more akin to art than rationality, even if the transformation of the former into the latter is taking place steadily, driven by the acquisition economy. Although profit slowly is becoming a cultural category for peasants, economizing and thrift continue to be central values. The house economy is fueled not by acquisition but by material activities the central principle of which is to care for the base. Included in the base are not only natural resources and material things but also culturally known ways of doing, people, habits, and habitats.

In the maintenance of the livelihood economy—as in Taussig's "use-value" orientation—can be seen a form of resistance that springs from the sheer fact of cultural difference. Peasant cultures in Latin America still evidence a significant contrast to dominant cultures of European origin, in terms of cultural constructs and practices regarding the land, food, and the economy. This contrast is greatest in indigenous cultures but is also found to varying degrees among mestizo and black subcultures. Cultural difference serves as the base for current theorizations and politics of various kinds, particularly politics of self-affirmation. Some claim that in the Peruvian Andes, for instance, some preconquest practices might still be alive. This particular group of intellectuals and activists (Proyecto Andino de Tecnologías Campesinas [PRATEC]) seeks not to explain the nature of Andean society in terms of abstract frameworks but to show phenomenologically— through a sort of hermeneutics based on staging peasant discourse—some of the qualities of Andean culture and their validity for the majority of the people in the Peruvian Andes today. Their aim is to contribute to the affirmation and autonomy of Andean culture.

Within the Andean worldview—in PRATEC's exposition[3]—the peasant world is conceived of as a living being, with no separation between people and nature, between individual and community, between society and the gods. This live world continually re-creates itself through mutual caring by all living beings. This caring depends on an intimate and ongoing dialogue between all living beings (including, again, people, nature, and the gods), a sort of affirmation of the essence and will of those involved. This dialogue is maintained through continual interactions that are social and historical. Each plot, for instance, demands different cultivation routines, different practices of caring. No standardized recipes or "packages"—such as those of IRD or the homogenized U.S. agriculture—can hope to encompass this diversity. The prescription of norms for "proper" cultivation is alien to Andean agriculture. Practices and events are never repeated out of a preestablished scheme; on the contrary, knowledge is continually re-created as part of a commitment to strengthening and enriching reality, not to transforming it. Language is alive, its meaning always dictated by the context; language is never permanent or stable. Conversation implies the reenactment of events talked about; words refer to what has been lived rather than to far-off happenings.

PRATEC activists recognize that Andean knowledge and practices have been eroded, yet they emphatically assert the validity of many long-standing practices among rural communities. They believe that peasants have learned to use the instruments of modernity without losing much of their vision of the world. Their project contemplates a process of affirmation and restructuring of Peruvian society following the criteria of anti-imperialism, repeasantization, and a sort of pan-Andean heteregeneous re-ethnicization; it is a strategy of decolonization, agrocentric and geared toward self-sufficiency in food. In the Pacific Coast region of Colombia, mobilized black communities are struggling to articulate and set into motion a process of cultural affirmation that includes, among its guiding principles, the search for ethnic identity, autonomy, and the right to decide on their own perspectives on development and social practice generally. Similar efforts are continually taking place in the Third World, often in contradictory ways, through actions of limited scope and visibility.

The process of gauging experiences such as these from Western perspectives is not easy. Two extremes must be avoided: to embrace them uncritically as alternatives; or to dismiss them as romantic expositions by activists or intellectuals who see in the realities they observe only what they want to see, refusing to acknowledge the crude realities of the world, such as capitalist hegemony and the like. Academics in the West and elsewhere are too apt to fall into the second trap, and progressive activists are more likely to fall into the former. Instead of true or false representations of reality, these accounts of cultural difference should be taken as instances of discourse and counterdiscourse. They reflect struggles centered on the politics of difference, which often—as in the Colombian Pacific Coast—include an explicit critique of development.

As Ana María Alonso (1992) remarked in the context of another peasant struggle at another historical moment, one must be careful not to naturalize "traditional" worlds, that is, valorize as innocent and "natural" an order produced by history (such as the Andean world in PRATEC's case or many of the grassroots alternatives spoken about by activists in various countries). These orders can also be interpreted in terms of specific effects of power and meaning. The "local," moreover, is neither unconnected nor unconstructed, as it is thought at times. The temptation to "consume" grassroots experiences in the market for "alternatives" in the Western academe should also be avoided. As Rey Chow warns (1922), one must resist participating in the reification of Third World experiences that often takes place under such rubrics as multiculturalism and cultural diversity. This reification hides other mechanisms:

> The apparent receptiveness of our curricula to the Third World, a receptiveness that makes full use of non-Western human specimens as instruments for articulation, is something we have to practice and deconstruct at once. . . . We [must] find a resistance to the liberal illusion of the autonomy and independence we can "give" the other. It shows that social knowledge (and the responsibility that this knowledge entails) is not simply a matter of empathy or identification with "the other" whose sorrows and frustrations are being made part of the spectacle. . . . This means that *our* attempts to "explore the 'other' point of view" and "to give it a chance to speak for itself," as the passion of many current discourse goes, must always be distinguished from the other's struggles, no matter how enthusiastically we assume the nonexistence of that distinction. (111, 112)

At the end of chapter 4 I concluded that the struggle over representation and for cultural affirmation must be carried out in conjunction with the struggle against the exploitation of and domination over the conditions of local, regional, national, and global political economies. The two projects are, indeed, one and the same. Capitalist regimes undermine the reproduc-

tion of socially valued forms of identity; by destroying existing cultural practices, development projects destroy elements necessary for cultural affirmation. In World Bank discourse, peasants have to be regulated by new technologies of power that transform them "into the docile subject of the epic of
progress" (Alonso 1992, 412). In many parts of the Third World, however,
rural life is significantly different from what the World Bank would have us
believe. Perhaps the manifold local models that researchers and activists
have begun to describe in recent years can serve as a basis for other regimes
of understanding and practice.

ENGENDERING VISION:
THE DISCOVERY OF WOMEN IN DEVELOPMENT

Women: The Invisible Farmers

The characterization of Colombia's rural population produced by the World
Bank mission of 1949 starts as follows:

> If we exclude housewives, domestic servants, and indefinite categories from the
> 3,300,000 rural people classified in the 1938 census, there were in that year
> about 1,767,000 economically active persons on the 700,000 farms in villages
> under 1,500. (International Bank 1950, 64)

Modern discourses have refused to recognize the productive role of
women. This is a general problem to which feminist scholars have paid close
attention for quite some time. Of more recent concern has been the role
women played in development and the effect of development policies on
them. Beginning with Ester Boserup's *Women's Role in Economic Development* (1970), a number of studies have shown that development has not only
rendered invisible women's contribution to the economy, it has had a detrimental effect on women's economic position and status.[4] Not only have
women's living conditions become more difficult, women's work load has
tended to increase as a result of development interventions. In many cases,
the status of women's work has worsened following their exclusion from
agricultural development programs. The reason for this exclusion is related
to the male bias of both development and the model chosen, that of U.S.
agriculture:

> Development planners have tended to assume that men are the most produc-
> tive workers. There has been worldwide failure to evaluate the contribution of
> women to productive activity. Approaching agricultural development from a
> Western perspective, planners define the U.S. agricultural system as the ideal.
> Women's contribution to agricultural production in the United States has re-
> mained invisible. . . . Programs for women have been in health, family planning,
> nutrition, child care and home economics. . . . For women, the consequences of

development include increased work loads, loss of existing employment, changes in the reward structures for their work, and loss of control of land. (Sachs 1985, 127)

In short, women have been the "invisible farmers." Or, to be more precise, women's visibility has been organized by techniques that consider only their role as reproducers. As Sachs aptly put it, development has practiced "agriculture for men and home economics for women." Up the end of the 1970s, women appeared for the development apparatus only as mothers engaged in feeding babies, pregnant or lactating, procuring water for cooking and cleaning, dealing with children's diseases, or, in the best of cases, growing some food in the home garden to supplement the family diet. Such was the extent of women's lives in most development literature. Only men were considered to be engaged in productive activities, and, consequently, programs intended to improve agricultural production and productivity were geared toward men. In cases where there was training for women, this took place in areas considered natural for them, such as sewing or handicrafts.

This allocation of visibilities was and continues to be embedded in concrete practices, despite the changes I will discuss shortly. Most agriculture experts and extension agents are male, trained by male experts, and prepared to cater and interact chiefly with male farmers; male farmers are the beneficiaries of whatever social and technological improvements take place in agriculture: they are the recipients of innovations, are allocated the best lands, concentrate on the production of crops that have a higher market content, and participate more fully in local and regional cash economies. Inevitably, the status of women's work declines as women are relegated to subsistence activities. When technical improvements occur in productive activities that are dominated by women, these are usually transferred to men; for instance, when a crop grown by women becomes mechanized, the control of tractors or tools goes not to women but to men. If there is labor displaced by new technologies, it is usually women who are disposed of first. Where there is a technological innovation that may ease the burden of women's work—grain mills replacing the mortar and pestle—women tend to be left jobless or proletarianized in the most precarious conditions. Women's work is not viewed as skilled, and if it is, it may be in the process of being deskilled. If malnutrition exists in a household, it is seen primarily as the responsibility of the mother; and when food is distributed in the family, usually the man of the house (if there is one) is served first. All of these effects have had negative consequences for the well-being of women and children (Latham 1988).

International training supported by FAO and U.S. AID followed the same division of intellectual labor: agriculture for men, home economics for women. As some feminist writers observe, development managed to modernize patriarchy, with grave consequences for Third World women (Mitter 1986; SID 1986). Modernized patriarchy also hides the fact that women's unpaid and low-paid labor has provided much of the basis for "modernization" (Simmons 1992). The invisibility of women in rural development programs was more paradoxical if we consider that according to an FAO estimate about 50 percent of the world's food for direct consumption is produced by women, and that increasingly rural households are headed by women—for instance, in Colombia 23 percent of urban households and 16 percent of rural households are headed by women (León, Prieto, and Salazar 1987, 137). We may assume that this was the result of a type of blindness that the development apparatus could easily correct, but it is perhaps more accurate to contend that development finds support in existing patriarchal structures (both in developed and in developing countries) to organize a particular economy of visibilities.

In some cases, women farmers' resistance to development interventions gives an indication of patriarchal power at work. Taussig (1978), for instance, found that women farmers resisted the adoption of the rural development strategy that the government has pushed since the early 1970s in the Cauca Valley region of Colombia. This strategy was based on monoculture and production for the market. Women farmers preferred to continue with their local practice, which included a more systemic pattern of cultivation, based on intercropping and growing both cash and food crops, a combination that ensured steady, even if little, income and the spread of labor evenly throughout the year. Government agents insisted that fruit trees should be cut, a practice that women farmers adamantly opposed. Most male farmers, however, embraced the new approach, lured by the prospects of producing for the market and having access to cash.

As in many other parts of the Third World, this strategy led to a further concentration of landholdings and the proletarianization of a larger segment of the local population. Women farmers did not adopt the new approach, in part because they were not pursued by male agents and in part because they foresaw the dangers involved in switching to production solely for the market. It is likely that they would have accepted credit and technical assistance had these been provided with different criteria, more consonant with their interests and ways of cultivation and on a equal footing with male farmers. The fact that this was not the case resulted, as Rubbo's (1975) research in the same region showed, in the deterioration of the position of women throughout the 1970s and 1980s, both in an economic sense and in relation to men. Continued proletarianization and male-biased government policy reconstituted sex roles to facilitate the discipline of the female work force, which was required for the expansion of capitalism in the region. In the process, not only class and labor relations but also gender relations were altered, in many ways to women's disadvantage.

In some countries, development has turned invisible the contribution of women to agricultural production which was locally visible before. Staudt's work on agricultural policy in Kenya has shown that even preindependence agricultural policy was more attentive to women's crucial role in production. This started to change in the 1950s, when land registration and training began to favor men, and took a definite turn against women after independence in 1963, when the country fully embarked on the road to development. Despite the fact that the introduction of improved seeds, for instance, placed added demands on women's labor, agricultural policy had already erased women from its field of visibility. International agencies did not help at all. They typically placed men and women in agriculture and home economics. A Home Economics Division was created within the Ministry of Agriculture with the help of U.S. AID, and this agency provided training in home economics in the United States for its top female officers (Staudt 1984). But one must not get the idea that under colonial rule the situation was necessarily different. Even if development policies seemingly were more detrimental to women than to their colonial counterparts in some countries, the process of destroying women-centered agricultural production practices started with colonialism. This was particularly true in settler states such as Rhodesia, where white patriarchal colonialists colluded with small groups of African men to control and "modernize" not only women but the majority of African men as well (Page 1991).

The situations Staudt and Page described are found in Senegambia, where women-centered rice-production systems were first disrupted with the introduction of peanuts by colonial powers in the nineteenth century. This expansion of commodity production had noticeable consequences for the more egalitarian traditional gender divisions of agricultural labor, shifting labor from task- to crop-specific gender roles. Two of these consequences were a decrease in food self-sufficiency, as land was diverted from rice to peanut production, and increased demand on the labor of women, who were in charge of rice production but under more difficult conditions. As in Kenya, colonial authorities also paid more attention to women farmers, in an attempt to convert the Gambia into a rice bowl that could export great quantities of rice. Beginning in the 1940s, however, men were brought in growing numbers to rice cultivation, a move that women resisted. After World War II, when the British pushed mechanized rice cultivation, women were relegated to wage labor in nonmechanized farm activities, a move they again opposed. In sum, the attempt by colonial powers and the postindependence state to create a reliable paddy peasantry involved the restructuring of gender, conjugal, and family relations. Women's labor power and their knowledge of agro-ecology production, however, remain central to this date, and gender-based struggles continue to shape the trajectory of agrarian change (Carney and Watts 1991). As this brief discussion of African experiences shows, it would be more accurate to say that both colonialism and development have utilized patriarchal practices in their construction of disciplined peasant farmers in the Third World, although the concrete mechanisms of capture have changed throughout the times.

One final aspect of the effect of economic development strategies on women involves the relationship between gender and the changing international division of labor. This has been of growing concern to feminist political economists since the late 1970s, when scholars began to theorize the emergence of an international division of labor based on the shift of manufacturing production to free trade zones and export platforms in the Third World. Rising labor costs in the North, additional costs such as pollution control and higher energy bills, intensification of worldwide competition, and a shift to the right in center states led to a new structure of accumulation based on reproletarianization and de-development in the North and the shift of certain activities to the South (periphery and semiperiphery). This shift was made possible by advances in transportation and communications, the fragmentation of the labor process (which allowed corporations to transfer the labor-intensive parts of a given production process to the Third World while retaining the knowledge-intensive tasks in the center), and a host of concessions given to MNCs by Third World states, such as tax breaks, exemptions on pollution controls, and, more important, a steady supply of docile, cheap workers (Fröbel, Heinrichs, and Kreye 1989; Borrego 1981; Mies 1986).

The fact that young women ended up being the optimal, and preferred, "docile, cheap labor force" was neither a coincidence nor the result of a sudden change of heart on the part of male planners and Third World elites (Benería and Sen 1981; Benería 1982; Fuentes and Ehrenreich 1983; Fernandez Kelly 1983; Ong 1987; Benería and Roldán 1987; Benería and Feldman 1992).[5] The promotion of industrialization in the Third World through export platforms and free trade zones was happening at the same time that calls for "intergrating women into development" were being hailed by international organizations (see the next section). The inclusion of women, however, was based on, and resulted in, the strenghtening of sexist and racist beliefs and practices, which is not the point to discuss here (see especially Fuentes and Ehrenreich 1983; Mies 1986; Ong 1987). Despite the fact that women who worked in factories obtained some independence due to their new source of income, feminist scholars studying this phenomenon agree that the process has been generally detrimental not only to women but to the popular classes of the Third World as a whole. The feminization of the labor force in some industries continues, and it is linked to development schemes; such is the case, for instance, with women in shrimp-

packaging plants in the port of Tumaco in Colombia. The vast majority of
women working in these plants come from rural families who have lost their
lands; they now work under precarious conditions.

In their sustained effort to unveil the twisted rationality and effects of
these processes, Lourdes Benería and other political economists recently
have focused on the effects on women of so-called structural adjustment
policies (SAPs) forced by the World Bank and the IMF on Third World
countries since the early 1980s. The general finding is that the burden of
SAP, although affecting drastically the middle and popular classes as a
whole, has fallen harder on poor women. Yet the studies also document the
creativity of households in coming up with survival strategies that allow
them to get by on a day-to-day basis. Persistent and aggravated poverty,
however, is changing the character of households and gender relations. The
household has indeed become a place in which families negotiate daily survival strategies; for women, this has meant either greater exposure to the
vagaries of the labor market under conditions of superexploitation or increased participation in the informal sector, under more flexible yet increasingly deteriorating conditions. In many cases, SAPs have led to the intensification of domestic work for women. On the positive side, some case studies
show that the new conditions in the household and the economy at large can
serve as catalysts for social change, such as greater female autonomy in the
family and the community (Benería and Feldman 1992).

It is clear that the new conditions of accumulation and reproduction are
leading to important cultural reconstructions in social and gender relations.
The extent to which these reconstructions alter the social systems that define identity is yet to be seen, although some of the effects are disturbing.
For instance, although in some countries, such as Peru, Bolivia, and Chile,
the crisis has tended to bring women together in various ways, in others
such as Mexico the struggle for survival has been increasingly privatized;
this privatization happens at the expense of the extended family and the
community (Benería 1992). This follows the ideology of privatization espoused by Reagan-Bush economics and the IMF; moreover, it facilitates the
process of flexible accumulation (read: freedom of superexploitation) that
has become so dear to the IMF and the post-Fordist regime of accumulation. We cannot be mistaken about the negative effects of this conquest,
which are felt more by poorer households, many of which are disintegrat-
ing. Benería helps us keep in mind what it is like to live under these conditions. She reports on a conversation she had in Mexico City with a struggling
twenty-three-year-old mother who was wondering whether she and her
family could survive their situation. Benería explains:

> As the mother of four children and housewife of a household classified under
> "extreme poverty," the situation she was referring to actually meant that there
> were no chairs in the house for the interviewers to sit, the children did not wear

shoes, the roof leaked, the floor was not paved, the inside walls were extremely dirty by any standard, the house had only three small rooms (kitchen, dining room, and a bedroom) while some extra space, with very poor conditions, was rented to another large family for very little money. Job insecurity for the father and only occasional paid work for the mother were a constant source of anxiety and even despair. . . . In all cases, the depth of the crisis was felt in a way that escaped statistics and analytical quantification. (1992, 91)

It is extremely important to maintain an awareness of this suffering and yet resist two conclusions. The first is that these women are totally helpless and unable to do anything for themselves. As Ruth Behar has said in her study of a poor market woman from Mexico, we must resist seeing Latin American poor women in terms already fixed in much of the academic and media discourse—as "beasts of burden," mothers and wives, staunch traditionalists, or heroic guerrilla fighters. "If looked from a cultural perspective," Behar continues, "Latin American women can emerge as thinkers, cosmologists, creators of worlds" (1990, 225). Household survival strategies are part of this creativity. However, as Brinda Rao (1991) cautions, the focus on the household should be accompanied by an interpretive account, similar to Behar's, of what household means to women. "Household" must be located within local and transnational paradigms of gender, people, and nature. Similarly, "survival startegies" must not be discussed at the cost of ignoring changes in the subjective dimensions of women's lives. The language of "coping mechanisms" and "survival strategies," although an important step in making visible women's agency, may still contribute to maintaining the image of women as victims, as their dynamism is reduced to short-term defenses of their life conditions within the economic domain (Rao 1991).

The second temptation we must resist is the conclusion that what poor women need is development (modernized patriarchy), which has been exactly the answer given by the international development establishment. In the next section, we study the rationality and danger of this reponse from the perspective of the discursive critique of development; we also look at the responses of some feminists who attempt to develop the discursive critique of WID without losing sight of the harsh conditions under which Third World women live. We then move to Colombian planning circles as they construct, this time, the lives and troubles of peasant women.

The WID Discourse and the Bureaucratization of Feminist Knowledge

The Women in Development (WID) strategy is susceptible of the same kind of analysis applied to the development discourse as a whole. The practice of WID, in other words, is characterized by processes of discursive formation, professionalization, and institutionalization; it also produces instrument-effects that affect women's lives—the women who are the object of the interventions as much as the women planners designing the programs.

According to Nüket Kardam (1991), a WID scholar and practitioner, the term "women in development" was coined by the women's committee of the Washington, D.C., chapter of the largest development nongovernmental organization (NGO), the Society for International Development. This group was influential in shaping U.S. AID's New Directions legislation in 1973, as a result of which the Office of Women in Development was established with the aim of integrating women into the agency's mainstream programming. WID activities also started to increase within the UN system in the early 1970s, leading to the 1975 World Conference in Mexico and the launching of the UN Decade for Women. At the time of the Nairobi Conference (1985), which marked the Decade's end, "there was no question of the consolidation of an international women's movement on a global basis" (Kardam 1991, 10); more specifically, "the discourse about women and development emphasized the contribution women would make to the attainment of general development goals" (12). Many believed that the success of the WID movement would depend on the extent to which it could be successfully institutionalized. To quote Kardam again:

> The responses of development agencies to women in development (WID) issues are shaped by the nature of their relations with other actors of the development assistance regime and by how well these new issues fit into organizational goals and procedures. "Policy entrepreneurs" within agencies can and do act on behalf of WID issues, framing them in ways that will be consistent with organizational goals and procedures, taking advantage of their agency's position in relation to other members of the regime, and developing political clout in order to influence policymaking. Through these means, WID advocates are able to promote a meaningful response. (1991, 2)

A meaningful response to WID issues, indeed, was what Kardam found among the agencies she studied, the United Nations Development Program (UNDP), the World Bank, and the Ford Foundation, even if with variations and limitations. At the World Bank, a Division for Women in Development was established in 1987, although more limited WID activities had begun several years earlier; guidelines for project appraisal on women in development were issued in 1989, accounting among other things for limitations imposed on women's work capacity "by culture and tradition" and making the appeal to "invest in women" as a "cost-effective route to broader development objectives such as improved economic performance, reduction of poverty, greater family welfare, and slower population growth" (quoted in Kardam 1991, 51). These policy formulations echo old home economics conceptions, although this time couched in the language of economic efficiency, motivated by the fact that "investments in human capital for women have a high payoff" (in Kardam 1991, 52). The first WID adviser within the World Bank was a population economist, and the office is housed within the Population and Human Resources Department; this is no coincidence.

By the early 1990s, the Division of Women in Development already had six professional staff members. Although this has given WID issues greater visibility within the organization, its effects are still limited due to a number of institutional constraints; one of these constraints is the lack of corresponding WID specialists within operational departments, which means that WID policy does not necessarily make it into concrete implementable policies and the project circuit. Kardam also found that "WID issues have received a more favorable response from staff members when they were introduced and justified on the basis of economic viability. The more the indispensability of WID components to the economic success of projects can be demonstrated, the more staff members are likely to pay attention" (80). Indeed, as a World Bank economist had put it earlier, the question is to decide how "female labor markets" can be rationalized to ensure more equitable participation by women (Lele 1986). Neoliberal economics and well-intentioned but generally ineffective policy proclamations joined forces in launching WID at the World Bank.

As Adele Mueller's ground-breaking work on WID has made apparent (1986, 1987a, 1987b, 1991), this institutionalized and state-linked development structure has become the organizational basis for the production of knowledge about women in the Third World, filtering in important ways what feminists in developed countries can know about Third World women. Building on Dorothy Smith's work, Mueller takes as a point of departure the insight that the topics with which the WID discourse deals "are not entities in the real world, merely there to be discovered, but rather are already constructed in procedures of rule" carried out by institutions (1987b, 1). This does not mean that many of the conditions of women WID researchers described are not real. It means that this reality serves only as a partial basis for another, institutionally constructed reality that is consonant with conceptualizations of the problems of development already put together in Washington, Ottawa, Rome, and Third World capitals. This power of the development apparatus to name women in ways that lead us to take for granted certain descriptions and solutions has to be made visible, for in the very process of naming, as Mohanty (1991b) says, habitates the possibility of a colonialist effect.

When feminist researchers and development experts take for granted, as the nature of their problem and the focus of their work, the category women in development as it is constructed by the development apparatus, Mueller insists, they take up with it a certain social organization of ruling. The use of standardized procedures and statistics makes inevitable a certain erasure of women's experience. Typified descriptions become "a way of knowing and a way of *not* knowing, a way of talking *about* women and a way of silencing women from speaking about the experience of their own lives as they are organized by unseen and uncontrollable outside forces" (1987b, 8). For Mueller, this has important consequences on two levels: the strengthening of the development apparatus, and the relations between First World feminists and Third World women. Mueller does not hesitate to call the development apparatus "one of the biggest, most male-dominated, most world-dominating institutions" (1991, 1). This does not mean that the work of feminists within WID has been without results. As Mueller is quick to mention, the results of WID in terms of improving women's conditions in the Third World or even providing jobs for women professionals in the United States have been meager. Yet the growth of knowledge and expertise during the last fifteen years, achieved in part as a result of WID, has changed the ground on which women's work, and their effort to reform development, now takes place.

This does not do away with the fact that, as Pam Simmons (1992) states, the call to "integrate" did not come from Third World women, whose position at the end of the UN Decade had worsened. It was development institutions that quickly adopted "the idea that women are good to have around if you are involved in project development" (Simmons 1992, 18). This generates powerful contradictions for feminists working within the development apparatus, as Mueller indicates:

> When the issues and political aims of the women's movement become knotted up with the ruling apparatus, it is no longer on the side of women in the Third World *or* the First World. I want to be very clear: this is not a damnation of feminism as in itself imperialist, but a recognition of the power of ruling forces to appropriate our topics, our language, our action for imperialist purposes which can never be our own. (Mueller 1991, 6)

The WID discourse partakes of all the major practices of development (creation of client categories, structured agendas, bureaucratics, and so on). This effect is well illustrated by the Colombian National Food and Nutrition Plan. Health and nutrition programs permitted PAN to organize a significant part of women's lives; it set in place a series of simultaneous operations to instruct women on the rules of proper nutrition, health, and hygiene; and it rationalized an existing sexual division of labor within the household. In integrating these interventions in a novel fashion, PAN contributed to the regulation of the lives of peasant women. Was all this bad? To answer this complex question, we would have to analyze how these programs fared vis-à-vis gender, class, and cultural relations, a point to which I will come back. But we cannot forget that programs such as PAN participate in the deployment of a type of biopolitics through which a multiplicity of problems are regulated as part of a greater web of power.

Another aspect of Mueller's concern is the mediation that is effected by the development apparatus of the relations between First World feminists and Third World women.[6] Mueller starts by quoting two African women, Marjorie Mbilinyi and Katherine Namuddu, who argue that as women become identified as a problem for capitalist development and WID funding, inevitably "Africa and Africans are recast by non-Africans as research data, or instances of a theory, or cases of a project, all of which come out of and feed directly into centralized information systems" (Mueller 1991, 5). The history and culture of the South are discovered and translated in the journals of the North, only to come back, reconceptualized and repackaged, as development interventions. This troubling aspect of transcultural knowledge creation—which orginates in the objectifying and detached nature of Western knowledge—is not restricted to feminist knowledge. It has been endemic to anthropology and the social sciences (Said 1989; Clifford 1989); despite some progress in the 1980s in terms of imagining new forms of representation, anthropology has yet to give satisfactory answers to the question of the production of knowledge about the "other."

Mueller invites First World feminists to face this predicament by advancing beyond matters of sex bias and integration into development to questioning the very procedures and structures of development as an institution of ruling. This is the only way to resist the bureaucratization of feminist knowledge and start the process of its decolonization. The starting place should be the standpoint of women, "where an interested and located investigation of the social world must begin: at the place where the knower herself sits. The knowers here are the professionals, academics, and bureaucrats who call themselves feminists and Women in Development practitioners" (Mueller 1991, 7). Borrowing from the title of a book, *In and Against the State*—authored by government social workers in London pondering the rationality of women's welfare programs—Mueller advises WID feminists to work "in and against development." Working as an insider implies trying to get at "how things work," that is, "how our practices contribute to and are articulated with the relations that overpower our lives" (Smith 1990, 204).

The risks of this strategy are clear, according to Mueller: exclusion, co-optation, "ghettoization." The prescription for working "in and against" development, however, is epistemologically and politically insightful. It entails examining the modes of knowing that are intensified by participating in specific social systems (Mani 1989), including professional training. It demands resistance to translating Third World realities into a standardized, orderly discourse and bureaucratic courses of action, which assumes in turn resistance to seeing the world only through the conceptualizations provided by professional expertise. It requires, finally, an acute awareness of the professionals' position as mediator between the "needs" of a particular group of women in the Third World and First World agencies. This last aspect—the role of the professional as producer of "expert discourses" that mediate between needs articulation and needs satisfaction—is as crucial to the state as it is to social movements (Fraser 1989).

For Mueller, "in and against" development is a place to begin, a space in which to pursue a more radical strategy of doing one's work from and within "a different social, economic, political and cultural space from that which is provided by Development institutions" (1987b, 2; see also Ferguson 1990, 279–88). The choice does not have to be either/or, nor is it possible to suggest across-the-board strategies. Mueller's shift of focus from Third World women and our need to "help" them to the ruling apparatus is politically promising. One must keep in mind as well the actions of Third World women—whether middle-class feminists or grassroots activists or both—for cues about how power operates and is resisted by women in the Third World. If it is true that women "are good to have around" if you are involved in project development, it is equally true, as Simmons reminds us, that "at the receiving end of [development] projects and plans, however, people are loudly protesting" (1992, 19). Perhaps it is also true that "if women go on defending economic growth, then they are also, by default, defending patriarchal privilege" (19), which does not mean that it is not necessary to contribute to women's struggle for better living conditions. Let us see how Colombian women have engaged in this struggle in and against the WID discourse.

The Struggle for Visibility and Empowerment:
The Program for Development with Peasant Women in Colombia

As in the case of DRI with respect to IRD discourse, programs for peasant women in Colombia have followed a route not completely charted by the international WID discourse, although WID has been an important force in shaping conceptions and policies. The 1988–1993 Programa de Desarrollo Integral Campesino (Program for Integral Peasant Development)—to be implemented as part of DRI's third phase in Colombia—included the Program for Development *with* Peasant Women (Programa para el Desarrollo con la Mujer Campesina [PDMC]). Conceived as one of three parts within the most important component of the Program for Integral Peasant Development, namely, its production strategy, the PDMC represented an important step in the development of policies for rural women in Colombia (DNP/UEA 1988; Fondo DRI 1989a, 1989b, 1989c). The document describing the program starts with the following caution:

> Among the elements considered for DRI III, the most difficult to formulate is
> perhaps the specific component for peasant women. There still exists, on the
> one hand and in the best of cases, skepticism regarding programs with peasant

women. On the other hand, to raise the question of the discrimination or subordination of women is always uncomfortable, since it touches the consciousness
of everybody. Yet once the responsibility to implement programs on behalf of
women is assumed, the awareness of this very situation generates the necessary
conviction and strength to persist in the endeavor, even if this represents a daily
struggle at all levels. This by itself justifies the allocation of resources to direct
actions with and on behalf of peasant women. (Fondo DRI 1989c, 1)

Feminists in many parts of the world will recognize and identify with this
statement. From the 1949 characterization of the Colombian population by
the World Bank mission, which made women invisible, to this formulation,
most certainly written by a female planner, there is a great distance. The
PDMC has also gained some distance from the traditional women's programs conceived along the lines of home economics principles. In fact, most
of the resources for the program are to be devoted to aspects such as production, credit, and technological assistance for agricultural production.
Women, in other words, are recognized in the program as active and independent producers, not only as home makers and secondary breadwinners.

The transition from home economics approaches to strategies of rural development for and with women occurred in a few years. It is important to
analyze this transformation from the prespectives of the politics of discourse,
gender, and the economy. Let us start with a review of the most important
events that led to the new strategy. Until the mid-1970s, government programs for women were conventionally conceived and of limited scope.
Whether they addressed questions of nutrition, health, hygiene, or education—such as the health and nutrition programs carried out by the Colombian Institute for Family Welfare (ICBF), or the home garden projects run
by the Colombian Agricultural Institute (ICA)—state policies for poor
women were based on a perception of women as restricted to the domestic
domain. This perception continued throughout the 1970s as "income-gener-
ating" projects introduced in the wake of the United Nations Decade for
Women (1975–1985) devoted resources to projects such as home improvement, manufacturing of handicrafts, and sewing. The projects sought to
make women more productive in those activities considered natural for
them. Although some improvements in areas such as nutrition did take
place, because these projects "accepted as a fact a [certain] sexual division of
labor, they contributed to the subordination of women" (León 1987, 123).

In the early 1980s, a new situation emerged as a result of a complex set of
factors. It is impossible to give an answer valid for all countries. The Colombian case suggests that the state's response to this new situation was shaped
by complex processes involving the increasing presence of women planners
in the government apparatus, the availability of studies conducted by Colombian and Latin American feminist researchers, new macroeconomic situ-

ations, and an international climate favorable to policies targeting women. Let us start with this last factor. Many commentators, particularly in the North, have pointed at the United Nations Decade for Women as the single most important factor fostering the new visibility of women. The UN Decade and WID, in this view, were instrumental in creating spaces for Third World women in which to organize and pursue their agendas, either on their own or through state institutions. They promoted research on women, channeled funds to women's projects, and put First World feminists in touch with Third World women activists, who, in turn, disseminated feminist knowledge among the women groups with which they worked. In addition, the international climate was instrumental in catapulting the issue of the participation of women in development onto the public sectors of the Third World. The fact that international organizations made clear their interest in formulating women's policies at the official level pushed governments in the Third World in this direction.

Feminists in many parts of the Third World recognize the importance of the UN Decade and WID as a factor in the greater scope and visibility their work achieved during the 1980s. As we saw, however, the WID discourse was a mixed blessing, a fact that Third World feminists have also discussed. The international climate also happened to coincide with two other phenomena of the early 1980s: a worsening of the food situation in many countries and declining availability of funding for social services under the impact of the debt crisis. It was thus that states "discovered" rural women (León 1986, 1987). The way in which this took place in Colombia was complicated. As late as 1983, there was no official policy for women in the agricultural sector, let alone women in general. Yet a series of developments were under way that prepared the ground for the adoption at the highest level of government of a National Policy for Development with Peasant Women (DNP/UEA 1984; Ministerio de Agricultura de Colombia 1985). The National Food and Nutrition Plan and the Integrated Rural Development Program, let it be recalled, had merged in 1982. As part of this reorganization, planners had to decide what to do with the few programs for women that existed, principally those at PAN and the National Agriculture Institute. A first attempt to dismantle these programs, opposed by several DRI/PAN women planners, led to the their reformulation on a more stable, although still precarious, basis. During the process, a high-level DRI female planner proposed that the upcoming national meeting of DRI users be convened explicitly in the name of both peasant men and peasant women. Although some women met separately at this meeting, an articulate peasant woman was elected national chair of the DRI Peasant Users' Association.[7]

Also invited to participate in the meeting by the planner in question was an accomplished scholar of rural issues and advocate of the rights of rural women, Magdalena León. León's career as a scholar had already given her a prominent place in the expert community on agrarian issues discussed in the previous chapter. The fact that she was invited to this meeting, however, reveals another set of issues. Although the participation of women in the public sector in Colombia is generally high by many standards, it is particularly so in the country's planning apparatus, which is staffed by highly qualified and trained professionals.[8] As in the case of many other countries in Latin America, most women planners do not see themselves as feminist, yet at times their practice contributes to the advancement of what could be called women's or, in some cases, feminist issues; this takes place as they pursue questions that arise out of their concrete planning practice. In some instances, as in the case just mentioned, planners approach feminist researchers in search of conceptual insights and support for their actions. Feminist researchers not infrequently participate in planning circles, mostly as consultants for research or evaluation of programs dealing with women, under contract with planning agencies, NGOs, or international organizations.

In Colombia, works by feminist scholars in the 1980s was crucial to both making visible the contribution of women to agricultural production and to articulating a set of policies for women (see León 1980, 1985, 1986, 1987, 1993; Rey de Marulanda 1981; León 1982; López and Campillo 1983; Campillo 1983; Bonilla 1985; León and Deere 1986; Bonilla and Vélez 1987; León, Prieto, and Salazar 1987; Medrano and Villar 1988). These works not only gave intellectual legitimacy to studies of peasant women but also provided the basis on which much of state policy was built. Among the most important results of these studies was the documented critique of the assumptions that development is gender neutral and that women are not engaged in agricultural production to any significant degree. Women researchers presented ample evidence to undermine these assumptions.

The work of two women at the Ministry of Agriculture, Cecilia López and Fabiola Campillo (1983), carried out with funding from UNICEF and FAO, was the centerpiece for the design of what became the National Policy for Development with Peasant Women, approved by CONPES in 1984.[9] The avatars of the resulting state policy, however, are another matter. After an initial period of enthusiasm and support during the Betancur administration (1982–1986), and following the departure of López and Campillo, the programs entered a period of disarray while funding for them languished. During the late 1980s, various programs for women were maintained at institutions such as DRI, ICA, and the Agrarian Reform Institute, mostly because they were in the agenda of international agencies. The advent of the Gaviria administration (1990–1994) marked a renaissance for women's policies at the highest level. This time the thrust of the policy was to provide compensatory measures for those groups perceived to be most vulnerable to the ongoing neoliberal adjustment process, namely, women, youth, and the elderly among the popular classes. DRI's PDMC was again reinforced and expanded as significant financial resources were devoted to policies for women.[10]

It is difficult to assess the significance of these policies and the results achieved so far. Because Colombia is one of the first countries to design and implement this type of policies for women, there are no parallels to be drawn yet with experiences in other nations. Although the assumption of gender neutrality has not been abandoned, a certain "gender distension" has taken place, allowing institutional support for women's projects (León 1993). The scope of policies for women has widened throughout the years, to include poor urban women in a limited way and transcend the agricultural focus. A new promising angle has emerged as a result of the move toward decentralization and local autonomy: the possibility of strengthening local and regional organizations as they take charge of the implementation of the new policies. In fact, it was the peasant women organizations that kept alive the debate during the ebbing years of the policy. This move, however, coincides with neoliberal pressures to scale down state operations and privatize welfare and development operations. Women are gaining spaces, yet many of these spaces are narrowing.

As León (1986, 1987, 1993) concludes, Colombian policies for rural women, despite their relative merits, still face important structural limitations. Like Fajardo, León sees access to land as a prerequisite to achieving significant improvements for rural people. In this way, as many other Latin American feminists do, León stresses the fact that class and gender cannot be separated from each other. Class and gender are "at a crossroads," to use Benería and Roldán's (1987) expression. Yet there are also important gender-specific obstacles to the success of the policies, which arise from the persistence of patriarchal structures in the society; some of these factors include continuing sexual divisions of labor within the household, a slow reponse to the incorporation of gender on the part of the staff of implementing agencies due to their own unexamined gender identities, and, in general, the lack of articulation of techno-economic strategies seeking to incorporate women into development with explicit measures to undermine patriarchal ideology and culture. In the context of stringent macroeconomic policies, productivist programs for women—often small and isolated from one another—not infrequently represent an added burden to women that do not compensate for their efforts (León 1993). The productivist logic of the opening to world markets is intended more to make women produce and reproduce efficiently than to support women's lives as autonomous human beings.

The reach of state policies vis-à-vis gender subordination is generating important debates among Latin American researchers. In discussing the Nicaraguan experience during the 1980s, Paola Pérez Alemán, for instance, distinguished among three kinds of situations: the incorporation of women "into the world of men," say, in agrarian cooperatives or predominantly male peasant organizations; the organization of women along the lines of traditional gender roles (that is, in the sphere of "reproduction"); and the creation of organizations, particularly in communal and educational areas, that allowed for greater questioning of traditional gender roles. Although the first two types may have been important in creating spaces for women to discuss their problems and share experiences as women, only in the third type of situation could practical gender interests (those directly linked to questions of survival and quality of life, in areas such as food, water, and health) and strategic gender interests (those derived specifically from gender subordination) be articulated (Pérez Alemán 1990).

The distinction between practical and strategic gender interests, originating in the work of Maxine Molyneux (1986), although helpful at some levels, is also problematic. As Amy Lind (1992) maintains, implicit in this approach is the assumption that women's "basic needs" are separate from their "strategic needs," and that a "practical" or a "survival strategy" cannot simultaneously be a political strategy that challenges the social order. This scenario also tends to assume that most poor women are concerned only with their "daily survival" and therefore have no strategic agenda beyond their immediate economic struggles. This type of analysis overlooks the critical contributions and challenges that organized poor women represent to the social order. Like Behar (earlier), Lind reminds us that poor women also negotiate power, construct collective identities, and develop critical perspectives on the world in which they live. Women's (and others') struggles to "put food in their mouths" might entail cultural struggles.

In the 1990s, most feminists accept that the division between practical and strategic gender interests is not so easily perceived. Two new strategies are being pursued: to replace "women in development" by "gender in development" as the organizing principle for women's efforts within development; and to complement the productivist approaches that are in vogue with empowerment strategies. The first goal reflects the continued assumption on the part of states that macroeconomic policies are gender neutral; it is intended to mainstream women's issues into the conception and design of economic policy as a whole—to push states into recognizing the real differences that exist between women and men as social subjects, and the need to consider the effect of macro policies on the sexual division of labor. The empowerment approach seeks "to transform the terms under which women are linked to productive activities in such a way that the economic, social and cultural equality of their participation is insured" (León 1993, 17). The result would be public policies with a gender perspective that does not subordinate empowerment to the goals of productivity. It is a question of making sure that biological differences cease to entail gender subordination.

In other words, the participation of women in social production is necessary but not sufficient to overcome women's subordination. Even if the new policies provided spaces for this to happen—to the extent that they might generate changes in the social and political relations between women and men and by strengthening women's organizations at all levels—only the development of gender-based forms of consciousness and organization can provide a firm basis for a lasting improvement of women's condition. This requires specific articulations, for instance, between training programs for peasant women and the development of gender consciousness; and between the promotion of women's organizations and greater gender autonomy (León 1986, 57–60). Only by becoming a new type of social subject, León concludes, can women construct a new development model. This would be a holistic, noneconomistic approach, more humane and just, and would include women's needs as perceived by women themselves; a sort of "Development as if Women Mattered" (Benería and Roldán 1987). But then, perhaps, WID itself will have to be transformed into something different altogether.

One final aspect to be discussed in terms of the relation of women to the development apparatus is whether WID does not entail a certain idea of "liberation" for Third World women. This is another aspect of the relationship between First World feminists and Third World women that is being discussed in hopeful ways, as a way of bringing together, rather than dividing, women across cultures. The critique of universalizing and Eurocentric tendencies within the women's movement and feminist scholarship advanced significantly during the 1980s in the United States (Spelman 1988; Trinh 1989; Mani 1989; hooks 1990; Anzaldúa 1990). The general belief is that the adoption of modern languages of liberation in order to look at Third World women is problematic. "Organizations for the promotion of women's rights," says an African woman quoted by Trinh T. Minh-ha (1989, 107), "tend to . . . assimilate us into a strictly European mentality and historical experience. The African woman, at least in the pre-colonial society, is neither a reflection of man, nor a slave. She feels no need whatsoever to imitate him in order to express their personality."

As Trinh warns, however, caution must be exercised in case this probing into the limitations of the modern languages of women's liberation plays into the defense of male privileges. The first precaution is to avoid assuming the existence of pure, gendered vernacular societies, free of domination. It must be acknowledged, nevertheless, that in many parts of Asia, Africa, and Latin America relations between women and men are gendered in ways that respond to local histories more than to modern structures. The specificity of these relations cannot be subsumed into Western patterns. The languages and practices of modernity, however, have permeated Third World societies to such an extent that it might make necessary the strategic use of modern languages of liberation, along with local idioms; but this use must be accompanied with attempts at showing the historical and culturally specific character of these languages. The fact that women in many parts of the Third World want modernization has to be taken seriously, yet the meaning of this modernization must not be taken for granted. Often it means something quite different from what it means in the West and has been constructed and reconstructed as part of the development encounter.

The study of gender as difference (Trinh 1989) has to be told from a non-ethnocentric feminist perspective. The difficulties are clear enough, for this entails developing languages through which women's oppression can be made visible cross-culturally without reinforcing—actually disallowing—the thought that women have to be developed and traditions revamped along Western lines. The work of some feminist anthropologists and Third World feminists seems to be going in this direction. Frédérique Apffel-Marglin (1992), for instance, has reinterpreted taboos surrounding menstruation in Orissa, India, as a way to challenge the discourse of development. Developmentalists oppose these taboos in the name of liberating women and bringing their communities "out of the past." Apffel-Marglin's complex interpretation, on the contrary, explains the menstrual taboos as arising from interrelated practices linking nature, gods and goddesses, community, and women and men as part of the cycle of life in a gendered society that still practices noncommodified ways of knowing. It is only from the perspective of the commodified individual, Apffel-Marglin concludes, that many traditional practices such as the taboos of menstruation are seen as curtailing freedom and dignity. These revised accounts, to be sure, can be challenged from other perspectives; yet they provide a warning against the uncritical use of Western conceptions.

As in the work of some Third World feminists such as Vandana Shiva (1989, 1992), there is a convergence of interests between feminism and the resistance to modernity that needs to be further explored as part of modernity's anthropology. The possibility that the concept of woman as the subject of liberal humanism may not be appropriate to many Third World contexts, and the refusal to separate women and men in some Third World feminisms, needs to be entertained. Marilyn Strathern has perhaps gone farthest in formulating a nonethnocentric approach to feminist anthropology. For her, "the commodity view of women as 'naturally' objects of men's schemes because of their power to reproduce becomes understandable from certain assumptions inherent in practices of Western knowledge" (1988, 316). In terms of the concept of reproduction so central to much of feminist theory, Strathern's reading of the highly relational Melanesian world entails that Melanesian women "do not make babies"; that is, "women do not replicate raw material, babies in the form of unfashioned natural resources, but produce entities which stand in a social relation to themselves. . . . Children are the outcome of the interaction of multiple others" (316). In the Melanesian society in question, people are not concerned with self-replacement at all; it is persons in relations with others rather than individuals in and of themselves who are the basis of social life.

Within this type of analogic gender, even relations such as mother-child are not autonomous but are produced out of others. Similarly, contrary to most appearances, it is not men's activity that creates society or culture or man's values that become the values of society at large. Even more, one cannot talk of men or women in the abstract. For Strathern, this abstract talk derives from our unexamined notion of society:

> It is when men's collective life is interpreted as a kind of sanctioning or authoritative commentary of life in general that it is assimilated to our organizing metaphor, "society." It is this metaphor which prompts questions about why men should be in the privileged position of determining ideology or creating the very foundations of social order to their advantage. I have suggested that the forms of Melanesian collective life are not adequately described through the Western model of a society, and that however men are depicted it cannot be as authors of such an entity. . . . Melanesian social creativity is not predicated upon a hierarchical view of a world of objects created by natural processes *upon which* social relations are built. Social relations are imagined as a precondition for action, not simply a result of it. (Strathern 1988, 319, 321)

The consequences of this critique of the pillar construct of society—which in anthropology is reflected in the assumption that all societies struggle with the same givens of nature, and thus organized to the same ends—are enormous (see Strathern 1988, 288–344). Strathern's notion of analogic gender also provides a corrective to Ivan Illich's useful theory of vernacular gender, to the extent that the latter still says little about the relational aspect of gendered domains and practices. More generally, it points to the need to develop new languages for examining domination, resistance, and liberation in nonmodern or hybrid ways.

This theoretical detour further exposes the problematic character of the WID discourse, to which we should return to conclude this section. Mexican anthropologist Lourdes Arizpe encapsulated well the logic of the WID discourse. "Everybody," she wrote, "seems to be nowadays preoccupied about the *campesinas*, but very few people are interested in them" (1983, 3). Women, in other words, have become a problem, a subject of preoccupation, but according to interests defined by others. The WID discourse, by conceiving of peasants as "food producers," fragments peasant lives according to a compartmentalization that rural people do not experience and that they resist. Indeed, the rich lives of Third World women are reduced to the prosaic status of human resources for boosting food production. Hence the importance, as Arizpe emphasizes, of creating spaces in which rural women can speak and be heard. We should be mindful that it is in the rearrangement of visibilities and statements that power configurations are changed. This brings us back to the question with which we started this chapter, that of visuality.

Why visuality in relation to women? Rey Chow provides an approximation:

> One of the chief sources of the oppression of women lies in the way they have been consigned to visuality. This consignment is the result of an epistemological mechanism which produces social difference by a formal distribution of positions and which modernism magnifies with the availability of technologies such as cinema. . . . If we take visuality to be, precisely, the nature of the social object that feminism should undertake to criticize, then it is incumbent upon us to analyze the epistemological foundation that supports it. It is, indeed, a foundation in the sense that a production of the West's "others" depends on a logic of visuality that bifurcates "subjects" and "objects" into the incompatible positions of intellectuality and specularity. (1992, 105)

For Chow, this regime of visuality results in constructions that are beyond the individual's grasp and that turn her into a spectacle whose "aesthetic" value increases with its/her increasing helplessness. Placing the human body (or human groups) into a field of vision within the panoptic/enframing logic of modern knowledge systems entails a certain dehumanization and violence. This is patently clear in the case of media representations of women, but also, say, of victims of famine in the Sahel, Irakis or Palestinians in the Middle East, and even Juan Valdez arising at 5 A.M. to pick coffee in "the Colombian Andes" which is destined to help along the work force of the U.S. at the beginning of the day. This, too, is about pornography and scopophilia, where intellectuality and historical agency are placed only on the side of the (Western) viewer, and specularity on that of the passive other. As in the war media, the development apparatus enframes peasants, women, and nature (next section) in a techno-gaze that "signifies the unmarked positions of Man and White" (Haraway 1988, 581). The apparatus "allows the 'others' to be seen, but would not pay attention to what they say" (Chow 1992, 114).

The articulation of the visible and the expressible allowed by the development apparatus is of a different order altogether. This order is constructed so that those who come under its orbit—peasants, women, nature, and a variety of spectacularized Third World others—can "begin the long journey into the world economy" (Visvanathan 1991, 382). The journey, however, is far from complete, and people struggle in manifold ways to break away from the grand avenue of progress. In the rhizomic layout that results from the micropolitics of the social field, there might emerge (in fact, there are always emerging) multiple articulations of statements and visibilities that differ from those dreamed of by bureaucrats at the World Bank and planning offices all over the world.

SUSTAINABLE DEVELOPMENT: THE DEATH OF NATURE
AND THE RISE OF ENVIRONMENT

The Gluttony of Vision and
the Problematization of Global Survival

The opening paragraph of the 1987 report *Our Common Future*, prepared by the World Commission on Environment and Development convened by the United Nations under the chairmanship of the former prime minister of Norway, Gro Harlem Bruntland, starts with the following proposition:

> In the middle of the 20th century, we saw our planet from space for the first time. Historians may eventually find that this vision had a greater impact on thought than did the Copernican revolution of the 16th century, which upset the human self-image by revealing that the earth is not the center of the universe. From space, we saw a small and fragile ball dominated not by human activity and edifice, but by a pattern of clouds, oceans, greenery, and soils. Humanity's inability to fit its doings into that pattern is changing planetary systems, fundamentally. Many such changes are accompanied by life-threatening hazards. This new reality, from which there is no escape, must be recognized—and managed. (World Commission 1987, 1)

Our Common Future launched to the world the strategy of sustainable development as the great alternative for the end of the century and the beginning of the next. Sustainable development would make possible the eradication of poverty and the protection of the environment in one single feat of Western rationality. The discourse is based on cultural histories that are not difficult to trace. Seeing the Earth from space was no great revolution, despite the commission's claim. The vision from space belongs to the paradigm defined by the scientific gaze of the nineteenth-century clinician. But in the same way that "the figures of pain are not conjured away by means of a body of neutralized knowledge; they [are] redistributed in the space in which bodies and eyes meet" (Foucault 1975, 11), the degradation of the Earth is only redistributed and dispersed in the professional discourses of environmentalists, economists, and politicians. The globe and its problems have finally entered rational discourse. Disease is housed in nature in a new manner. And as the medicine of the pathological led to a medicine of the social space (the healthy biological space was also the social space dreamed of by the French Revolution), so will the "medicine of the Earth" result in new constructions of the social that allow nature's health to be preserved. This new construction of the social is what the concept of sustainable development attempts to bring into place.

The Bruntland report inaugurated a period of unprecedented gluttony in the history of vision and knowledge with the concomitant rise of a global "ecocracy." Some might argue that this is too harsh a judgment, so we should carry the argument step by step. The opening paragraph makes clear another important aspect of the sustainable development discourse, the emphasis on management. Management is the twin of gluttonous vision, particularly now when the world is theorized in terms of global systems. The category "global problems" is of recent invention, deriving its main impetus from the ecological fervor fostered by the Club of Rome reports of the 1970s, which provided a distinct vision of the world as a global system where all the parts are interrelated (Sachs 1988). Management has to be of planetary proportions, because we are talking about a "fragile ball." Carrying the baton from Bruntland, *Scientific American*'s September 1989 special issue on managing planet Earth reveals, at its surface, the essence of the managerial attitude. Whether it is the Earth as a whole, its industrial or agricultural systems, its climate, water, or population, what is at stake for these groups of scientists and businessmen—all of them men—is the continuation of the models of growth and development through appropriate management strategies. "What kind of planet do we want? What kind of planet can we get?", asks the author in the opening article (Clark 1989, 48). "We" have the responsibility to manage the human use of planet Earth. "We" "need to move peoples and nations towards sustainability" by effecting a change in values and institutions that parallels the agricultural or industrial revolutions of the past. The question in this discourse is what kind of new manipulations can we invent to make the most of the Earth's "resources."

But who is this "we" who knows what is best for the world as a whole? Once again, we find the familiar figure of the Western scientist turned manager. A full-page picture of a young Nepalese woman "planting a tree as part of the reforestation project" is exemplary of the mind-set of this "we." It is not the women of the Chipko movement in India, for instance—with their militancy, their radically different forms of knowledge and practice of forestry, defending their trees politically and not through carefully managed "reforestation" projects—who are portrayed, but an ahistorical young dark woman, whose control by masculinist and colonialist sciences, as Vandana Shiva (1989) has shown, is ensured in the very act of representation. It is still assumed that the benevolent (white) hand of the West will save the Earth; it is up to the fathers of the World Bank, mediated by Gro Harlem Bruntland, the matriarch scientist, and a few cosmopolitan Third Worlders who made it to the World Commission, to reconcile "humankind" with "nature."

The Western scientist continues to speak for the Earth. God forbid that a Peruvian peasant, an African nomad, or a rubber tapper of the Amazons should have something to say in this regard.

But can reality be "managed"? The concepts of planning and management embody the belief that social change can be engineered and directed, produced at will. Development experts have always entertained the idea that poor countries can more or less smoothly move along the path of progress through planning. Perhaps no other concept has been so insidious, no other idea gone so unchallenged, as modern planning (Escobar 1992a). The narratives of planning and management, always presented as "rational" and "objective," are essential to developers. In this narrative, peasants appear as the half-human, half-cultured benchmark against which the Euro-American world measures its achievements. A similar blindness to these aspects of planning is found in environmental managerialism. The result is that, as they are being incorporated into the world capitalist economy, even the most remote communities in the Third World are torn apart from their local context and redefined as "resources."

It would be tempting to assign the recent interests in the environment on the part of mainstream development experts and politicians to a renewed awareness of ecological processes, or to a fundamental reorientation of development, away from its economistic character. Some of these explanations are true to a limited extent. The rise of the ideology of sustainable development is related to modification in various practices (such as assessing the viability and impact of development projects, obtaining knowledge at the local level, development assistance by NGOs), new social situations (the failure of top-down development projects, unprecedented social and ecological problems associated with that failure, new forms of protest, deficiencies that have become accentuated), and identifiable international economic and technological factors (new international divisions of labor with the concomitant globalization of ecological degradation, coupled with new technologies to measure such degradation). What needs to be explained, however, is precisely why the response to this set of conditions has taken the form that it has, "sustainable development," and what important problems might be associated with it.

Four aspects should be highlighted in this regard. First, the emergence of the concept of sustainable development is part of a broader process of the problematization of global survival that has resulted in a reworking of the relationship between nature and society. This problematization has appeared as a response to the destructive character of post–World War II development, on the one hand, and the rise of environmental movements in both the North and the South, on the other, resulting in a complex internationalization of the environment (Buttel, Hawkins, and Power 1990). What is problematized, however, is not the sustainability of local cultures and realities but rather that of the global ecosystem. But again, the global is defined according to a perception of the world shared by those who rule it. Liberal ecosystems professionals see ecological problems as the result of complex processes that transcend the cultural and local context. Even the slogan Think globally, act locally assumes not only that problems can be defined at a global level but that they are equally compelling for all communities. Ecoliberals believe that because all people are passengers of spaceship Earth, all are equally responsible for environmental degradation. They rarely see that there are a great differences and inequities in resource problems between countries, regions, communities, and classes; and they usually fail to recognize that the responsibility is far from equally shared.

A second aspect regulating the sustainable development discourse is the economy of visibility it fosters. Over the years, ecosystems analysts have discovered the "degrading" activities of the poor but seldom recognized that the problems are rooted in development processes that displaced indigenous communities, disrupted peoples' habitats and occupations, and forced many rural societies to increase pressure on the environment. Although in the seventies ecologists saw that the problem was economic growth and uncontrolled industrialization, in the eighties many of them came to perceive poverty as a problem of great ecological significance. The poor are now admonished for their "irrationality" and their lack of environmental consciousness. Popular and scholarly texts alike are populated with representations of dark and poor peasant masses destroying forests and mountainsides with axes and machetes, thus shifting visibility and blame away from the large industrial polluters in the North and South and from the predatory way of life fostered by capitalism and development to poor peasants and "backward" practices such as swidden agriculture.

Third, the ecodevelopmentalist vision expressed in mainstream sustainable development reproduces the central aspects of economism and developmentalism. Discourses do not replace each other completely but build upon each other as layers that can be only partly separated. The sustainable development discourse redistributes many of the concerns of classical development: basic needs, population, resources, technology, institutional cooperation, food security, and industrialism are all found in the Bruntland report, reconfigured and reshuffled. The report upholds ecological concerns, although with a slightly altered logic. By adopting the concept of sustainable development, two old enemies, growth and the environment, are reconciled (Redclift 1987). The report, after all, focuses less on the negative consequences of economic growth on the environment than on the effects of environmental degradation on growth and potential for growth. It is growth (read: capitalist market expansion), and not the environment, that has to be sustained. Furthermore, because poverty is a cause as well as an effect of environmental problems, growth is needed with the purpose of eliminating poverty, with the purpose, in turn, of protecting the environment. The Bruntland Commission purports that the way to harmonize these conflicting objectives is to establish new forms of management. Environmental managerialism becomes a panacea of sorts.

Fourth, this reconciliation is facilitated by the new concept of "the environment," the importance of which in ecological discourse has grown steadily in the post–World War II period. The development of ecological consciousness that accompanied the rapid growth of industrial civilization also effected the transformation of "nature" into "environment." No longer does nature denote an entity with its own agency, a source of life and discourse; for those committed to the world as resource, the environment becomes an indispensable construct. As the term is used today, environment includes a view of nature according to the urban-industrial system. Everything that is relevant to the functioning of this system becomes part of the environment. The active principle of this conceptualization is the human agent and his/her creations, while nature is confined to an ever more passive role. What circulates are raw materials, industrial products, toxic wastes, "resources"; nature is reduced to stasis, a mere appendage to the environment. Along with the physical deterioration of nature, we are witnessing its symbolic death. That which moves, creates, inspires—that is, the organizing principle of life—now resides in the environment (Sachs 1992).

The ultimate danger of accepting the sustainable development discourse is highlighted by a group of environmental activists from Canada:

> A genuine belief that the Bruntland Report is a big step forward for the environmental/green movement . . . amounts to a selective reading, where the data on environmental degradation and poverty are emphasized, and the growth economics and "resource" orientation of the Report are ignored or downplayed. This point of view says that given the Bruntland Report's endorsement of sustainable development, activists can now point out some particular environmental atrocity and say, "This is not sustainable development." However, environmentalists are thereby accepting a "development" framework for discussion. (Green Web 1989, 6)

Becoming a new client of the development apparatus, in other words, brings with it more than is bargained for: it affirms and contributes to the spread of the dominant economic worldview. This affirmation relies on the inscription of the economic onto the ecological, an inscription that takes place through ecosystems analysis and ecodevelopment. These perspectives accept the scarcity of natural resources as a given, which leads their proponents to stress the need to find the most efficient forms of using resources without threatening the survival of nature and people. As the Bruntlant Report bluntly put it, it is a matter of finding the means to "produce more with less" (World Commission on Environment and Development 1987, 15). The

World Commission is not alone in this endeavor. Year after year, this dictum is reawakened by the World Watch Institute in its *State of the World* report, one of the chief sources for ecodevelopers. Ecology, as Wolfgang Sachs (1988) perceptively says of these reports, is reduced to a higher form of efficiency. Unlike the discourse of the 1970s, which focused on "the limits to growth," the 1980s discourse becomes fixated on the "growth of the limits" (Sachs 1988).

Liberal ecologists and ecodevelopmentalists do not seem to perceive the cultural character of the commercialization of nature and life that is integral to the Western economy, nor do they seriously account for the cultural limits that many societies posed to unchecked production. It is not surprising, then, that their policies are restricted to promoting the "rational" management of resources. As long as environmentalists accept this presupposition, they also accept the imperatives for capital accumulation, material growth, and the disciplining of labor and nature. The epistemological and political reconciliation of economy and ecology proposed by sustainable development is intended to create the impression that only minor adjustments to the market system are needed to launch an era of environmentally sound development, hiding the fact that the economic framework itself cannot hope to accommodate environmental considerations without substantial reform.[11] Furthermore, by rationalizing the defense of nature in economic terms, green economists continue to extend the shadow that economics casts on life and history. These economists "do more than simply propose new strategies; they also tell people how to see nature, society and their own actions. . . . They promote the sustainability of nature and erode the sustainability of culture" (Sachs 1988, 39).

This effect is most clear in the World Bank's approach to sustainable development; this approach is based on the belief that, as the president of the World Bank put it shortly after the publication of the Bruntland report, "sound ecology is good economics" (Conable 1987, 6). The establishment in 1987 of a top-level Environment Department, and the Global Environment Facility (GEF) (read: the Earth as a giant market/utility company under Group of Seven and World Bank control) created in 1992, reinforced the managerial attitute toward nature. "Environmental Planning," said Conable in the same address, "can make the most of nature's resources so that human resourcefulness can make the most of the future" (3). In keeping with 1980s neoliberal orientation, a central role is reserved for the market. As a Harvard economist put it at the 1991 World Bank Annual Conference on Development Economics,

> The source of environmental degradation and sustainability is not growth at all. It is policy and market failures. . . . Show me a depleted resource or a degraded environment and I will show you a subsidy or a failure to establish the basic

conditions that would enable the market to function efficiently. . . . If I had to
present the solution in one sentence, it would be this: All resources should have
titles, and all peoples should have entitlements. (Panayatou 1991, 357, 361)

This is admittedly an extreme view, but it does reflect the tendency toward
the privatization of resources, under the benign but insidious label "intellectual property rights." This discourse—one of the hottest debates in the development literature at the moment—seeks to guarantee control by corporations of the North of the genetic material of the world's biological species,
the majority of which are in the South. Hence the insistence on the part of
corporations and many international organizations and governments of the
North that patents on stock currently in genetic banks or developed in the
future be allowed. Biotechnology thus introduces life fully into industrial
production, to the joy of some and the dismay of many (Hobbelink 1992).
Biotechnology "will be to the Green Revolution what the Green Revolution
was to traditional plant varieties and practices. . . . [It] will significantly
change the context within which technological change in the Third World is
conceptualized and planned" (Buttel, Kenney, and Kloppenburg 1985, 32).

Biotechnology, biodiversity, and intellectual property rights represent a
new turn in sustainable development discourse, as we will see shortly. Shiv
Visvanathan has called the world of Bruntland and sustainable development
a disenchanted cosmos. The Bruntland report is a tale that a disenchanted
(modern) world tells itself about its sad condition. As a renewal of the contract between the modern nation-state and modern science, its vision of the
future is highly impoverished. Visvanathan is particularly concerned with
the potential of sustainable development for colonizing the last areas of
Third World social life that are not yet completely ruled by the logic of the
individual and the market, such as water rights, forests, and sacred groves.
What used to be called the commons is now halfway between the market
and the community, even if economics cannot understand the language of
the commons because the commons have no individuality and do not follow
the rules of scarcity and efficiency. Storytelling and analysis must be generated around the commons in order to replace the language of efficiency with
that of sufficiency, the cultural visibility of the individual with that of community. "What one needs is not a common future but the future as commons" (383). Visvanathan is also concerned with the ascendancy of the sustainable development discourse among ecologists and activists. It is fitting
to end this section with his call for resistance to cooptation, somewhat remi-
niscent of Adele Mueller's warning of the bureaucratization of feminist
knowledge:

> Bruntland seeks a cooptation of the very groups that are creating a new dance
> of politics, where democracy is not merely order and discipline, where earth is
> a magic cosmos, where life is still a mystery to be celebrated. . . . The experts
> of the global state would love to coopt them, turning them into a secondary,

second-rate bunch of consultants, a lower order of nurses and paramedics still assisting the expert as surgeon and physician. It is this that we seek to resist by creating an explosion of imaginations that this club of experts seeks to destroy with its cries of lack and excess. The world of official science and the nation-state is not only destroying soils and silting up lakes, it is *freezing the imagina-tion*. . . . We have to see the Bruntland report as a form of published illiteracy and say a prayer for the energy depleted and the forests lost in publishing the report. And finally, a little prayer, an apology to the tree that supplied the paper for this document. Thank you, tree. (Visvanathan 1991, 384; emphasis added)

The Capitalization of Nature: Two Forms of Ecological Capital

In a recent article, Martin O'Connor (1993) suggests that capital is under-going a significant change in form and is entering an ecological phase. No longer is nature defined and treated as an external, exploitable domain; through a new process of privatization, effected primarily by a shift in repre-sentation, previously uncapitalized aspects of nature and society become, themselves, internal to capital; they become stocks of capital. "Correspond-ingly, the primary dynamic of capitalism changes form, from accumulation and growth feeding on an external domain, to ostensible self-management and conservation of the *system of capitalized nature* closed back on itself" (M. O'Connor 1993, 8). This new form entails a more pervasive semiotic conquest and incorporation of nature as capital, even if calling for the sus-tainable use of resources; it appears when brute appropriation is contested, chiefly by social movements.

Capital's modern form—the conventional, reckless way of appropriating and exploiting resources as raw materials—is thus now accompanied, and potentially being replaced, by this second, postmodern "ecological" form. This section develops the following argument, based on the two forms of capital in its ecological phase: (a) both forms, modern and postmodern, are necessary to capital, given the conditions in the late twentieth century worldwide; (b) both forms require complex discursive articulations that make them possible and legitimate; (c) both forms take on different but in-creasingly overlapping characteristics in the First and Third worlds and must be studied simultaneously; (d) social movements and communities are increasingly faced with the dual task of building alternative productive ra-tionalities and strategies, on the one hand, and resisting semiotically the inroads of the new forms of capital into the fabric of nature and culture, on the other.

The modern form of ecological capital. The first form capital takes in the ecological phase operates according to the logic of modern capitalist ratio-nality; it is being theorized in terms of what James O'Connor calls the sec-ond contradiction of capitalism. The starting point of Marxist crisis theory, let it be remembered, is the contradiction between capitalist productive forces and production relations, or between the production and realization of value and surplus value. This first contradiction is well known to political economists. But there is a second aspect of capitalism that although present since its inception has become pressing only with the aggravation of the ecological crisis and the social forms of protest generated by such a crisis. This is the second contradiction of capitalism (O'Connor 1988, 1989, 1992). The central insight is that we need to refocus on the role of the *conditions of production* for capital and capitalist restructuring, insufficiently theorized by Marx but placed at the center of inquiry by Polanyi (1957b) in his critique of the self-regulating market. Why? Because it has become clear not only that capitalism impairs or destroys the social and environmental conditions on which it relies (including nature and labor) but also that capitalist restructuring increasingly takes place at the expense of those conditions. A "condition of production" is defined as everything that is treated as if it were a commodity even if it is not produced as a commodity according to the laws of value and the market. Labor power, land, nature, urban space, and so on, fit this definition. Recall that Polanyi called land (that is, nature) and labor (that is, human life) fictitious commodities. The history of modernity and capitalism, in this way, must be seen as the progressive capitalization of production conditions. Trees produced capitalistically on plantations can be taken as an exemplar of this process of capitalization, which also includes the scientific and administrative conquest of most domains of economic and social life specific to modernity.

The capitalization of nature is greatly mediated by the state; indeed, the state must be seen as an interface between capital and nature, human beings and space. The capitalization of nature has been central to capitalism ever since primitive accumulation and the enclosure of the commons. The history of capital is thus the history of exploitation of production conditions, including the ways in which capital impairs or destroys its own conditions.[12] Capital's threatening of its own conditions elicits attempts to restructure those conditions in order to reduce costs or defend profits. This restructuring takes place through technological change and by making raw materials and more disciplined labor available more cheaply. These changes, however, often require a higher degree of cooperation and state intervention, as in the case of government development plans and controls to corporations, and as in the case of the World Bank's insistence that countries develop "national environmental plans" (even if for capital's sustained profits). The existence of more visible policies of this type means that these processes are becoming more social and potentially the rallying points for political struggles. Lobbies by NGOs and Third World environmental groups to control the World Bank, for instance, are a reflection of this greater socialization of the process of capital.

Social struggles generated around the defense of production conditions—such as occupational health and safety movements, women's movements around the politics of the body or basic needs, mobilization against toxic waste dumping in poor neighborhoods of the North or poor countries in the South—also make more visible the social character of the production (and necessary reconstruction) of life, nature, and space. These struggles tend to alter the social relations of reproduction of production conditions. There are two sides to these struggles: the struggle to protect the conditions of production and life itself in the face of capital's recklessness and excess; and the struggle over the policies of capital and the state to restructure production conditions (usually via further capitalization and privatization). In other words, social movements have to face simultaneously the destruction of life, the body, nature, and space and the crisis-induced restructuring of these conditions (J. O'Connor 1988).

Struggles against poverty and exploitation can be ecological struggles to the extent that the poor attempt to keep natural resources under communal, not market, control and resist the crematistic valorization of nature. The rural poor in particular, because of their different culture, practice a certain "ecologism," contributing to the conservation of resources (Martínez Alier 1992). Often ecological struggles are also gender struggles. Many aspects of the destruction of production conditions—arising from deforestation and the damming of rivers, for example, and reflected in increasingly difficult access to food, water, and fuel, all of which are women's tasks in many parts of the world—affect women particularly and contribute to restructuring class and gender relations.[13] Women sometimes are able to seize these conditions to struggle for the defense of production conditions and their identities. Generally speaking, women's struggles against the capitalization of nature and patriarchal control have remained largely invisible. There is a great need to incorporate gender and women's struggles into the theorization of capital and nature. Many of the questions that feminists have addressed to development are yet to be tackled by green economists and other environmentalists (Harcourt 1994).

This question is perceived to some extent as a debate between essentialism and materialism.[14] Although critical of essentialism, some ecofeminists (Mellor 1992; Holland-Cunz in Kuletz 1992) nevertheless highlight the need to address "the central question of how we theorize the very real question of the finite nature of the planet and the biological differences of women and men" (Mellor 1992, 46). The relevance of biological differences has been overlooked in political economy; "what is incorporated into the sphere of 'production' does not just represent the interest of capital, it represents the interest of men" (51). A feminist green socialism must start by recognizing that men have stakes in controlling women's sexuality and relations to life and nature. Some feminists have moved toward a synthesis of materialist and essentialist perspectives, even if recognizing the limitations of the latter. The key to this synthesis is to arrive at materialist and nonpatriarchal formulations of the historical proximity of women and nature which do not overlook the fact that human beings are cultural and biological entities, material and emotional at the same time (Holland-Cunz in Kuletz 1992).

A related aspect, also undeveloped in most ecological conceptions, is the role of culture and discourse in organizing and mediating nature and production conditions. Behind this question is the relationship between natural and historical processes. Mexican ecosocialist Enrique Leff believes that we do not have yet adequate conceptualizations of the mutual inscription of nature and history. True, as the ecological becomes part of the accumulation process, the natural is absorbed into history and thus can be studied by historical materialism. Yet culture still remains an important mediating instance; capital's effects and modes of operation are always shaped by the practices of the culture in which such transformation takes place (Godelier 1986; Leff 1986a). When a culture that becomes dominant seeks to maximize not continuity and survival but material benefits, then a certain articulation between the biological and the historical is obtained. For Leff, capital accumulation requires the articulation of the sciences to the production process, so that the truths they produce become productive forces in the economic process. Environmental sciences participate in reinscribing nature into the law of value; the lack of epistemological vigilance has resulted in a certain disciplining of environmental themes which has precluded the creation of concepts useful for the formulation of alternative ecological and economic rationalities (Leff 1986b).

The role of sustainable development in articulating conceptions and practices regarding production conditions is clear. Production conditions are not just transformed by capital. They have to be transformed in and through discourse. The sustainable development movement is a massive attempt, perhaps not witnessed since the rise of empirical sciences (Merchant 1980), to resignify nature, resources, the Earth, and human life itself. It is a somewhat clumsy and shortsighted attempt, as we will see briefly when we compare it with the reinvention of nature currently effected by biotechnology, but its importance should not be minimized. Sustainable development is the last attempt to articulate modernity and capitalism before the advent of cyberculture. The resignification of nature as environment; the reinscription of the Earth into capital via the gaze of science; the reinterpretation of poverty as effect of destroyed environments; and the new lease on management and planning as arbiters between people and nature, all of these are effects of the discursive construction of sustainable development. As more and more professionals and activists adopt the grammar of sustainable development, the reinvention of production conditions will be more effective. Institutions, again, will continue to reproduce the world as seen by those who rule it. The accumulation and expanded reproduction of capital also require the accumulation of discourse and cultures, that is, their increased normalization. This normalization is resisted, thus perhaps introducing a contradiction not considered by political economists.[15]

Political economy is a master narrative indebted at the cultural level to the reality that it seeks to sublate, modern capitalism. To be sure, Euro-centered historical materialism and feminisms provide us with illuminating views of the conversion of nature and women into objects of work and production; to this extent they are extremely important. At the same time, however, an effort should be made to understand social life in the Third World (and in the West) through frameworks that do not rely solely on these intellectual achievements. Highlighting the mediation of discourse in capital's modern form is a way to start.

The postmodern form of ecological capital.   Public policy in many parts of the Third World continues to operate on the basis of conventional development, even if increasingly there are areas of the world sold to sustainable development. Martin O'Connor is right, however, in pointing to a qualitative change in the form of capital. If with modernity one can speak of the progressive semiotic conquest of social and cultural life, today this conquest is extended to the very heart of nature and life. Once modernity is consolidated and the economy becomes a seemingly ineluctable reality—a true descriptor of reality for most—capital must broach the question of the domestication of all remaining social and symbolic relations in terms of the code of production. It is no longer capital and labor per se that are at stake, but the reproduction of the code. Social reality becomes, to borrow Baudrillard's (1975) expression, "the mirror of production."

The rising discourse of biodiversity in particular achieves this feat. In this discourse, nature becomes a source of value in itself. Species of flora and fauna are valuable not so much as resources but as reservoirs of value that research and knowledge, along with biotechnology, can release for capital and communities. This is one of the reasons why ethnic and peasant communities in the tropical rain-forest areas of the world are finally being recognized as owners of their territories (or what is left of them), but only to the extent that they accept to treat it—and themselves—as reservoirs of capital. Communities and social movements in various parts of the world are being enticed by biodiversity projects to become "stewards of the social and natural 'capitals' whose sustainable management is, henceforth, both their responsibility and the business of the world economy" (M. O'Connor 1993, 5). Once the semiotic conquest of nature is completed, the sustainable and rational use of the environment becomes an imperative. Here lies the underlying logic of sustainable development and biodiversity discourses.

This new capitalization of nature does not only rely on the semiotic conquest of territories (in terms of biodiversity reserves and new schemes for land ownership and control) and communities (as "stewards" of nature); it also requires the semiotic conquest of local knowledges, to the extent that "saving nature" demands the valuation of local knowledges of sustaining nature. Modern biology is beginning to find local knowledge systems to be useful complements. In these discourses, however, knowledge is seen as something that exists in the "minds" of individual persons (shamans, sages, elders) about external "objects" (plants, species), the medical or economic "utility" of which their bearers are supposed to "transmit" to the modern experts. Local knowledge is not seen as a complex cultural construction, involving not objects but movements and events that are profoundly historical and relational. These forms of knowledge usually have entirely different modes of operation and relations to social and cultural fields (Deleuze and Guattari 1987). By bringing them into the politics of science, local forms of knowledge are recodified by modern science in utilitarian ways.

A brief example will illustrate the logic of the two forms of capital in its ecological phase. The Pacific Coast region of Colombia is one of the areas with the highest biological diversity in the world. Covering about 5.4 million hectares, it is populated by about eight hundred thousand Afro-Colombians and forty thousand indigenous people belonging to various ethnic groups, particularly Emberas and Waunanas. Since the early 1980s, the government has been intent on developing the region and has formulated ambitious development plans (DNP 1983, 1992). Capital has been flowing to parts of the region in the form of investment in African palm oil, large-scale shrimp cultivation, mining, timber, and tourism. The plans and the investments operate in the modern form of capital. They contribute to ecological degradation and the displacement and proletarization of local people. Parallel to this development, however, the government has also launched a more modest but symbolically ambitious project for the protection of the region's almost legendary biological diversity (GEF-PNUD 1993). This project forms part of the global strategy for the protection of biodiversity advanced by the World Bank's Global Environment Facility (GEF) and the United Nations. The project has an innovative design, including aspects such as the systematization of both modern and traditional knowledge of biodiversity and the promotion of organizational forms by the black and indigenous communities of the region.

The biodiversity project obeys the logic of the second form of capital. It has become possible not only due to international trends but also because of increased mobilization by black and indigenous communities in the context of the rights newly accorded to them by the constitutional reform of 1991, which recognizes the rights of ethnic minorities to territorial and cultural autonomy. Moreover, the project has had to accept the communities as important interlocutors, and several black leaders have been able to insert themselves into the project staff. These professionals/activists are aware of the risks involved in participating in such an enterprise, yet they believe that the project presents a space of struggle they cannot afford to ignore. Are these activists merely assisting capital in the semiotic conquest of nature and communities? Are they contributing to the superficial greening of economics and communities? Or, on the contrary, or simultaneously, can they engage in cultural resistance and articulate their own productive strategies? One thing is certain: these processes are taking place in a number of countries with high degrees of biological diversity where GEF is operating. Activists and communities in these countries are faced with the dire need to come up with their own visions or being swept away by developmentalism and biotechnology. It is too soon to tell what the outcome of these struggles will be. The growing black movement in Colombia is an indication that organized communities have more power than most observers will admit, despite the magnitude of the forces that oppose them.

The tasks of articulating alternative productive strategies—autonomous, culturally grounded, and democratic—is difficult. Worldwide, there is no clarity about what those alternatives might look like, even if some general principles have been put forward. For Leff, "There does not exist yet a sufficiently worked out theory of sustainable development based on an ecological rationality" (1992, 62). As we saw, the liberal sustainable development discourse is based, on one hand, on an economistic, not ecological, rationality. Ecosocialism, on the other hand, has not incorporated culture as a mediating instance between the social and the ecological. Leff's attempt is geared toward an integration of the ecological, the technological, and the cultural in what he terms an alternative productive rationality. For Leff, every culture includes a principle of productivity, the basis of a production paradigm that, in the case of many ethnic groups, "is not economistic yet pertains to political economy" (1993, 50). The environment thus must be seen as the articulation of cultural, ecological, economic, and technological processes that must be woven together to generate a balanced and sustained productive system.[16]

The difficulties ahead in the task of building a culture-specific productive strategy are tremendous, beyond the obvious opposition by established interests. Should organized communities, for instance, put prices on biodiversity resources? Develop patents? Impose "sustainable use" of forest resources on their people? Conversely, can they afford not to put prices on their resources? What would be the economic, political, and cultural consequences of either course of action? Can they contribute to the deconstruction of market mechanisms through cultural resistance while playing into the marketing of nature? The worst for these communities would be to opt for conventional development; most already know that. To accede to postdevelopment, communities need to experiment with alternative productive strategies and, simultaneously, practice semiotic resistance to capital's and modernity's restructuring of nature and society. Economic decentralization, debureaucratization of environmental management, political pluralism, cultural autonomy, and ecological productivity can serve as overall criteria to advance this type of strategy. More on this in the concluding chapter.

Cyberculture and the Postmodern Reinvention of Nature

The discourses of biodiversity and biotechnology can be situated within the framework of what Donna Haraway calls the postmodern reinvention of nature. This reinvention is being fostered by sciences such as molecular biology, genetics, and immunology, research trends such as the human genome project, and artificial intelligence and biotechnology. We could be moving from a regime of "organic" (premodern) and "capitalized" (modern) nature to a regime of "constructed" nature effected by novel forms of science and technology (Escobar 1994). In this regime, nature would be built by manifold biopractices.[17]

Haraway's critical reading of twentieth-century science narratives such as primatology and sociobiology intends to make explicit the connection between the content of science and its social context, a connection that is usually rendered invisible through practices of writing and reading that are constitutive of the making of science.[18] If before World War II the dominant idioms of biology were borrowed from human engineering, personality studies, and scientific management, after the war the language of systems analysis became dominant. The new conceptual tools speak of systems and cybernetic machines, feedback mechanisms, optimization and information theory, population genetics, ergonomics, and sociobiology. This shift in paradigms is linked to the logic of control appropriate to postwar capitalism. Machine and market recur as organizing principles but couched in the language of systems and cybernetics. Living beings are conceptualized no longer in terms of hierarchically organized and localized organisms but in terms of coded texts, engineered communications systems, command-control networks, purposeful behavior, and probabilistic outcomes. Pathology comes to be the result of stress and communications breakdown, and the entire immune system is modeled as a battlefield (Haraway 1989b, 1991).

The language of this discourse is decidedly postmodern; it is not inimical to the post-Fordist regime of accumulation, with its cultural order of "flexible labor" that would keep dark invaders at a distance, or quickly phagocytize them if they come close enough or become numerous enough to pose the threats of contagion and disorder. Haraway reads in these developments the denaturalization of the notions of "organism" and "individual," so dear to pre–World War II modern science and political economy, and the emergence of a new entity, the cyborg—a hybrid of organism and machine "appropriate to the late twentieth century" (1991, 1)—which arises to fill the vacuum. In the language of sustainable development, one would say that cyborgs do not belong in/to nature; they belong in/to the environment, and the environment belongs in/to systems.

Taking Simone de Beauvoir's declaration that "one is not born a woman" to the postmodern domain of late-twentieth-century biology, Haraway states that "one is not born an organism. Organisms are made; they are constructs of a world-changing kind" (1989b, 10). Organisms make themselves and are made by history. This deeply historicized account of life is difficult to accept if one remains within the modern traditions of realism, rationalism, and organic nature. The historicized view assumes that what counts as nature and what counts as culture in the West ceaselessy change according to complex historical factors, although in every case nature "remains a crucially important and deeply contested myth and reality" (1989a, 1). Bodies, organisms, and nature are not just passive receptors of the naming power of science; their specificity and affectivity mean that they have an active part in the production of knowledge about them. They must thus be seen as "material-semiotic" actors, rather than as mere objects of science preexisting in purity. But there are other actors in the construction of organisms as objects of knowledge, including humans and machines (visualization technologies, the lab), medical and business practices, and cultural productions of various kinds (narratives of science, origins, systems, and the like). Haraway refers to this complex system that accounts for the construction of organisms as "the apparatus of bodily production" (1989b, 1992). The apparatus reminds us that organisms "are made in world-changing techno-scientific practices by particular collective actors in particular times and places" (1992, 297).

The apparatus of bodily production implies that the boundaries between the organic, the technical, and the textual that make it up are quite permeable. These three domains are no longer neatly separated; any giving organism that becomes an object of science is already a mixture of the three. Although nature, bodies, and organisms certainly have an *organic* basis, they are increasingly produced in conjunction with *machines*, and this production is always mediated by scientific and cultural *narratives*. Nature is a co-construction among humans and nonhumans. We thus have the possibility of engaging in new conversations with and around nature, involving humans and nonhumans together in the reconstruction of nature as public culture. If the cyborg can be seen as the imposition of a new grid of control on the planet, it also represents new possibilities for potent articulations among humans, animals, and machines.

The grasping of this possibility has tremendous implications for Haraway. To begin with, the search for natural matrices and organic wholes—based on the dichotomies between mind and body, machine and organism, animal and human—has to be abandoned or drastically reformed. The possibility that the organic is not opposed to the technological must be entertained; even more, "there are great riches for feminists in explicitly embracing the possibilities inherent in the breakdown of clean distinctions between organism and machine and similar distinctions structuring the Western self" (Haraway 1985, 92).[19] Cyborgs are not necessarily the enemy. This also means that socialists, feminists, and others should devote attention to the social relations of science and technology, to the extent that they mediate and shape the construction of ourselves, our bodies, and nature. Haraway's call is to embrace "the skillfull task of reconstructing the boundaries of daily life, in partial connection with others [humans, organisms, and machines], in communication with all our parts" (1985, 100). This requires new imaginations, figurations of difference stemming from those opposed to the unmarked category of the white male, the universal norm against which others have to measure their achievements.

The historicization of nature's construction has been the object of discussion by others in various traditions. Adorno's and Benjamin's dialectic of nature and history, of naturalized history and historicized nature, showed what was radically new about industrialism and modernity: the experience of nature as commodity, that is, as an arrested form of history (to the extent that it reflects the displacement of nature's transiency onto commodities); the "veil" thrown onto nature by the ideology of nature as object to be appropriated (enframing); and what these authors considered the prehistoric, barbaric state of modern history. Also adumbrated by Benjamin were the possibility of working through this prehistory (from Marx) through a new dialectics of seeing, of bringing about new configurations of nature and history that reveal the ways in which nature is inevitably inmersed in history, the agency and aliveness of nature itself, the ways in which natural objects "do not submit to language signs meekly, but have the semantic strength to set the signs into question" (Buck-Morss 1990, 60).[20]

Like Haraway, Benjamin would like us to join the technological capacity to produce with the utopian capacity to dream, and vice versa; that is, to transform the ruins inherited from historical nature (as in Haraway's readings of modern artifacts and discourses) and the fossils of naturalized history (such as the body as commodity) in order to infuse new life into mythic (fetishized) history and mythic nature (the images of cyberspaces to be created) through a dialectics of dreaming and waking. Haraway's language and vision are perhaps more appropriate for our age. They also highlight aspects that are important to other cultures, such as nature's agency and the belief that nature is a co-construction between humans and nonhumans (including the mythic and the spiritual). One chief difference is the separation of humans and nature present in Haraway's work, even if she calls on us to see nature as subject. This is a reflection of a contextual difference between the First and Third World.

Critics of the new technologies usually paint a bleak future. But perhaps the birth of cyberculture—as a truly postindustrial and postmodern society—also entails a certain cultural promise for more just social configurations. But the obstacles and risks ahead are clear. New knowledge and power configurations are narrowing down on life and labor, particularly in biotechnology. These practices are perhaps exemplified by the human genome project, an initiative intended to map the entire human genome. The new genetics "will prove to be an infinitely greater force for reshaping society and life than was the revolution in physics, because it will be embedded throughout the social fabric at the micro-level by medical practices and a variety of other discourses" (Rabinow 1992, 241). The new regime of biosociality, as Paul Rabinow has named it, implies that "nature will be modeled on culture understood as practice. Nature will be known and remade through technique and will finally become artificial, just as culture becomes natural" (241).

This might bring with it the dissolution of modern society and of the nature/culture split. Genetics, immunology, and environmentalism "are the leading vehicles for the infiltration of technoscience, capitalism and culture into what the moderns call 'nature'" (245). According to Evelyn Fox Keller (1992), the new genetics, besides summoning again the ghost of biological determinism, signals the dawn of an era in which nature and culture are radically reconceived. A new "malleability of nature" is proclaimed by molecular biology, which is seen as holding the key to greater happiness for humankind through the promise of the cure for a panoply of genetic diseases, many of which, as Keller rightly notes, are questionably labeled as such. The "right to healthy genes" might well become the battle cry of a host of medical reformers which will require grids of examination more pervasive than those Foucault unveiled in his study of the birth of the clinic (1975).

What all this means for the Third World has yet to be examined. This examination has to start with inventing a new language to speak of these issues from Third World perspectives. Sustainable development will certainly not do. Calls for "catching up" with the West in the production of new technologies, lest the latter's dominance in this domain throw the Third World into even greater forms of dependence (Castells 1986), are also inadequate. The hypothetical proposition that emerging nations could skip industrialization and develop postindustrial societies based on information and biological technologies is attractive but probably unworkable at this point. To the extent that new social practices are being constructed around the new technologies, it is crucial for the Third World to participate in the global conversations that generate such practices; local groups must position themselves in relation to the processes of material and symbolic globalization in ways that allow them to overcome their position of subordination as actors in the global scene.

What are the requirements of knowledge to advance this strategy? Scientific work can produce knowledge that contributes to popular causes and interests. There are types of analyses that are helpful and at times essential to social movements. Some agro-ecologists, for instance, plea for the need to consider multiple perspectives, build communication between different popular groups worldwide, and design institutions capable of accepting a plurality of viewpoints and options (Altieri 1987). These criteria are being proposed by social movements themselves about the work of experts. At the theory level, there is the need to articulate a poststructuralist political economy of ecology and biology. This need goes beyond recognizing that nature is socially constructed to insist that the constructs of political economy and science be analyzed discursively. It reiterates the connection and evolution of bodies, organisms, and communities with the making and evolution of narratives about them. As we saw, the two forms of capital are linked to known discourses. From this perspective, there cannot be a materialist analysis that is not at the same time a discursive analysis.

This chapter has shown the system of transformation of development. Integrated rural development, WID, and sustainable development exhibit features that betray their origin in a common discursive practice. This "endoconsistency" (Deleuze and Guattari 1993) of concepts such as development refers to the concept's systematicity, despite the heterogeneity of the elements that inhabit the space it creates. The repeated bifurcation of development—into discourses such as those analyzed in this chapter—reflect the appearance of new problems, even if the new discourses exist in the same plane of the original concept, and thus contribute to the discourse's self-creation and autoreferentiality. Nothing has really changed at the level of the discourse, even if perhaps the conditions for its continued reproduction have been altered. "Development" continues to reverberate in the social imaginary of states, institutions, and communities, perhaps more so after the inclusion of women, peasants, and nature into its repertoire and imaginative geographies.

Under the title "The Lesson that Rio Forgets," the cover picture of the issue of *The Economist* that appeared the week before the Earth Summit (the United Nations World Conference on Environment and Development held in Rio de Janeiro in June 1992) shows an undifferentiated mass of dark people, the "teeming masses" of the Third World. The "lesson" is population: the expanding masses of the Third World have to be curbed if sustainable development is to be achieved. The fact that the populations of the industrialized world consume a strikingly higher percentage of world resources than their Third World counterparts does not enter into *The Economist*'s equation. By a curious optical twist, the consumption of people of the North is rendered invisible, whereas the dark hordes of the South are consigned to a new round of gluttonous vision.

Worldwide, the new biotechnologies further capitalize nature by planting value into it through scientific research and development. Even human genes become part of the conditions of production, an important arena for capitalist restructuring and, so, for contestation. The reinvention of nature currently under way, effected by and within webs of meaning and production that link the discourses of science and capital, should be incorporated into a political economy of ecology appropriate to the new age whose dawn we are already witnessing. Social movements, intellectuals, and activists have the opportunity to create discourses in which the problematizations of food, gender, and nature are not reduced to one more problem of development, to one more chapter in the history of economic culture. Far from Bruntland, the picture of Earth from space should serve as a basis for visions that allows us to reawaken the awareness of life and the living, to reimagine the relationship between society and nature, and to reconnect life and thought at the level of myth.

Chapter 6

CONCLUSION:
IMAGINING A POSTDEVELOPMENT ERA

> We don't know exactly when we started to talk about
> cultural difference. But at some point we refused to go on
> building a strategy around a catalogue of "problems" and
> "needs." The government continues to bet on democracy
> and development; we respond by emphasizing cultural
> autonomy and the right to be who we are and have our own
> life project. To recognize the need to be different, to build
> an identity, are difficult tasks that demand persistent work
> among our communities, taking their very heterogeneity
> as a point of departure. However, the fact that we do not
> have worked out social and economic alternatives makes
> us vulnerable to the current onslaught by capital. This is
> one of our most important political tasks at present: to
> advance in the formulation and implementation of
> alternative social and economic proposals.
> —Libia Grueso, Leyla Arroyo, and Carlos Rosero,
> the Organization of Black Communities
> of the Pacific Coast of Colombia,
> January 1994

Statistics (1980s)

THE INDUSTRIALIZED COUNTRIES, with 26 percent of the population, account
for 78 percent of world production of goods and services, 81 percent of
energy consumption, 70 percent of chemical fertilizers, and 87 percent of
world armaments. One U.S. resident spends as much energy as 7 Mexicans,
55 Indians, 168 Tanzanians, and 900 Nepalis. In many Third World countries, military expenditures exceed expenditures for health. The cost of one
modern fighter plane can finance forty thousand rural health centers. In
Brazil, the consumption of the 20 percent richest is thirty-three times that of
the 20 percent poorest, and the gap between rich and poor is still growing.
Forty-seven percent of the world's grain production is used for animal feed.
The same amount of grain could feed more than 2 billion people. In Brazil

the area planted with soybeans could feed 40 million people if sown with corn and beans. The world's six larger grain mechants control 90 percent of the global trade of grain, whereas several million people have died of hunger in the Sahel region as a result of famines during the 1980s alone. The tropical rain forest provides about 42 percent of the worlds's plant biomass and oxygen; 600,000 hectares of rain forest are destroyed annually in Mexico alone, 600,000 in Colombia. The amount of coffee that producing countries had to export to obtain one barrel of oil doubled between 1975 and 1982. Third World workers who are in the textile and electronic industries are paid up to twenty times less than their counterparts in Western Europe, the United States, or Japan for doing the same job with at least the same productivity. Since the Latin American debt crisis broke in 1982, Third World debtors have been paying their creditors an average of $30 billion more each year than they have received in new lending. In the same period, the food available to poor people in the Third World has fallen by about 30 percent. One more: the vast majority of the more than 150 wars that have been waged in the world since 1945 have taken place in the Third World, as reflections of superpower confrontations. Even those taking place since the end of the cold war continue to be a reflection of the effects of the struggle for power among the industrialized nations.

One could continue.[1] Statistics tell stories. They are techno-representations endowed with complex political and cultural histories. Within the politics of representation of the Third World, statistics such as these function to entrench the development discourse, often regardless of the political aim of those displaying them. Toward the end of this book, however, one should be able to draw a different reading from these figures: not the reading that reproduces the tale of populations in need of development and aid; nor the reductive interpretation of these figures in terms of pressing needs that call for the "liberation" at any cost of poor people from their suffering and misery; perhaps not even the narrative of exploitation of the South by the North, in the ways in which this story was told up to a decade ago. Instead, one should be able to analyze counting in terms of its political consequences, the way in which it reflects the crafting of subjectivities, the shaping of culture, and the construction of social power—including what these figures say about surplus material and symbolic consumption in those parts of the world that think of themselves as developed. Not the perverse reading, finally, of the International Monetary Fund—insisting on "austerity measures" for the Third World, as if the majority of people in the Third World had known anything but material austerity as a fundamental fact of their daily existence—but a renewed awareness of the suffering of many, of the fact that "the modern world, including the modernized Third World, is built on the suffering and brutalization of millions" (Nandy 1989, 269).

The Third World and the Politics of Representation

"Today something that we do will touch your life." This Union Carbide motto became ironically real after the December 1984 gas leak in Bhopal, India, which affected two hundred thousand people and left at least five thousand dead. Bhopal is not only a reminder of the connection between the choices and power of some and the chances of others, a connection firmly established by the global economy with a deadly appearance of normalcy; as Visvanathan (1986) has suggested, Bhopal is also a metaphor of development as a disater of sorts which demands that the casualties be forgotten and dictates that a community that fails to develop is obsolescent. An entire structure of propaganda, erasure, and amnesia on Bhopal was orchestrated by science, government, and corporations which allowed the language of compensation as the only avenue of expression of outrage and injustice— and even compensation was precarious at best. If, as in the Sahelian famines, those affected cannot be accommodated within the languages of the market, salvation (by U.S. marines or international troops), and semisecularized Christian hope, so much the worse for them. In these examples, the clinical, military, and corporate gazes join their efforts to launch allegedly beneficent and sanitized operations for the good of Mankind (with a capital M, that of Modern Man). Restore Hope, Desert Storm, Panama, and Granada are signs of a so-called new world order.[2]

The development discourse, as this book has shown, has been the central and most ubiquitous operator of the politics of representation and identity in much of Asia, Africa, and Latin America in the post–World War II period. Asia, Africa, and Latin America have witnessed a succession of regimes of representation—originating in colonialism and European modernity but often appropriated as national projects in postindependence Latin America and postcolonial Africa and Asia—each with its accompanying regime of violence. As places of encounter and suppression of local cultures, women, identities, and histories, these regimes of representation are originary sites of violence (Rojas de Ferro 1994). As a regime of representation of this sort, development has been linked to an economy of production and desire, but also of closure, difference, and violence. To be sure, this violence is also mimetic violence, a source of self-formation. Terror and violence circulate and become, themselves, spaces of cultural production (Girard 1977 and Taussig 1987). But the modernized violence introduced with colonialism and development is itself a source of identity. From the will to civilization in the nineteenth century to today, violence has been engendered through representation.

The very existence of the Third World has in fact been wagered, managed, and negotiated around this politics of representation. As an effect of the dicursive practices of development, the Third World is a contested reality whose current status is up for scrutiny and negotiation. For some, the Third World "can be made a symbol of planetary intellectual responsibility . . . it can be read as a text of survival" (Nandy 1989, 275). After the demise of the Second World, the Third and First worlds necessarily have to realign their places and the space of ordering themselves. Yet it is clear that the Third World has become the other of the First with even greater poignancy.[3] "To survive, 'Third World' must necessarily have negative *and* positive connotations: negative when viewed in a vertical ranking system . . . positive when undestood sociopolitically as a subversive, 'non-aligned' force" (Trinh 1989, 97). The term will continue to have currency for quite some time, because it is still an essential construct for those in power. But it can also be made the object of different reimaginings. "The Third World is what holds in trust the rejected selves of the First and the [formerly] Second Worlds . . . before envisioning the global civilization of the future, one must first own up the responsibility of creating a space at the margins of the present global civilization for a new, plural, political ecology of knowledge" (Nandy 1989, 273, 266).

As we will see, however, the Third World should in no way be seen as a reservoir of "traditions." The selves of the Third World are manifold and multiple, including selves that are becoming increasingly illegible according to any known idiom of modernity, given the growing fragmentation, polarization, violence, and uprootedness that are taking hold of various social groups in a number of regions.[4] It is also possible, even likely, that radically reconstituted identities might emerge from some of those spaces that are traversed by the most disarticulating forces and tensions. But it is too soon even to imagine the forms of representation that this process might promote. Instead, at present one seems to be led to paying attention to forms of resistance to development that are more clearly legible, and to the reconstruction of cultural orders that might be happening at the level of popular groups and social movements.

Since the middle and late 1980s, for instance, a relatively coherent body of work has emerged which highlights the role of grassroots movements, local knowledge, and popular power in transforming development. The authors representing this trend state that they are interested not in development alternatives but in alternatives to development, that is, the rejection of the entire paradigm altogether. In spite of significant differences, the members of this group share certain preoccupations and interests:[5] an interest in local culture and knowledge; a critical stance with respect to established scientific discourses; and the defense and promotion of localized, pluralistic grassroots movements. The importance and impact of these movements are far from clear; yet, to use Sheth's (1987) expression, they provide an arena for the pursuit of "alternative development as political practice." Beyond, in spite of, against development: these are metaphors that a number of Third

World authors and grassroots movements use to imagine alternatives to development and to "marginalize the economy"—another metaphor that speaks of strategies to contain the Western economy as a system of production, power, and signification.

The grassroots movements that emerged in opposition to development throughout the 1980s belong to the novel forms of collective action and social mobilization that characterized that decade. Some argue that the 1980s movements changed significantly the character of the political culture and political practice (Laclau and Mouffe 1985; Escobar and Alvarez 1992). Resistance to development was one of the ways in which Third World groups attempted to construct new identities. Far from the essentializing assumptions of previous political theory (for example, that mobilization was based on class, gender, or ethnicity as fixed catagories), these processes of identity construction were more flexible, modest, and mobile, relying on tactical articulations arising out of the conditions and practices of daily life. To this extent, these struggles were fundamentally cultural. Some of these forms and styles of protest will continue throughout the 1990s.

Imaging the end of development as a regime of representation raises all sorts of social, political, and theoretical questions. Let us start with this last aspect by recalling that discourse is not just words and that words are not "wind, an external whisper, a beating of wings that one has difficulty in hearing in the serious matter of history" (Foucault 1972, 209). Discourse is not the expression of thought; it is a practice, with conditions, rules, and historical transformations. To analyze development as a discourse is "to show that to speak is to do something—something other than to express what one thinks; . . . to show that to add a statement to a pre-existing series of statements is to perform a complicated and costly gesture" (1972, 209). In chapter 5, for instance, I showed how seemingly new statements about women and nature are "costly gestures" of this sort, ways of producing change without transforming the nature of the discourse as a whole.

Said differently, changing the order of discourse is a political question that entails the collective practice of social actors and the restructuring of existing political economies of truth.[6] In the case of development, this may require moving away from development sciences in particular and a partial, strategic move away from conventional Western modes of knowing in general in order to make room for other types of knowledge and experience. This transformation demands not only a change in ideas and statements but the formation of nuclei around which new forms of power and knowledge might converge. These new nuclei may come about in a "serial" manner.[7] Social movements and antidevelopment struggles may contribute to the formation of nuclei of problematized social relations around which novel cultural productions might emerge. The central requirement for a more lasting transformation in the order of discourse is the breakdown of the basic organization of the discourse (chapter 2), that is, the appearance of new rules of formation of statements and visibilities. This may or may not entail new objects and concepts; it may be marked by the reappearance of concepts and practices discarded long ago (new fundamentalisms are a case in point); it may be a slow process but it may also happen with relative rapidity. This transformation will also depend on how new historical situations—such as the divisions of social labor based on high technology—alter what may be constituted as objects of discourse, as well as on the relation between development and other institutions and practices, such as the state, political parties, and the social sciences.

Challenges to development are multiplying, often in dialectical relation to the fragmentary attempts at control inherent in post-Fordist regimes of representation and accumulation; post-Fordism necessarily connects or disconnects selectively regions and communities from the world economy; although always partial, disconnection not infrequently presents attractive opportunities from poor people's perspectives. Some of this is going on in the so-called informal economies of the Third World (the label is an attempt by economic culture to maintain the hold on those realities that exist or emerge at its limits). As local communities in the West and the Third World struggle for incorporation into the world economy, they still might have to develop creative and more autonomous practices that could be more conducive to renegotiating class, gender, and ethnic relations at the local and regional levels.

The process of unmaking development, however, is slow and painful, and there are no easy solutions or prescriptions. From the West, it is much more difficult to perceive that development is at the same time self-destructing and being unmade by social action, even as it continues to destroy people and nature. The dialectic here tends to push for another round of solutions, even if conceived through more radical categories—cultural, ecological, politicoeconomic, and so on. This will not do. The empty defense of development must be left to the bureaucrats of the development apparatus and those who support it, such as the military and (not all of) the corporations. It is up to us, however, to make sure that the life span of the bureaucrats and the experts as producers and enforcers of costly gestures is limited. Development unmade means the inauguration of a discontinuity with the discursive practice of the last forty years, imagining the day when we will not be able to say or even entertain the thoughts that have led to forty years of incredibly irresponsible policies and programs. In some parts of the Third World, this possibility may already be (in some communities it always was) a social reality.

Hybrid Cultures and Postdevelopment in Latin America

It is said that during the 1980s Latin American countries experienced the harshest social and economic conditions since the conquest. But the 1980s also witnessed unprecedented forms of collective mobilization and theoretical renewals of importance, particularly in social movements and in the analysis of modernity and postmodernity. The specificity of the Latin American contribution to the discussions of modernity stems from two main sources: the social and temporal heterogeneity of Latin America modernity, that is, the coexistence—in a coeval way, even if emerging from different cultural temporalities—of premodern, modern, and even antimodern and amodern forms; and the urgency of social questions, coupled with a relatively close relation between intellectual and social life. This basis for critical intellectual work is reflected in the forms and products of analysis, particularly in the following areas: the linking of analyses of popular culture with social and political struggles, for instance in the literature on social movements; the willingness to take up the questions of social justice and of the construction of new social orders from the vantage point of postmodernity; a novel theorization of the political and its relation to both the cultural and the democratization of social and economic life; the reformulation of the question of cultural identity in nonessentialist ways; and a keen interest in the relation between aesthetics and society.

The point of departure is a challenging reinterpretation of modernity in Latin America. In Latin America, "where the traditions have not yet left and modernity has not settled in," people doubt whether "to modernize ourselves should be our principal objective, as politicians, economists and the publicists of the new technologies do not cease to tell us" (García Canclini 1990, 13). Neither on the way to the lamentable erradication of all traditions nor triumphantly marching toward progress and modernity, Latin America is seen as characterized by complex processes of cultural hybridization encompassing manifold and multiple modernities and traditions. This hybridization, reflected in urban and peasant cultures composed of sociocultural mixtures that are difficult to discern, "determines the modern specificity of Latin America" (Calderón 1988, 11). Within this view, the distinctions between traditional and modern, rural and urban, high, mass, and popular cultures lose much of their sharpness and relevance. So does the intellectual division of labor, of anthropology as the science of stubborn traditions and sociology as the study of overpowering modernity, for instance. The hypothesis that emerges is no longer that of modernity-generating processes of modernization that operate by substituting the modern for the traditional but of a hybrid modernity characterized by continuous attempts at renovation, by a multiplicity of groups taking charge of the multitemporal heterogeneity preculiar to each sector and country.[8]

Accounts of successful hybrid experiences among popular groups are becoming numerous. These accounts reveal the ineluctable traffic between the traditional and the modern that these groups have to practice and the growing importance of transnational visual archives for popular art and struggles. The Kayapo's use of video cameras and planes to defend their culture and ancestral lands in the Brazilian rain forest is already becoming legendary. Peasants in northern Peru are also found to combine, transforming and reinventing them, elements of long-standing peasant culture, modern urban culture, and translational culture in their process of political organization (Starn 1992). The study of this complex semiotics of protest and of the hybrid and inventive character of popular daily life presents challenging questions to anthropologists and others. The question that arises is how to understand the ways in which cultural actors—cultural producers, intermediaries, and the public—transform their practices in the face of modernity's contradictions. Needless to say, inequalities in access to forms of cultural production continue, yet these inequalities can no longer be confined within the simple polar terms of tradition and modernity, dominators and dominated.

The analysis in terms of hybrid cultures leads to a reconceptualization of a number of established views. Rather than being eliminated by development, many "traditional cultures" survive through their transformative engagement with modernity. It becomes more appropriate to speak of popular culture as a present-oriented process of invention through complex hybridizations that cut across class, ethnic, and national boundaries. Moreover, popular sectors rarely attempt to reproduce a normalized tradition; on the contrary, they often exhibit an openness toward modernity that is at times critical and at times transgressive and even humorous. Not infrequently, what looks like authentic practice or art hides, on close inspection, the commodification of types of "authenticity" that have long ceased to be sources of cultural insights. If we continue to speak of tradition and modernity, it is because we continually fall into the trap of not saying anything new because the language does not permit it. The concept of hybrid cultures provides an opening toward the invention of new languages.[9]

Several disclaimers must accompany this theorization of popular culture. First, it should not be imagined that these processes of hybridization necessarily unmake long-standing traditions of domination. In many cases, the harshness of conditions reduces hybridization to mundane adaptations to increasingly oppressive market conditions. Economic reconversion overdetermines cultural reconversions that are not always felicitous. Paradoxically, however, the groups with a higher degree of economic autonomy and "insertion" into the market have at times a better chance of successfully affirming their ways of life than those clinging to signs of identity the social force of which has been greatly diminished by adverse economic conditions (García Canclini 1990). What is essential in these cases—for example, musicians and producers of handicrafts such as weavers and potters who incorporate transnational motifs into traditional designs—is the mediation new elements effect between the familiar and the new, the local and that which comes from afar, which is ever closer. This cultural hybridization results in negotiated realities in contexts shaped by traditions, capitalism, and modernity.

The second qualification is that the concept of hybridization should in no way be interpreted as the exhaustion of Third World imagery, cosmology, and mythical-cultural traditions; despite the pervasive influence of modern forms, the weighty presence of magic and myth in the social life of the Third World is still extremely significant, as writers and artists continue to make patently clear. As Taussig (1987) suggests, the vitality, magic, wit, humor, and nonmodern ways of seeing that persist among popular groups can be best understood in terms of dialectical images produced in ongoing contexts of conquest and domination. At the level of daily life, these popular practices represent a counterhegemonic force that opposes the instrumentalizing and reactionary attempts of the church, the state, and modern science to domesticate popular culture. These practices resist narrative ordering, flashing back and forth between historical times, self and group, and alienation from and immersion in magic.[10]

This also means that cultural crossings "frequently involve a radical restructuring of the links between the traditional and the modern, the popular and the educated, the local and the foreign. . . . What is modern explodes and gets combined with what is not, is affirmed and challenged at one and the same time" (García Canclini 1990, 223, 331). Let us be sure about one thing: the notion of hybrid cultures—as a biological reading might suggest—does not imply the belief in pure strands of tradition and modernity that are combined to create a hybrid with a new essence; nor does it amount to the combination of discrete elements from tradition and modernity, or a "sellout" of the traditional to the modern. Hybridity entails a cultural (re)creation that may or may not be (re)inscribed into hegemonic constellations. Hybridizations cannot be celebrated in and of themselves, to be sure; yet they might provide opportunities for maintaining and working out cultural differences as a social and political fact. By effecting displacements on the normal strategies of modernity, they contribute to the production of different subjectivities.

More than the biological metaphor, hybrid cultures call forth what Trinh T. Minh-ha calls the hyphenated condition. The hyphenated condition, she writes, "does not limit itself to a duality between two cultural heritages. . . . [it] requires a certain freedom to modify, appropriate, and reappropriate without being trapped in imitation" (1991, 159, 161). It is a "transcultural between-world reality" that requires traveling simultaneously backward—into cultural heritage, oneself, one's social group—and forward, cutting across social boundaries into progressive elements of other cultural formations. Again, it is necessary to point out that there is nothing here that speaks of the "preservation of tradition" in the abstract. Hybrid cultures are not about fixed identities, even if they entail a shifting between something that might be construed as a constant, long-standing presence (existing cultural practices) and something else construed as a transient, new, or incoming element (a transnational element or force). It is also necessary to point out that everything that is happening in the Third World can by no means be considered a hybrid culture in the terms just specified. In a similar vein, the progressive (or conservative) character of specific hybridizations is not given in advance; it rests on the articulations they may establish with other social struggles and discourses. Precisely, it is the task of critical research to learn to look at and recognize hybrid cultural differences of political relevance, a point to which I will return.[11]

Unlike major analytical tendencies in the West, the anthropology of modernity in terms of hybrid cultures does not intend to provide a solution to the philosophy of the subject and the problem of subject-centered reason— as Habermas (1987) defined the project of the critical discourses on modernity from Nietzsche to Heidegger, Derrida, Bataille, and Foucault—nor a recasting of the Enlightenment project, as in the case of Touraine (1988) and Giddens (1990) and Habermas's own project of communicative reason. In Habermas's account, the Third World will have no place, because sooner or later it too will be completely transformed by the pressures of reflexivity, universalism, and individuation that define modernity, and because sooner or later its "lifeworld" will be fully rationalized and its "traditional nuclei" will "shrink to abstract elements" (1987, 344) after being fully articulated and stabilized by and through modern discourses. In the Third World, modernity is not "an unfinished project of Enlightenment." Development is the last and failed attempt to complete the Enlightenment in Asia, Africa, and Latin America.[12]

Latin America's anthropology of modernity retakes the question of the reconstitution of social orders through collective political practice. For some, this process has to be based on the belief that Latin Americans "have to stop being what we have not been, what we will never be, and what we do not have to be," namely, (strictly) modern (Quijano 1990, 37). In the face of worsening material conditions for most people and the rising hegemony of technocratic and economic neoliberalism as the new dogma of modernity in the continent, the call to resist modernization while acknowledging the existence of hybrid cultures that harbor modern forms seems utopian. There is, indeed, a utopian content to this admonition, but not without a theory of the history that makes it possible. This historical sense includes a cultural theory that confronts the logics of capital and instrumental reason.[13]

It is clear that the technological gap between rich and poor countries is growing in the wake of the global economic restructuring of the 1980s and the advent of cyberculture. Should this phenomenon be interpreted as a "new dependency" (Castells and Laserna 1989)? Is the choice really between a dynamic renegotiation of dependency—one that may allow Latin America to accede to the production of some of the new technologies—or the further marginalization from the world economy with the concomitant progressive decomposition of social and economic structures (Castells 1986; Castells and Laserna 1989)? If it is true, as Castells and Laserna state, that the Third World is more and more subjected to types of economic integration that are coupled with greater social disintegration; that entire regions in the Third World are in peril (is it necessarily a peril?) of becoming totally irrelevant to the world economy (marginalized from its benefits even if integrated into its effects); that, finally, this whole state of affairs seems to bring with it "sociocultural perversion" and political disarticulation; if all of these processes are taking place, in sum, can one accept, with these authors, that the answer should be "a policy capable of articulating social reform with technological modernization in the context of democracy and competitive participation in the world economy" (1989, 16)? Or are there other possible perspectives, other ways of participating in the conversations that are reshaping the world?

Ethnography, Cultural Studies, and the Question of Alternatives

One of the most common questions raised about a study of this kind is what it has to say about alternatives. By now it should be clear that there are no grand alternatives that can be applied to all places or all situations. To think about alternatives in the manner of sustainable development, for instance, is to remain within the same model of thought that produced development and kept it in place. One must then resist the desire to formulate alternatives at an abstract, macro level; one must also resist the idea that the articulation of alternatives will take place in intellectual and academic circles, without meaning by this that academic knowledge has no role in the politics of alternative thinking. It certainly does, as we will see shortly.

Where, then, lies "the alternative"? What instances must be interrogated concerning their relation to possible alternative practices? A first approach to these questions is to look for alternative practices in the resistance grassroots groups present to dominant interventions. This was the predominant approach to the question of alternatives during the 1980s, both in anthropology and critical development studies, even if the relationship between resistance and alternatives was not fully articulated as such. A different, perhaps complementary approach can be gleaned from the ethnographies discussed at the end of chapter 2. Those ethnographies sought to investigate the concrete forms that concepts and practices of development and modernity take in specific communities. This type of research might be taken as a point of departure for the investigation of alternatives from anthropological perspectives. In other words, ethnographies of the circulation of discourses and practices of modernity and development provide us, perhaps for the first time, with a view of where these communities are culturally in relation to development. This view may be taken as a basis for interrogating current practices in terms of their potential role in articulating alternatives. Notions of hybrid models and communities of modelers (chapter 3) are ways of giving form to this research strategy.

Said differently, the nature of alternatives as a research question and a social practice can be most fruitfully gleaned from the specific manifestations of such alternatives in concrete local settings. The alternative is, in a sense, always there. From this perspective, there is not surplus of meaning at the local level but meanings that have to be read with new senses, tools, and theories. The deconstruction of development, coupled with the local ethnographies just mentioned, can be important elements for a new type of visibility and audibility of forms of cultural difference and hybridization that researchers have generally glossed over until now. The subaltern do in fact speak, even if the audibility of their voices in the circles where "the West" is reflected upon and theorized is tenuous at best. There is also the question of the translatability into theoretical and practical terms of what might be read, heard, smelled, felt, or intuited in Third World settings. This process of translation has to move back and forth between concrete proposals based on existing cultural differences—with the goal of strengthening those differences by inserting them into political strategies and self-defined and self-directed socioeconomic experiments—and the opening of spaces for destabilizing dominant modes of knowing, so that the need for the most violent forms of translation is diminished. In other words, the process must embrace the challenge of simultaneously seeing theory as a set of contested forms of knowledge—originating in many cultural matrices—and have that theory foster concrete interventions by the groups in question.[14]

The crisis in the regimes of representation of the Third World thus calls for new theories and research strategies; the crisis is a real conjunctional moment in the reconstruction of the connection between truth and reality, between words and things, one that demands new practices of seeing, knowing, and being. Ethnography is by no means the sole method of pursuing this goal; but given the need to unmake and unlearn development, and if one recognizes that the crucial insights for the pursuit of alternatives will be found not in academic circles—critical or conventional—or in the offices of institutions such as the World Bank but in a new reading of popular practices and of the reappropriation by popular actors of the space of hegemonic sociocultural production, then one must at least concede that the task of conceptualizing alternatives must include a significant contact with those whose "alternatives" research is supposed to illuminate. This is a conjunctural possibility that ethnography-oriented research might be able to fulfill, regardless of the discipline.

Can the project of cultural studies as political practice contribute to this project of figuration? If it is true, as Stuart Hall proposes, that "movements provoke theoretical moments" (1992, 283), it is clear that the movement for refiguring the Third World has generated neither the intellectual momentum nor the political intention necessary for its proper theoretical moment to arise. This moment, moreover, can be crafted not merely as a moment pertaining to the Third World but as a global moment, the moment of cybercultures and hybrid reconstructions of modern and traditional orders, the moment of possible (truly) postmodern and posthumanist landscapes. The Third World has unique contributions to make to these figurations and intellectual and political efforts, to the extent that its hybrid cultures or "rejected selves" may provide a vital check and different sense of direction to the trends of cyberculture now dominant in the First World (Escobar 1994). The shifting project of cultural studies—its "arbitrary closure," to use Hall's expression—must beging to take into account the various ongoing attempts at refiguring the Third World.

Some of this is starting to happen. Critiques of development produced in the Third World are beginning to circulate in the West. This aspect deserves some attention, because it raises other complex questions, beginning with "what is the West." As Ashis Nandy writes, the "West is now everywhere, within the West and outside: in structures and minds" (1983, xii). There is sometimes a reluctance on the part of some of the Third World authors who call for the dismantling of development to acknowledge this fact—that is, to keep on seeing strong traditions and radical resistance in places where perhaps there are other things going on as well. But there is also a reluctance on the part of academic audiences in the First World—particularly the progressive audiences who want to recognize the agency of Third World people—to think about how they appropriate and "consume" Third World voices for their own needs, whether it is to provide the expected difference, renew hope, or think through political directions.

If Third World intellectuals who travel to the West must position themselves in a more self-conscious manner vis-à-vis both their Third World constituencies and their First World audiences—that is, with respect to the political functions they take on—European and American audiences must be more self-critical of their practices of reading Third World voices. As Lata Mani (1989) suggests, we all have to be more reflective of the modes of knowing that are intensified because of our particular location (see also Chow 1992). This is doubly important because theory is no longer simply produced in one place and applied in another; in the post-Fordist world, theorists and theories travel across discontinuous terrains (Clifford 1989), even if, as this book has shown, there are identifiable centers of production of dominant knowledges. But even these knowledges are far from being just applied without substantial modifications, appropriations, and subversions.

If one were to look for an image that describes the production of development knowledge today, one would use not epistemological centers and peripheries but a decentralized network of nodes in and through which theorists, theories, and multiple users move and meet, sharing and contesting the socioepistemological space.

At the bottom of the investigation of alternatives lies the sheer fact of cultural difference. Cultural differences embody—for better or for worse, this is relevant to the politics of research and intervention—possibilities for transforming the politics of representation, that is, for transforming social life itself. Out of hybrid or minority cultural situations might emerge other ways of building economies, of dealing with basic needs, of coming together into social groups. The greatest political promise of minority cultures is their potential for resisting and subverting the axiomatics of capitalism and modernity in their hegemonic form.[15] This is why cultural difference is one of the key political facts of our times. Because cultural difference is also at the root of postdevelopment, this makes the reconceptualization of what is happening in and to the Third World a key task at present. The unmaking of the Third World—as a challenge to the Western historical mode to which the entire globe seems to be captive—is in the balance.

Despite flexibility and contradictions, it is clear that capital and new technologies are not conducive to the defense of minority subjectivities—minority seen here not only as ethnicity but in relation to its opposition to the axiomatics of capitalism and modernity. Yet everything indicates at the same time that the resurgence and even reconstitution of subjectivities marked by multiple traditions is a distinct possibility. The informational coding of subjectivities in today's global ethnoscapes does not succeed in erasing completely singularity and difference. In fact, it relies more and more on the production of both homogeneity and difference. But the dispersion of social forms brought about by the deterritorialized information economy nevertheless makes modern forms of control difficult. This might offer unexpected opportunities that groups at the margin could seize to construct innovative visions and practices. At the same time, it must be recognized that this dispersal takes place at the cost of the living conditions of vast numbers of people in the Third World and, increasingly, in the West itself. This situation must be dealt with at many levels—economic, cultural, ecological, and political.[16]

Popular groups in many parts of the Third World seem to be increasingly aware of these dilemmas. Caught between conventional development strategies that refuse to die and the opening of spaces in the wake of ecological capital and discourses on cultural plurality, biodiversity, and ethnicity, some of these groups respond by attempting to craft unprecedented visions of themselves and the world around them. Urged by the need to come up with alternatives—lest they be swept away by another round of conventional development, capitalist greed, and violence—the organizing strategies of these groups begin to revolve more and more around two principles: the defense of cultural difference, not as a static but as a transformed and transformative force; and the valorization of economic needs and opportunities in terms that are not strictly those of profit and the market. The defense of the local as a prerequisite to engaging with the global; the critique of the group's own situation, values, and practices as a way of clarifying and strengthening identity; the opposition to modernizing development; and the formulation of visions and concrete proposals in the context of existing constraints, these seem to be the principal elements for the collective construction of alternatives that these groups seem to be pursuing.[17]

Postdevelopment and cyberculture thus become parallel and interrelated processes in the cultural politics of the late-twentieth century. For what awaits both the First and the Third World, perhaps finally transcending the difference, is the possibility of learning to be human in posthumanist (postman and postmodern) landscapes. But we must be mindful that in many places there are worlds that development, even today and at this moment, is bent on destroying.

NOTES

CHAPTER 1

1. For an interesting contemporary analysis of this document, see Frankel (1953, 82–110).

2. Some trends in the 1960s and 1970s were critical of development, although, as will become clear shortly, they were unable to articulate a rejection of the discourse that struck at its roots. Among these, it is important to mention Paulo Freire's "pedagogy of the oppressed" (Freire 1970); the birth of Liberation Theology at the Latin American Bishops' Conference held in Medellín in 1964; and the critiques of "intellectual colonialism" (Fals Borda 1970) and economic dependency (Cardoso and Faletto 1979) of the late 1960s and early 1970s. The most perceptive cultural critique of development was by Illich (1969). All of these critiques were important for the discursive approach of the 1980s and 1990s analyzed in this book.

3. "According to the same learned white man [Ivan Illich], the concept that is currently named 'development' has gone through six stages of metamorphosis since late antiquity. The perception of the outsider as the one who needs help has taken on the successive forms of the barbarian, the pagan, the infidel, the wild man, the 'native,' and the underdeveloped" (Trinh 1989, 54). See Hirschman (1981, 24) for a similar idea and set of terms. It should be pointed out, however, that the term *underdeveloped*—linked from a certain vantage point to equality and the prospects of liberation through development—can be seen in part as a response to more openly racist conceptions of "the primitive" and "the savage." In many contexts, however, the new term failed to correct the negative connotations implied by the earlier qualifiers. The "myth of the lazy native" (Alatas 1977) is still alive today in many quarters.

4. Mohanty's work can be situated within a growing critique by feminists, especially Third World feminists, of ethnocentrism in feminist scholarship and the feminist movement. See also Mani (1989); Trinh (1989); Spelman (1988); and hooks (1990). The critique of the women in development discourse will be discussed at length in chapter 5.

5. The study of a discourse along these axes is proposed by Foucault (1986, 4). The forms of subjectivity that development produced are not explored in this book in a significant manner. An illustrious group of thinkers, including Franz Fanon (1967, 1968), Albert Memmi (1967), Ashis Nandy (1983), and Homi Bhabha (1990), have produced increasingly enlightening accounts of the creation of subjectivity and consciousness under colonialism and postcolonialism.

6. On the violence of representation, see also de Lauretis (1987).

7. Article-length analyses of development as discourse include Escobar (1984, 1988); Mueller (1987b); Dubois (1991); Parajuli (1991); and St-Hilaire (1993).

8. The group responsible for this "dictionary of toxic words" in the development discourse includes Ivan Illich, Wolfgang Sachs, Barbara Duden, Ashis Nandy, Vandana Shiva, Majid Rahnema, Gustavo Esteva, and myself among others.

9. This group, convened under the sponsorship of the United Nations World Institute for Development Economics Research (WIDER) and headed by Stephen Marglin and Frédérique Apffel-Marglin, has been meeting for several years and includes some of the people mentioned in the previous note. One edited volume has already been published as a result of the project (Apffel-Marglin and Marglin 1990), and a second one (Apffel-Marglin and Marglin 1994) is in press.

10. A collection by Jonathan Crush (Queens University, Canada) on discourses of development is in the process of being compiled; it includes analyses of "languages of development" (Crush, ed. 1994). Discourse analyses of development fields is the subject of the project "Development and Social Science Knowledge," sponsored by the Social Science Research Council (SSRC) and coordinated by Frederick Cooper (University of Michigan) and Randall Packard (Tufts University). This project began in the spring of 1994 and will probably continue for several years.

11. Sikkink rightly differentiates her institutional-interpretive method from "discourse and power" approaches, although her characterization of the latter reflects only the initial formulation of the discursive approach. I feel that both methods—the history of ideas and the study of discursive formations—are not incompatible. Although the former method pays attention to the internal dynamics of the social generation of ideas in ways that the latter sometimes overlooks (thus giving the impression that development models are just "imposed on" the Third World, not produced from the inside as well), the history of ideas tends to ignore the systematic effects of discourse production, which in important ways shapes what counts as ideas in the first place. For a differentiation between the history of ideas and the history of discourses, see Foucault (1972, 135–98; 1991b).

12. This is the case with the organization Cultural Survival, for example, and its advocacy anthropology (Maybury-Lewis 1985). Its work, however, recycles some problematic views of the anthropologist speaking on behalf of "the natives" (Escobar 1991). See also Price (1989) for an example of anthropologists opposing a World Bank project in defense of indigenous peoples.

13. See, for instance, Ulin (1991); Sutton (1991); hooks (1990); Said (1989); Trinh (1989); Mascia-Lees, Sharpe, and Cohen (1989); Gordon (1988, 1991); and Friedman (1987).

14. Discussions on modernity and postmodernity in Latin America are becoming a central focus of research and political action. See Calderón, ed. (1988); Quijano (1988, 1990); Lechner (1988); García Canclini (1990); Sarlo (1991); and Yúdice, Franco, and Flores, eds. (1992). For a review of some of these works, see Montaldo (1991).

15. Throughout the book, I refer to one country, Colombia, and one problem area, malnutrition and hunger. This should ground the reader in the geopolitical and social aspects of development.

Chapter 2

1. Foucault (1979, 1980a, 1980b, 1991a) refers to this aspect of modernity—the appearance of forms of knowledge and regulatory controls centered on the production and optimization of life—as "biopower." Biopower entailed the "governmentalization" of social life, that is, the subjection of life to explicit mechanisms of produc-

tion and administration by the state and other institutions. The analysis of biopower and governmentality should be an integral component of the anthropology of modernity (Urla 1993).

2. Root's words also reflect a salient feature of North American consciousness, namely, the utopian desire to bring progress and happiness to all peoples not only within the confines of their own country but beyond their shores as well. At times, within this kind of mentality the world becomes a vast surface burdened with problems to be solved, a disorganized horizon that has to be set "on the path of ordered liberty" once and for all, "with or without the consent" of those to be reformed. This attitude was also at the root of the dream of development.

3. For an in-depth treatment of U.S. foreign policy toward Latin America and the Third World, see Kolko (1988) and Bethell (1991). See also Cuevas Cancino (1989); Graebner (1977); Whitaker (1948); Yerguin (1977); Wood, B. (1985); and Haglund (1985). It must be pointed out that most scholars have missed the significance of the emergence of the development discourse in the late 1940s and early 1950s. López Maya, on whose work the account of three conferences is based, is an exception.

4. Ethnocentric remarks were at times expressed quite openly during the first half of the century. Wilson's ambassador to England, for instance, explained that the United States would intervene in Latin America to "make'em vote and live by their decisions." If this did not work, "We'll go in again and make'em vote again. . . . The United States will be there for two hundred years and it can continue to shoot men for that little space till they learn to vote and rule themselves" (quoted in Drake 1991, 14). The "Latin mind" was believed to "scorn democracy" and be ruled by emotion, not by reason.

5. Cardoso and Faletto (1979) discuss some of these changes for Latin America as a whole. The rise of social movements in Colombia in the 1920s is analyzed in Archila (1980).

6. The interpretation of this period of Colombia's history is highly disputed. Economic historians (see, for instance, Ocampo, ed. 1987) generally believe that the Great Depression and World War II pushed the ruling class toward industrialization as the only viable alternative for development. This view, held by many in Latin America, has been disputed recently. Sáenz Rovner (1989, 1992) rejects the idea that growth and development were goals that the Colombian elite shared in the 1940s, adding that the government did not seriously consider the Currie report. Antonio García's (1953) paper provides important clues to assess the status of planning in Colombia with reference to the Currie mission. For García, planning activities in the 1940s were highly ineffective not only because of narrow conceptions of the planning process but because the various planning bodies had no power to implement the desired goals and programs. Although he found the Currie report unobjectionable from the economic viewpoint, he took issue with it on social grounds, advocating instead the kind of planning process that Jorge Eliécer Gaitán presented to congress in 1947.

By the late 1940s, García had a fully worked out alternative to capitalist development models, which has not been given the attention it merits by economic and social historians (see García 1948, 1950). This alternative, based on a sophisticated structural and dialectical interpretation of "backwardness"—in ways that resembled and presaged Paul Baran's (1957) work of a few years later—was based on a distinction between economic growth and the overall development of society. This was revolutionary, given the fact that a liberal model of development was becoming consolidated at this point, as Pécaut (1987) has shown in detail. More research needs to be done on this period from the perspective of the rise of development. Although nineteenth-century-style "economic essay" was the rule until the 1940s—for instance, in the works of Luis López de Mesa (1944) and Eugenio Gómez (1942)—in the 1930s several authors were calling for new styles of inquiry and decision making, based on greater objectivity, quantification, and programming. See, for instance, López (1976) and García Cadena (1956). Some of these issues are dealt with in Escobar (1989).

7. On the origins of the notions of development and Third World, see Platsch (1981); Mintz (1976); Wallerstein (1984); Arndt (1981); Worsley (1984); and Binder (1986). The term *development* existed at least since the British Colonial Development Act of 1929, although, as Arndt insists, its usage at this early moment was quite different from what it came to signify in the 1940s. The expression *underdeveloped countries* or *areas* came into existence in the mid-1940s (see, for instance, the documents of the Milbank Memorial Fund of this period). Finally, the term *Third World* did not come into existence until the early 1950s. According to Platsch, it was coined by Alfred Sauvy, a French demographer, to refer—making an analogy to the Third Estate in France—to poor and populous areas of the world.

8. Samir Amin refers to the Bandung Plan as the "bourgeois national plan for the Third World of our age" (1990, 46). Even if Bandung represented a "third world path of development," Amin contends, it fitted well into the "unbroken succession of national bourgeois attempts, repeated abortions and surrender to the demands of the subordination" to international powers (47).

9. A detailed account of U.S. foreign assistance during the war is found in Brown and Opie (1953). See also Galbraith (1979).

10. On the economic changes during this period, see Williams (1953) and Copland (1945). The political economy of these changes is analyzed in some detail in chapter 3.

11. Bataille's interpretation of the Marshall Plan is questionable on economic grounds. As Payer (1991) remarks, the United States had little choice but to reactivate the European economy; otherwise its own economy would collapse sooner or later for lack of trading partners, particularly given the excess-production capacity generated during the war. But Bataille's argument runs much deeper. For him, the essential point about the Marshall Plan was the fact that an improved standard of living might make possible the increase of "energy resources" of the human being, and hence his/her self-consciousness. This would make possible the setting in place of a type of human existence in which "consciousness will cease to be consciousness of *something*; in other words, of becoming conscious of the decisive meaning of an instant in which increase (the acquisition of *something*) will resolve into expenditure; and this will be precisely *self-consciousness*, that is, a consciousness that henceforth has *nothing as its object*" (190). This belief is at the basis of his notion of a "general economy," to which *The Accursed Share* is devoted. For a useful discussion of Bataille's work as a critical discourse of modernity, see Habermas (1987).

12. Truman had made this clear in 1947. "The problems of countries in this [American] Hemisphere are different in nature and cannot be relieved by the same means and the same approaches which are in contemplation for Europe" (quoted in

López Maya 1993, 13); he went on to extol the virtues of private investment in the Latin American case.

13. See, for instance, Hatt (1951); Lewis (1955); Buchanan and Ellis (1951); Political and Economic Planning (1955); Sax (1955); and Coale and Hoover (1958). On the use of population models and statistics, see United Nations, Department of Social and Economic Affairs (1953); Liebenstein (1954); Wolfender (1954); and Milbank Memorial Fund (1954).

14. Malthusian overtones were often quite blatant, as in the following example: "As Malthus pointed out long ago, the supply of people easily outruns the supply of food. . . . Where men have become more numerous in relation to food, the men are cheap; where food is still plentiful in relation to men, men are dear. . . . What is a dear man? One who has cost much to bring up; one who has acquired many expensive habits, among which are skills other people are willing to buy at high rates. . . . At least 75 million Americans have been, with some ups and downs, having this kind of life. . . . We Americans have on hand 22,796 tons of coal for each and every person. The Italians have only six for each and every person. Why wonder that the Italians are cheap and we are dear? Or that the Italians all try to move in with us? We have about 60 times as much iron and 200 as much coal than the Japanese. Of course the Japs are cheap" (Pendell 1951, viii). Other well-known Malthusian books of the period are by Vogt (1948) and Osborn (1948).

15. See, for instance, Dennery ([1931] 1970). This book deals with population growth in India, China, and Japan and its consequences for the West.

16. I am indebted to Ron Balderrama for sharing with me his analysis of the change that took place in the discourse on race in the 1940s and 1950s. This discourse relied on the scientific knowledge of population biology, genetics, and the like.

17. It is important to emphasize that this concern did not address the structural causes of poverty but lent itself to imperialist or elitist "population control" policies, particularly against indigenous people and popular classes (Mamdani 1973). Although access to contraception may certainly constitute an important improvement, particularly for women, it should not be incompatible with the struggle against poverty and for better health systems, as women insist in many parts of Latin America. See, for instance, Barroso and Bruschini (1991).

18. For a review of modernization theories of development, see Villamil, ed. (1979); Portes (1976); Gendzier (1985); and Banuri (1990).

19. For a debate on the subject, see von Hayek's (1944) frontal attack on all kinds of intervention on the economy and Finer's (1949) response to Hayek. See also Lewis (1949), particularly his reasoning for "why plan in backward countries."

20. The influence of the TVA was by no means restricted to Colombia. River-basin development schemes with direct TVA participation were devised in many countries. This history has yet to be written.

21. The methodology for the study of discourse used in this section follows Foucault's. See especially Foucault (1972 and 1991b).

22. The loan agreements (Guarantee Agreements) between the World Bank and recipient countries signed in the late 1940s and 1950s invariably included a commitment on the part of the borrower to provide "the Bank," as it is called, with all the information it requested. It also stipulated the right of Bank officials to visit any part

of the territory of the country in question. The "missions" that this institution period-ically sent to borrowing countries was a major mechanism for extracting detailed information about those countries, as is shown in detail in chapter 4.

23. Although most Latin American professionals avidly gave themselves to the task of extracting the new knowledge from their countries' economies and cultures, in time the transnationalization of knowledge resulted in a dialectic through which the call for a more autonomous social science was advanced (Fals Borda 1970). This dialectic contributed to intellectual and social efforts such as dependency theory and Liberation Theology.

24. I owe this helpful comparison—the "landing of the experts" in the Third World in the early post–World War II period to the landing of the Allies in Nor-mandy—to Chilean sociologist Edmundo Fuenzalida.

25. This brief description of the effect of development in the Pacific Coast of Colombia is based on fieldwork I did there in 1993.

26. The coherence of effects of the development discourse should not signify any sort of intentionality. As the discourses discussed by Foucault, development must be seen as a "strategy without strategists," in the sense that nobody is explicitly master-minding it; it is the result of a historical problematization and a systematized re-sponse to it.

CHAPTER 3

1. Heidegger makes the case that modern Europe was the first society to produce a structured image of itself and the world, what he calls a world picture. The modern world picture entails an unprecedented way of objectifying the world; the world comes to be what it is "to the extent that it is set up by man. . . . For the first time there is such a thing as a 'position' for man" (1977, 130, 132). See also Mitchell (1988, 1989).

2. Culturalist and poststructuralist critiques of economics are barely beginning. As far as I know, only Tribe (1981), Gudeman (1986; Gudeman and Rivera 1990, 1993), and McCloskey (1985) have paid significant attention to economics as dis-course and culture. The implications of Foucault's work for the history of economic thought has been explored by Vint (1986) and Sanz de Santamaría (1984). Millberg (1991) has recently broached the subject of the relevance of poststructuralism to Marxist and post-Keynesian economics. This chapter is meant to contribute to the cultural critique of economics started by these authors.

3. Foucault defines the disciplines as the methods that "made possible the metic-ulous control of the operations of the body, which assured the constant subjection of its forces and imposed upon them a relation of docility-utility" (1979, 137). The disci-plines were in ascension in the seventeenth century in factories, military barracks, schools, and hospitals. These institutions brought the human body into a new ma-chinery of power; the body became the object of a "political anatomy."

4. Marx's philosophy was a product of the modern age and Western cosmology, marked by atavistic notions of progress, rationalism, and the goals of objectivity and even universality. It placed the center of the world in the Occident, and that of history in modernity, as the crucial transition period to the end of prehistory and the inauguration of true history.

5. This is an extremely succinct account of the Western economy as an ensemble of systems of production, power, and signification. A more thorough exposition is found in chapter 3 of my doctoral dissertation, "Power and Visibility: The Invention and Management of Development in the Third World" (University of California at Berkeley, 1987). This chapter was left out of the present book version. On the rise of the market, see Polanyi (1957a); Polanyi, Arensberg, and Pearson, eds. (1957); Braudel (1977); Hicks (1969); Wallerstein (1974); and Dobb (1946). The concept of market culture is discussed in Reddy (1987). On the questions of discipline, the social, and the individual, see particularly Foucault (1979, 1991a); Burchell, Gordon, and Miller, eds. (1991); Donzelot (1979); Procacci (1991); and Landes (1983). The best account of the emergence of the economy and of economic ideology is still Dumont (1977); see also Foucault (1972) and Baudrillard (1975) for discussions of production as an epistemic order and a code of signification.

6. Marx's revolutionary promise reversed Ricardo's pessimism by positing the possibility of the reapprehension and reconstitution of humanity's essence by the dispossessed. On the suspension of development in economics, see Foucault (1973, 261).

7. The analysis in this section is based on Schumpeter (1954), Dobb (1946, 1973), Blaug (1978), Deane (1978), Bell and Kristol (1981), and Foucault (1973).

8. Foucault (1973) emphasizes the fact that for Ricardo labor became the basis of both production and economic knowledge. People labor and exchange because they experience needs and desires and, above all, because they are subject to time, toil, and, ultimately, death. Foucault refers to this aspect of modernity as "the analytic of finitude."

9. The utility theory of value—perfected by Walras, Marshall, and the economists of the Austrian School, and the origins of which Schumpeter (1954, 909–44) finds in Aristotle and the Scholastic doctors—echoed the major tenets of the philosophical doctrine of utilitarianism. Vilfredo Pareto would attempt, at the turn of the century, to purge the theory of its connections with utilitarianism by emphasizing its logical and purely formal character. He proposed the concept of ordinal utility (the individual's ability to array goods in a scale of preference without measuring them) and worked out a theory of value that (especially as further developed by Allen and Hicks) is still the fundament of contemporary theory of value as it appears in today's microeconomic textbooks. As is well known, these textbooks start with a discussion of the "rational" economic agent who seeks to maximize his or her utility.

10. Schumpeter, who despite his sociohistorical approach was fond of "pure analysis," called the Walrasian general-equilibrium theory "the only work by an economist that will stand comparison with the achievements of theoretical physics" (1954, 827). Joan Robinson called the same theory "the most extravagant claim of Western orthodoxy" (1979, 13). This did not deter the Nobel Committee from granting the Nobel Prize to mathematical economists such as Arrow and Debreu for "perfecting" such a law.

11. It should be pointed out, however, that by this time capital had already defeated its enemies; microeconomic theory thus emerged as the theory of "efficiency," that is, the maximum exploitation of labor.

12. Besides Maier's book (1975), see Aldcroft (1977); Gramsci (1971) on Americanism and Fordism; and Harvey (1989) on the Fordist regime of accumulation.

13. Say's classical law that "supply creates its own demand" was another target of Keynes's theory. Similarly, for Keynes the interest rate would be no longer the instrument that automatically would balance savings and investment but a money rate under the influence of monetary policy and the current expectations about future movements.

14. In this section I use the terms *core, periphery,* and *semiperiphery* as derived from world systems and dependency theories. The countries of the core (also called center countries in some versions) are those that became industrialized in the nineteenth century, roughly the so-called developed countries of today (Western Europe, the United States, Canada, Australia, New Zealand, and South Africa); the periphery is composed of most Third World countries, whereas the semiperiphery has changed since the advent of what world system theorists call the capitalist world economy in the 1650s. Today, the semiperiphery includes a few of the largest countries in the Third World and the so-called New Industrializing Countries, NICs (South Korea, Taiwan, Hong Kong, and Singapore, with a handful of countries waiting to be formally admitted to the club, such as Malaysia, Thailand, and Chile). For a more elaborate explanation of these terms, see Braudel (1977) and Wallerstein (1974, 1984).

15. The analysis in this section is based on the following works: Borrego (1981), Amin (1976, 1990), Wallerstein (1974), Hopkins and Wallerstein (1987), and Cardoso and Faletto (1979).

16. These economic changes were paralleled by unprecedented cultural and social changes. In Latin America socialist, Communist, anarchist, and to a lesser extent feminist and student movements emerged in a number of countries. Creativity in art and literature reached unprecedented levels (for instance, Mexican murals and the first wave of writings by women). Cutting the umbilical cord that had tied the landed oligarchy to London, and not yet having established the tight connection that was inevitably to unite them with New York after the Second World War, Latin Americans delved into their own past for newer certainties (*indigenismo*), developed eclectic views inspired by socialism and Marxism (Mariátegui, Haya de la Torre, and Jorge Eliécer Gaitán), and concentrated on internal economic conditions to develop healthy national economies (import substitution industrialization). This intellectual ferment was frustrated by the counteroffensive the United States launched via development and the Alliance for Progress.

17. I owe this final contextualization of the pioneers of development economics to Stephen Marglin (conversation in 1992).

18. A good summary of the early economic development theories, accessible to nonspecialists, is found in Meier (1984). See also Seers (1983); Meier and Seers, eds. (1984); Hirschman (1981); and Bauer (1984). A well-known textbook is Todaro (1977).

19. Joseph Love (1980) has explored the possible connections between debates on economic development held in Eastern Europe in the 1920s by economists such as Rosenstein-Rodan and those held in Latin America in the late 1930s and 1940s, particularly within the ambit of the UN Economic Commission for Latin America (CEPAL).

20. For instance, Albert Hirschman lived in Bogotá from 1952 to 1956 as financial adviser to the National Planning Board. Lauchlin Currie went back to live in Colombia, became a Colombian citizen in the late 1950s, and continued to be a major presence in development-planning circles in Colombia and elsewhere. Arthur Lewis

was economic adviser to the prime minister of Ghana and deputy director of the UN Special Fund in the late 1950s. Rosenstein-Rodan became assistant director of the economics department of the World Bank in 1947. Ragnald Nurkse and Jabob Viner delivered lectures in Brazil in 1951 and 1953 respectively, where they had a fruitful dialogue with Brazilian economists. (According to Celso Furtado, in a conversation I had with him in 1984, this dialogue with Brazilian economists was instrumental for Nurkse and Viner in the development of their respective theories.)

21. Other influences were at play in the exclusion of Schumpeter's view; for instance, the fact that development economics was almost exclusively an affair of Anglo-American academic institutions, to which Schumpeter's systemic thinking—arising from a different intellectual tradition—was somewhat alien; and the fact that his theory did not lend itself easily to the sort of mathematical elaborations for which a number of development economists were developing a special fondness.

22. The belief that making the rich richer is an effective way of activating the economy was also at the basis of Reagan-Bush economics. There will always be economists who will defend this view as logical from the point of view of economic rationality.

23. For a presentation of CEPAL's theories, see what has been termed the *CEPAL Manifesto* (Economic Commission for Latin America 1950), authored by CEPAL's first director and inspiring force, Raúl Prebisch. As a radicalization of CEPAL's theory, dependency theory emerged in the late 1960s. See the principal dependency texts, Sunkel and Paz (1970), Furtado (1970), and Cardoso and Faletto (1979).

24. A number of excellent critical accounts of the birth and evolution of CEPAL's thinking are available. See Hirschman (1961), Di Marco, ed. (1974), Cardoso (1977), Rodríguez (1977), Love (1980), and Sikkink (1991).

25. From the point of view of discourse, "concepts such as those of surplus value and the falling rate of profit, as found in Marx, may be described on the basis of the system of positivity that is already in operation in the work of Ricardo; but these concepts (which are new, but whose rules of formation are not) appear—in Marx himself—as belonging at the same time to a quite different discursive practice. . . . This positivity is not a tranformation of Ricardo's analysis; it is not a new political economy; it is a discourse that occurred around a derivation of certain economic concepts, but which, in turn, defines the conditions in which the discourse of economists takes place, and may therefore be valid as a theory and a critique of political economy" (Foucault 1972, 176).

26. Among the exceptions are Irma Adelman and Cynthia Tafts Morris, whose work on income distribution in developing countries (1973) has been influential. See also Joan Robinson (1979).

27. On development planning in Colombia, see García (1953); Cano (1974); Perry (1976); López and Correa (1982); de la Torre, ed. (1985); and Sáenz Rovner (1989). See also the development plans published by the various presidential administrations of the last three decades.

28. See particularly the following: Seers (1979); Hirschman (1981); Little (1982); Livingstone (1982); Chenery (1983); Meier (1984); Bauer (1984); Flórez (1984); Meier and Seers (1984); and Lal (1985).

29. In Prebisch's (1979) view, the general-equilibrium theory overlooks two fundamental phenomena: the surplus and power relations. The surplus grows faster than

the product, and the capital accumulation process is hindered by the appropriation of surplus by a privileged minority. In addition, the gains of technical progress spread not according to marginal productivity but through the power structure, which leads to a distributional crisis. This was why for Prebisch neoclassical economics was irrelevant to explaining the phenomena of the periphery. It is what he called the frustration of neoclassicism.

30. The search for paradigms and research programs in economics serves to legitimize economic science and policy; it allows economists to postulate notions of structure, change, and progress in the development of their knowledge; and it privileges certain theoretical choices (neoclassical economics) by superimposing the same choice on the historical archive. This type of assessment, moreover, cannot account for the formation of the discursive fields—the economy, development—on which the science is based.

31. In Colombia, the total opening of the economy took off in 1991 and unleashed an unprecedented number of strikes by workers in many branches of the economy, civil servants, and agriculturalists, which continued to the end of 1993 (at the time I am writing these lines). The government's commitment to the *apertura* has not been shaken.

32. Gudeman and Rivera restricted their work to mestizo peasants in the Colombian Andes. Other historicocultural conversations and matrices would have to be considered with indigenous and Afro-Colombian groups in the same country, or with peasant groups in countries like Peru, Guatemala, and Bolivia, where the pre-Columbian influence is still strong.

33. Gudeman and Rivera's model of house and corporation can be related to Deleuze and Guattari's (1987) concepts of nomad and state forms of knowledge, technology, and economic organization.

34. The classical economists, argue Gudeman and Rivera (1990), derived some of their insights from the "folk conversations" of European peasants. The corporate model of the economy thus relied at least in part on observations of the house model as it existed at the time in Europe. This movement from folk voice to centric text was important in the theoretical elaboration of classical political economy (17).

35. There is a troubling aspect in Amin's call for socialism: "If there is a positive side to the universalism created by capitalism, it is not to be found at the level of economic development (since this by nature remains unequal), but definitely at the level of a popular, cultural and ideological universalism, boding for the 'post-capitalist' stage, a genuine socialist outlook" (1990, 231). This statement is all the more puzzling given the fact that in the next section he calls for "the plurality of productive systems, political visions and cultures" (233).

36. Participatory action research is based on a similar principle. See Fals Borda (1988) and Fals Borda and Rahman, eds. (1991).

CHAPTER 4

1. However, it is at the local level that the discord between the needs of the institutions and those of the local people come out more clearly. This discord is often felt as a personal and anguishing conflict among local development workers, which they resolve in various ways (from turning a deaf ear to it to deciding to leave the

development apparatus to become a community activist). Even among the university-trained staff of development organizations one finds this type of conflict, as I witnessed in Colombia among professionals working in rural development.

2. The best known of these experimental projects of the late 1960s and early 1970s include those carried out in Narangwal (Johns Hopkins School of Hygiene and Public Health and the Indian Council of Medical research), Jamkhed (carried out by Indian physicians), and Morinda (Cornell-MIT International Nutrition Program and the Indian Food and Nutrition Board), all in India; Cali, Colombia (University of Michigan and Universidad del Valle Medical School); and Guatemala (Institute of Nutrition of Central America and Panama [INCAP], a UN-sponsored research institute established in cooperation with MIT's Department of Nutrition and Food Science). Some of them were conceived as research projects on the etiology of malnutrition and the determinants of nutritional status; others as pilot projects on health, nutrition, and family planning. A brief discussion of some of these projects is found in Berg (1981); see also Levinson (1974). A state-of-the-art volume on nutrition intervention—based on five separate volumes prepared by the Harvard Institute of International Development for the Office of Nutrition of U.S. AID—is Austin, ed. (1981).

3. Some of this history is sketched in Scrimshaw and Wallerstein, eds. (1982).

4. Nevin Scrimshaw was at the time and for many years the head of the Department of Nutrition and Food Science at MIT. Along with Alan Berg of the World Bank's nutrition division, Scrimshaw was the most influential figure in setting research and policy agendas in international nutrition. Scrimshaw had substantial links with the Rockefeller Foundation, the United Nations University, and organizations such as the FAO and WHO. Alan Berg had been involved in the 1960s with U.S. AID's nutrition intervention programs and research in India, before moving to the Brookings Institution and, in the mid-1970s, the World Bank. Berg also was closely affiliated with MIT's International Nutrition Program.

5. See the reviews of nutrition-planning models by Lynch (1979); Hakim and Solimano (1976); and Field (1977).

6. See, besides the volumes cited, Joy and Payne (1975); Anderson and Grewald, eds. (1976); FAO/WHO (1976); Winikoff, ed. (1978); Joy, ed. (1978); Mayer and Dwyer, eds. (1979); Aranda and Sáenz, eds. (1981); Teller, ed. (1980); Berg (1981); Austin and Esteva, eds. (1987).

7. Conveniently, two books, one written by a senior World Bank official (Berg 1981) and the other prepared for the World Bank by one Harvard and two Stanford professors (Timmer, Falcon, and Pearson 1983), declared the demise of FNPP in the early 1980s, closing a cycle and at the same time opening a new one, this time with a more pragmatic emphasis on food policy. Integrated rural development programs, however, unlike their nutrition counterparts, continue to exist in some countries.

8. This and all other translations from Spanish are my own.

9. See the PIA/PNAN reports of activities for the period 1975–1980, including PIA/PNAN (1975a, 1975b, 1977).

10. This controversy has taken place around various issues, such as Reutlinger and Selowsky's macro estimates of malnutrition (1976). See Payne's review of this book (1977), plus the subsequent correspondence between Payne and Reutlinger/Selowski in the November 1977 issue of the same journal. Another important area of debate has been the so-called small but healthy models of malnutrition of the early to mid-

1980s, in which it was asserted that previous figures for malnutrition based on measurements of height and weight for a given age overestimated the prevalence of malnutrition because they did not take into account certain adaptations in body size to low food intake (see n. 19 for a definition of methods of nutritional assessment). If these adaptations were taken into account, the authors of this model argue, many of today's malnourished children would be found to be small but healthy. The implications of this argumentation can be enormous, ranging from the denial of the problem to a redirection of policy away from food and nutrition programs toward health and environmental interventions (the implication that the authors of the model favor). See, for instance, Sukhatme and Margen (1978); Payne and Cutler (1984).

11. This analysis of the Colombian National Food and Nutrition Plan (PAN) and the Integrated Rural Development Program (DRI) is based on fieldwork I did in Bogotá and Cali during the following periods: June 1981–May 1982; December 1983–January 1984; summer 1990, 1993. During the first prolonged period, I participated daily in the activities of PAN and DRI planners and collected information on all aspects of plan design, implementation, and evaluation for the period 1971–1982. Besides participant observation, I conducted interviews with planners at the Department of National Planning (DNP), PAN, DRI, the ministries of agriculture and health, the Colombian Institute for Family Welfare (ICBF), and the regional PAN office in Cali. Changes in policy and programming were updated in 1983–1984 and again in 1990.

12. The author of this assessment, Guillermo Varela, directed between 1971 and 1975 the design of what was to become the National Food and Nutrition Plan. At that time, Varela was part of the staff of the Division of Population and Nutrition of the Department of National Planning. Varela's retrospective study was commissioned by U.S. AID and the PIA/PNAN.

13. My first contact with Varela took place in September 1975. Having gone to his Bogotá office for an unrelated reason, I established an animated conversation about the FAO documents I spotted on the shelves in his office. I had been reading the same documents in the library of the Universidad del Valle in Cali, where I had just finished my undergraduate degree in chemical engineering. Out of this conversation emerged the possibility of applying for a PAN/DRI scholarship for graduate work in food and nutrition, which I subsequently earned. I then went to Cornell University for a two-year master's program. After my return from Cornell in January 1978, I worked with PAN for eight months.

14. In some instances, the studies of the 1960s and 1970s led to politicized interventions by activists and dissenting intellectuals, particularly in public health. See, for instance, the work of Yolanda Arango de Bedoya (Department of Social Medicine of the Universidad del Valle in Cali) on primary health care (1979) and Juan César García (1981) in the Dominican Republic on the history of the institutionalization of health. In the United States, Marxist-inspired studies of health and underdevelopment were also important, particularly those published in the *International Journal of Health Services*. See, for instance, Navarro (1976). This book had some repercussions in Latin America.

15. An account of the early public health and hygiene activities of the Rockefeller Foundation in the South of the U.S. (particularly the hookworm program) and abroad (campaigns against hookworm, yellow fever, malaria, and the training of public

health personnel) is found in Brown (1976). The establishment of medical schools in Latin American universities with support from the Rockefeller Foundation in the 1950s (for instance, the Universidad del Valle Medical School in Cali) was also an important factor in the promotion of nutrition and public health research and activities. Some of the nutrition programs carried out in the Cauca Valley under Rockefeller sponsorship, and their consequences for local peasants, are discussed by Taussig (1978).

16. For an analysis of Colombian agriculture during the period, see Kalmanovitz (1978); Arrubla, ed. (1976); Bejarano (1979, 1985); Rojas and Fals Borda, eds. (1977); Moncayo and Rojas (1979); Fajardo (1983); Perry (1983); Ocampo, Bernal, Avella, and Errázuriz (1987); and Zamocs (1986). This presentation is based chiefly on the works of Kalmanovitz and Fajardo. The analysis of the agrarian political economy is based on Kalmanovitz (1978); Fajardo, ed. (1991); de Janvry (1981); and Crouch and de Janvry (1980).

17. For contemporary critical analyses of the green revolution, particularly in relation to nutrition, see Almeida (1975); Franke (1974); and Cleaver (1973).

18. In Colombia and elsewhere, the semiproletarian peasants spend part of the year working on their own plots and migrate to several parts of the country as seasonal work becomes available, such as the harvesting of coffee and cotton or the cutting of sugarcane.

19. Methods for the assessment of the nutritional status at this point were derived from anthropometry (particularly measurements of weight for age, height for age, arm circumference, and skinfold thickness). The best-known classification was the so-called Gómez classification, which distinguished among three degrees of malnutrition (mild, moderate, and severe), in terms of weight for age measurement in relation to a given standard. Although for many years the standard (normal) growth charts were derived from a Harvard study of well-to-do children in Cambridge, Massachusetts, many countries started to develop their own standards in the 1960s and 1970s. For assessments of the nutritional status of the Colombian population, see Pardo (1984) and Mora (1982).

20. CIAT was set up in 1967 by the Rockefeller Foundation as one of the spearheads of the green revolution in the heart of the rich Cauca River Valley of Colombia. At the time of the conference the region was witnessing increased proletarianization of the black peasantry, which Michael Taussig (1978, 1980) was by then researching. It was the same region where the Rockefeller Foundation was active, in cooperation with the local medical establishment, in nutrition, family plannning, and health research; the same region where I was doing my undergraduate studies in science and engineering. All of these events were not coincidental. They were framed by the development process.

21. Medical professionals were particularly entrenched in the Colombian Institute for Family Welfare (ICBF). Their views on the struggle over the definition of nutrition can be gleaned from the writings of some of the most illustrious physician-nutritionists, all of them associated at one point or another with ICBF, particularly Obdulio Mora, Franz Pardo, Leonardo Sinisterra, R. Rueda Williamson, and R. Grueso. See, for instance, the papers presented at this conference by Pardo (1973) and Grueso (1973).

22. On the early planning stages, see DNP/UDS (1974a, 1974b, 1974c, 1974d, and

1975). I reconstructed this part of the story based on archives and interviews conducted in 1981 and 1982 with planners who participated in the process.

23. See DNP (1975b); see also the July 1975 DNP letter to Lawrence Casazza of the World Bank (circulated in an internal memo), which included several annexes on program design and funding. The influence of funding procedures on program design and implementation has not been studied. Disbursement procedures of World Bank funds for PAN and DRI are detailed in DNP/PAN (1979a).

24. This was part of a struggle between the director of the Coordinating Group and Miguel Urrutia, the head of DNP at the time, which resulted in the former's dismissal and the depoliticization of the plan.

25. See the following program descriptions: DNP/PAN (1975b, 1976b, 1976c, 1976d, 1976e, 1976f, and 1977); DNP-PAN/IICA (1977).

26. An Office of Community Participation was set up in 1976 within the Ministry of Health. The participation component was riddled with problems, and by the middle of 1982 it had not taken off the ground. A National Plan for Community Participation was instituted in that year, as if participation could be effected by decree. Interviews with Edgar Mendoza and María Beatriz Duarte, from the Direction of Participation of the Ministry of Health (November 1981). See also Ministerio de Salud (1979, 1982).

27. A number of Colombians received advanced training at MIT's International Nutrition Planning Program; one of its graduates became PAN's head in 1979. I spent two years at Cornell's International Nutrition Program on a PAN scholarship.

28. As part of its evaluation program, PAN contracted several surveys with a private institute. See Instituto SER (1980b, 1981). Surveys conducted before the 1979 survey, however, had serious sampling or methodological problems, so that a baseline could not be constructed (interview with Franz Pardo, of PAN's evaluation unit, November 6, 1981). In 1981, a national survey conducted by the National Statistics Department (DANE), in cooperation with PAN and DRI, allowed planners to have a more disaggregated view of the food and nutrition situation of the country (Pardo 1984). Both PAN and DRI produced routine annual evaluation reports, although they were mostly restricted to items such as the financial disbursement of resources, the building of health facilities, and so on.

29. Interview with Germán Perdomo, head of the health division, DNP (March 1982).

30. These projects, in countries like Mexico (Puebla), Colombia (Cáqueza and García Rovira), Peru (Cajamarca), and Honduras have not been sufficiently studied from the perspective of their influence on the discourse of rural development. For an analysis of these projects from a conventional political economy perspective, see de Janvry (1981).

31. In DRI's case, the most important of these institutions were the Agrarian Bank (Caja Agraria), the Colombian Agricultural Institute (ICA), the Colombian Agrarian Reform Institute (INCORA), the National Institute of Natural Resources (INDERENA), the National Services of Vocational Learning (SENA), the Agriculture Livestock Marketing Institute (IDEMA), the Ministries of Health and Education, the Colombian Institute for Family Welfare (ICBF), the Colombian Institute of Energy (ICEL), the National Institue of Health (INS), and the Rural Road Fund. These organizations had a long tradition of rivalry.

32. The 1982 reorientation is detailed in four key publications; see DNP/DRI-PAN (1982a, 1982b, 1983) and DNP/UEA (1982a). For a thorough insider's account of DRI policy changes from 1976 to 1989, see Fajardo, Errázuriz, and Balcázar (1991).

33. The view of the commercial growers' associations at the time is represented in Junguito (1982); see also DNP/UEA (1982b). The evolution of the most powerful organization of capitalist farmers in the twentieth century, the Sociedad de Agricultores de Colombia (SAC), is recounted in Bejarano (1985).

34. One of the most celebrated events DRI organized was the International Seminar of Peasant Economy, carried out in a small town a few hours' drive from Bogotá on June 3–6, 1987. Papers were presented at the seminar by well-known scholars from all over Latin America. Attended by more than twelve hundred people, including representatives of peasant organizations, scholars, and government personnel, the seminar was convened "with the common purpose of studying the conditions to strengthen, within a pluralist framework, national and international policies on behalf of peasant producers." See Bustamante, ed. (1987).

35. The DRI evaluation group in Bogotá carried out evaluations of socioeconomic impact of the first phase in four main districts (Rionegro, Lorica, Sincelejo, and Valle de Tenza), based on its own formulation for program evaluation (DNP/DRI 1976a). In 1983, DRI contracted more thorough and rigorous evaluations with some of the major universities in the country (Universidades Nacional, Javeriana, Andes, de Antioquia, y del Valle). See, for instance, Arango et al. (1987) for the evaluation of the Rionegro, Lorica, and Sincelejo carried out by a team from the Universidad de Antioquia in Medellín. For a review of the various evaluations, see Fajardo, Errázuriz, and Balcázar (1991, 200–32).

36. For instance, in one region, onions replaced a combination of corn and beans; in another, beans replaced a combination of corn and beans; in yet another, potatoes were replaced by dairy cattle; plantains or manioc replaced corn or tobacco, and so on. In general, however, the shift to monoculture (which the government had encouraged in the early 1970s) was avoided, promoting instead the practice of polyculture, although this time keeping the several crops in separate parts of the farm or planting some parts in intercropping and others in monocropping. The concrete recommendations were arrived at through empirical research on items such as crop rotation, sowing density, fertilization methods, and pest control and following the principles of productivity and cost effectiveness. See Fajardo, Errázuriz, and Balcázar (1991, 225, 226).

37. This contrasts sharply, say, with the World Bank, where room for dissent is nonexistent. Colombia also contrasts in this respect with countries like Chile or Argentina, where for historical reasons neoliberal economists, under the aegis of the so-called Chicago Boys, have become dominant. This is changing rapidly in Colombia as well.

38. A debate of this type is being carried out, for instance, between a group gathered around the work of José Antonio Ocampo, a neoclassical economist and economic historian, and Marxist-inspired political economists such as Salomón Kalmanovitz. See Kalmanovitz (1989) for a summary of the debate.

39. The bottom 85 percent of peasant holders, with farm sizes between 0 and 20 hectares, account for only about 15 percent of the land. Farmers with holdings be-

tween 5 and 20 hectares (that is, actual or potential DRI beneficiaries), representing 20 percent of total owners, control 10 percent of the land; those with holdings between 100 and 500 hectares (3 percent of owners) control 27.4 percent of the land; finally, those with holdings larger than 500 hectares (0.55 percent of owners) account for 32.6 percent of the land. The figures are for 1984; they show a tendency toward increased concentration of land ownership with respect to 1960 and 1970 figures. See Fajardo, Errázuriz, and Balcázar (1991, 136).

40. This phrase of Deleuze's, referring to Foucault as the first "to teach us something fundamental: the indignity of speaking for others" (Foucault and Deleuze 1977, 209), is invoked by Sanz de Santamaría in his reflection on the DRI evaluation process.

41. The researcher's life was threatened, and several of his coresearchers were assassinated. It must be said that this was happening at the height of the so-called dirty war of the 1980s, an episode of heightened repression for progressive intellectuals, and union and peasant leaders by local elites and security forces in various regions of the country.

CHAPTER 5

1. Comment written by Donna Haraway on Elizabeth Bird's paper (1984).
2. Electronic mail from Stacy Leigh Pigg, August 1992.
3. This presentation is based on Grillo (1990, 1992); Grillo, ed. (1991); Valladolid (1989); Chambi and Quiso C. (1992); de la Torre (1986).
4. Some of the landmarks in this literature are Benería and Sen (1981); Benería, ed. (1982); León, ed. (1982); León and Deere, eds. (1986); Sen and Grown (1987); Gallin, Aronoff, and Ferguson, eds. (1989); Gallin and Ferguson, eds. (1990); A. Rao, ed. (1991). Useful reviews of the vast literature in the field are found in the edited volumes by Gallin, Aronoff, and Ferguson (1989), and Gallin and Ferguson (1990). For related works see Bourque and Warren (1981); Nash and Safa, eds. (1986); Mies (1986); Benería and Roldán (1987); Jelin, ed. (1990); Benería and Feldman, eds. (1992).
5. See also some of the articles in Rao, ed. (1991) and the special issue on women in the *Review of Radical Political Economy* 23 nos. 3–4.
6. An important variant of this question is the relationship between First and Third World feminists. Feminists in the Third World, like the Colombian researchers to be discussed shortly, often find themselves in a difficult situation, between their own subversiveness as women and "the more familiar, oppressive discursive prowess of the First World" (Chow 1992, 111). This postmodern cultural situation in which Third World feminists find themselves—at once resisting patriarchy and the West and having to use at times Eurocentric languages—is a difficult one. For them, "the question is never that of asserting power as woman alone, but of showing how the concern for women is inseparable from other types of cultural oppression and negotiation" (111; see also Mani 1989). The constraints under which Third World WID researchers work are real, even if they vary widely according to country. For the Zambian case, Hansen and Ashbaugh (1990) found that the precarious conditions under which they lived forced local women professionals to conform closely to the

terms specified by the discourse of international WID agencies, thus curtailing greatly these women's efforts at critique.

7. Conversation with María Cristina Rojas de Ferro (DRI planner at the time), Northampton, Mass., July 1992.

8. Studies on the participation of women in the public sector in Latin America are scarce, although it seems true that this participation is high in Colombia and Venezuela, compared with many other Latin American countries. It also seems, however, that a certain "feminization" of the labor force in the public sector has taken place since the early 1980s, as highly trained men migrated to higher-paying jobs in the private sector in the wake of the debt crisis. In Colombia, for instance, a woman was appointed for the first time in the mid-1980s director of the Department of National Planning, one of the most important and coveted posts of the country, even if she did not pursue in any particular way women's issues. There seems to be some pressure for women in high-level positions not to engage in "women's issues." As far as PAN and DRI are concerned, the participation of women, mostly economists, at PAN was very high; women represented at least 50 percent of the professional staff. Women's participation at DRI (staffed mostly by agricultural economists, agronomists, and rural sociologists) was significantly lower. This perhaps reveals, again, a perception that PAN dealt with nutrition and health—"women's issues"—whereas DRI dealt with masculinized production. I owe these observations to Patricia Prieto, a former member of DRI's evaluation group and now an independent consultant (conversation held in Bogotá on July 26, 1992).

9. The highest decision-making body in Colombia is the National Council for Social and Economic Policy (CONPES), composed of the president, all cabinet members, and the head of the Department of National Planning.

10. Conversation with Patricia Prieto, July 26, 1992.

11. The methodological individualism of economics, for instance, makes it extremely difficult to raise questions of intergenerational equity (Norgaard 1991a), and its discursive monism precludes significant dialogue among the disciplines that comprise environmental sciences, particularly ecology (Norgaard 1991b). Similarly, internal critiques of economics often suggest that the cure for market failure is more and better markets (privatization), or that the cure for externalities, increasing returns to scale, or imperfect competition that cause markets to fail is the imitation of market outcomes—getting prices right, reformed cost-benefit analysis, and the like (Marglin 1992).

12. Examples given by O'Connor include global warming and acid rain destroying nature; salinization of water tables and the pesticide treadmill impairing agriculture; congestion, pollution, and high rents resulting from the capitalization of urban space impairing capital's own conditions; and rising health costs destroying labor power. The costs of this destruction are borne disproportionately by poor people, the Third World, and governments.

13. Brinda Rao (1989, 1991) gives an example of the creation of "water scarcity" in the Pune district of the state of Maharashtra in India. This phenomenon was a result of government projects that favored large farmers, and it has affected women in ways that go well beyond the increased distance they have to travel daily to fetch water. Because water is associated with the feminine principle, water scarcity has contrib-

uted to the erosion of traditional power by women. To complicate matters, accelerating deforestation has led to the disappearance of medicinal plants and has increased infant mortality, sometimes now attributed to women's witchcraft.

14. Part of the debate was carried out in the last few years in the pages of the Santa Cruz journal *Capitalism, Nature, Socialism*. The charge of "essentialism" in relation to ecofeminism stems chiefly from its association with spiritualist and culturalist strands of feminism, particularly the latter's emphasis on the superiority of women's culture, rooted in a feminine principle and women's essential "nature." Feminists of as diverse origin and practice as Susan Griffin, Vandana Shiva, Petra Kelly, and Mary Daly have been accused of essentialism. Ecofeminists argue that the critique of essentialism allows critics to disregard the contributions and force of spiritual and cultural feminists without considering them seriously. See Mellor (1992) and Merchant (1990) for summaries of the debate.

15. A third contradiction? Capital impairing and destroying cultures by seeking to homogenize them through discipline, normalization, and the like, including the forms of resistance to renewed attempts at cultural restructuring by capital.

16. Less clear in Leff's case is whether notions such as production and rationality can be theorized from the perspective of different cultural orders.

17. Science fiction writers have captured well the character of this transformation. Their landscapes are populated with cyborgs of all kinds, cyberspaces and virtual realities, and new possibilities of being human through an amazing set of new technological and social options. They show how artificial intelligence and biotechnologies are beginning to reshape biological and social life.

18. For Haraway's reading of primatology, see (1989a), especially chs. 3 and 7, and (1991), chs. 2 and 5. Narratives of immunology and bioengineering are discussed in (1989b, 1985); of sociobiology in (1991), especially chs. 3 and 4.

19. Haraway ambivalently interprets the ecofeminist defense of the organic as an oppositional ideology fit for twentieth-century capitalism. Her challenge to eco-feminists, however, is clear and fundamental. Perhaps one can say that the affirmation of nature and the organic (and similar instances, such as the indigenous) is an epochal strategy, dictated by the continuing importance of industrialism and modernity for present-day societies. This possibility is increasingly precluded by the rising cyberculture.

20. This kinship between the projects of Haraway and Benjamin is drawn from a reading of Susan Buck-Morss's book on Benjamin (1990, especially chapters. 3 and 5 and pp. 205–15).

CHAPTER 6

1. Most of these figures come from Strahm (1986). Some come from World Bank sources. On statistics as political technologies, see Urla (1993).

2. Generally speaking, "Attempts to introduce the language of liberation to those who do not speak it, as a precondition for the latter qualifying for what the moderns call liberation, is a travesty of even the normatives of the modern concept of liberation. . . . To the lesser mortals, being constantly sought to be liberated by a minority within the modern world, the resistance to the categories imposed by the dominant language of dissent is part of the struggle for survival" (Nandy 1989, 269).

3. Here I am talking primarily about the geographical Third World, or South, but also the Third World within the First. The connection between the Third World within and without can be important in terms of building a cultural politics in the West.

4. I have in mind, for instance, the profound breakdown and reconstitution of identities and social practices fostered by drug money and drug-related violence in countries like Colombia and Peru, or the social geographies of many large Third World cities, with their fortified sectors for the rich—connected with a growing number of electronic media to transnational cyberspaces—and massively pauperized and eroded sectors for the poor. These social geographies resemble more and more *Blade Runner*–type science fiction scenarios.

5. Among the most visible members of this group are Ashis Nandy (1983, 1989); Vandana Shiva (1989); D. L. Shet (1987); Shiv Visvanathan (1986, 1991); Majid Rahnema (1988a, 1988b); Orlando Fals Borda (1984, 1988; Fals Borda and Rahman (1991); Gustavo Esteva (1987); and Pramod Parajuli (1991). A more complete bibliography and treatment of the works of these authors is found in Escobar (1992b).

6. "A change in the order of discourse," wrote Foucault in the conclusion of *The Archaeology of Knowledge*, "does not presuppose 'new ideas,' a little invention and creativity, a different mentality, but transformations in a practice, perhaps also in neighbouring practices, and in their common articulation. I have not denied—far from it—the possibility of changing discourse: I have deprived the sovereignty of the subject of the exclusive and instantaneous right to it" (1972, 209).

7. "The substitution of one formation by another is not necessarily carried out at the level of the most general or most easily formalized statements. Only a serial method, as used today by historians, allows us to construct a series around a single point and to seek out other series which might prolong this point in different directions on the level of other points. There is always a point in space or time when series begin to diverge and become redistributed in a new space, and it is at this point that a break takes place. . . . And when a new formation appears, with new rules and series, it never comes all at once, in a single phrase or act of creation, but emerges like a series of 'building blocks,' with gaps, traces and reactivations of former elements that survive under the new rules" (Deleuze 1988, 21).

8. Although there are significant differences among the authors reviewed in this section, they share common themes and positions. The work of CLACSO's (Latin American Social Science Council) Working Group on Cultural Politics has been instrumental in advancing this line of research. The coordinator of this group, Néstor García Canclini, has produced what is perhaps the most important text in this regard, under the poetic title *Culturas Híbridas: Estrategias Para Entrar y Salir de la Modernidad*. Many of these debates are carried out in the journals *David y Goliath*, published by CLACSO in Buenos Aires, and *Nueva Sociedad*, published in Caracas. See also García Canclini, ed. (1987); Bartra (1987); Calderón, ed. (1988); Quijano (1988, 1990); Lechner (1988); Sarlo (1991); and Britto García (1991). Some of these texts are reviewed in Montaldo (1991). The only text available in English that deals with this literature is Yúdice, Franco, and Flores, eds. (1992).

9. Related theorizations of popular culture have appeared in the United States and Europe, chiefly in cultural studies. See particularly the works of de Certeau (1984), Fiske (1989a, 1989b), Willis (1990), and Angus and Jhally, eds. (1989).

10. García Marquez emphasizes that everything he has written is strictly real. "Daily life in Latin America shows us that reality is filled with extraordinary things. . . . It is sufficient to glance at the newspapers to realize that extraordinary events are always happening" (1982, 36). Neruda spoke of Mexico as the last magic country, in ways that apply to many places in the Third World.

11. Some of these points became clear to me in discussions with Trinh T. Minh-ha and Rey Chow at faculty seminars held in Northampton, Massachusetts, on January 20–22, 1993, and organized by the women's studies program at Smith College.

12. Habermas's tour de force (1987) shows the shortcomings of the various attempts since Nietzsche at overcoming subject-centered reason by relying on reason, even if he does it in order to prepare the ground for his own attempt (communicative action), probably no less flawed according to his own criteria than those he critiques. One quick note on Habermas's treatment of Foucault (1987, chs. 9 and 10): although Habermas is right in saying that Foucault does not succeed in providing a fully satisfactory account of the genealogy of the social, Foucault's (1986) notion of "problematizations of truth" (games of truth and power) as the source of specific configurations of social life does not entail positing power as a transcendental that arrives from nowhere, as Habermas imputes to Foucault. Laclau and Mouffe's (1985) notion of "field of discursivity" from which all social reality emerges through articulations—derived from a reformulation of Foucault's notion of discursive formation—and Deleuze's interpretation of Foucault's work in terms of mathematical concepts such as strata, foldings, topology, and the outside are meant to give an idea of the sources of power.

13. "Utopia is what connects philosophy to its epoch . . . it is with utopia that philosophy becomes political, carrying to its extreme the critique of the epoch" (Deleuze and Guattari 1993, 101; my translation from the Spanish version).

14. This is a risky question—one that oscillates between unreflective interventionism based on the belief that one can "liberate" others, on the one hand, and a total disregard for the role of intellectual work in social life, on the other. There is also the danger, as bell hooks put it, that "cultural studies could easily become the space for the informers" (1990, 9). For hooks, only a significant exchange between the critic and the people he or she writes about "will insure that it [cultural studies] is a location that enables critical intervention" (9).

15. "The response of the States, or of the axiomatic, may obviously be to accord the minorities regional or federal or statutory autonomy, in short, to add axioms. But this is not the problem: this operation consists only in translating the minorities into denumerable sets or subsets, which would enter as elements into the majority, which could be counted among the majority. . . . What is proper to the minority is to assert a power of the nondenumerable, even if that minority is composed of a single member. This is the formula for multiplicities" (Deleuze and Guattari 1987, 470).

16. A discussion of some of these questions is found in the visionary articles written by Guattari in the last months of his life. See Guattari (1993) for a Spanish-language collection of these works. In these writings, Guattari introduced the notion of ecosophy, an ethico-political perspective on diversity and alterity that requires economic, ecological, psychological, scientific, and social transformations. He spoke of the need to "construct new transcultural, transnational, and transversalist lands,

and value universes freed from the allure of territorialized power" as the only way to overcome the current planetary predicament (1993, 208).

17. I have in mind, for instance, the organization of black communities in the Pacific Coast region of Colombia, which are confronted by growing forces destructive to their culture and tropical rain-forest environment. Their social movement is framed by large-scale government plans for the "sustainable development" of the region; projects for the conservation of the region's almost legendary biological diversity; capitalist pressures for the control of land; the integration of the country into the Pacific Basin economies; and a political opening for the defense of minority rights, territories, and cultures.

REFERENCES

Adas, Michael. 1989. Machines as the Measure of Men. Ithaca: Cornell University Press.

Adelman, Irma, and Cynthia Tafts Morris. 1973. Economic Growth and Social Equity in Developing Countries. Stanford: Stanford University Press.

Alatas, Syed Hussein. 1977. The Myth of the Lazy Native. London: Frank Cass.

Aldcroft, Derek. 1977. From Versailles to Wall Street, 1919–1929. Berkeley: University of California Press.

Almeida, Silvio. 1975. Analysis of Traditional Strategies to Combat World Hunger and Their Results. International Journal of Health Services 5 (1): 121–41.

Alonso, Ana María. 1992. Gender, Power, and Historical Memory: Discourses of Serrano Resistance. In Feminists Theorize the Political, edited by Judith Butler and Joan Scott, 404–25. Boulder: Westview Press.

Altieri, Miguel, ed. 1987. Agroecology. The Scientific Basis of Alternative Agriculture. Boulder: Westview Press.

Amin, Samir. 1976. Unequal Development. London: Monthly Review Press.

———. 1985. Delinking. London: Zed Books.

———. 1990. Maldevelopment. London: Zed Books.

Anderson, M. A., and T. Grewald, eds. 1976. Nutrition Planning in the Developing World. Bogotá: Programas Editoriales.

Angus, Ian, and Sut Jhally, eds. 1989. Cultural Politics in Contemporary America. New York: Routledge.

Anzaldúa, Gloria, ed. 1990. Making Face, Making Soul: Haciendo Caras. San Francisco: Aunt Lute Foundation.

Apffel-Marglin, Frédérique. 1992. Women's Blood: Challenging the Discourse of Development. The Ecologist 22 (1): 22–32.

———, and Stephen Marglin, eds. 1990. Dominating Knowledge: Development, Culture, and Resistance. Oxford: Clarendon Press.

———. 1994. Decolonizing Knowledge: From Development to Dialogue. Oxford: Clarendon Press.

Appadurai, Arjun. 1991. Global Ethnoscapes: Notes and Queries for a Transnational Anthropology. In Recapturing Anthropology: Working in the Present, edited by Richard Fox, 191–210. Santa Fe: School of American Research.

Apthorpe, Raymond. 1984. Agriculture and Strategies: The Language of Development Policy. In Room for Manoeuvre, edited by Edward Clay and Bernard Shaffer, 127–41. Rutherford: Fairleigh Dickinson University Press.

Aranda, J., and L. Sáenz, eds. 1981. El Proceso de Planificación de Alimentación y Nutrición. Guatemala: INCAP.

Arango, Mariano, et al. 1987. Economía Campesina y Políticas Agrarias en Colombia. Medellín: Universidad de Antioquia.

Arango de Bedoya, Yolanda. 1979. Reflexiones sobre la Atención Primaria en Salud. Educación Médica en Salud 13 (4): 341–49.

Archila, Mauricio. 1980. Los Movimientos Sociales entre 1920 y 1924: Una Aproximación Metodológica. Cuadernos de Filosofía y Letras 3 (3): 181–230.

Arizpe, Lourdes. 1983. Las Campesinas y el Silencio. FEM 8 (29): 3–6

Arndt, H. W. 1978. The Rise and Fall of Economic Growth. Chicago: University of Chicago Press.

―――. 1981. Economic Development: A Semantic History. Economic Development and Cultural Change 29 (3): 457–66.

Arrubla, Mario, ed. 1976. La Agricultura Colombiana en el Siglo XX. Bogotá: Colcultura.

Asad, Talal. 1973. Introduction. In Anthropology and the Colonial Encounter, edited by Talal Asad, 9–20. Atlantic Highlands, N.J.: Humanities Press.

Austin, James, ed. 1981. Nutrition Intervention in Developing Countries: An Overview. Cambridge, Mass.: Oelgeschlager, Gunn & Hain Publishers.

―――, and Gustavo Esteva, eds. 1987. Food Policy in Mexico. Ithaca: Cornell University Press.

Bacon, Robert. 1916. For Better Relations with Our Latin American Neighbors. Washington, D.C.: Carnegie Endowment for Peace.

Banco de la República de Colombia. 1979. Colombia en el Grupo de Consulta 1979. Bogotá: Banco de la República.

Banuri, Tariq. 1990. Development and the Politics of Knowledge: A Critical Interpretation of the Social Role of Modernization. In Dominating Knowledge: Development, Culture and Resistance, edited by Frédérique Apffel-Marglin and Stephen Marglin, 29–73. Oxford: Clarendon Press.

Baran, Paul. 1957. The Political Economy of Growth. New York: Monthly Review Press.

―――. 1958. On the Political Economy of Backwardness. In The Economics of Underdevelopment, edited by A. N. Agarwala and S. P. Singh, 75–91. Bombay: Oxford University Press.

Barroso, Carmen, and Cristina Bruschini. 1991. Building Politics from Personal Lives: Discussions on Sexuality among Poor Women in Brazil. In Third World Women and the Politics of Feminism, edited by Chandra Mohanty, 153–72. Bloomington: Indiana University Press.

Bartra, Roger. 1987. La Jaula de la Melancolía. México, D.F.: Grijalbo.

Basadre, Jorge. [1949] 1967. Latin American Courses in the United States. Reprinted in Latin American History: Essays on Its Study and Teaching, 1895–1965, edited by Howard Cline, 413-59. Austin: University of Texas Press.

Bataille, Georges. 1991. The Accursed Share. New York: Zone Books.

Baudrillard, Jean. 1975. The Mirror of Production. St. Louis: Telos Press.

Bauer, Peter. 1984. Reality and Rhetoric: Studies in the Economics of Development. Cambridge: Harvard University Press.

―――, and Basil Yamey. 1957. The Economics of Underdeveloped Countries. Chicago: University of Chicago Press.

Behar, Ruth. 1990. Rage and Redemption: Reading the Life Story of a Mexican Marketing Woman. Feminist Studies 16 (2): 223–58.

Bejarano, Jesús Antonio. 1979. El Régimen Agrario de la Economía Exportadora a la Economía Industrial. Bogotá: Editorial La Carreta.

―――. 1985. Economía y Poder. Bogotá: Fondo Editorial CEREC.

————. 1987. La Economía Campesina como una Opción de Desarrollo. *In* Seminario Internacional de Economía Campesina y Pobreza Rural, edited by Jorge Bustamante, 60–65. Bogotá: Fondo DRI.

Bell, Daniel, and Irving Kristol. 1981. The Crisis in Economic Theory. New York: Harper Colophon Books.

Benería, Lourdes. 1992. The Mexican Debt Crisis: Restructuring the Economy and the Household. *In* Unequal Burden, edited by Lourdes Benería and Shelley Feldman, 83–104. Boulder: Westview Press.

————, ed. 1982. Women and Development: The Sexual Division of Labor in Rural Societies. New York: Praeger/ILO.

————, and Gita Sen. 1981. Accumulation, Reproduction and Women's Role in Economic Development: Boserup Revisited. Signs 7 (2): 279–98.

————, and Martha Roldán. 1987. The Crossroads of Class and Gender. Chicago: University of Chicago Press.

————, and Shelly Feldman, eds. 1992. Unequal Burden. Economic Crisis, Persistent Poverty, and Women's Work. Boulder: Westview Press.

Berg, Alan. 1973. The Nutrition Factor. Washington, D.C.: The Brookings Institution.

————. 1981. Malnourished People: A Policy View. Washington, D.C.: The World Bank.

————, and Robert Muscatt. 1973. Nutrition Program Planning: An Approach. *In* Nutrition, National Development and Planning, edited by A. Berg, N. Scrimshaw, and D. Call, 247–74. Cambridge: MIT Press.

————, Nevin Scrimshaw, and David Call, eds. 1973. Nutrition, National Development and Planning. Cambridge: MIT Press.

Bethell, Leslie. 1991. From The Second World War to the Cold War: 1944–1954. *In* Exporting Democracy: The United States and Latin America, edited by Abraham F. Lowenthal, 41–71. Baltimore: Johns Hopkins University Press.

Bhabha, Homi. 1990. The Other Question: Difference, Discrimination, and the Discourse of Colonialism. *In* Out There: Marginalization and Contemporary Cultures, edited by Russell Ferguson, et al., pp.71–89. New York: New Museum of Contemporary Art; and Cambridge: MIT Press.

Biersteker, Thomas. 1991. Linkages between Development and the Social Sciences. Presented at the Social Science Research Council Meeting on Development and Social Science. Berkeley, Calif. November 15–16.

Binder, Leonard. 1986. The Natural History of Development Theory. Comparative Studies in Society and History 28 (1): 3–33.

Bird, Elizabeth. 1984. Green Revolution Imperialism. Photocopy. History of Consciousness Program, University of California, Santa Cruz.

Blaug, Mark. 1976. Kuhn versus Lakatos *or* Paradigms versus Research Programmes in the History of Economics. *In* Method and Appraisal in Economics, edited by Spiro Latsis, 149–80. Cambridge: Cambridge University Press.

————. 1978. Economic Theory in Retrospect. Cambridge: Cambridge University Press.

Bonilla, Elsy, ed. 1985. Mujer y Familia en Colombia. Bogotá: Plaza & Janés.

————, and Eduardo Vélez. 1987. Mujer y Trabajo en el Sector Rural Colombiano. Bogotá: Plaza & Janés.

Borrego, John. 1981. Metanational Capitalist Accumulation and the Emerging Paradigm of Revolutionist Accumulation. Review 4 (4): 713–77.

Boserup, Ester. 1970. Women's Role in Economic Development. New York: St. Martin's Press.

Bourque, Susan, and Kay Warren. 1981. Women of the Andes. Ann Arbor: University of Michigan Press.

Braudel, Fernand. 1977. Afterthoughts on Material Civilization and Capitalism. Baltimore: Johns Hopkins University Press.

Britto García, Luis. 1991. El Imperio Contracultural: Del Rock a la Postmodernidad. Caracas: Nueva Sociedad.

Brown, Richard. 1976. Public Health in Imperialism: Early Rockefeller Programs at Home and Abroad. American Journal of Public Health 66 (9): 897–903.

Brown, William, and Redvers Opie. 1953. American Foreign Assistance. Washington, D.C.: Brookings Institution.

Buchanan, Norman, and Howard Ellis. 1951. Approaches to Economic Development. New York: Twentieth Century Fund.

Buck-Morss, Susan. 1990. The Dialectics of Seeing. Cambridge: MIT Press.

Burbach, Roger, and Patricia Flynn. 1980. Agribusiness in the Americas. New York: Monthly Review.

Burchell, Graham, Colin Gordon, and Peter Miller, eds. 1991. The Foucault Effect. Chicago: University of Chicago Press.

Burgin, Miron. [1947] 1967. Research in Latin American Economics and Economic History. Reprinted in Latin American History: Essays on Its Study and Teaching, 1895–1965, edited by Howard Cline, 465–76. Austin: University of Texas Press.

Bustamante, Jorge, ed. 1987. Seminario Internacional de Economía Campesina y Pobreza Rural. Bogotá: Fondo DRI.

Buttel, Frederick, Martin Kenney, and Jack Kloppenburg. 1985. From Green Revolution to Biorevolution: Some Observations on the Changing Technological Bases of Economic Transformation in the Third World. Economic Development and Cultural Change 34 (1): 31–55.

———, A. Hawkins, and G. Power. 1990. From Limits to Growth to Global Change: Contrasts and Contradictions in the Evolution of Environmental Science and Ideology. Global Environmental Change 1 (1): 57–66.

Calderón, Fernando, ed. 1988. Imágenes Desconocidas: La Modernidad en la Encrucijada Postmoderna. Buenos Aires: CLACSO.

Campillo, Fabiola. 1983. Situación y Perspectivas de la Mujer Campesina en Colombia. Propuesta de una Política para su Incorporación al Desarrollo Rural. Bogotá: Ministerio de Agricultura.

Cano, Augusto. 1974. Antecedentes Constitucionales y Legales de la Planeación en Colombia. In Lecturas Sobre Desarrollo Económico Colombiano, edited by Hernando Gomez and Eduardo Wiesner, 221–71. Cali: Fundación para La Educación Superior y el Desarrollo.

Cardoso, Fernando Henrique. 1977. The Originality of a Copy: CEPAL and the Idea of Development. CEPAL Review 1977 (2): 7–40.

———, and Enzo Faletto. 1979. Dependency and Development in Latin America. Berkeley: University of California Press.

Carney, Judith, and Michael Watts. 1991. Disciplining Women? Rice, Mechanization, and the Evolution of Mandinga Gender Relations in Senegambia. Signs 16 (4): 651–81.

Castells, Manuel. 1986. High Technology, World Development, and Structural Transformations: The Trends and the Debates. Alternatives 11 (3): 297–344.

———, and Roberto Laserna. 1989. La Nueva Dependencia: Cambio Tecnológico y Reestructuración Socioeconómica en Latinoamérica. David y Goliath 55:2–16.

Chambi P., Néstor, and Víctor Quiso C. 1992. Estudio sobre Cosmovisión, Conocimiento Campesino y Tecnología Tradicional de los Criadores Aymaras. Documento de Estudio no. 24. Lima: PRATEC.

Chenery, Hollis. 1983. Interaction between Theory and Observation in Development. World Development 11 (10): 853–61.

Chow, Rey. 1992. Postmodern Automatons. In Feminists Theorize the Political, edited by Judith Butler and Joan Scott, 101–17. New York: Routledge.

Clark, William. 1989. Managing Planet Earth. Scientific American 261 (3): 46–57.

Clay, Edward, and Bernard Shaffer, eds. 1984. Room for Manoeuvre: An Exploration of Public Policy Planning in Agricultural and Rural Development. Rutherford: Fairleigh Dickinson University Press.

Cleaver, Harry. 1973. The Contradictions of the Green Revolution. In The Political Economy of Development and Underdevelopment, edited by Charles Wilber, 187–96. New York: Random House.

Clifford, James. 1986. Introduction: Partial Truths. In Writing Culture: The Poetics and Politics of Ethnography, edited by James Clifford and George Marcus, 1–27. Berkeley: University of California Press.

———. 1988. The Predicament of Culture. Cambridge: Harvard University Press.

———. 1989. Notes on Theory and Travel. Inscriptions 5:177–88.

Coale, Ansley, and Edgar Hoover. 1958. Population Growth and Economic Development in Low Income Countries. Princeton: Princeton University Press.

Cobos, A., and S. Góngora. 1977. Guía Metodológica para la Identificación y Análisis de Sistemas de Producción Agropecuaria en Areas de Pequeños Productores. Bogotá: ICA.

Comaroff, Jean. 1985. Body of Power, Spirit of Resistance. Chicago: University of Chicago Press.

———, and John Comaroff. 1991. Of Revelation and Revolution. Chicago: University of Chicago Press.

Conable, Barber. 1987. Address to the World Resources Institute. Washington, D.C.: World Bank.

Cooper, Frederick. 1991. Development and the Remaking of the Colonial World. Paper presented at SSRC meeting on Social Science and Development, Berkeley, Calif., November 15–16.

———, and Ann Stoler. 1989. Introduction: Tensions of Empire: Colonial Control and Visions of Rule. American Ethnologist 16 (4): 609–22.

Copland, Douglas. 1945. The Road to High Employment. Harvard: Oxford University Press.

Crouch, Luis, and Alain de Janvry. 1980. The Class Basis of Agricultural Growth. Food Policy 5 (1): 3–13.

Crush, Jonathan, ed. 1994. Discourses of Development. New York: Routledge. Forthcoming.

Cuevas Cancino, Francisco. 1989. Roosevelt y la Buena Vecindad. México, D.F.: Fondo de Cultura Económica.

Currie, Lauchlin. 1967. Obstacles to Development. East Lansing: Michigan State University Press.

Dahl, G., and A. Rabo, eds. 1992. Kam-Ap or Take-Off: Local Notions of Development. Stockholm: Stockholm Studies in Social Anthropology.

Deane, P. 1978. The Evolution of Economic Ideas. Cambridge: Cambridge University Press.

De Castro, Josué. [1952] 1977. The Geography of Hunger. New York: Monthly Review Press.

De Certeau, Michel. 1984. The Practice of Everyday Life. Berkeley: University of California Press.

De Janvry, Alain. 1981. The Agrarian Question and Reformism in Latin America. Baltimore: Johns Hopkins University Press.

De la Torre, Ana. 1986. Los dos Lados del Mundo y del Tiempo. Lima: Centro de Investigación, Educación y Desarrollo.

De la Torre, Cristina, ed. 1985. Modelos Económicos de Desarrollo Colombiano. Bogotá: Editorial Oveja Negra.

De Lauretis, Teresa. 1987. Technologies of Gender. Bloomington: Indiana University Press.

Deleuze, Gilles. 1988. Foucault. Minneapolis: University of Minnesota Press.

———, and Félix Guattari. 1987. A Thousand Plateaus. Minneapolis: University of Minnesota Press.

———. 1993. Qué es la Filosofía? Barcelona: Editorial Anagrama.

Dennery, Etienne. [1970] 1931. Asia's Teeming Millions. Washington, D.C.: Kennikat Press.

Diawara, Manthia. 1990. Reading Africa through Foucault: V. Y. Mudimbe's Reaffirmation of the Subject. October 55:79–104.

Dietz, James, and Dilmus James, eds. 1990. Progress toward Development in Latin America. Boulder: Lynne Rienner.

Di Marco, Luis Eugenio, ed. 1974. Economía Internacional y Desarrollo: Estudios en Honor de Raúl Prebisch. Buenos Aires: Ediciones Depalma.

DNP (Departamento Nacional de Planeacion de Colombia). 1975a. Plan Nacional de Alimentación y Nutrición. Bogotá: DNP.

———. 1975b. Para Cerrar la Brecha: Plan de Desarrollo Social, Económico y Regional 1975–1978. Bogotá: DNP.

———. 1983. Plan de Desarrollo Integral para la Costa Pacífica. Cali: CVC.

———. 1992. Plan Pacífico: Una Estrategia de Desarrollo Sostenible para la Costa Pacífica Colombiana. Bogotá: DNP.

DNP/DRI. 1975a. Síntesis del Programa de Desarrollo Rural Integrado. Bogotá: DNP/DRI

———. 1975b. Estudio de Formas Asociativas en las Areas del Program de Desarrollo Rural Integrado. Bogotá: DNP/UDA.

———. 1976a. Bases para la Evaluación del Programa de Desarrollo Rural Integrado. Bogotá: DNP/DRI.

———. 1976b. Normas Generales para la Organización del Program de Desarrollo Rural Integrado. Bogotá: DNP/DRI; rev. ed. 1979.

_____. 1979. El Subsector de Pequeña Producción y el Programa DRI. Bogotá: DNP/DRI.

DNP/DRI-PAN. 1982a. Realizaciones de los Programas DRI-PAN. Bogotá: DRI-PAN.

_____. 1982b. Propuesta para las Ejecuciones del Programa DRI-PAN. Bogotá: DRI-PAN.

_____. 1983. Nuevas Orientaciones. Bogotá: DRI-PAN.

DNP/PAN. 1975a. Proyecto de Regionalización. Indice de Información Recolectada en los Departamentos. Bogotá: DNP/PAN.

_____. 1975b. Programa de Alimentos Procesados de Alto Valor Nutricional y Bajo Costo. Bogotá: DNP/PAN.

_____. 1976a. Regionalización del País para su Aplicación. Bogotá: DNP/PAN.

_____. 1976b. Distribución Subsidiada de Alimentos. Programa Cupones. Bogotá: DNP/PAN.

_____. 1976c. Programa de Distribución Subsidiada de Alimentos. Subprograma de Distribución Directa. Bogotá: DNP/PAN.

_____. 1976d. Programa de Educación Nutricional. Proyecto de Educación Interpersonal. Bogotá: DNP/PAN.

_____. 1976e. Proyecto de Educación Nutricional para el Nivel Profesional, Asistencia Técnica y Proyectos Pilotos. Bogotá: DNP/PAN.

_____. 1976f. Programa de Huertas Escolares y Caseras. Bogotá: DNP/PAN.

_____. 1977. Programa de Evaluación. Bogotá: DNP/PAN.

_____. 1979a. Procedimiento para Retiro de Recursos BIRF. Convenio de Préstamo 1487-CO (segunda versión). Bogotá: DNP/PAN.

DNP-PAN/IICA. 1977. Seminario de Evaluación de Programas de Huertas Escolares y Pancoger. Bogotá: DNP-PAN/IICA.

DNP/UDS (Departamento Nacional de Planeación de Colombia, Unidad de Desarrollo Social). 1973. Bases para una Política de Alimentación y Nutrición en Colombia. Bogotá: DNP/UDS.

_____. 1974a. Esbozo General del Plan de Nutrición. Bogotá: DNP/UDS.

_____. 1974b. Selección de Variables para el Análisis. Bogotá: DNP/UDS.

_____. 1974c. Selección de Alimentos. Bogotá: DNP/UDS.

_____. 1974d. Objetivos, Estrategias y Mecanismos del Plan Nacional de Alimentación y Nutrición (Cuadro Resúmen). Bogotá: DNP/UDS.

_____. 1975. Circular no. 1. Bogotá: DNP/UDS.

DNP/UEA. 1982a. Experiencias de la Fase I del Programa DRI y Recomendaciones para la Fase II. Bogotá: DNP/UEA.

_____. 1982b. Plan de Integración Nacional. Política Agropecuaria y el Sistema de Alimentos. Bogotá: DNP/UDA.

_____. 1984. Política sobre el Papel de la Mujer Campesina en el Desarrollo Agropecuario. Bogotá: DNP/UEA.

_____. 1988. Programa de Desarrollo Integral Campesino (1988–1993).

Dobb, Maurice. 1946. Studies in the Development of Capitalism. London: Routledge and Kegan Paul.

_____. 1973. Theories of Value and Distribution Since Adam Smith. Cambridge: Cambridge University Press.

Donzelot, Jacques. 1979. The Policing of Families. New York: Pantheon Books.

Donzelot, Jacques. 1988. The Promotion of the Social. Economy and Society 17 (3): 217–34.

———. 1991. Pleasure in Work. In The Foucault Effect, edited by Graham Burchell, Colin Gordon, and Peter Miller, 251–80. Chicago: University of Chicago Press.

Drake, Paul. 1991. From Good Men to Good Neighbors: 1912–1932. In Exporting Democracy: The United States and Latin America, edited by Abraham F. Lowenthal, 3–41. Baltimore: Johns Hopkins University Press.

Dubois, Marc. 1991. The Governance of the Third World: A Foucauldian Perspective of Power Relations in Development. Alternatives 16 (1): 1–30.

Dumont, Louis. 1977. From Mandeville to Marx: The Genesis and Triumph of Economic Ideology. Chicago: University of Chicago Press.

Economic Commission for Latin America. 1950. The Economic Development of Latin America and Its Principal Problems. New York: United Nations.

Emmanuel, Arghiri. 1972. Unequal Exchange: A Study of the Imperialism of Trade. London: New Left Books.

Escobar, Arturo. 1984. Discourse and Power in Development: Michel Foucault and the Relevance of His Work to the Third World. Alternatives 10 (3): 377–400.

———. 1987. Power and Visibility: The Invention and Management of Development in the Third World. Ph.D. diss., University of California, Berkeley.

———. 1988. Power and Visibility: Development and the Invention and Management of the Third World. Cultural Anthropology 3 (4): 428–43.

———. 1989. The Professionalization and Institutionalization of "Development" in Colombia in the Early Post–World War II Period. International Journal of Educational Development 9 (2): 139–54.

———. 1991. Anthropology and the Development Encounter: The Making and Marketing of Development Anthropology. American Ethnologist 18 (4): 16–40.

———. 1992a. Planning. In The Development Dictionary, edited by Wofgang Sachs, 112–45. London: Zed Books.

———. 1992b. Reflections on "Development": Grassroots Approaches and Alternative Politics in the Third World. Futures 24 (5): 411–36.

———. 1994. Welcome to Cyberia: Notes on the Anthropology of Cyberculture. Current Anthropology. Forthcoming.

———, and Sonia E. Alvarez, eds. 1992. The Making of Social Movements in Latin America: Identity, Strategy, and Democracy. Boulder: Westview Press.

Esteva, Gustavo. 1987. Regenerating People's Space. Alternatives 12 (1): 125–52.

Fabian, Johannes. 1983. Time and the Other: How Anthropology Makes Its Object. New York: Columbia University Press.

Fajardo, Darío. 1983. Haciendas, Campesinos y Políticas Agrarias en Colombia, 1920–1980. Bogotá: Editorial Oveja Negra.

———. 1984. Apuntes para una Política de Reforma Agraria y Seguridad Alimentaria. Lecturas de Economía 15:221–40.

———. 1987. Desarrollo Rural y Decentralización. In Seminario Internacional de Economía Campasina y Pobreza Rural, edited by Jorge Bustamante, 208–22. Bogotá: Fondo DRI.

———, ed. 1991. Campesinos y Desarrollo en América Latina. Bogotá: Tercer Mundo Editores y Fondo DRI.

———, María Errázuriz, and Fernando Balcázar. 1991. La Experiencia del DRI en

Colombia. *In* Campesinos y Desarrollo en América Latina, edited by Darío Fajardo, 125–259. Bogotá: Tercer Mundo Editores y Fondo DRI.

Fals Borda, Orlando. 1970. Ciencia Propia y Colonialismo Intelectual. México, D.F.: Editorial Nuestro Tiempo.

————. 1984. Resistencia en el San Jorge. Bogotá: Carlos Valencia Editores.

————. 1988. Knowledge and People's Power. Delhi: Indian Social Science Institute.

————, and Anisur Rahman, eds. 1991. Action and Knowledge: Breaking the Monopoly with Participatory Action-Research. New York: Apex Press.

Fanon, Franz. 1967. Black Skin, White Masks. New York: Grove Press.

————. 1968. The Wretched of the Earth. New York: Grove Press.

FAO. 1974a. Assessment of the World Food Situation. Rome: FAO.

————. 1974b. The World Food Problem: Proposals for National and International Action. Rome: FAO.

FAO/WHO Expert Committee on Nutrition. 1976. Food and Nutrition Strategies in National Development. Rome: FAO; Geneva: WHO.

Feder, Ernest. 1977. Agribusiness and the Elimination of Latin America's Rural Proletariat. World Development 5 (5–7): 559–71.

————. 1983. Perverse Development. Quezon City: Foundation for Nationalist Studies.

Ferguson, James. 1990. The Anti-Politics Machine: "Development," Depoliticization, and Bureaucratic Power in Lesotho. Cambridge: Cambridge University Press.

Fernández Kelly, María Patricia. 1983. For We Are Sold, I and My People: Women and Industry in Mexico's Frontier. Albany: SUNY Press.

Field, John Osgood. 1977. The Soft Underbelly of Applied Knowledge: Conceptual and Operational Problems in Nutrition Planning. Food Policy 2 (3): 228–39.

Finer, Herman. 1949. Road to Reaction. Boston: Little, Brown.

Fishlow, Albert. 1985. The State of Latin American Economics. Stanford-Berkeley Occasional Papers in Latin American Studies, no. 11.

Fiske, John. 1989a. Understanding the Popular. Boston: Unwin Hyman.

————. 1989b. Reading the Popular. Boston: Unwin Hyman.

Flórez, Luis B. 1984. Una Reflexión Sobre la Economía del Desarrollo y el Desarrollo Económico. Cuadernos de Economía (Bogotá) 7:65–82.

Fondo DRI. 1989a. Programa de Desarrollo Integral Campesino. Bogotá: Ministerio de Agricultura/Fondo DRI.

————. 1989b. Programa de Desarrollo Integral Campesino. Evaluación del Programa. Bogotá: Ministerio de Agricultura/Fondo DRI.

————. 1989c. Programa de Desarrollo Integral Campesino. Mujer Campesina. Bogotá: Fondo DRI.

Foucault, Michel. 1972. The Archaeology of Knowledge. New York: Harper Colophon Books.

————. 1973. The Order of Things. New York: Vintage Books.

————. 1975. The Birth of the Clinic. New York: Vintage Books.

————. 1979. Discipline and Punish. New York: Vintage Books.

————. 1980a. Power/Knowledge. New York: Pantheon Books.

————. 1980b. The History of Sexuality. Introduction. New York: Vintage Books.

Foucault, Michel. 1980c. Truth and Power. *In* Power/Knowledge, edited by Colin Gordon, 109–33. New York: Pantheon Books.

———. 1986. The Use of Pleasure. New York: Pantheon Books.

———. 1991a. Governmentality. *In* The Foucault Effect, edited by Graham Burchell, Colin Gordon, and Peter Miller, 87–104. Chicago: University of Chicago Press.

———. 1991b. Politics and the Study of Discourse. *In* The Foucault Effect, edited by Graham Burchell, Colin Gordon, and Peter Miller, 53–72. Chicago: University of Chicago Press.

———, and Gilles Deleuze. 1977. Intellectuals and Power: A Conversation. *In* Language, Counter-memory, Practice, edited by Donald Bouchard, 205–17. Ithaca: Cornell University Press.

Fox, Richard, ed. 1991. Recapturing Anthropology: Working in the Present. Santa Fe, N.M.: School of American Research.

Franke, Richard. 1974. Miracle Seeds and Shattered Dreams in Java. Natural History 83 (1): 10–18, 84–88.

Frankel, Herbert. 1953. The Economic Impact on Underdeveloped Societies. Cambridge: Harvard University Press.

Fraser, Nancy. 1989. Unruly Practices. Minneapolis: University of Minnesota Press.

Freire, Paulo. 1970. Pedagogy of the Oppressed. New York: Herder and Herder.

Friedman, Jonathan. 1987. Beyond Otherness or: The Spectacularization of Anthropology. Telos 71:161–70.

Fröbel, Folker, Jurgen Heinrichs, and Otto Kreye. 1989. The New International Division of Labor. Cambridge: Cambridge University Press.

Fuentes, Annette, and Barbara Ehrenreich. 1983. Women in the Global Factory. Boston: South End Press.

Fuenzalida, Edmundo. 1983. The Reception of "Scientific Sociology" in Chile. Latin American Research Review 18 (2): 95–112.

———. 1987. La Reorganización de Las Instituciones de Enseñanza Superior e Investigación en América Latina entre 1950 y 1980 sus Interpretaciones. Estudios Sociales 52 (2): 115–38.

Fuglesang, Minou. 1992. No Longer Ghosts: Women's Notions of "Development" and "Modernity" in Lamu Town, Kenya. *In* Kap-Am or Take-Off: Local Notions of Development, edited by G. Dahl and A. Rabo, 123–56. Stockholm: Stockholm Studies in Social Anthropology.

Furtado, Celso. 1970. Economic Development of Latin America. Cambridge: Cambridge University Press.

Galbraith, John Kenneth. 1979. The Nature of Mass Poverty. Cambridge: Harvard University Press.

Galli, Rosemary. 1981. Colombia: Rural Development as Social and Economic Control. *In* The Political Economy of Rural Development, edited by Rosemary Galli, 27–87. Albany: SUNY Press.

Gallin, Rita, Marilyn Aronoff, and Anne Ferguson, eds. 1989. The Women and International Development Annual. Vol. 1. Boulder: Westview Press.

———, and Anne Ferguson, eds. 1990. The Women and International Development Annual. Vo. 2. Boulder: Westview Press.

García, Antonio. 1948. Bases de la Economía Contemporánea. Elementos para una Economía de la Defensa. Bogotá: RFIOC.

———. 1950. La Democracia en la Teoría y en la Práctica. Una Posición Frente al Capitalismo y al Comunismo. Bogotá: Iqueíma.

———. 1953. La Planificación de Colombia. El Trimestre Economico 20:435–63.

———. 1972. Atraso y Dependencia en América Latina. Buenos Aires: El Ateneo.

García, Juan César. 1981. Historia de las Instituciones de Investigación en Salud en América Latina, 1880–1930. Educación Médica en Salud 15 (1): 71–88.

García Cadena, A. 1956. Unas Ideas Elementales sobre Problemas Colombianos. Bogotá: Banco de la República.

García Canclini, Néstor. 1990. Culturas Híbridas: Estrategias para Entrar y Salir de la Modernidad. México, D.F.: Grijalbo.

García de la Huerta, Marcos. 1992. La Técnica y la Difusión del Ideal de Modernidad. In Estudios sobre Sociedad y Tecnología, edited by J. Sanmartín et al., 131–60. Barcelona: Editorial Anthropos.

García Márquez, Gabriel. 1982. El Olor de la Guayaba. Bogotá: La Oveja Negra.

Garfinkel, H. 1967. Studies in Ethnomethodology. Englewood Cliffs, N.J.: Prentice-Hall.

GEF (Global Environment Facility)/PNUD. 1993. Proyecto Biopacífico. Plan Operativo. Bogotá: Biopacífico.

Gendzier, Irene. 1985. Managing Political Change: Social Scientists and the Third World. Boulder: Westview Press.

George, Susan. 1986. More Food, More Hunger: Development. Seeds of Change 1986 (1/2): 53–63.

Giddens, Anthony. 1990. The Consequences of Modernity. Stanford: Stanford University Press.

Girard, René. 1977. Violence and the Sacred. Baltimore: Johns Hopkins University Press.

Godelier, Maurice. 1986. The Mental and the Material. London: Verso.

Gómez, Eugenio. 1942. Problemas Colombianos. Sociología e Historia. Bogotá: Editorial Santa Fé.

Goodman, David, Bernardo Sorj, and John Wilkinson. 1987. From Farming to Biotechnology: A Theory of Agro-Industrial Development. Oxford: Basil Blackwell.

Gordon, Deborah. 1988. Writing Culture, Writing Feminism: The Poetics and Politics of Experimental Ethnography. Inscriptions 3/4:7–26.

———. 1991. Engendering Ethnography. Ph.D. diss. Board of Studies in History of Consciousness, University of California, Santa Cruz.

Graebner, Norman. 1977. Cold War Diplomacy: American Foreign Policy, 1945–1975. New York: D. Van Nostrand.

Gramsci, Antonio. 1971. Americanism and Fordism. In Selection from the Prison Books. New York: International Publishers.

Gran, Guy. 1986. Beyond African Famines: Whose Knowledge Matters? Alternatives 11 (2): 275–96.

Green Web. 1989. Sustainable Development: Expanded Environmental Destruction. Green Web Bulletin, no. 16.

Grillo, Eduardo. 1990. Visión Andina del Paisaje. In Sociedad y Naturaleza en los Andes. Vol.1, edited by Eduardo Grillo, 133–67. Lima: PRATEC/UNEP.

———. 1992. Desarrollo o Descolonización en los Andes? Presented at the meeting on Alternatives to the Greening of Economics, Amherst, Mass., June 19–24.

Grillo, Eduardo, ed. 1991. Cultura Andina Agrocéntrica. Lima: PRATEC.

Grueso, R. 1973. La Situación Nutricional y Alimentaria de Colombia. Presented at the Primer Seminario Intersectorial de Alimentación y Nutrición, Palmira, December 9–12. Bogotá: ICBF.

———. N.d. El Programa Integrado de Nutrición Aplicada (PINA) en Colombia. Bogotá: ICBF.

Guatari, Felix. 1993. El Constructivismo Guattariano. Cali: Universidad del Valle Press.

Gudeman, Stephen. 1986. Economics as Culture: Models and Metaphors of Livelihood. London: Routledge and Kegan Paul.

———. 1992. Remodelling the House of Economics: Culture and Innovation. American Ethnologist 19 (2): 141–54.

———, and Alberto Rivera. 1990. Conversations in Colombia: The Domestic Economy in Life and Text. Cambridge: Cambridge University Press.

———. 1993. Caring for the Base. Presented at the meeting on Alternative Approaches to the Greening of Economics, Bellagio, Italy, August 2–6.

Guha, Ranajit. 1988. The Prose of Counter-Insurgency. In Selected Subaltern Studies, edited by Ranajit Guha and Gayatri Spivak, 37–44. Delhi: Oxford University Press.

———. 1989. Dominance without Hegemony and Its Historiography. In Subaltern Studies. Vol. 6, edited by Ranajit Guha, 210–309. Delhi: Oxford University Press.

Gutman, Nancy. 1994. The Economic Consequences of Pragmatism: A Re-interpretation of Keynesian Doctrine. In Decolonizing Knowledge: From Development to Dialogue, edited by Frédérique Apffel-Marglin and Stephen Marglin. Oxford: Clarendon Press. Forthcoming.

Habermas, Jürgen. 1987. The Philosophical Discourse of Modernity. Cambridge: MIT Press.

Hacking, Ian. 1991. How Should We Do the History of Statistics? In The Foucault Effect, edited by Graham Burchell, Colin Gordon, and Peter Miller, 181–96. Chicago: University of Chicago Press.

Haglund, David. 1985. Latin America and the Transformation of U.S. Strategic Thought. Albuquerque: University of New Mexico Press.

Hakim, Peter, and Georgio Solimano. 1976. Nutrition and National Development: Establishing the Connections. Food Policy 1 (3): 249–59.

Hall, Stuart. 1992. Cultural Studies and Its Theoretical Legacies. In Cultural Studies, edited by Lawrence Grossberg, Cary Nelson, and Paula Treichler, 286–94. New York: Routledge.

Hancock, Graham. 1989. Lords of Poverty. New York: Atlantic Monthly Press.

Hansen, Karen, and Leslie Ashbaugh. 1990. Women on the Front Line: Development Issues in Southern Africa. In The Women and International Development Annual. Vol. 2, edited by Rita Gallin and Anne Ferguson, 205–29. Boulder: Westview Press.

Haraway, Donna. 1985. A Manifesto for Cyborgs: Science, Technology, and Socialist Feminism in the 1980s. Socialist Review 80:65–107.

———. 1988. Situated Knowledges: The Science Question in Feminism and the Privilege of Partial Perspective. Feminist Studies 14 (3): 575–99.

———. 1989a. Primate Visions. New York: Routledge.

————. 1989b. The Biopolitics of Postmodern Bodies: Determinations of Self in Immune System Discourse. Differences 1 (1): 3–43.

————. 1991. Simians, Cyborgs, and Women: The Reinvention of Nature. New York: Routledge.

————. 1992. The Promises of Monsters: A Regenerative Politics of Inappropriate(d) Others. In Cultural Studies, edited by Lawrence Gorssberg, Cary Nelson, and Paula Treichler, 295–337. New York: Routledge.

Harcourt, Wendy. 1994. A Feminist Alternative to Greening Economics. VENA Journal. Forthcoming.

Harvey, David. 1989. The Condition of Postmodernity. Oxford: Basil Blackwell.

Hatt, Paul. 1951. World Population and Future Resources. New York: American Book.

Hayek, Friedrich A. von. 1944. The Road to Serfdom. Chicago: Chicago University Press.

Heidegger, Martin. 1977. The Question Concerning Technology. New York: Harper and Row.

Hicks, John. 1969. A Theory of Economic History. Oxford: Clarendon Press.

Hirschman, Albert. 1958. The Strategy of Economic Development. New Haven: Yale University Press.

————. 1961. Latin American Issues. New York: Twentieth Century Fund.

————. 1981. Essays in Trespassing: Economics to Politics and Beyond. Cambridge: Cambridge University Press.

Hobbelink, Henk. 1992. La Diversidad Biológica y la Biotecnología Agrícola. Ecología Política 4:57–72.

hooks, bell. 1990. Yearning: Race, Gender, and Cultural Politics. Boston: South End Press.

Hopkins, Terence, and Immanuel Wallerstein. 1987. Capitalism and the Incorporation of New Zones into the World-Economy. Review 10 (3): 763–79.

Hunt, Geoffrey. 1986. Two Methodological Paradigms in Development Economics. The Philosophical Forum 18 (1): 52–68.

Illich, Ivan. 1969. Celebration of Awareness. New York: Pantheon Books.

Instituto SER. 1980a. Jerarquización de los Municipios del País. Bogotá: SER.

————. 1980b. Análisis Encuesta PAN-77. Bogotá: SER.

————. 1981. Análisis de la Encuesta PAN-79. Bogotá: SER.

International Bank for Reconstruction and Development. 1950. The Basis of a Development Program for Colombia. Baltimore: Johns Hopkins University Press.

————. 1955. The Autonomous Regional Corporation of the Cauca and the Development of the Upper Cauca Valley. Washington, D.C.: IBRD.

James, Thomas. 1984. Exiled Within: The Schooling of Japanese-Americans, 1942–1945. Ph.D. diss., Stanford University.

Jay, Martin. 1988. Scopic Regimes of Modernity. In Vision and Visuality, edited by Hal Foster, 3–28. Seattle: Bay Press.

Jelin, Elizabeth, ed. 1990. Women and Social Change in Latin America. London: Zed Books.

Joy, Leonard, ed. 1978. Food and Nutrition Planning: The State of the Art. Guilford, England: IPC Science and Technology Press.

————, and Philippe Payne. 1975. Food and Nutrition Planning. Rome: FAO.

Junguito, R. 1982. Alternativas para el Manejo de la Política Agropecuaria. Bogotá: DNP/UEA.

Kalmanovitz, Salomón. 1978. Desarrollo de la Agricultura en Colombia. Bogotá: Editorial La Carreta.

———. 1989. La Encrucijada de la Sinrazón. Bogotá: Tercer Mundo.

Kardam, Nüket. 1991. Bringing Women In: Women's Issues in International Development Program. Boulder: Lynne Rienner Publishers.

Keller, Evelyn Fox. 1992. Nature, Nurture, and the Human Genome Project. In The Code of Codes: Scientific and Social Issues of the Human Genome, edited by Daniel Kevles and Leroy Hood, 281–99. Cambridge: Harvard University Press.

Kolko, Gabriel. 1988. Confronting the Third World: United States Foreign Policy, 1945–1980. New York: Pantheon Books.

Kuletz, Valerie. 1992. Eco-Feminist Philosophy: Interview with Barbara Holland-Cunz. Capitalism, Nature, Socialism 3 (2): 63–78.

Kulick, Don. 1992. "Coming Up" in Gapun: Conceptions of Development and Their Effect on Language in a Papua New Guinean Village. In Kam-Ap or Take-Off: Local Notions of Development, edited by G. Dahl and A. Rabo, 10–34. Stockholm: Stockholm Studies in Social Anthropology.

Laclau, Ernesto, and Chantal Mouffe. 1985. Hegemony and Socialist Strategy. London: Verso.

Lal, Deepak. 1985. The Poverty of "Development Economics." Cambridge: Harvard University Press.

Landes, David. 1983. Revolution in Time: Clocks and the Making of the Modern World. Cambridge: Harvard University Press.

Lappé, Frances Moore, Joseph Collins, and David Kinley. 1980. Aid as Obstacle. San Francisco: Institute for Food and Development Policy.

Lasswell, Harold. 1945. World Politics Faces Economics. New York: McGraw-Hill.

Latham, Michael. 1988. Western Development Strategies and Inappropriate Modernization as Causes of Malnutrition and Ill Health. In Hunger and Society. Vol. 1, edited by Michael Latham, 75–95. Cornell International Nutrition Monograph Series, no. 17.

Latour, Bruno, and Steve Woolgar. 1979. Laboratory Life: The Social Construction of Scientific Facts. Princeton: Princeton University Press.

Laugier, Henry. 1948. The First Step in the International Approaches to the Underdeveloped Areas. Milbank Memorial Fund Quarterly 26 (3): 256–59.

Lechner, Norbert. 1988. Los Patios Interiores de la Democracia. Subjetividad y Política. Santiago: FLACSO.

Leff, Enrique. 1986a. Ecología y Capital. México, D.F.: UNAM.

———. 1986b. Ambiente y Articulación de Ciencias. In Los Problemas del Conocimiento y la Perspectiva Ambiental del Desarrollo, edited by Enrique Leff, 72–125. México, D.F.: Siglo XXI.

———. 1992. La Dimensión Cultural y el Manejo Integrado, Sustentable y Sostenido de los Recursos Naturales. In Cultura y Manejo Sustentable de los Recursos Naturales, edited by Enrique Leff and Julia Carabias. México, D.F.: CIIH/UNAM.

———. 1993. Marxism and the Environmental Question: From the Critical Theory of Production to an Environmental Rationality for Sustainable Development. Capitalism, Nature, Socialism 4 (1): 44–66.

Lele, Uma. 1986. Women and Structural Transformation. Economic Development and Cultural Change 34 (2): 195–219.

León, Magdalena. 1980. Mujer y Capitalismo Agrario. Bogotá: ACEP.

————. 1985. La Medición del Trabajo Femenino en América Latina: Problemas Teóricos y Metodológicos. In Mujer y Familia en Colombia, edited by Elssy Bonilla, 177–204. Bogotá: Plaza y Janés.

————. 1986. Política Agraria en Colombia y Debate Sobre Políticas para la Mujer Rural. In La Mujer y la Política Agraria en América Latina, edited by Magdalena León y Carmen Diana Deere, 43–59. Bogotá: Siglo XXI.

————. 1987. Política Agraria y su Impacto en la Mujer Rural, Como Actor Social de la Economía Campesina. In Seminario Internacional de Economía Campesina y Probreza Rural, edited by Jorge Bustamante, 119–26. Bogotá: Fondo DRI.

————. 1993. Neutralidad y Distensión de Género en la Política Pública de América Latina. Presented at the Nineteenth Congreso Latinoamericano de Sociología, Caracas, May 30–July 4.

————, ed. 1982. Las Trabajadoras del Agro. Vol. 2, Debate Sobre la Mujer en América Latina y el Caribe. Bogotá: ACEP.

————, and Carmen Diana Deere, eds. 1986. La Mujer y La Política Agraria en América Latina. Bogotá: Siglo XXI.

————, Patricia Prieto, and María Cristina Salazar. 1987. Acceso de la Mujer a la Tierra en América Latina y el Caribe: Panorama General y Estudio de Caso de Honduras y Colombia. Bogotá: Informe Presentado a la Organización de las Naciones Unidas para la Agricultura y la Alimentación (FAO).

Levinson, James. 1974. Morinda: An Economic Analysis of Malnutrition Among Young Children in Rural India. Cambridge: Cornell/MIT International Nutrition Policy Series.

Lewis, W. Arthur. 1949. The Principles of Economic Planning. London: D. Dobson.

————. 1955. The Theory of Economic Growth. Homewood, Ill.: R. D. Irwin.

————. [1954] 1958. Economic Development with Unlimited Supply of Labor. In The Economics of Underdevelopment, edited by Amar Narin Agarwala and S. P. Singh. Bombay: Oxford University Press.

Liebenstein, Harvey. 1954. A Theory of Economic-Demographic Development. Princeton: Princeton University Press.

————. 1957. Economic Backwardness and Economic Growth. New York: Wiley.

Lind, Amy. 1992. Power, Gender, and Development: Popular Women's Organization and the Politics of Needs in Ecuador. In The Making of Social Movements in Latin America, edited by Arturo Escobar and Sonia E. Alvarez, 134–49. Boulder: Westview Press.

Little, Ian M. 1982. Economic Development: Theory, Policy and International Relations. New York: Basic Books.

Livingstone, Ian. 1982. The Development of Development Economics. In Approaches to Development Studies, edited by Ian Livingstone, 3–28. Hampshire, England: Gower.

Londoño, Juan Luis, and Guillermo Perry. 1985. El Banco Mundial, El Fondo Monetario y Colombia: Análisis Crítico de sus Relaciones. Coyuntura Económica 15 (3): 209–43.

López, Alejandro. 1976. Escritos Escogidos. Bogotá: Colcultura.

López, Cecilia, and Fabiola Campillo. 1983. Problemas Teóricos y Operativos de la Ejecución de una Política para la Mujer Campesina. Bogotá: DNP/UEA.

López, Gustavo A., and Luis F. Correa. 1982. La Planeación en Colombia. Cincias Humanas 2 (3): 3–34.

López de Mesa, Luis. 1944. Posibles Rumbos de la Economía Colombiana. Bogotá: Imprenta Nacional.

López Maya, Margarita. 1993. Cambio de Discursos en la Relacion entre los Estados Unidos y América Latina de la Segunda Guerra Mundial a la Guerra Fría (1945–1948). Presented at the Thirty-fourth Annual Convention of the International Studies Association, Acapulco, March 23–27.

Love, Joseph. 1980. Raúl Prebisch and the Origins of the Doctrine of Unequal Exchange. Latin American Research Review 15 (3): 45–70.

Lynch, Lowell. 1979. Nutrition Planning Methodologies: A Comparative Review of Types and Applications. Food and Nutrition Bulletin 1 (3): 1–14.

McCloskey, Donald. 1985. The Rhetoric of Economics. Madison: University of Wisconsin Press.

McKay, Harrison, H. McKay, and Leonardo Sinisterra. 1978. Improving Cognitive Ability in Chronically Deprived Children. Science 200 (4339): 270–78.

McNamara, Robert. 1975. The Nairobi Speech. In Assault on World Poverty. The World Bank, 90–98. Baltimore: Johns Hopkins University Press.

Maier, Charles. 1975. Recasting Bourgeois Europe. Princeton: Princeton University Press.

Mamdani, Mahmood. 1973. The Myth of Population Control. New York: Monthly Review.

Mani, Lata. 1989. Multiple Mediations: Feminist Scholarship in the Age of Multinational Reception. Inscriptions 5:1–24.

Manzo, Kate. 1991. Modernist Discourse and the Crisis of Development Theory. Studies in Comparative International Development 26 (2): 3–36.

Marcus, George, and Michael Fischer. 1986. Anthropology as Cultural Critique. Chicago: University of Chicago Press.

Marglin, Stephen. 1990. Toward the Decolonization of Mind. In Dominating Knowledge, edited by Stephen Marglin and Frédérique Apffel-Marglin, 1–28. Oxford: Clarendon Press.

———. 1992. Alternative Approches to the Greening of Economics: A Research Proposal. Photocopy.

Martínez Alier, Juan. 1992. Ecología y Pobreza. Barcelona: Centre Cultural Bancaixa.

Mascia-Lees, Frances, F. P. Sharpe, and C. Ballerino Cohen. 1989. The Postmodernist Turn in Anthropology: Cautions from a Feminist Perspective. Signs 15 (1): 7–33.

Maybury-Lewis, David. 1985. A Special Sort of Pleading: Anthropology at the Service of Ethnic Groups. In Advocacy and Anthropology: First Encounters, edited by Robert Paine, 131–48. St. John's, New Foundland: Memorial University of New Foundland.

Mayer, Jean, and Johanna Dwyer, eds. 1979. Food and Nutrition Policy in a Changing World. Oxford: Oxford University Press.

Medrano, Diana, and Rodrigo Villar. 1988. Mujer Campesina y Organización Rural en Colombia. Bogotá: CEREC.

Meier, Gerald. 1984. Emerging from Poverty: The Economics that Really Matters. New York: Oxford University Press.

———, and Dudley Seers, ed. 1984. Pioneers in Development. Oxford: Oxford University Press.

Mellor, Mary. 1992. Eco-Feminism and Eco-Socialism: Dilemmas of Essentialism and Materialism. Capitalism, Nature, Socialism 3 (2): 43–62.

Memmi, Albert. 1967. The Colonizer and the Colonized. Boston: Beacon Press.

Merchant, Carolyn. 1980. The Death of Nature: Women, Ecology and the Scientific Revolution. New York: Harper and Row.

———. 1990. Ecofeminism and Feminist Theory. In Reweaving the World: The Emergence of Ecofeminism, edited by Irene Diamond and Gloria Ferman Orenstein, 100–105. San Francisco: Sierra Club Books.

Metz, Christian. 1982. The Imaginary Signifier. Bloomington: Indiana University Press.

Mies, Maria. 1986. Patriarchy and Accumulation on a World Scale. London: Zed Books.

Milbank Memorial Fund. 1948. International Approaches to Problems of Underdeveloped Countries. New York: Milbank Memorial Fund.

———. 1954. The Interrelationships of Demographic, Economic and Social Problems in Underdeveloped Areas. New York: Milbank Memorial Fund.

Millberg, William. 1991. Marxism, Poststructuralism, and the Discourse of Economists. Rethinking Marxism 4 (2): 93–104.

Ministerio de Agricultura de Colombia. 1985. Proyecto Desarrollo con la Mujer Campesina, Convenio DRI-PAN-INCORA. Bogotá: Ministerio de Agricultura.

Ministerio de Salud, Dirección de Participación de la Comunidad. 1979. Apuntes para la Participación de la Comunidad en Salud. Bogotá: Ministerio de Salud.

———. 1982. Plan Nacional de Participación de la Comunidad en Atención Primaria en Salud. Bogotá: Ministerio de Salud.

Mintz, Sidney. 1976. On the Concept of a Third World. Dialectical Anthropology 1 (4): 377–82.

Mitchell, Timothy. 1988. Colonising Egypt. Cambridge: Cambridge University Press.

———. 1989. The World as Exhibition. Comparative Studies in Society and History 31 (2): 217–36.

———. 1991. America's Egypt: Discourse of the Development Industry. Middle East Report (March-April): 18–34

Mitter, Swasti. 1986. Toys for the Boys. Development: Seeds of Change 1986 (3): 66–68.

Mohanty, Chandra. 1991a. Cartographies of Struggle: Third World Women and the Politics of Feminism. In Third World Women and the Politics of Feminism, edited by Chandra Mohanty, Ann Russo, and Lourdes Torres, 1–47. Bloomington: Indiana University Press.

———. 1991b. Under Western Eyes: Feminist Scholarship and Colonial Discourses.

In Third World Women and the Politics of Feminism, edited by Chandra Mohanty, Ann Russo, and Lourdes Torres, 51–80. Bloomington: Indiana University Press.

Molyneux, Maxine. 1986. Mobilization without Emancipation? Women's Interests, State and Revolution. *In* Transition and Development: Problems of Third World Socialism, edited by Richard Fagen, Carmen Diana Deere, and José Luis Coraggio, 280–302. New York: Monthly Review Press.

Moncayo, Víctor Manuel, and Fernando Rojas. 1979. Producción Campesina y Capitalismo. Bogotá: Editorial CINEP.

Montaldo, Graciela. 1991. Estrategias del Fin de Siglo. Nueva Sociedad, no. 116:75–87.

Mora, Obdulio. 1982. Situación Nutricional de la Población Colombiana en 1977–1980. Bogotá: Ministerio de Salud y ASCOFAME.

Morandé, Pedro. 1984. Cultura y Modernización en América Latina. Santiago: Universidad Católica.

Mudimbe, V. Y. 1988. The Invention of Africa. Bloomington: Indiana University Press.

Mueller, Adele. 1986. The Bureaucratization of Feminist Knowledge: The Case of Women in Development. Resources for Feminist Research 15 (1): 36–38.

———. 1987a. Peasants and Professionals: The Social Organization of Women in Development Knowledge. Ph.D. diss. Ontario Institute for Studies in Education.

———. 1987b. Power and Naming in the Development Institution: The "Discovery" of "Women in Peru." Paper presented at the Fourteenth Annual Third World Conference, Chicago.

———. 1991. In and Against Development: Feminists Confront Development on Its Own Ground. Photocopy.

Murphy, Craig, and Enrico Augelli. 1993. International Institutions, Decolonization, and Development. International Political Science Review 14 (1): 71–85.

Namuddu, Katherine. 1989. Problems of Communication between Northern and Southern Researchers in the Context of Africa. Paper presented at the Seventh World Congress of Comparative Education, Montreal, June 26–30.

Nandy, Ashis. 1983. The Intimate Enemy: Loss and Recovery of Self under Colonialism. Delhi: Oxford University Press.

———. 1987. Traditions, Tyranny, and Utopias. Delhi: Oxford University Press.

———. 1989. Shamans, Savages, and the Wilderness: On the Audibility of Dissent and the Future of Civilizations. Alternatives 14 (3): 263–78.

Nash, June. 1979. We Eat the Mines and the Mines Eat Us. New York: Columbia University Press.

———, and Helen Safa, eds. 1986. Women and Change in Latin America. South Hadley, Mass.: Bergin & Garvey Publishers.

Navarro, Vicente. 1976. Medicine under Capitalism. New York: Prodist.

Norgaard, Richard. 1991a. Sustainability as Intergenerational Equity. Washington, D.C.: World Bank Internal Discussion Paper, no. IDP 97.

———. 1991b. Sustainability: The Paradigmatic Challenge to Agricultural Economics. Paper presented at the Twenty-first Conference of the International Association of Agricultural Economists, Tokyo, August 22–29.

Nurkse, Ragnald. 1953. Problems of Capital Formation in Underdeveloped Countries. Oxford: Oxford University Press.

O'Connor, James. 1988. Capitalism, Nature, Socialism: A Theoretical Introduction. Capitalism, Nature, Socialism 1 (1): 11–38.

———. 1989. Political Economy of Ecology of Socialism and Capitalism. Capitalism, Nature, Socialism 1 (3): 93–108.

———. 1992. A Political Strategy for Ecology Movements. Capitalism, Nature, Socialism 3 (1): 1–5.

O'Connor, Martin. 1993. On the Misadventures of Capitalist Nature. Capitalism, Nature, Socialism 4 (3): 7–40.

Ocampo, José Antonio, ed. 1987. Historia Económica de Colombia. Colombia: Siglo XXI.

———, et al. 1987. La Consolidación del Capitalismo Moderno. In Historia Económica de Colombia, edited by José Antonio Ocampo, 243–331. Bogotá: Siglo XXI.

Ong, Aihwa. 1987. Spirits of Resistance and Capitalist Discipline. Albany: SUNY Press.

Orr, John Boyd. 1953. The White Man's Dilemma. London: G. Allen and Unwin.

Osborn, Fairfield. 1948. Our Plundered Planet. Boston: Little, Brown.

Pacey, A., and Philip Payne, eds. 1985. Agricultural Development and Nutrition. Boulder: Westview Press.

Packard, Randall. 1989. The "Healthy Reserve" and the "Dressed Native": Discourses on Black Health and the Language of Legitimation in South Africa. American Ethnologist 16 (4): 686–704.

Page, Helán. 1991. Historically Conditioned Aspiration and Gender/Race/Class Relations in Colonial and Post-Colonial Zimbabwe. Photocopy.

Panayatou, Theodor. 1991. Roundtable Discussion: Is Economic Growth Sustainable? In Proceedings of the World Bank Annual Conference on Development Economics, edited by Lawrence Summers and Shekhar Shah, 353–62. Washington, D.C.: The World Bank.

Parajuli, Pramod. 1991. Power and Knowledge in Development Discourse. International Social Science Journal 127:173–90.

Pardo, Franz. 1973. La Producción Agropecuaria y las Necesidades Alimentarias de la Población Colombiana. Presented at the Primer Seminario Intersectorial de Alimentación y Nutrición, Palmira, December 9–12. Bogotá: ICBF.

———. 1984. La Situación Alimentaria de la Población Colombiana. Encuesta Nacioopnal de Alimentación, Nutrición y Vivienda. Bogotá: DANE-DNP-DRI-PAN.

Payer, Cheryl. 1982. The World Bank. New York: Monthly Review Press.

———. 1991. Lent and Lost: Foreign Credit and Third World Development. London: Zed Books.

Payne, Philip. 1977. Review of Malnutrition and Poverty, by S. Reutlinger and Marcelo Selowsky. Food Policy 2 (2): 164–65.

———, and Peter Cutler. 1984. Measuring Malnutrition: Technical Problems and Ideological Perspectives. Economic and Political Weekly 19 (34): 1485–91.

Pécaut, Daniel. 1987. Orden y Violencia: Colombia 1930–1954. Bogotá: Siglo XXI Editores.

Pendell, Elmer. 1951. Population on the Loose. New York: W. Funk.

Pérez Alemán, Paola. 1990. Organización, Identidad y Cambio. Las Campesinas en Nicaragua. Managua: CIAM.

Perry, Guillermo. 1976. El Desarrollo Institucional de la Planeación en Colombia. Derecho Financiero 2 (2): 65–91.

Perry, Santiago. 1983. La Crisis Agraria en Colombia, 1950–1980. Bogotá: El Ancora Editores.

PIA/PNAN (Proyecto Interagencial de Promoción de Políticas de Alimentación y Nutrición). 1973a. Guía Metodológica para Planificación de Políticas Nacionales de Alimentación y Nutrición. Santiago: PIA/PNAN.

———. 1973b. Reunión Interagencial de Consulta Sobre Políticas Nacionales de Alimentación y Nutrición en las Américas, Santiago, 12–22 de Marzo de 1973 (Informe Final). Santiago: PIA/PNAN.

———. 1975a. Informe Sobre la Primera Etapa, Marzo 1971–Julio 1975. Santiago: PIA/PNAN.

———. 1975b. Plan de Operaciones. Santiago: PIA/PNAN.

———. 1977. Actividades Segundo Semestre 1976. Informe y Evaluación. Santiago: PIA/PNAN.

Pigg, Stacy Leigh. 1992. Constructing Social Categories through Place: Social Representations and Development in Nepal. Comparative Studies in Society and History 34 (3): 491–513.

Platsch, Carl. 1981. The Three Worlds, or the Division of Social Scientific Labor, circa 1950–1975. Comparative Studies in Society and History 23 (4): 565–90.

Polanyi, Karl. 1957a. The Great Transformation. Boston: Beacon Press.

———. 1957b. The Economy as Instituted Process. In Trade and Market in the Early Empires, edited by Karl Polanyi, Conrad Arensberg, and Harry Pearson, 243–70. Glencoe, Ill: Free Press.

———, Conrad Arensberg, and Harry Pearson, eds. 1957. Trade and Market in the Early Empires. Glenco, Ill: Free Press.

Political and Economic Planning. 1955. World Population and Future Resources. New York: American Book.

Portes, Alejandro. 1976. On the Sociology of National Development Theories and Issues. American Journal of Sociology 2 (1): 55–85.

———, and Douglas Kincaid. 1989. Sociology and Development in the 1990s: Critical Challenges and Empirical Trends. Sociological Forum 4 (4): 479–503.

Prebisch, Raúl. 1979. The Neo-Classical Theories of Economic Liberalism. CEPAL Review 7:167–88.

Pred, Alan, and Michael Watts. 1992. Reworking Modernity. New Brunswick: Rutgers University Press.

Price, David. 1989. Before the Bulldozer. Washington, D.C.: Cabin John Press.

Procacci, Giovanna. 1991. Social Economy and the Government of Poverty. In The Foucault Effect, edited by Graham Burchell, Colin Gordon, and Peter Miller, 151–68. Chicago: University of Chicago Press.

Quijano, Aníbal. 1988. Modernidad, Identidad y Utopía en América Latina. Lima: Sociedad y Política Ediciones.

———. 1990. Estética de la Utopía. David y Goliath 57:34–38.

Rabinow, Paul. 1986. Representations Are Social Facts: Modernity and Post-Modernity in Anthropology. In Writing Culture: The Poetics and Politics of Ethnography, edited by James Clifford and George Marcus, 234–61. Berkeley: University of California Press.

————. 1989. French Modern: Norms and Forms of the Social Environment. Cambridge: MIT Press.

————. 1992. Artificiality and Enlightenment: From Sociobiology to Biosociality. In Incorporations, edited by Jonathan Crary and Sanford Kwinter, 234–52. New York: Zone Books.

————, and William Sullivan, eds. 1987. Interpretive Social Science: A Second Look. Berkeley: University of California Press.

Rahnema, Majid. 1986. Under the Banner of Development. Development: Seeds of Change, nos. 1–2:37–46.

————. 1988a. Power and Regenerative Processes in Micro-Spaces. International Social Science Journal 117:361–75.

————. 1988b. On a New Variety of AIDS and Its Pathogens: Homo Economicus, Development, and Aid. Alternatives 13 (1): 117–36.

————. 1991. Global Poverty: A Pauperizing Myth. Interculture 24 (2): 4–51.

Rao, Aruna, ed. 1991. Women's Studies International: Nairobi and Beyond. New York: Feminist Press at the City University of New York.

Rao, Brinda. 1989. Struggling for Production Conditions and Producing Conditions of Emancipation: Women and Water in Rural Maharashtra. Capitalism, Nature, Socialism 1 (2): 65–82.

————. 1991. Dominant Constructions of Women and Nature in Social Science Literature. Santa Cruz: CES/CNS Pamphlet 2.

Rau, Bill. 1991. From Feast to Famine. London: Zed Books.

Redclift, Michael. 1987. Sustainable Development: Exploring the Contradictions. London: Routledge.

Reddy, William. 1987. Money and Liberty in Modern Europe. Cambridge: Cambridge University Press.

Reinhardt, Nola. 1988. Our Daily Bread: The Peasant Question and Family Farming in the Colombian Andes. Berkeley: University of California Press.

Reutlinger, Shlomo, and Marcelo Selowsky. 1976. Malnutrition and Poverty: Magnitude and Policy Options. Baltimore: Johns Hopkins University Press (published for the World Bank).

Rey de Marulanda, Nora. 1981. El Trabajo de la Mujer. Documento CEDE 064. Bogotá: CEDE/Universidad de los Andes.

Richards, Paul. 1984. Indigenous Agricultural Revolution. Boulder: Westview Press.

Robinson, Joan. 1979. Aspects of Development and Underdevelopment. Cambridge: Cambridge University Press.

Rocha, Glauber. 1982. An Aesthetic of Hunger. In Brazilian Cinema, edited by Randal Johnson and Robert Stam, 68–71. Rutherford: Fairleigh Dickinson University Press.

Rodríguez, Octavio. 1977. On the Conception of the Centre-Periphery System. CEPAL Review 1:195–239.

Rojas, Humberto, and Orlando Fals Borda, eds. 1977. El Agro en el Desarrollo Histórico Colombiano. Bogotá: Punta de Lanza.

Rojas de Ferro, María Cristina. 1994. A Political Economy of Violence. Ph.D. diss., Carleton University, Ottawa.

Root, Elihu. 1916. Addresses on International Subjects. Cambridge: Harvard University Press.

Rostow, W. W. 1952. The Process of Economic Growth. New York: W. W. Norton.

———. 1960. The Stages of Economic Growth: A Non-Communist Manifesto. Cambridge: Cambridge University Press.

Rubbo, Anna. 1975. The Spread of Capitalism in Rural Colombia: Effects on Poor Women. In Towards an Anthropology of Women, edited by Rayna Reiter, 333–57. New York: Monthly Review Press.

Sachs, Carolyn. 1985. Women: The Invisible Farmers. Totowa: Eowman and Allanheld.

Sachs, Wolfgang. 1988. The Gospel of Global Efficiency. IFDA Dossier, no. 68:33–39.

———. 1990. The Archaeology of the Development Idea. Interculture 23 (4): 1–37.

———. 1992. Environment. In The Development Dictionary, edited by Wolfgang Sachs, 26–37.

———, ed. 1992. The Development Dictionary: A Guide to Knowledge as Power. London: Zed Books.

Sáenz Rovner, Eduardo. 1989. Industriales, Proteccionismo y Política en Colombia: Intereses, Conflictos y Violencia. Universidad de los Andes. Facultad de Administración. Monografía no. 13.

———. 1992. La Ofensiva Empresarial. Industriales, Políticos y Violencia en los Años 40 en Colombia. Bogotá: Tercer Mundo.

Said, Edward. 1979. Orientalism. New York: Vintage Books.

———. 1989. Representing the Colonized: Anthropology's Interlocutors. Critical Inquiry 15:205–25.

Sanz de Santamaría, Alejandro. 1984. Discurso Económico y Poder. Texto y Contexto 2:155–84.

———. 1987. Epistemology, Economic Theory and Political Democracy: A Case Study in a Colombian Rural Community. Ph.D. diss., University of Massachusetts, Amherst.

———, and L. A. Fonseca. 1985. Evaluación de Impacto del Programa DRI en el Distrito de Málaga. Bogotá: Universidad de los Andes (Research Report).

Sarlo, Beatriz. 1991. Un Debate Sobre la Cultura. Nueva Sociedad, no. 116:88–93.

Sax, Karl. 1955. Standing Room Alone. Boston: Beacon Press.

Scheper-Hughes, Nancy. 1992. Death without Weeping. Berkeley: University of California Press.

Schultz, Theodore. 1964. Transforming Traditional Agriculture. New Haven: Yale University Press.

Schumpeter, Joseph. 1934. The Theory of Economic Development. Cambridge: Harvard University Press.

———. 1954. History of Economic Analysis. Oxford: Oxford University Press.

Scott, James. 1985. Weapons of the Weak: Everyday Forms of Peasant Resistance. New Haven: Yale University Press.

———. 1990. Domination and the Arts of Resistance. New Haven: Yale University Press.

Scrimshaw, Nevin, and M. B. Wallerstein, eds. 1982. Nutrition Policy Implementation. New York: Plenum Press.

Seers, Dudley. 1979. Birth, Life, and Death of Development Economics. Development and Change 10:707–19.

_____. 1983. The Political Economy of Nationalism. Oxford: Oxford University
Press.

Sen, Gita, and Caren Grown. 1987. Development, Crises, and Alternative Visions:
Third World Women's Perspectives. New York: Monthly Review Press.

Shackle, G.L.S. 1967. The Years of High Theory: Tradition and Innovation in Economic Thought, 1926–1939. Cambridge: Cambridge University Press.

Shaffer, Bernard. 1985. Policy Makers Have Their Needs Too: Irish Itinerants and
the Culture of Poverty. Development and Change 16 (3): 375–408.

Sheth, D. L. 1987. Alternative Development as Political Practice. Alternatives 12 (2):
155–71.

Shiva, Vandana. 1989. Staying Alive. Women, Ecology and Development. London:
Zed Books.

_____. 1992. The Seed and the Earth: Women, Ecology and Biotechnology. The
Ecologist 22 (1): 4–8.

Shonfield, Andrew. 1950. Attack on World Poverty. New York: Random House.

SID (Society for International Development). 1986. Latin American Regional
Women's Workshop. Modernized Patriarchy: The Impact of the Crisis on Latin
American Women. Development: Seeds of Change 3:22–23.

Sikkink, Kathryn. 1991. Ideas and Institutions: Developmentalism in Brazil and Argentina. Ithaca: Cornell University Press.

Simmons, Pam. 1992. "Women in Development": A Threat to Liberation. The Ecologist 22 (1): 16–21.

Slater, David. 1993. The Geopolitical Imagination and the Enframing of Development Theory. Photocopy.

Smith, Dorothy. 1974. The Social Construction of Documentary Reality. Sociological
Inquiry 44 (4): 257–68.

_____. 1984. Textually Mediated Social Organization. International Social Science
Journal 36 (1): 59–75.

_____. 1986. Institutional Ethnography: A Feminist Method. Resources for Femi-
nist Research 15 1): 6–13.

_____. 1987. The Everyday World as Problematic: A Feminist Sociology. Boston:
Northeastern University Press.

_____. 1990. The Conceptual Practices of Power. Boston: Northeastern University
Press.

Soedjatmoko. 1985. Patterns of Armed Conflict in the Third World. Alternatives 10
(4): 474–94.

Soja, Edward. 1989. Postmodern Geographies. London: Verso.

Spelman, Elizabeth. 1988. Inessential Woman: Problems of Exclusion in Feminist
Thought. Boston: Beacon Press.

St-Hilaire, Colette. 1993. Canadian Aid, Women and Development. The Ecologist
23 (2): 57–63.

Starn, Orin. 1992. "I Dreamed of Foxes and Hawks": Reflections on Peasant Protest,

New Social Movements, and the *Rondas Campesinas* of Northern Peru. *In* The Making of Social Movements in Latin America: Identity, Strategy, and Democracy, edited by Arturo Escobar and Sonia Alvarez, 89–111. Boulder: Westview Press.

Staudt, Kathleen. 1984. Women's Politics and Capitalist Transformation in Sub-Saharan Africa. Women in Development Working Paper Series, no. 54. East Lansing: Michigan State University.

Stoler, Ann. 1989. Making Empire Respectable: The Politics of Race and Sexual Morality in Twentieth Century Colonial Cultures. American Ethnologist 16 (4): 634–61.

Strahm, Rudolf. 1986. Por Qué Somos Tan Pobres? México, D.F.: Secretaría de Educación Pública.

Strathern, Marilyn. 1988. The Gender of the Gift. Berkeley: University of California Press.

Sukhatme, P. V., and Sheldon Margen. 1978. Models for Protein Deficiency. American Journal of Clinical Nutrition 31 (7): 1237–56.

Summers, Lawrence, and Shekhar Shah, eds. 1991. Proceedings of the World Bank Annual Conference on Development Economics. Washington, D.C.: World Bank.

Sunkel, Osvaldo. 1990. Reflections on Latin American Development. *In* Progress Toward Development in Latin America, edited by James Dietz and Dilmus James, 133–58. Boulder: Lynne Rienner.

————, and Pedro Paz. 1970. El Subdesarrollo Latinoamericano y la Teoría del Desarrollo. México, D.F.: Siglo XXI.

Sutton, David. 1991. Is Anybody Out There? Anthropology and the Question of Audience. Critique of Anthropology 11 (1): 91–104.

Taussig, Michael. 1978. Destrucción y Resistencia Campesina. El Caso del Litoral Pacífico. Bogotá: Punta de Lanza.

————. 1980. The Devil and Commodity Fetishism in South America. Chapel Hill: University of North Carolina Press.

————. 1987. Shamanism, Colonialism, and the Wild Man. Chicago: University of Chicago Press.

Taylor, Charles. 1985. Philosophical Papers of Charles Taylor. Vol. 2, Philosophy of the Human Sciences. Cambridge: Cambridge University Press.

Teller, C., ed. 1980. Interrelación Desnutrición, Población y Desarrollo Social y Económico. Guatemala: INCAP.

Timmer, Peter, Walter Falcon, and Scott Pearson. 1983. Food Policy Analysis. Baltimore: Johns Hopkins University Press (published for the World Bank).

Todaro, Michael. 1977. Economic Development in the Third World. New York: Longman.

Touraine, Alain. 1988. The Return of the Actor. Minneapolis: University of Minnesota Press.

Tribe, Keith. 1981. Genealogies of Capitalism. Atlantic Highlands, N.J.: Humanities Press.

Trinh T. Minh-ha. 1989. Woman, Native, Other. Bloomington: Indiana University Press.

————. 1991. When the Moon Waxes Red. New York: Routledge.

Truman, Harry. [1949] 1964. Public Papers of the Presidents of the United States: Harry S. Truman. Washington, D.C.: U.S. Government Printing Office.

Ulin, Robert. 1991. Critical Anthropology Twenty Years Later: Modernism and Post-modernism in Anthropology. Critique of Anthropology 11 (1): 63–89.

United Nations, Department of Social and Economic Affairs. 1953. The Determinants and Consequences of Population Change. New York: United Nations.

———. 1951. Measures for the Economic Development of Underdeveloped Countries. New York: United Nations.

Uribe, Consuelo. 1986. Limitations and Constraints of Colombia's National Food and Nutrition Plan (PAN). Food Policy 11 (1): 47–70.

Urla, Jacqueline. 1993. Cultural Politics in the Age of Statistics: Numbers, Nations, and the Making of Basque Identities. American Ethnologist 20 (4): 818–43.

Valladolid, Julio. 1989. Concepción Holística de la Agricultura Andina. Documento de Estudio, no. 13. Lima: PRATEC.

Varas, Augusto. 1985. Democratization, Peace, and Security in Latin America. Alternatives 10 (4): 607–24.

Varela, Guillermo. 1979. El Plan Nacional de Alimentación y Nutrición de Colombia: Un Nuevo Estilo de Desarrollo. Bogotá: Departamento Nacional de Planeación.

Villamil, José, ed. 1979. Transnational Capitalism and National Development. Atlantic Highlands, N.J.: Humanities Press.

Vint, John. 1986. Foucault's Archaeology and Economic Thought. The Journal of Interdisciplinary Economics 1 (1): 69–85.

Visvanathan, Shiv. 1986. Bhopal: The Imagination of a Disaster. Alternatives 11 (1): 147–65.

———. 1991. Mrs. Bruntland's Disenchanted Cosmos. Alternatives 16 (3): 377–84.

Vogt, William. 1948. Road to Survival. New York: W. Sloan Associates.

Wallerstein, Immanuel. 1974. The Modern World System. Vols. 1 and 2. New York: Academic Press.

———. 1984. The Politics of the World Economy. Cambridge: Cambridge University Press.

Watts, Michael. 1983. Silent Violence: Food, Farming, and Peasantry in Northern Nigeria. Berkeley: University of California Press.

Whitaker, Arthur. 1948. The United States and South America: The Northern Republics. Cambridge: Harvard University Press.

Williams, John Henry. 1953. Economic Stability in a Changing World. New York: Oxford University Press.

Williams, Patricia. 1991. The Alchemy of Race and Rights. Cambridge: Harvard University Press.

Williams, Raymond. 1973. The Country and the City. New York: Oxford University Press.

Willis, Paul. 1990. Common Culture. Boulder: Westview Press.

Wilson, Harold. 1953. The War on World Poverty. London: Gollancz.

Winikoff, Beverly, ed. 1978. Nutrition and National Policy. Cambridge: MIT Press.

Wolfender, Herbert. 1954. Population Statistics and Their Compilation. Chicago: University of Chicago Press.

Wood, Bryce. 1985. The Dismantling of the Good Neighbor Policy. Austin: University of Texas Press.

Wood, Geof. 1985. The Politics of Development Policy Labelling. Development and Change 16 (3): 347–73.

World Bank. 1975. Rural Development. Sector Policy Paper. Washington, D.C.: World Bank.

―――. 1977. Colombia: Appraisal of an Integrated Nutrition Improvement Project. Report no. 1583-CO. Washington, D.C.: World Bank.

―――. 1981. Accelerated Development in Sub-Saharan Africa: An Agenda for Action. Washington, D.C.: World Bank.

―――. 1991. World Development Report. New York: Oxford University Press.

World Commission on Environment and Development. 1987. Our Common Future. New York: Oxford University Press.

Worsley, Peter. 1984. The Three Worlds: Culture and World Development. Chicago: University of Chicago.

Yanagisako, Silvia, and Jane Collier. 1989. Gender and Kinship: Toward a Unified Analysis. Stanford: Stanford University Press.

Yerguin, Daniel. 1977. Shattered Peace: The Origins of the Cold War and the National Security State. Boston: Houghton Mifflin.

Yúdice, George, Jean Franco, and Juan Flores, eds. 1992. On Edge: The Crisis of Contemporary Latin American Culture. Minneapolis: University of Minnesota Press.

Zamocs, León. 1986. The Agrarian Question and the Peasant Movement in Colombia. Cambridge: Cambridge University Press.

INDEX

PRINCETON STUDIES IN
CULTURE/POWER/HISTORY

High Religion:
A Cultural and Political History of Sherpa Buddhism
by Sherry B. Ortner

A Place in History:
Social and Monumental Time in a Cretan Town
by Michael Herzfeld

The Textual Condition
by Jerome J. McGann

Regulating the Social:
The Welfare State and Local Politics in Imperial Germany
by George Steinmetz

Hanging without a Rope:
Narrative Experience in Colonial and Postcolonial Karoland
by Mary Margaret Steedly

Modern Greek Lessons:
A Primer in Historical Constructivism
by James Faubion

The Nation and Its Fragments:
Colonial and Postcolonial Histories
by Partha Chatterjee

Culture/Power/History:
A Reader in Contemporary Social Theory
edited by Nicholas B. Dirks, Geoff Eley, and Sherry B. Ortner

After Colonialism:
Imperial Histories and Postcolonial Displacements
edited by Gyan Prakash

Encountering Development:
The Making and Unmaking of the Third World
by Arturo Escobar

Social Bodies: Science, Reproduction, and Italian Modernity
by David G. Horn

Revisioning History:
Film and the Construction of a New Past
edited by Robert A. Rosenstone

The History of Everyday Life:
Reconstructing Historical Experiences and Ways of Life
edited by Alf Ludtke

The Savage Freud and Other Essays on Possible and Retrievable Selves
by Ashis Nandy

Children and the Politics of Culture
edited by Sharon Stephens

Intimacy and Exclusion: Religious Politics in Pre-Revolutionary Baden
by Dagmar Herzog

What Was Socialism, and What Comes Next?
by Katherine Verdery

Citizen and Subject:
Contemporary Africa and the Legacy of Late Colonialism
by Mahmood Mamdani

Colonialism and Its Forms of Knowledge:
The British in India
by Bernard S. Cohn

Charred Lullabies:
Chapters in an Anthropology of Violence
by E. Valentine Daniel

Theft of an Idol:
Text and Context in the Representation of Collective Violence
by Paul R. Brass

Essays on the Anthropology of Reason
by Paul Rabinow

Vision, Race, and Modernity:
A Visual Economy of the Andean Image World
by Deborah Poole

Children in "Moral Danger" and the Problem of Government
in Third Republic France
by Sylvia Schafer